CU00758576

for an honour, never
nour, never wear one.

DE ROTHSCHILD

*I*t takes practice and skill
to live without regret.

OSCAR WILDE

Il fout toujours gâter un peu un tableau pour le finir.

You must always spoil a painting a little to finish it.

EUGÈNE DELACROIX

is forever.

EX

*I*nstead of trekking to Nepal,
I love going to Palm Beach and Long Island.
Some people call that boring, I call it classic.

DIANA VREELAND

use; nor is there
essity for it. Yet
t do without it.

REUD

There is one fundamental fact about lighting:
where there is no light, there is no beauty.

BILLY BALDWIN

Signature SPACES

Signature SPACES

WELL-TRAVELLED INTERIORS
by Paolo Moschino & Philip Vergeylen

VENDOME SCRIPTUM

*I'm going to make everything around me **beautiful** – that will be my *life*.*

ELSIE DE WOLFE

To our parents.

Foreword

By Min Hogg

*W*ell-Travelled Interiors, the subtitle to this book, expresses perfectly the lives and thinking behind the London-based decorating duo that compiled it, Paolo Moschino and Philip Vergeylen.

Alongside pictures of their work the book includes scattered spreads of snapshots taken while travelling the world, from which they derive inspiration and later translate into the various client schemes, or to their in-house fabric collection. These collages contain a mix of interesting textures, colour combinations, single objects, joinery, plasterwork, patterns, people and architecture.

Thus we can follow a three-dimensional stone façade seen on the walls of The Gesu Nuovo Church in Naples interpreted later in wood panelling to line the walls of a townhouse stairwell, or find the meandering line of Rome's River Tiber as a raised moulding winding its way across the fitted cupboard doors of an Italian client, and the plasterworked pattern of geometric tracery from a room by Madeleine Castaign in Paris reproduced in paint for a bathroom.

They have abandoned the norm of text running throughout by substituting appropriate quotations, or 'bon mots' uttered by famous and infamous, past and present, members of the artistic worlds, and which chime with their own ethos. For example, *'I'm going to make everything around me beautiful, that will be my life'* – Elsie de Wolf.

There are splashes of eccentricity too. Who could predict a client's wish for a stuffed polar bear to grace an interior to be fulfilled within weeks? By contacting London's Zoo the decorators joined a waiting list for the next bear to drop dead. There was astonishment all round when shortly one did, and they rushed it to a taxidermist.

The skilfully varied approach, be it for the luscious or the strict, in each and every job shows sympathy towards both tastes and needs of the owners. Attention to the original architecture and its location are matched by a welcome emphasis on the provision of generous storage – can one ever have enough? And to an enviable finish throughout.

Incidentally, they are rather good fun too.

Style is a simple way of saying complicated things.

JEAN COCTEAU

Introduction

By Philip Vergeylen and Paolo Moschino

We have both always been passionate about design, although neither of us set out to become designers. Paolo is Italian and studied political science, then came to London aged 23 for a few months. He ended up running an interiors shop – and never left. Philip is Belgian, and says his parents gave him three choices of profession: doctor, banker or lawyer. But, while pretending to study in his first year at university, he found ten years' worth of a design magazine in his grandmother's library and eagerly read every issue cover to cover. (This might have been a clue to his real interests.) Much later, after a high-powered career in financial services, he met Paolo and began to help him with some interior design work coming his way. Now he runs the company's interior design studio.

Perhaps our lack of formal study is what keeps us so impassioned about our work. For us, design isn't a job – it's our life. We are always studying, always absorbing, always looking at design, art and architecture. We designed our first apartment together about 20 years ago, when Paolo was running the shop he had bought from the designer Nicky Haslam. People – customers, friends – would come to the apartment, and then to the shop, and say, won't you do my house? That's how it slowly started, and it just grew organically. Today we have projects on every continent.

As our company has grown over the years, we have been very fortunate to be surrounded by great people, and we are proud to have built a strong team that fully shares our passion. Working in our office often feels like being in a pressure cooker, but luckily we all love what we do and the pressure is always mixed with lots of laughter. Nobody in our team walks – we RUN! We are both workaholics, but, then again, when your work is your passion, it doesn't always feel like work.

~

We have strong feelings about everything – we either love or hate, we are rarely indifferent. That's contagious for clients. When they see that we have bold reactions, it gives them confidence to have their own opinions. We don't mind at all if people think differently to us; what's important is to have the confidence to express what you like and don't like. If you're reluctant to take risks, you will end up with something half-baked. Go with your instincts, we say, and run!

We don't think of ourselves as having a specific style as designers. If you can walk into a house and say, 'Philip and Paolo did that,' it would be a failure for us. What's important to us is to really understand our clients, and for them to trust us. We spend a lot of time with them, talking, planning, shopping. Often we become friends because we all get to know each other so well. Sometimes someone will spend an afternoon deciding on a lampshade; other times, people make key decisions very quickly because they are extremely busy. We like both extremes. The only thing that really matters to us is that the trust is there.

~

People come to us through different channels. They read about us, have been referred, or have seen our work at a friend's house. Best of all is when we've already done a project with them and they come back.

Starting a new project is the most exciting challenge. We will visit to get an idea of the location, scale and complexity of the undertaking. Location is important: you can't do the same kind of house in the tropics as you would in the mountains. At the same time, that doesn't mean that because a house is in Texas you need to build a ranch – but it does need to be suitable for its environment. Absorbing the space and surroundings, and getting to know the client, gives us an adrenaline high that makes the wheels turn at super speed in our heads.

Our list of clients looks like the United Nations, and we find it endlessly fascinating to work with people of different backgrounds. (This is also reflected in the mix of nationalities of the members of our team.) What do they like? What do they dislike? How will they live and use the space? Do they want a showhouse that will knock your socks off, or something understated, calm and serene? Is it going to be a cosy family home that's not precious? Or do they need a very formal house with plenty of space for entertaining? It's very important to understand these factors in great detail from the beginning. Then ideas and concepts start accumulating, ready for editing at a later stage. This is what makes us jump out of bed in the morning. (When Philip is off on a creative whirlwind, with ideas sparking in every direction, Paolo is always there to keep his feet on the ground.)

~

Then comes the time to make ideas reality. Needless to say, this sometimes comes with challenges (although we never accept the statement that something is impossible) and construction delays. But challenges often make the outcome better. You can have rooms with tiny windows in a corner and everything off-balance, underground areas with no natural light, limited possibilities for outdoor space. You need to look at it, and say: how do I create order when everything is wonky? Our own dining room in London was a terrible room, with windows and doors in odd corners, but we put in fake doors and balanced the proportions, and now you would never know.

Proportion is hugely important to us; we will literally pick up half a centimetre if it is wrong in the balance of a room. It's very important to establish the difference between interior design and simply furnishing a house. We like to create the bones, to think about the interior architecture, how everything works together. After all of that is thought-through, *then* you can decorate. And how gratifying it is when you see progress and watch your designs come to life!

~

Once the essential structural elements are in place, we like to twist what you see. Philip is particularly good at visualising every project down to the smallest detail. He says that when he finds it difficult to 'see' a room in his head, he knows there is something wrong and that we need to change our approach. Essentially, our mantra is: architecture takes a lot of effort, should be perfect and look perfect; interior design takes an equal amount of effort, should be perfect, but never look perfect. Perfection in architecture is beautiful, but in interior design, it can be very sterile and lack personality. What we like in interiors is some order with an unexpected twist. We try to avoid rooms that look staged, and are always looking for an element of surprise and humour.

In one project – a dining room with a seventeenth-century reclaimed church stone floor and Georgian panelling – we used Georgian chairs, but instead of putting in a chandelier, which might have been the obvious route, we suspended a contemporary sculpture by Saraceno made of Perspex and aluminum. And, in one of our current projects – a massive reception room in a mansion of grand proportions in London – we are putting in a twisted neon light inspired by Lucio Fontana. When one or two items are unexpected, the room doesn't look like it has been designed in one day. We like strong design bones, but comfort too, so that you get the right mixture of allure and charm. What we don't like are contrived or self-conscious interiors, or bland ones that don't reflect the personality of the owner.

Clients play their part too. We are happy to use everything that our clients own; we don't take jobs to sell furniture, but to create an environment that is perfect for them. Often someone will have a really weird pair of armchairs, or some other item that makes you initially think 'oh no'. But ultimately that can make the room, because it's idiosyncratic and represents their personality. Of course, you also have times when people get overly focused on using something they spent a lot of money on and which doesn't really work. You have to know when not to throw good money after bad, and that's also advice we might offer.

We love to juxtapose styles and eras. If you want a perfect eighteenth-century French interior, you don't need a designer, you need a scholar and curator. We rarely match things or use pairs, except for bedside tables! We travel a great deal, and are always thinking about every project. For us, they never really finish. Sometimes we'll find a lamp four years after a house was completed, and ring the owners to tell them it would be perfect in such-and-such a room. That's how it should be; houses live and breathe and change, like their owners, and this is something you want to feel as soon as you enter a home.

~

For us, there are two elements that make a house sing: books and art. We always look at the books people have, what they are reading, what interests them. And we consider putting art on the wall to be part of our remit. Philip spends at least an hour a day looking at catalogues, and works closely with galleries and auction houses.

Working with art is one of the most exciting elements of our job – but art is a very subjective area. Some people have huge collections, and it's a real privilege to work with that. But other clients are much more tentative, with little experience or a lack of confidence about buying art. Enthusiasm, however, is contagious, and we find that – with some encouragement – people get caught up and inspired when they start to buy art. It can take a while; if you have never bought art, and aren't familiar with the market and how it all works, it can be a pricey learning curve. And this is where our experience can help.

If clients are uncertain about their tastes, we encourage them to start off in one medium, like photography. After a while they start to say, 'I like this, not that.' Then, if they are interested in taking it to the next level, we encourage them to look more widely. We love eclectic collections of art, sculpture and objects. Art has been created for thousands

of years; let's show that! In one project we put a colossal Roman torso in front of a Louis Morris painting, and Bruegel and Warhol paintings of flowers next to each other. Those juxtapositions can be really revealing, and make you see the artworks differently. (And we firmly believe that you can always find space; we're not known for our minimalist streak!) But what's most important is that the art is meaningful for our clients. We would rather find a place for a mediocre painting that someone loves than a Picasso they are indifferent to.

The maxim that good pieces will work together is true also for furniture; you can put an eighteenth-century commode alongside two 1950s armchairs, and it will look great if each item has integrity. Our tastes tend towards antique and vintage furniture, rather than contemporary pieces, although we frequently commission custom-made pieces. We love the crafts of upholstery, boiserie, carpentry, metal-work. People are constantly coming up with new materials and new ways to work with older materials, which we find so exciting.

~

These innovations inspire us, but so do books, travel, artworks and people. Sometimes the way someone describes a house in a novel or memoir makes you feel you can almost smell and see those interiors. Or it can be a piece of art. Philip has an enduring memory of an abstract white sculpture by the French-German artist Jean Arp, that he saw floating on a lake when he was 12 years old. He says that, for him, this was the discovery of pure beauty, and of an emotion of wonder that he tries to recapture in his work. Coming across these moments – when an object, image or situation really speaks to you – is important to our work, although we never use anything literally. A good example of the way we want to use these inspirations is a gorgeous drawing of the Silver Room in the Amalienburg Pavilion in Munich, by the great illustrator Jeremiah Goodman (page 122). It loses the details of the building, but captures the spirit; it allows you to dream.

The Ballets Russes era is also a big influence for us, and you'll see a picture of Nijinsky and a drawing by Bakst amongst the collection of images that show some of our favourite sources of inspiration. Again, it's not so much that what Bakst designed is a direct reference; it's more about a creative moment, a few years in European culture when everything exploded. Stravinsky, Picasso, Cocteau, Ravel; they broke all the rules and gave us new pathways for creativity.

For us, it's all about creative energy. Cy Twombly, Maurizio Cattelan, Balthus, Velasquez – these are all artists who create work that punches you in the stomach. Or Francis Bacon, whose use of colour is just genius, and who is able to take an existing masterpiece and transform and reinterpret it, as in his portrait of Pope Innocent X, shown in this book, so that it is 100% his own. As Yves St Laurent once said: reinterpretation is creation. That is a very liberating idea.

Look at the picture of Cocteau's desk on page 9. Paolo took the photo because he loved the fact that it was messy, yet beautiful, and incongruously set against leopard-print wallpaper. Cocteau wasn't 'decorating'. He has pinned up various pictures, written on the board, and his working tools are on the table. Nothing is planned or staged, none of his own work is shown, but it is filled with personality, and tells you so much about him. That is the challenge for us as designers. We don't want to create pretty stages; we want houses that reflect the essence of our clients.

Travel can also be a great source of inspiration for us – even virtual travel. We have a picture here of a man in a bright yellow jacket, sitting under a huge antique sculpture, which comes from one of our favourite movies, *La Grande Bellezza* ('The Great Beauty') by Paolo Sorrentino. It is set in Rome, and has the most wonderful witty dialogue, music and scenery. It gives you a deliciously sarcastic view of the city, its society, fashion and art. We also have pictures of some real trips, including one of a man in a headscarf that Paolo took during a cruise on the Nile. We were virtually the only people on the boat because there had just been a crisis in Egypt, and it was a magical trip.

We are also often inspired by historical figures. Take Eugenia Errazuriz, a Chilean heiress who came to Europe, was a patron of Picasso and Diaghilev, and had an enormous influence on the design aesthetic of the twentieth century. She bought a farmhouse in Biarritz, painted everything white and hung unlined linen curtains. Her friends thought she had gone mad; where were the tassels? The velour? But she could see the beauty in materials and in ordinary objects, like a watering can. She was the first society person to have, say, a spectacular Louis XVI commode and put a wicker basket with a plant on it. Now, we take that sort of thing for granted, but at the time it was revolutionary. She sought the beauty of simplicity, and we try to pay tribute to that idea.

Cecil Beaton is another fascinating figure for us. When he was living in Wiltshire, he decided to throw a *fête champêtre* for his friends, but he didn't have much money and felt his house looked a bit drab. So he spent the whole night sewing buttons on to his curtains. How creative! How different! The lesson is about thinking outside of the box, and understanding that you can turn ordinary things into something fabulous.

~

What is most important for us is to keep a spirit of openness and play. We are a good mix, because we tend to look at things from a different perspective, but in the end we both enjoy ourselves. We take design and decoration very seriously – but it's also serious fun.

Our passion for design, and the pleasure we get from seeing beauty, takes us on a non-stop journey. With this book we want to take you, the reader, along with us.

*Le grand ennemi
de l'art, c'est le bon goût.*

The great enemy of art is good taste.

MARCEL DUCHAMP

Fidel Castro

Elegance is elimination.

EUGENIA ERRAZURIZ

Everyone was usually an actor, but when she made her entrance, they automatically became spectators …

ALBERTO MARTINI ON THE MARCHESA CASATI

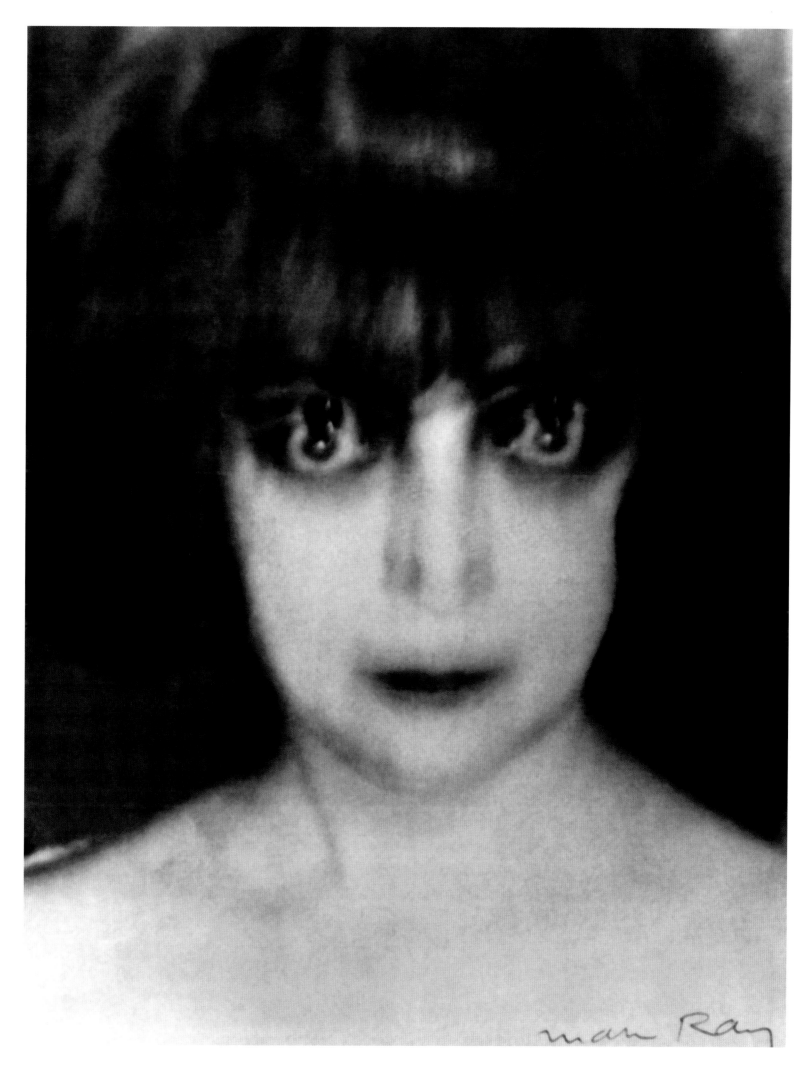

The wilder the idea, the newer, the farther out, the more it demands that you know why you want it. If you fall in love with something, that's all that matters.

BILLY BALDWIN

To *look* at a thing is very different from *seeing* a thing.

OSCAR WILDE

eople who collect out of love are exempt from the dictates that govern traditional design, for there are no rules for true lovers.

ROSE TARLOW

On the books: HORSHAM *A History* HAINES

The real voyage of discovery consists not in seeking new landscapes, but in having new eyes.

MARCEL PROUST

Le laid peut être beau, le joli, jamais.

The ugly can be beautiful, the pretty never will.

PAUL GAUGUIN

If you can dream it,
you can make it!

WALT DISNEY

All I want is the best of everything and there's very little of that left.

LUCIUS BEEBE

I have *not* yet, *indeed,*
thought of a remedy for *luxury.*
BENJAMIN FRANKLIN

Remember, *colour* is not just *colour*, but **mood**, *temperature* and **structure**.

VAN DAY TRUEX

Writing has laws of perspective, of light and shade, just as painting does, or music. If you are born knowing them, fine. If not, learn them. Then rearrange the rules to suit yourself.

TRUMAN CAPOTE

163

Never copy.
Be yourself.

The world worships the original.

LUISA CASATI

One must always draw, draw with the eyes, when one cannot draw with a pencil.

BALTHUS

Je ne peins pas ce que je vois,
Je peins ce que je pense.

I don't paint what I see,
I paint what I think.

PABLO PICASSO

Whisky, gambling and Ferraris are better than housework.

FRANÇOISE SAGAN

Picture Credits

Page 2: Clive Nichols

Pages 4–5: Nicholas Haslam Ltd

Page 6: Clive Nichols

Inspirational:

Page 9: Jean Cocteau's Study by Phillipe Petit © Getty Images

Inspirational:

Page 10: Simon Upton/The Interior Archive

Page 15: Simon Brown/*House & Garden* © The Condé Nast Publications Ltd.

Pages 16–17: Simon Upton/The Interior Archive

Pages 18–19: Simon Upton/The Interior Archive

Pages 20–21: Clive Nichols

Pages 22–23: Tim Beddow

Page 24: Simon Upton/The Interior Archive

Page 25: Tim Beddow

Pages 26–27: Simon Upton/The Interior Archive

Pages 28–29: Simon Upton/The Interior Archive

Pages 30-31: *Scrapbook: from left to right:*

Top row: Etienne George/Getty Images, Paolo Moschino, Nicholas Haslam Ltd, Nicholas Haslam Ltd, G. Dagli Orti/Getty Images

Centre row: Art Media/Getty Images, Nicholas Haslam Ltd, Tom duBrock/Verdura NY, Nicholas Haslam Ltd, Time Life Pictures/Getty, *Berger des nuages, Shepard of Clouds* by Jean Arp 1953 and floating water sculpture by Marta Pan. Photo © Collection Kröller-Müller Museum, Otterlo, the Netherlands

Bottom row: Paolo Moschino, Pictorial Press/Alamy Stock Photos, Paolo Moschino, Nicholas Haslam Ltd, Nicholas Haslam Ltd, Cecil Beaton/Conde Nast

Pages 32–33: Simon Upton/The Interior Archive

Pages 34-35: Simon Upton/The Interior Archive

Inspirational:

Page 37: Bust of Cecil Beaton in front of reproduction Button Curtains © Roger Barnard/*'Cecil Beaton At Home' Exhibition*/Beaudesert Ltd

Pages 38–39: Simon Upton/The Interior Archive

Pages 40–41: Simon Upton/The Interior Archive

Pages 40–43: Clive Nichols

Pages 44–45: Simon Upton/The Interior Archive

Pages 46–47: Simon Upton/The Interior Archive

Inspirational:

Pages 48–49: Museum, *After the Deluge* series © David LaChapelle/Art + Commerce

Pages 50–51: Simon Upton/The Interior Archive

Pages 52–53: Clive Nichols

Page 54: *top left;* Jan Baldwin/Narratives, *bottom left;* Tim Beddow, *centre* Simon Upton/The Interior Archive

Page 55: *top right;* Jan Baldwin/Narratives, *bottom right;*

Nicholas Haslam Ltd

Pages 56–57: Tim Beddow, Nicholas Haslam Ltd

Pages 58–59: Simon Upton/The Interior Archive

Inspirational:

Page 61: Eugenia Errazuriz, circa 1930, by Man Ray; © Man Ray Trust/ADAGP

Pages 62–63: Gemma/Nicholas Haslam Ltd?

Page 64: Simon Upton/The Interior Archive

Page 65: Jan Baldwin/Narratives

Page 66–67: Clive Nichols

Page 68: Simon Upton/The Interior Archive

Page 69: Simon Upton/The Interior Archive

Inspirational:

Page 71: Marquise Casati, 1920, by Man Ray; © Man Ray Trust/ADAGP, Paris and DACS, London

Pages 72–73: Simon Upton/The Interior Archive

Inspirational:

Page 74: TK Coral Ballroom, Palazzo Brandolini © Contour/Getty Images

Page 75: Jan Baldwin/Narratives

Pages 76–77: Simon Upton/The Interior Archive

Page 78: Simon Upton/The Interior Archive

Page 79: Clive Nichols

Page 80: Clive Nichols

Page 81: Tim Beddow

Page 82: Simon Upton/The Interior Archive

Page 83: Jan Baldwin/Narratives

Inspirational:

Page 84: Neon structure by Lucio Fontana at the Museo Del Novecento © Mondadori/Getty Images

Pages 85–86: Simon Upton/The Interior Archive

Pages 87–88: Simon Upton/The Interior Archive

Inspirational:

Page 90: Babe Paley by Horst P. Horst © Getty Images

Pages 92–93: Simon Upton/The Interior Archive

Pages 94–95: Simon Upton/The Interior Archive

Pages 96: Nicholas Haslam Ltd

Pages 97: Paolo Moschino

Pages 98–99: Jan Baldwin/Narratives

Page 100: Jan Baldwin/Narratives

Inspirational:

Page 101: Sculpture by Mittoraj © Francesco Venturi

Pages 102–103: Simon Upton/The Interior Archive

Page 104: Simon Upton/The Interior Archive

Page 105: Clive Nichols, Nicholas Haslam Ltd

Page 106: Tim Beddow

Page 107: Simon Upton/The Interior Archive

Page 108: Simon Upton/The Interior Archive, *bottom;* Jan Baldwin/Narratives

Page 110–111: Simon Upton/The Interior Archive

Page 112: Nicholas Haslam Ltd

Page 113: Simon Upton/The Interior Archive

Inspirational:

Pages 114–115: Hall of Mirrors, Villa Palagonia, Bagheria, Sicily, Italy © DeAgostini/Getty Images

Pages 116–117: Belgrave Square?

Pages 118–119: Simon Upton/The Interior Archive

Pages 120–121: Simon Upton/The Interior Archive

Inspirational:

Page 122: Illustration by Jeremiah Goodman of the Silver Room at the Nymphenburg Palace, courtesy of Jeremiah Goodman Studio Archive.

Pages 124–125: Simon Brown/*House & Garden* © The Condé Nast Publications Ltd.

Pages 126–127: Clive Nichols

Pages 128–129: Simon Upton/The Interior Archive

Pages 130–131: Clive Nichols

Inspirational:

Page 133: *Pope Innocent X*, study after Velasquez, Francis Bacon, 1953 © Bridgeman Images/Des Moines Art Center

Pages 134–135: Clive Nichols

Pages 136–137: Simon Upton/The Interior Archive

Page 138: Clive Nichols

Inspirational:

Page 139: The television room at Ferrieres, home of Baron and Helene de Rothschild by Hort P. Horst © Getty Images

Inspirational:

Page 140: *Sunbaker* by Max Dupain, 1937 © Art Gallery of NSW

Pages 142–143: Simon Upton/The Interior Archive

Page 144: Nicholas Haslam Ltd

Inspirational:

Page 145: Cecil Beaton (1904–1980) at Reddish House, his home in Broad Chalke, Wiltshire, 1951 by Paul Popper © Popperfoto/Getty Images)

Inspirational:

Pages 146–147: *Man's Conquest* mural, Rockefeller, NY by Jose Maria Sert © Ann E Parry/Alamy Stock Photo

Page 148: Simon Upton/The Interior Archive

Page 149: Tim Beddow

Pages 150–151: Simon Upton/The Interior Archive

Inspirational:

Page 152: Palace of Versailles, Door to the Salon d'Apollon, Palace of Versailles by Raphael Gaillarde © Invictus SARL/Alamy Stock Photo

Inspirational:

Page 153: The stairs of the Petit Trianon in Versailles © 2011 Gamma-Rapho

Acknowledgements

Pages 154–155: Simon Upton/The Interior Archive

Pages 156–157: Clive Nichols

Pages 158–159: Simon Upton/The Interior Archive

Pages 160–161: Clive Nichols

Inspirational:

Page 163: Writer Truman Capote reclining in his apartment by Constantin Joffe © Conde Nast/Getty Images

Pages 164–165: Simon Upton/The Interior Archive

Inspirational:

Pages 166–167: Novecento, laxidermied horse, leather saddlery, rope, and pulley by Maurizio Cattelan, 1997. Photo © Paolo Pellion di Persano. Courtesy Maurizio Cattelan's Archive.

Page 168: Nicholas Haslam Ltd

Page 169: Clive Nichols

Inspirational:

Page 170: *Boy Leading a Horse*, 1906, oil on Canvas by Pablo Picasso © Granger, NYC./Alamy Stock Photo

Inspirational:

Page 171: *Prince Balthazar Carlos*, c.1634, oil on canvas by Diego Velazquez. Photo © Universal History Archive/UIG via Getty images.

Pages 172–173: Tim Beddow

Pages 174–175: Clive Nichols

Pages 176–177: Simon Upton/The Interior Archive

Inspirational:

Pages 178–179: *Fifty Days at Iliam: The Fire that Consumes All before It*, 1978, oil, oil crayon & graphite on canvas by Cy Twombly. Photo © Bridgeman Images

Pages 180–181: Simon Upton/The Interior Archive

Pages 182–183: Simon Upton/The Interior Archive

Pages 184–185: Nicholas Haslam Ltd.

Page 186: Simon Upton/The Interior Archive

Page 187: Clive Nichols

Inspirational:

Pages 188–189: Yves Saint Laurent In Paris, 1964 by Robert Doisneau © Doisneau/Gamma-Rapho/Getty Images

Pages 190–191: Clive Nichols

Page 192: Clive Nichols

Page 193: Simon Upton/The Interior Archive

Page 194: Nicholas Haslam Ltd

Page 195: Simon Upton/The Interior Archive

Inspirational:

Pages 196–197: *The Living Room*, 1941–43, oil on canvas, by Balthus (Balthasar Klossowski de Rola.) © Brigdeman Images

Pages 198–199: Simon Upton/The Interior Archive

Page 200: *top left* and *centre*; Simon Upton/The Interior Archive, *bottom left*; Nicholas Haslam Ltd

Page 201: *top right*; Tim Beddow, *bottom right*; Simon Upton/The Interior Archive

Page 202: Nicholas Haslam Ltd

Page 203: Nicholas Haslam Ltd

Page 204–205: Simon Upton/The Interior Archive

Page 206: Clive Nichols

Page 207: Simon Upton/The Interior Archive

Pages 208–209: Clive Nichols

Pages 210–211: *Scrapbook: from left to right:*

Top row: Basilica Santa Chiara, Naples © Cindy Hopkins/Alamy Stock Photo, Set of La Grande Bellezza © Gianni Fiorito/ Getty Images, © Nicholas Haslam Ltd, Carlos de Beistegui Venetian Ball © Cecil Beaton/Condé Nast via Getty Images, © Nicholas Haslam Ltd

Centre row: © Nicholas Haslam Ltd, *lower left*; Michel Mercier © Silver Screen Collection/Getty Images, © Nicholas Haslam Ltd, © Nicholas Haslam Ltd, © Nicholas Haslam Ltd, © Nicholas Haslam Ltd, © Nicholas Haslam Ltd, *upper right*; Francoise Sagan ©/AFP/Getty Images

Bottom row: Ballet Russe © Emil Otto Hoppe/Ullstein Bild via Getty Images, © Nicholas Haslam Ltd, © Leeds Castle, © Nicholas Haslam Ltd, © Nicholas Haslam Ltd

Pages 212–213: Simon Upton/The Interior Archive

Pages 214–215: Simon Upton/The Interior Archive

Inspirational:

Page 216: Christian Berard Trompe l'oeil © Pol Baril courtesy of l'Insitut Guerlain.

Pages 218–219: Simon Upton/*House & Garden* © The Condé Nast Publications Ltd.

Pages 220–221: Paul Massey/*House & Garden* © The Condé Nast Publications Ltd.

Page 224: Brian Harrison/*House & Garden* © The Condé Nast Publications Ltd.

Page 225: Simon Upton/*House & Garden* © The Condé Nast Publications Ltd.

Pages 226–227: Simon Upton/*House & Gardenn* © The Condé Nast Publications Ltd.

Inspirational:

Pages 228–229: Piazza, Venice, 2008 © Michael Eastman. Courtesy of the Michael Eastman and Edwynn Houk Gallery, New York and Zurich.

Pages 230–231: Simon Upton/The Interior Archive

Pages 232–233: Simon Upton/The Interior Archive

Pages 235: Tim Beddow

Page 236–237: Nicholas Haslam Ltd

Page 240: Clive Nichols

The authors and the publishers would like to thank the following people, and organisations, for their help and support in the production of this book:

Jan Baldwin and Narratives
Roger Barnard of Beaudesert Limited
Tim Beddow
Karin Howes, the Interior Archive
Susan Kramer and Stan Schaap Carli McCasland, the Edwynn Houk Gallery, NY
and Michael Eastman
Gemma Miller
Clive Nichols
Astrid Obert
Sian Phillips, Bridgeman Images
Nancy Saul, DACS, London
Roslyn Sulcas
Roel van As-Krijgsman, Kröller-Müller Museum

First published in 2016 by VENDOME SCRIPTUM an imprint of

THE VENDOME PRESS
Suite 2043
244 Fifth Avenue
New York, NY 10011
www.vendomepress.com

CO & BEAR PRODUCTIONS (UK) LTD
63 Edith Grove
London,
UK, SW6 5EA
www.scriptumeditions.co.uk

Publishers: Beatrice Vincenzini, Mark Magowan & Francesco Venturi

Copyright © 2016 The Vendome Press LLC and Co & Bear Productions (UK) Ltd

Foreword: Min Hogg
Project Manager: David Shannon
assisted by Alexandra Lima
Design: Malcolm Smythe & Mr Cat
Production: Jim Spivey

All rights reserved. No part of the contents of this book
may be reproduced in whole or in part without prior written
permission from the publishers.

Distributed in North America by Abrams Books
Distributed in the rest of world by Thames & Hudson

ISBN: 978-0-86565-330-6

First Edition
1 3 5 7 9 10 8 6 4 2

Library of Congress Cataloging-in-Publication Data
Names: Moschino, Paolo, author. | Vergeylen, Philip, author.
Title: Signature spaces : well-traveled interiors / by Paolo Moschino &
Philip Vergeylen ; foreword by Min Hogg ; principal photography by Simon
Upton & Clive Nichols.
Description: New York : Vendome Press, 2016.
Identifiers: LCCN 2016033966 | ISBN 9780865653306 (hardback)
Subjects: LCSH: Moschino, Paolo--Themes, motives. | Vergeylen,
Philip--Themes, motives. | Interior decoration--Great Britain. | BISAC:
DESIGN / Interior Decorating. | ARCHITECTURE / Interior Design / General.
| DESIGN / Furniture.
Classification: LCC NK2047.6.M67 A4 2016 | DDC 747.0941--dc23
LC record available at https://lccn.loc.gov/2016033966

Printed and Bound in China by 1010 Printing International Ltd.

Nothing brings on jealousy like laughter.

FRANÇOISE SAGAN

One friend remembered going on holiday with her to Italy and on the first morning she appeared at breakfast totally shattered. When asked what the matter was, she said 'The Leaves!'. It seemed the geraniums outside her window had been 'Clattering together all night'.

SOFKA ZINOVIEFF
The Mad Boy, Lord Berners, My Grandmother and Me

More tears are shed over answered prayers
than unanswered ones.

SAINT TERESA OF AVILA

Une deception en amour s'oubli.
En amitié, elle ne se pardonne guère.

A disappointment in love may be forgotten;
a disappointment in friendship, never.

BONI DE CASTELLANE

Great m
others

WAS

Be daring, b
be anything
purpose and
the play-it-s
commonplac

Polite c

All our fir
state of m

CW00740977

DAMASCUS

The Parisians were astonished that Hottentots cut off a testicle
—whereas the Hottentots were astonished to see Parisians keep both.
Voltaire

But we cannot allow any such reflection to induce us to put
the truth aside in favour of what are supposed to be national interests.
Freud, *Moses and Monotheism*

Gérard Degeorge

DAMASCUS

Flammarion

Contents

Page 2. Map of Damascus illustrating a Latin translation of Ptolemy's *Geographia* by Jacopo D'Angiolo, Florence, c. 1470. Bibliothèque Nationale, Paris. Ms. latin 4802, f. 134v.

Facing page. Al-Wasiti, The *Maqamat* ("Get-together") of al-Hariri: Abu Zayd in the inn of Anah near Damascus famous for its wines, Baghdad, 1237 (634 H). Bibliothèque Nationale, Paris. Ms. arabe 5847, f. 33.

Page 6. Umayyad Mosque. Vestibule and west portico. Morning washing.

واخو العيلة المعيل اذا اخال لم يلم

قال الراوي فعرفت حينئذ انه ابو زيد ذو الريب ذوالعيب ومسود وجه الشيب

وساقي عظم منزه وقبح تورده فقلت له لسان الآنفة واذلال المعرفة الميان اك

ياشيخا ان تقلع عن الحا فتضجر وتمجر وتنكر وفكرت ثم قال انها ليلة مزاج

لا تلاح ونزه تشرب مزاج لا لحاح فعتد عا بدا الجى ان تلانى غدا لانى افارقه فقام من

Introduction

If a well-cultivated bit of land is in the middle of a desert, like the alleged paradise of Damascus in Syria, mere contrast enhances our idea of it.

Immanuel Kant[1]

Syria is that portion of the Middle East bordered on the west by the Mediterranean, separated from the Anatolian plateau by the Taurus Mountains and from Mesopotamia by the Euphrates, and which extends southwards into the Arabian Peninsula.[2] Its position on the world map at the juncture of the three continents of Europe, Asia, and Africa, its place on the great incense and silk trade routes linking India and the Mediterranean by way of the Persian Gulf and the Red Sea account for a history of such breadth and richness that European history pales by comparison into a poor relation in some distant backwater. In the heart of what is a magnificent region, there emerges, from the barren and glinting stones, a city synonymous with the land (in Arabic both bear the name "Sham"): Damascus. Protected from the western rains by the lofty ranges of the Lebanon and Anti-Lebanon,[3] sheltered from the chill gales of the north by the Qalamun and from the southern winds by the Druze *jabal*, the plain of Damascus is characterized by extreme aridity. From May to October, for six solid months, beneath a uniformly blue sky, it is gripped by a heat wave and the sun beats down unremittingly without a drop of rain to soften the blow. Located on the eight-inch (200-mm) isohyetal line (that separating steppe from desert proper), without the waters of the Barada river, Damascus would never have been more than an obscure caravansary. Rising 3,609 feet (1,100 m) above sea level at Zabadani, and joining forces with the runoff and melted snow from a mountainous area twenty-five miles (40 km) wide whose summits exceed 9,843 feet (3,000 m), the Barada winds through a narrow gorge and emerges close to the village of Rabweh in the Damascus floodplain before flowing a further twenty-two miles (35 km) and finally emptying into Lake 'Utayba to the east. In addition to water from a multitude of little springs and wadis running down the mountainside, thirteen miles (21 km) from the city the source 'Ayn al-Fija (in whose honor the Greeks struck coins) provides abundant supply. Even so, left to its own devices, the plain of Damascus could never have supported tree planting and would have been reduced in the best years to a

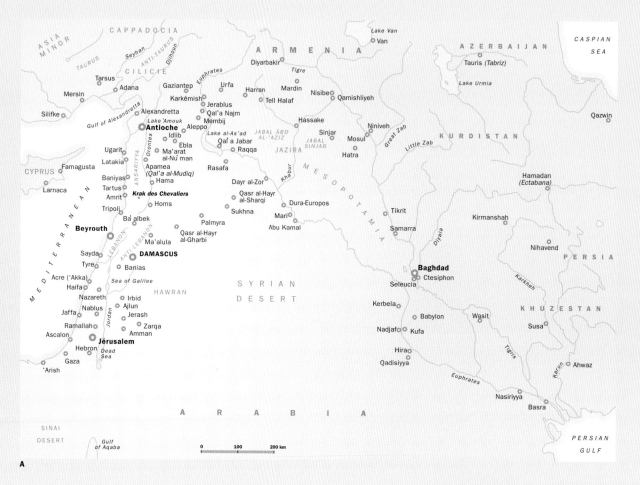

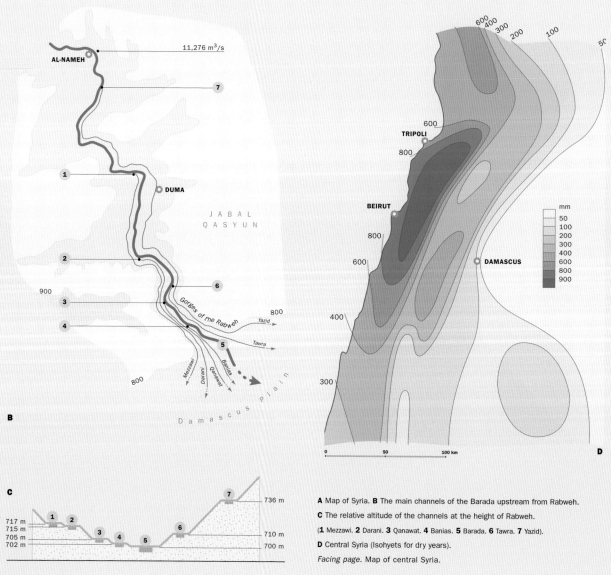

A Map of Syria. **B** The main channels of the Barada upstream from Rabweh.

C The relative altitude of the channels at the height of Rabweh.

(**1** Mezzawi. **2** Darani. **3** Qanawat. **4** Banias. **5** Barada. **6** Tawra. **7** Yazid).

D Central Syria (Isohyets for dry years).

Facing page. Map of central Syria.

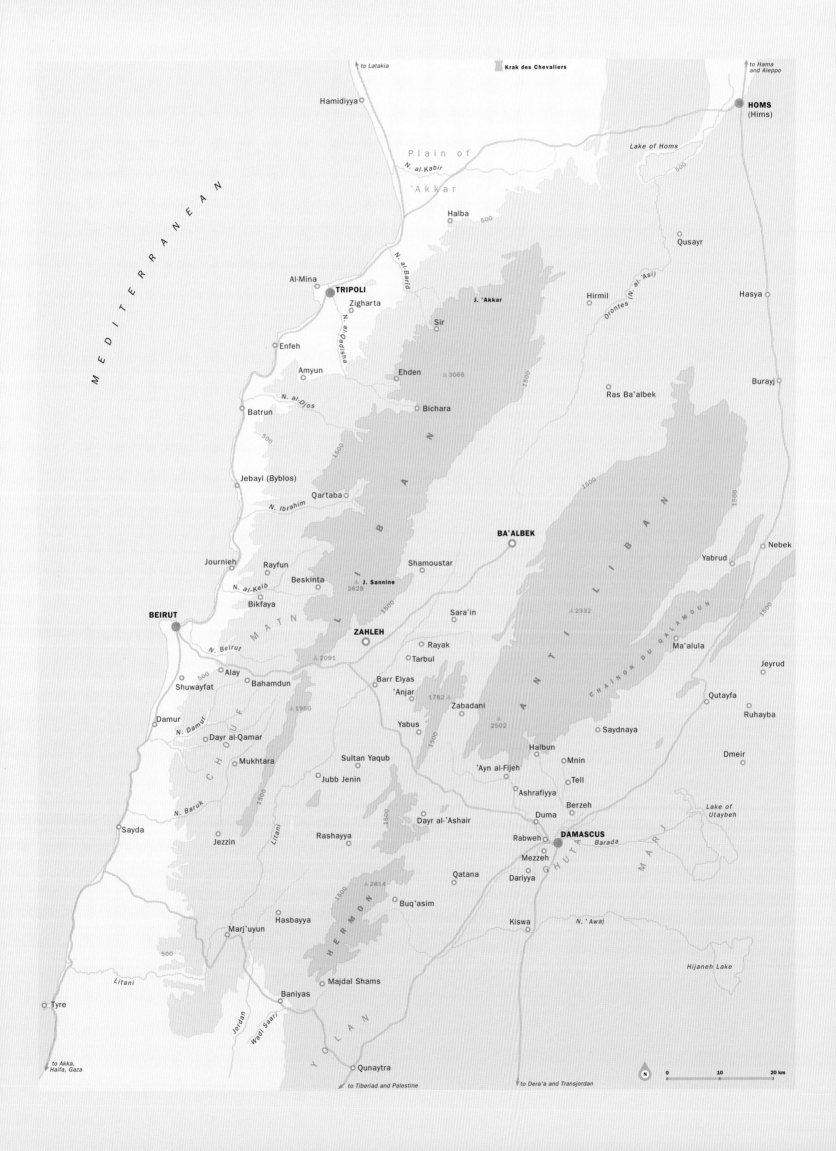

MEDITERRANEAN

to Latakia

Krak des Chevaliers

to Hama
and Aleppo

HOMS
(Hims)

Hamidiyya

Plain of
'Akkar

N. al-Kabir

Lake of Homs

500

Halba   500

Qusayr

N. al-Barid

Al-Mina

TRIPOLI

Zigharta

J. 'Akkar

Hirmil

Orontes (N. al-'Asi)

Hasya

Sir

Enfeh

N. al-Qadisha

Amyun

Ehden   △3066

Ras Ba'albek

Burayj

Batrun

N. al-Djos

Bichara

500

1500

Jebayl (Byblos)

Qartaba

N. Ibrahim

1500

BA'ALBEK

Nebek

Journieh

Rayfun

Shamoustar

Yabrud

Beskinta

J. Sannine

N. al-Kelb   2628   △

Bikfaya

Sara'in

△2332

Ma'alula

BEIRUT

MATN

1500

ZAHLEH

Jeyrud

N. Beirut   △2091

Rayak

Qutayfa

Alay   500

Tarbul

Ruhayba

Shuwayfat

Bahamdun

Barr Elyas

1782

Damur

△1950

'Anjar

Zabadani

Saydnaya

Dmeir

N. Damur

Yabus

2502 △

Dayr al-Qamar

Halbun

Mnin

Mukhtara

Sultan Yaqub

'Ayn al-Fijeh

Tell

Jubb Jenin

Ashrafiyya

Lake of
Utaybeh

1500

Dayr al-'Ashair

Berzeh

Rashayya

Duma

DAMASCUS

Barada

Sayda

Jezzin

Rabweh

N. Baruk

Litani

1500

Mezzeh

Qatana

Dariyya

MARJ

Hasbayya

2814 △

Buq'asim

Kiswa

N. 'Awaj

Marj'uyun

HERMON

Hijaneh Lake

500

Baniyas

Majdal Shams

Litani

Tyre

to Akka,
Haifa, Gaza

Jordan

Wadi Saar

JOLAN

Qunaytra

to Tiberiad and Palestine

to Dera'a and Transjordan

N   0   10   20 km

meager culture of barley or wheat. From earliest times, however, nature has benefited from the aid of human endeavor: at the latest in the Aramaean period, settlers started channeling the water on both sides of the *talweg* into a vast network of canals, thus ensuring a supply of water to the town and permitting the irrigation of thousands of acres of rich alluvial soil. Thus it was that, around the oldest continuously settled city in the world, there arose the most famous oasis in all the East: the Ghuta.[4]

All the main channels—two on the left bank, the Yazid and the Tawra, and four on right, the Mezzawi, the Darani, the Qanawat, and the Banias—stem from the principal bed upstream from Rabweh. The first two feed into the fields and districts on the left bank; the last two supply the quarters within the city walls, while the remaining channels irrigate local orchards and gardens. In such an unforgiving climate, the abundance of water has been a source of universal amazement. "Water flows everywhere, in houses and streets and in the baths," marveled the geographer Ibn Hawqal at the end of the tenth century.[5] "There is such provision of water in Damascus . . . that almost every man has a fountain in his garden as well as in his home," the French naturalist Belon du Mans enthused in 1555.[6] A second system of channels formed downstream in the vicinity of Bab Tuma provides for the eastern part of the Ghuta, and farther towards the east to the lower reach of the valley, the Zor. These main watercourses are seconded by two further and complementary sources: to the north, the waters of the Mnin, and to the south those of the River 'Awaj flowing from the heights of Mount Hermon, which a channel almost nineteen miles (30 km) long carries to the village of Dariyya, whence they disgorge into the principal network.[7]

View of the Ghuta east of Bab al-Sharqi.

From the beginning of April to the end of November, under the eagle eye of the *chawi*—specially appointed agents—each village is allowed access to water at intervals that vary with the type of agriculture concerned. Lying around a city that was already powerful by the first millennium B.C.E., and whose bounty had steadily grown through effort and patience, the vast fertile alluvial sheet stretching out at the foot of Mount Qasiyun has been transformed into one of the oldest and most productive agricultural regions in the entire Middle East.

The western part, where the water is regulated through irrigation and drainage, is the Ghuta—itself a "well-cultivated bit of land"—a mass of greenery extending over more than 20,000 acres (8,000 ha), almost sixteen miles (25 km) long by seven miles (10 km) broad, swathed in orchards and market-gardens, with apricot, pomegranate, walnut, apple, pear, plum, cherry, peach, and fig trees, with myrtle, cucumbers, zucchini, tomatoes, beans and chickpeas, aniseed and sesame, and so on. There then come extensive plantings of fruit-trees and cereals, followed by the Zor, where allotments stand amidst poplar trees and hemp fields. Farther to the east, in less well-irrigated grounds where the water cycle is longer, vines, cereals, and olive trees predominate. Beyond this, as water becomes scarcer still, extensive cultivation replaces plantations and the villages lie farther apart: this is the Marj—the "meadow"—twice the size of the Ghuta and less densely populated. A zone of pasture and cereal crops, a green plain in the spring, morose and dust-blown for the rest of the year, it imperceptibly peters out into the desert steppe, *al-badiya*, and then into the true desert, an immense rocky land that stretches out into Arabia.

Set in a vast crown of greenery, the city dominated by Mount Qasiyun[8] has never been more than a dot on the map.[9] Located at the opening of the alluvial plain on the right bank of the Barada and at some distance from the mountain—as a defensive precaution, no doubt—from east to west it stretches over less than one and a half miles (2 km) atop four tells about sixty-five feet (20 m) high, which are in fact man-made hillocks amassed over the centuries from the progressive accumulation of archeological debris. The highest and certainly the oldest of these—undoubtedly marking the site of the earliest Neolithic village—rises southeast of the Great Mosque less than half a mile (500 m) from the Barada; the second lies in the Christian quarter; the third in the Jewish area; and the fourth in a northern section of the district of Shaghur.[10] As a center of agricultural and craft production, a place of interchange between the Bedouin and sedentary populations, a crossing-point for caravan tracks and mountain corridors, a point of convergence for routes from the Indian and Chinese worlds, from East Africa, Anatolia, Central Asia, the Arabic Peninsula and the Red Sea, and maintaining close contacts with the Mediterranean region through its natural ports of Tyre and 'Akka (Acre), from time immemorial Damascus has enjoyed a political, commercial, and cultural vocation, affirming its position as Syria's chief city as early as the Aramaean period.

Its plentiful waters and teeming gardens have exerted singular fascination. For Muslim authors,

fruits and vegetables
cereals and olivetrees
fruits and cereals
cereals
vines
villages

QASIYUN

DAMASCUS

MARJ

N   0   1   5 km

Agriculture in the Damascus Ghuta.

Damascus is the living image of paradise. Tabari lists it as one of the four places of the world "full of delight and pleasures";[11] al-Muqaddasi places it among the four earthly paradises,[12] and Ibn Khurdadhbeh calls the city one of Nature's best-favored sites.[13] Dimashqi includes it among "the most salubrious, beautiful, and elegant cities on earth," comparing it to "a white bird settling in a vast meadow and drinking of the waters that flow up to it from every side." [14] According to the celebrated fourteenth-century traveler Ibn Battuta, it is "the city which surpasses all other cities in beauty and takes precedence of them in loveliness,"[15] while one poet was inspired to dub it "a beauty spot on the cheek of world."[16] For Europeans, it seemed an enchanting haven where one could rest easy after endless days of tramping through the desert: "Truly, there is no one who, laying eyes on Damascus, would not freely confess it to be the site of the most beautiful city in the world," wrote the French traveler Jean Palerne in 1582.[17] An evocation of its channels, orchards, and gardens was soon to become an obligatory purple passage in any description.

As if its exceptional location and the eminent role it has so often played in world history are not enough, Islamic tradition—not invariably exacting as to the trustworthiness of its sources—has further gilded the lily, and no exaggeration seems too far-fetched. Indeed, striving to augment its fame, glory, prestige, holiness, and nobility, anything and every-thing has been enlisted. Unknown and unknowable before modern archeology, the confusion sur-rounding its origins was extreme, and each in his own way attempted through interpolations and/or extrapolations—in the main tendentiously shored up by tall tales from the Bible—to push the date of its foundation back to remotest times. "Damascus was built by Dimashq, son of Qani, son of Malik, son of Arfakhshad, son of Sem, five years before the birth of Abraham," was al-Muqaddasi's estimate.[18] Undaunted, Ibn Rusteh, an author of the tenth century and originally from Isfahan, claimed to have it on good authority and not mere hearsay that "the first enclosing walls built on earth following the Flood were those of Harran, 'Babil' [Babylon], and then Damascus."[19] According to the talented tenth-century polygraph, Mas'udi, the city is supposed to have been founded by a certain Jayrun b. Sa'ad b.'Ad who settled on the shores of the Barada shortly after the episode of the Tower of Babel.[20] Mount Qasiyun, meanwhile, seems to have served as a magnet for legends. The "cave called by the name of Adam,"[21] is supposed to stand near its summit; then, in the vicinity of Berza, Abraham's native village, there is the "cave of blood," where Cain is supposed to have slaughtered his brother,[22] and to which Abraham, Moses, Jesus, Lot, and Job retreated to pray.[23] It was there too that Elijah found refuge from the kings of his tribe.[24] According to one tradition, the Messiah spent time there with his mother,[25] though another states that it was St. John the Baptist who came with his, while Christ is supposed to have prayed there in the company of his Apostles.[26]

The Ghuta has not been forgotten either, since it is here that Ya'qub (Jacob) is said to have put his sheep to graze.[27] In the village of Bayt Lahya to the east of Damascus, the father of Abraham, Azar, made the idols that the future biblical iconoclast was to become so intent on destroying.[28] Lastly, Ibn 'Asakir maintains that between Mount Qasiyun and Bab al-Faradis (one of the gates in the northern rampart) there lie the tombs of no fewer than seventy thousand prophets.[29]

Eschatology too raises its head, propelling the history of Damascus forwards from the Dawn of Ages to the End of Time: tradition has it that "it will be the final refuge of mankind at the outbreak of the bloody disorders marking the end of the world";[30] another version has Jesus descending down the great white minaret of Bab al-Sharqi on the Day of Judgment.[31] This biblically tinged farrago, which in all probability overlays still more ancient pagan traditions, attests to the fact that Damascus is not only an immensely venerable city, but also one that has always occupied a preeminent place in the Oriental imagination.

The gorges of the Barada and the Beirut–Damascus road (late nineteenth-century print).

N ORR Sc

From Neolithic village to imperial capital

The emergence of agriculture and settlements

In spite of numerous tall tales linking its origins with figures as fantastic as Abraham, Gog, and Noah, everything would indicate that Damascus began life as a Neolithic village. Between 12,000 and 10,000 B.C.E. in the whole of the Levant from the Nile to the Euphrates, a culture developed known as the Natufian, named for a wadi in Palestine—the wadi al-Natuf—where it was first discovered. Although not attested in the Damascus region, its presence is recorded in the mountainous regions bordering the Damascus basin, the Hawran, the Qalamun, and the area around Saydnaya. While the economy had not progressed beyond the Paleolithic stage of hunting and gathering and fishing, the first sedentary villages began to appear, with half-buried houses, circular in plan and roofed over with branches and reeds. It was against this backdrop of settlement in various localities over a strip of alluvial land between the steppe and the mountain linking the valley of the Jordan to that of the Euphrates via the Damascene,

that, in around 9000 B.C.E., the earliest experiments in agriculture were made. Hunting and gathering remained the main source of food, but humankind, exerting an increasing influence over its milieu and gradually sheltering itself from environmental risk, evolved from the state of predator to that of producer of its own food. Since excavations on the site of the city itself are now impossible, the only digs have been at tells in the immediate vicinity.

The village of Aswad was founded shortly before 9000 B.C.E. on the banks of Lake 'Utayba about twelve miles (20 km) to the southeast of present-day Damascus. The staple crop of emmer of a domesticated morphology—thus attesting to the presence of agriculture in the full sense—was to appear from the very outset of occupation and formed the basis of a diet supplemented by pulses such as peas and lentils, the spontaneous harvesting of barley and wild fruit, including pistachios, figs, capers, almonds, wild rosehip, and grapes, as well as local game taken by hunting—gazelle, wild boar, oxen, equines, deer, waterbirds, etc. Archeological material reflects the economic evolution. Stone tools consist primarily in blades, sickles, notched arrows, borers, gravers, and scrapers. Bone tools are rare but very diverse and include punches, needles, smoothing-tools or slickers, parers, spatulas, tool handles as well as pendants. Both stylized animal and human figurines and macropygian female statuettes, with their hands clasped over the abdomen below prominent breasts, were modeled in clay then hardened by fire. At the end of the tenth millennium, obsidian from Cappadocia, in the form of shards or lamellae, attest to relations between the Damascus region and areas several hundred miles distant. As to funerary arrangements, corpses were buried huddled in single-occupancy graves dug out of the bare ground. The village attained its greatest extent in the first half of the eighth millennium, by which time it had covered the entire tell. Control over agricultural techniques improved markedly and cereals—including the newly "domesticated" barley—came to occupy a more significant place as a foodstuff, as testified by the growing proportion of sickles among the stone tools found. The number of tools made from bone grew significantly, while the clay-modeled animal and female figurines in turn became ever more elaborate and varied. It was during this period that, about ten miles (15 km) farther to the north, groups probably originating in Aswad founded a new village on the Ghurayfah tell, whose occupation was barely to

last until 7000 B.C.E. Life there was virtually identical to that in Aswad, differing only in the domestication of the sheep recorded at the earliest phase of occupation of the site.

The final stage in the occupation of the Ghurayfah tell appears contemporary with the foundation of a new village about ten miles (15 km) to the southwest of Damascus on the site of the Ramad tell. Lying at the foot of Mount Hermon and near the confluence of two wadis in a zone where the level of rainfall allowed dry cultivation, the Ramad tell was located on a significant north-south transport route. There agricultural techniques were also making progress, with emmer and barley now being supplemented by the cultivation of lentils and flax. The number of domesticated animal species also increased, and included goats, sheep, oxen, pigs, and dogs.

Architecture likewise stood at a crossroads: if the houses, similar to those in Aswad and Ghurayfah, were still circular and half-buried at the initial level of occupation, thanks to increased mastery over building techniques, they were soon to adopt a rectangular plan. Aligned along lanes, the floors of dwellings were now pargeted; the foundations were in stone, the superstructure in unfired clay brick measuring $16 \times 12 \times 4$ inches ($40 \times 30 \times 8$ cm)—dimensions close to those produced by peasants in villages of the Damascus area today.[1] A new material made its appearance: lime, molded and smoothed, sometimes painted with red ornamental bands. This form of white pottery ("whiteware") identical to that in the contemporary levels at Ras Shamra, Byblos, al-Kowm, Buqras, and Abu Hurayra, testifies to improved control over firing processes that paved the way for the emergence of ceramics proper. In addition to animal and human stylized figurines, skulls removed from the skeleton after defleshing, modeled over with lime, and heaped together in pits, perhaps indicate a religious component—something like "ancestor worship," mirrored by a possible belief in the afterlife and an unprecedented sense of continuance and inheritance.

The main Neolithic sites in the Damascus region.

This practice was in any case widespread in the majority of contemporary villages in Neolithic Syria (Jericho, Baysamun, Kfar Ha Horesh, 'Ayn Ghazal), to which parallels can be found in parts of the world as remote as New Guinea. During the final period of occupation of the Ramad tell, which saw the advent of lusterware with incised decoration, the impoverishment of the tools and the disappearance of permanent dwellings bore witness, as in the rest of southernmost Syria, to the progressive extinction of sedentary settlement and its replacement, in all probability, by herding.

According to the current state of knowledge, sedentary life in the Damascus region seems to have been interrupted for more than one thousand years, taking up again only in the second half of the sixth millennium, almost two miles (3 km) from Aswad at the tell of al-Khazzami, where only sporadic provisional excavations have ever been carried out. Except for the al-Khazzami tell and some pottery collected on the surface at the Ramad tell, the upper strata of which appear to have been eroded away, nothing is known of the Damascus region during the sixth and fifth millennia.

From the sixth millennium, the so-called Ubaidian culture, originating in southern Mesopotamia and characterized by monochrome-painted ware, spread throughout the Middle East from the Mediterranean to the Persian Gulf. Together with the appearance of monumental buildings of a public nature[2] in conjunction with dwelling places, this marked a watershed in the development of agricultural societies. The village, with its insignificant differentiation in terms of topography and social life, gradually receded before more complex forms of social organization implying the accumulation of economic surpluses, a measure of standardization in craftsmanship, and an upsurge in interchange. The Neolithic "revolution"—a slow maturation that in fact stretched over millennia—led to an "urban revolution" that was indeed consolidated in a matter of generations.

Urban revolution

Seemingly without prompting, around 3300 B.C.E., while Syria was still languishing at the Neolithic stage of the agricultural village, flourishing agglomerations sprang up in the land of Sumer and neighboring Susiana—city-states extending over dozens of acres and possessed of both monumental architecture and extensive trading networks. Intensified exchange also created the ideal conditions for one of the crucial inventions in human history: writing. The phenomenon of urbanization gradually gained ground throughout Syria: by the end of the fourth millennium, Habuba Kabira, founded in the mid-valley of the Euphrates by emigrants from Uruk, had become an agglomeration of forty-five acres (18 ha) of regular plan surrounded by a rectilinear rampart flanked by rectangular turrets; at the beginning of the third millennium, in an effort to monitor river and caravan traffic a little downstream, Mari was founded, built on a circular plan. Nevertheless, compared to the startling conurbations in the land of Sumer, whose surface area could attain 100 acres (40 ha), the earliest Syrian towns seem both modest and late arrivals on the scene. To date, the oldest known example in interior Syria, Ebla, arose at the beginning of the third millennium, evolving progressively from an earlier settlement. It was to become a powerful regional state, whose territory extended from the plain of Antioch to Karkemish (Carchemish) in the north and Hama to the south. It is in the cuneiform records from this city written in Eblaite (a local branch of archaic Semitic[3]) that mention is first made of Damascus. Although no studies focusing on the Damascus region in the third millennium have yet been published, it would certainly have played a role—at least to some degree—in the rise of urban civilization underway in Syria during that period. In any case, excavations carried out in Damascus in 1965 within the enclosure of the present-day Umayyad mosque unearthed a vase dating from the mid-third millennium.

Bronze Age female terracotta figurine dating from the second half of the third millennium B.C.E. (excavation by the Franco-Syrian Mission). This figurine is the most ancient vestige unearthed to date on the site of the city itself.

the existence of a sizable city surrounded by a sturdy rampart almost ten feet (3 m) high, while Dayr Khabiyya possesses vestigial fortifications. In addition to being a caravan stage, Damascus was probably already a fortified economic center.

Pawn of the Great Empires—Egyptian, Mitanni, and Hittite

At the end of the third and beginning of the second millennium, Amorite nomads encroaching eastwards brought about a deterioration in urban life in many areas of Syria and marked the end of the last Sumerian dynasty in Mesopotamia. Belonging (linguistically speaking) to the family of the Semites from the west, the new arrivals gradually settled the area, founding a series of kingdoms with capitals at Karkemish, Aleppo, and Qatna (Katna). To the south of the latter city stood the land of Amurru, probably including the area of Damascus which at this time bore the name 'Apum. A cylinder seal, discovered in 1948 at Dayr Khabiyya around a dozen miles (20 km) southwest of Damascus, attests to relations between this area and Mesopotamia in the eighteenth century B.C.E.

In the absence of any mention in contemporary texts, nothing is known with certainty about Damascus in the first half of the second millennium. Nevertheless, the caravan routes attested to only a short time later were already surely in use, and considering its abundant water, agricultural resources, and site, Damascus must have been one of its most important staging posts. If, due to lack of excavation, the city itself has revealed nothing from this era, two tells in the vicinity have provided a trickle of evidence: the al-Salihiyya tell has revealed

By the second half of the second millennium, the Damascus region was designated by a slightly modified form: 'Api, transcribed in cuneiform as Upi.[4] Its geographical limits remain in doubt, however, and it is not even certain that Damascus was its capital. Nevertheless, like other contemporary cities, it was ruled by "kings," though the names of only two have come down to us: Ariwana and Zalaya. Knowledge of the city's history at this juncture derives from records of the conflicts opposing the three great powers of the time: Egypt, the Mitanni, and the Hittites. Ascending to the throne in 1490 B.C.E., Pharaoh Thutmose III bore Egyptian power to its apogee, triumphing in Syria at Meggido over a coalition led by the prince of Qadesh (Kadesh). The names of the 119 cities whose sovereigns were captured at the battle are carved on a pylon at the temple of Amon in Karnak, beside a monumental relief showing the pharaoh's enemies squirming at his feet as he seizes them by the hair. Appearing here for only the second time in history, Damascus is listed among the cities in the form *ta-mas-q*. In the reign of Amenophis III, as indicated by an inscription on a statue found in the funerary temple of the pharaoh at Thebes, *ta-mas-q* numbered among the towns in Syria subject to or on friendly terms with Egypt. According to diplomatic correspondence rediscovered at Akhenaton, the current tell of al-Amarna, dating from the reign of Amenophis IV (1379–1362 B.C.E.), Egypt preserved authority over southern Syria—including the country

Facing page. The Crossing of the Red Sea by the Hebrews. Fresco in the Synagogue at Dura-Europos. Damascus Museum.

of 'Api. Precious clues as to how this authority was exercised in the provinces also survive: as long as taxes and foodstuffs made their way to Egypt, the vassals could still wield power—though a small garrison commanded by an Egyptian officer would be posted in certain localities to arbitrate in case of dispute between rival cities. One letter mentions Damascus in connection with a quarrel between the kings of Amurru and Byblos. Unearthed in 1969 at Kumidi—present-day Kamid al-Lawz in the plain of the Beka'a—another was sent by the pharaoh to a certain Zalaya, "king of Damascus." One often encounters governors lamenting predations by armed outlaws, the Habiru—sometimes, and probably incorrectly, identified with the Hebrews[5]— and, more especially, an evidence of a growing concern with the threat posed by the mighty Hittites. As soon as he acceded to the throne in 1380, Suppiluliuma annexed a good part of Syria, including Egypt's subject territories, such as Ugarit, Amurru, Qadesh, and Damascus, whose King Ariwana was

sent into exile in Anatolia. After a century of conflict, a peace treaty signed between Ramses II and the Hittite king Hattusili III in 1283 roughly established the border between the two kingdoms on a line running south of Qadesh.

Capital of an Aramaean state

At the turn of the twelfth century, a haphazard confederation of populations from the north—the "Sea Peoples," as they were dubbed by the Egyptians who saw them arrive by boat—swept away the Hittite Empire and devastated Syria before Ramses III halted them at the gates of Egypt itself in 1182. Among these were the Pelesets, i.e. Philistines, who were to settle the southern Syrian littoral. After the passage of these "Sea Peoples," a veil of silence lasting several generations fell over Syria. When further documentation surfaced, the Syrian political scene had altered profoundly and, around the edges of the

desert, the Aramaeans—newly arrived seminomadic Semites—stood at the head of principalities, such as Bit Bakhiani, Bit 'Adini, Bit Agushi, and Bit Gabbari.

Although they had probably ranged over the borders of the Upper and Mid-Euphrates by the middle of the second millennium, their first appearance in history occurs in the chronicles of the Assyrian king Tiglat-Pileser I (1116–1076 B.C.E.): "Twenty-eight times I have crossed the Euphrates after the Aramaean Ahlamu. I defeated them from Tadmar, which is in the land of Amurru. . . . Their booty and their property I carried to my city of Assur."[6] Concerning central and southern Syria, the only feasible recourse is Biblical sources, though these demand the greatest prudence since their reliability is far from guaranteed. In effect, archeological discoveries in the last few decades have undermined many of the historical bases of the Biblical chronicle, in particular as regards the wanderings of the patriarchs, the exodus from Egypt, the conquest of Canaan, and the fabled empire of David and Solomon.[7] There is ample proof today that Deuteronomic history, far from being inspired by a god to a prophet in a bush, is no more than a prosaic account of the political ambitions of the kingdom of Judah during the reign of Josiah in the seventh century B.C.E.; that the two Books of Kings, so often quoted even in our time as indisputable authorities, are fables concocted in the seventh century and no historical record at all; that David and Solomon were no more than chiefs of hordes who roamed over a tiny mountain range; that, in the tenth century, Jerusalem remained a modest hamlet;[8] and that, as archeology and sources external to the Bible bear out, the earliest and true kingdom of Israel was that under Omri (884–873). The conquest of the Aramaean kingdom of Damascus by David (1004–965), so fulsomely reiterated in the Bible,[9] seems today little better than a forgery. Much the same patently goes for the conflict which, according to I Kings 11:23–25, is supposed to have raged between Rezon, king of Damascus, and

Israel throughout the "reign" of Solomon. A few years after the death of the latter, Bar-Hadad I was to elevate the Aramaean kingdom of Damascus into the top regional power.

According to I Kings 15:18–20 and 2 Chr. 16:1–6, Asa (911–870), king of Judah, during a border dispute with a rival, Basha (908–885), king of Israel, gathered together all his property—"took all the silver and the gold that were left in the treasures of the house of the Lord," as the Bible text has it—and packed it off to Bar-Hadad I with an invitation to sever the alliance with Basha. Overrunning the north of Israel, Bar-Hadad I forced Basha to withdraw the troops besieging Jerusalem, thus extending the hegemony of Damascus southwards for at least a decade. I Kings 20:1–34 records a prolonged conflict between Hadad-'idr of Damascus and Ashab, son of Omri, king of Israel,[10] that singularly fails to tally with Assyrian sources which, on the contrary, make mention of an alliance between the kings of Hamat, Damascus, and Israel to counter recurrent threats from the Assyrian monarch Salmanasar III (858-824). The inventory of the forces on the battlefield of Qarqar in 853 confirms the predominant role of Damascus in the coalition: while the army of Ashab marshaled 200 chariots and 10,000 foot soldiers and that of Irhuleni of Hamath, 700 chariots, 700 cavalry and 10,000 infantry, Hadad-'idr's numbered 1,200 chariots, 12,000 cavalry, and 20,000 infantrymen.[11] A little later, Hadad-'idr, having lost his life in somewhat mysterious circumstances, was replaced by a certain Hazael. Relations worsened between the erstwhile allies and they clashed at the battle of Ramoth-Galaad. Salmanasar III once again took to the warpath reaching the gates of Damascus, but—having failed to storm the city—cut down the trees in its gardens and laid waste to the hinterland. This siege, the first recorded in the histories, marked the beginning of a long series numbering more than one hundred. In 838, having gained an indecisive victory over the troops of Damascus, for a second time Salmanasar III was thwarted before the city.

Free from the Assyrian threat, Hazael could now concentrate his armies against Israel, which soon lost the majority of its possessions in Transjordan, marching on Jerusalem whose king, Jehoash (Joash) (800–784), according to 2 Kings 12:17–18, reverted to the stratagem used by his predecessor, Asa, and bought off the Aramaeans with treasure from the temple and his palace. The kingdom of Damascus was then left as the dominant power in southern Syria. Yet, enfeebled by their struggles, the states of Syria were not long in finally succumbing to the might of Assyria. Around 796 B.C.E., Bar Hadad III, son of Hazael, was forced to submit and pay tribute in his own palace to the Assyrian monarch Hadad-Ninari III. The inventory of this tribute testifies to the prosperity of Damascus by this time.[12] In 732,

following a forty-five day siege, Tiglat-Pileser III stormed Damascus, put to death its last king, Rahianu, devastated the orchards, and carted off a substantial proportion of its inhabitants. Contrary to Isaiah's oracle, Damascus was not reduced to a "ruinous heap,"[15] but it was fourteen centuries before the great Aramaean city would regain its status as a capital of an independent State, under the Arab dynasty of the Umayyad. In 722, Sargon II seized Samaria, whose population—in particular the craftsmen, notables, and military—were taken captive back to distant Assyria.[14] In 587, after devastating the countryside around Damascus, the king of Babylon, Nebuchadnezzar, took Jerusalem, set fire to the palace and the temple, flattened the city walls, and deported its people.

The Christian village of Maʻalula, whose inhabitants speak Aramaic to this day.

In spite of a lack of fieldwork on the actual site of the city, it is still possible to gather a cursory picture of Aramaean Damascus. Assyrian and biblical texts referred to previously present it as a powerful and prosperous place, endowed with a palace and staunchly defended behind ramparts whose exact disposition, however, remains unknown. A palace probably stood on a piece of raised ground—a tell built up from layers of archeological material and not a natural feature—approximately twenty feet (6 m) high and close to the center of the current intramural

city, a district whose Greco-Roman name, *al-Baris* ("the citadel"), was current at the time of the Islamic conquest and may preserve the memory of its onetime occupant.[15] The presence of gardens and orchards that the Assyrians did their utmost to dilapidate during successive sieges proves that a highly developed irrigation network was in place. Indeed, when 2 Kings 5:12 asks "are not Abana and Pharphar rivers of Damascus?" the latter is identifiable with the Barada and the former with one of its primary offshoots, the Banias. It is moreover probable that the channel denoted today by the Aramaean term *al-Tawra* ("the Bull"), already existed at the time on the slopes of Mount Qasiyun. As for the temple, it undoubtedly occupied the site of the present-day Umayyad mosque. There are incontrovertible sources stating that the mosque stands on the site of the Church of St. John the Baptist, which was merely a refurbishment of the temple of Jupiter Damascenus, itself built on the site of the temple of Zeus, an avatar of Hadad, the Aramaean god of storms, thunder, and rain. Furthermore the building is mentioned twice in the Bible, first at 2 Kings 5:18, in a passage relating the cure of Aramaean war chief Na'aman, then more especially at 2 Kings 16:10–12, detailing its wealth and prestige: when, in 732, Achaz (Ahaz), king of Judah, traveled to Damascus ahead of his ally Tiglat-Pileser III, he was so impressed by the temple altar that he had a model (together with plans of the entire building) sent to the priest Urias

Top. Fretwork ivory plaque of Arslan Tash, formerly Hadatu. To either side of a tree, a pair of affronted ram-headed sphinxes sporting the *pschent*, the Egyptian royal crown. Second half of the eighteenth century B.C.E. Aleppo Museum.

Bottom. Basalt orthostat found in 1948 during restoration work on the Umayyad Mosque. Ninth or eighth century B.C.E. Damascus Museum.

(Urijah) with orders to erect a similar one at the temple at Jerusalem. The earliest material evidence of the construction, a basalt orthostat later set up in the central wall of the hellenistic sanctuary, beneath the Umayyad mosque, came to light by chance in 1948. In addition to this orthostat, a series of carved ivory plaques found in the palace belonging to the Assyrian governor of the city of Hadatu (present-day Arslan Tash) might well originate—as the name Hazael inscribed on one of them implies—either from the tribute paid by Hadad-Ninari III, or from the sack of Damascus by Tiglat-Pileser.[16] If the political history of the Aramaeans was short-lived, their cultural influence was to endure for centuries. From the eighth century, Aramaic, a Semitic language close to Hebrew and Arabic, was to become the administrative language of first the Assyrian then the Persian Empires, imposing its currency from the Indus to the Bosphorus. The language of Jesus, in the form of Syriac, it remains today the liturgical language of several Christian communities in the Middle East. In the Ghuta, many villages still bear Aramaic names: Kafr Batna, Aqraba, etc.

Annexed by the Persian Empire during the reign of Cyrus (c. 550–c. 530), Syria constituted the satrap "beyond the river." Historical documentation on contemporary Damascus is meager, the only material vestiges being a handful of inscribed seals and two capitals that might have belonged to the palace of the governor. In the literary field, the city is mentioned but once by the Greek geographer Strabo who wrote at the dawn of the common era: "Then begins the Damascus region, a justly praised land whose chief town, Damascus, passed at the time of Persian domination for the most famous city in this entire region of Asia."[17] It was in any case to Damascus, stoutly defended behind ramparts and surely stationed by a Persian garrison, that Darius III dispatched his wives and treasure for safekeeping shortly before facing Alexander at the battle of Issus in 333 B.C.E.

The conquests of the Macedonian witnessed the onset of a period that—through his immediate successors, and then with Rome and Byzantium—lasted nearly a thousand years until the arrival of the Muslim Arabs in the seventh century C.E. Nevertheless, the Hellenization of Syria, pursuant on a determined policy of urbanization, was all in all a superficial phenomenon: Greek, the language of the court, administrators, lawyers, major traders, and more generally of all those who found it advantageous to assimilate the politically dominant culture, never percolated down to the mass of the population, who remained faithful to the old Aramaic idiom. Urban growth brought in its wake a vast development program in the countryside, where agricultural machinery improved markedly, with the introduction of watermills, Archimedes' screws, norias, and oil- and vine-presses, while modernized irrigation works increased the area available for cultivation. In the urban domain, no city, not even Alexandria, could hope to compete with Antioch, the new capital established by Alexander's successor Seleucos I, for the magnificence of its portico-bordered avenues, public services, and suburbs, including one named Daphne renowned throughout the Orient. As for Damascus, during the early era of Macedonian domination, eclipsed by more recently established settlements, it whiled away the time as a local trading center; then, at a date that remains somewhat doubtful, perhaps 111 B.C.E. when Antiochos IX made it his transitory capital, a Greco-Macedonian colony was set up without the city walls to the east of the Aramaean city. In accordance with the principles of Hippodamos of Milet, firmly endorsed by Aristotle,[18] the new districts adopted a regular plan with straight, orthogonal streets from about ten to sixteen feet (3–5 m) wide separating rectangular plots of approximately 328 × 148 feet (100 × 45 m), built with terraced houses, each reachable from the thoroughfare. Still today, whereas in the western zone no regularity in the street layout can be discerned, in the eastern part of intramural Damascus, and in spite of considerable modifications in plot division brought about by frequent rebuilding over the centuries, the average spacing of the streets—328 feet (100 m) for those lying east–west and 148 feet (45 m) for the north–south ones—is identical to that in other Hellenistic foundations in Syria, such as Laodicea, Antioch, and Aleppo.

These two adjoining towns—the old Aramaean city around its temple in the west and, in the east, the new Greco-Macedonian city centered on its agora—amalgamated only slowly, and it is likely that, at some unspecified date, the fusion of the two cities was sealed by the erection of new ramparts. There as elsewhere, Hellenism respected the local religions—all the more readily since its own divinities were largely Hellenized counterparts of Eastern gods. Zeus merged with the Aramaean Hadad and was worshipped in the great temple at Damascus that was probably rebuilt in Hellenistic style. An effigy of Zeus-Hadad appears on the reverse of a tetradrachm struck at Damascus in the reign of Antiochos XII. As

so often the case in Syria, during this period Damascus was given a string of Greek appellations: Philadelphos (285–246 B.C.E.), under Ptolemy II; it is also supposed to have been briefly known as Arsinoia and, at the beginning of the first century B.C.E., as Demetrias, when Demetrios III (88–85 B.C.E.) settled there temporarily. Greek mythographers—whose vein of inspiration is on a par with the Holy Scriptures—declare that it was founded by Damasco, son of Hermes and the nymph Alimede.

During the disorders attending the collapse of the Seleucid dynasty, in 84 B.C.E. the city entered the orbit of Nabatean Aretas III. Under this king, a new district was founded outside the walls to the east of the Hellenistic city, as seems proved by the slightly offset alignment of the north-south streets and the name this area bore in Islamic times: Hara al-Nabatiyyin, the "Nabatean quarter." In 72 B.C.E., it was seized by Tigranes, king of Armenia. Less than ten years later, in 64 B.C.E., the Roman proconsul Pompey excluded the last Seleucid sovereign, Antiochus XIII, from the throne, and turned Syria, with Antioch as its capital, into a Roman province. Rome was to lavish great care on what was a strategically important province for the safety of the empire, chasing pirates in the eastern

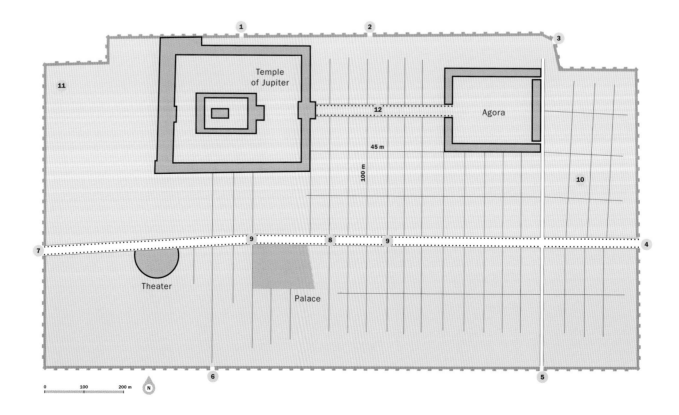

Bab al-Sharqi in a late nineteenth-century print. The central and south bays
of the Roman gate, not yet restored at that juncture, were filled in. Only a single dogleg
entryway existed in the northern bay to the right of the minaret.

"Western" interventions

Mediterranean, monitoring the border for nomads and incursions from Iran (Parthian until 224 C.E., and then Sassanian), repressing Jewish revolts, etc.

Although in the absence of systematic excavations, few material residua of the Damascus of earlier times (save an orthostat, some seals, and two capitals) have to date come to light, Roman Damascus is the oldest structure for which architectural elements in situ make it possible to form a relatively precise picture. Of the Roman enclosure—apart from the virtually intact three-bay eastern gate of Bab al-Sharqi—only scattered masonry underpinning subsists, and this is subsumed into later constructions. Erected during the Imperial epoch, the enceinte encompassed the ancient Aramaean city, the Hellenistic city, and the Nabatean quarter within a rectangle measuring approximately 4,920 × 2,460 feet (1,500 × 750 m), with straight sides except to the north where it hugged the meandering course of a secondary branch of the Barada. Built in coursed block in accordance with the tried and trusted methods of Roman fortification, it was pierced by seven gates, each dedicated to a planet. With the exception of Bab al-Sharqi, they were either refurbished, or, in the majority of cases, simply rebuilt in the Islamic period: in the south, Bab al-Saghir, dedicated to Mars and Bab Kaysan to Saturn; in the west, Bab al-Jabiya dedicated to Jupiter; in the north Bab al-Jiniq dedicated to the Moon, Bab al-Faradin to Mercury, and Bab Tuma to Venus.

As late as the beginning of the twentieth century, there stood, in front of this last, the vestiges of a Roman bridge that spanned the river. Connecting Bab al-Sharqi to Bab al-Jabiya, a broad, some 5,000-feet (1,500 m) long thoroughfare with porches lined with shops, the celebrated "Straight Street," or *via recta* of the Acts of the Apostles, cuts through the city from east to west, facilitating connections with outlying areas and communication between the three sectors—Aramaean, Hellenistic, and Nabatean—of the new city. This true *decumanus maximus* that ran through preexistent quarters, as in Palmyra, diverts from the

perfectly straight hippodamic grid in permitting itself two minor deviations each marked by a monumental structure. A second artery with porches perpendicular to the preceding—a veritable *cardo maximus*—connects Bab Tuma to Bab Kaysan, and was laid out on the site of the eastern flank of the Hellenistic wall that was probably destroyed when the Nabatean district was established under Aretas III. In the northeast corner, not far from Bab Tuma, stood the agora, a vast rectangular court shaded with porticos on all sides. By the time of Septimius Severus at the latest, the street linking this to the temple was transformed into a monumental road lined with colonnades.

While Damascus was famous for its prunes, figs, and alabaster,[20] it was to its temple dedicated to Jupiter Optimus Maximus Damascenus that it owed its immense prestige. It was not without reason that Emperor Julian, in the second half of the fourth century C.E. called "holy and vast Damascus" superior to all other towns in the beauty of its ceremonies and the size of its temples, "Jupiter's only worthy city and the cynosure of the Orient."[21]

Facing page. Plan of Roman Damascus. **1** Bab al-Faradis. **2** Bab al-Jiniq. **3** Bab Tuma. **4** Bab al-Sharqi. **5** Bab Kaysan. **6** Bab al-Saghir. **7** Bab al-Jabiya.
8 Straight Street (Via rector). **9** Arch. **10** Hara al-Nabatiyyn. **11** The site of the castrum. **12** Street with porticos linking the temple to the agora.

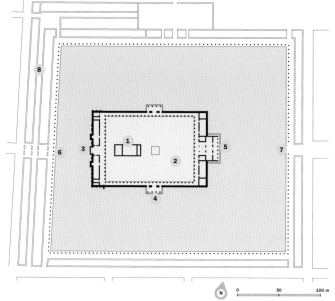

The cella, of which nothing subsists, was flanked by two roughly rectangular enclosures whose major axis lay east–west. Of the external concourse, only an immense quadrilateral approximately 1,247 × 1,017 feet (380 × 310 m) bordered internally by a portico, and some scattered, dilapidated fragments survive: segments of wall, column shafts, a door with a bay, and, more interestingly, in the center of the western side, a monumental gate with a pediment and curved architrave communicating with the "Gamma," a vast market hall skirting the north and west sides, so called because of its plan shaped like the Greek capital letter.

The inner enclosure, with its sober sequence of slightly projecting pilasters surmounted by Egyptian capitals with gorges is, on the other hand, relatively well preserved—except to the northern flank, because that has been used as an external wall for the

Umayyad mosque. Of the four gates in the middle of its side walls, three survive intact: that in the west, Bab al-Barid, which is used today as the main entrance to the Umayyad mosque; the eastern one, Bab Jayrun; and the southern, whose three bays were walled in when the mosque was created at the beginning of the eight century. Inaugurated under Tiberius, the building only attained its final shape towards the end of the first century.

According to the historian Flavius Josephus, Damascus would have possessed a theater and a gymnasium donated by Herod (40–4 B.C.E.), king of the Jews.[22] The existence of the theater, whose site Jean Sauvaget located by surface observation in 1949,[23] has been confirmed by the more recent discovery of significant fragments of its superstructure during the refurbishment of a luxury residence.

Above, left. Temple of Jupiter. Monumental west doorway to the outer compound. *Above, right, top.* Elevation of the east front of the peribolos (restitution by R. Dussaud). *Above, right, bottom.* Plan of the sanctuary. **1** Cella. **2** Temenos. **3** Bad al-Barid. **4** Triple south door. **5** Bad Jayrun. **6** West gate to the outer enceinte. **7** East gate to the outer enceinte. **8** The Gamma.

Built under Diocletian (284–305), the castrum was probably located within the city, at the northwest corner of the rampart, where the present citadel stands. An expanding population necessitated the boring of a new canal, the Nahr Qanawat, to provide water for intramural districts.

Hardly three years after the death of Christ, the most clamorous conversion in the whole history of religion occurred in the shadow of the Damascus city walls: a young Jewish fanatic whom the Sanhedrin had dispatched to seek out those of the faith who had begun to follow Jesus' teaching[24] and bring them back in chains to Jerusalem, saw a dazzling light in the sky and heard voices—shocked to the core and with his soul under extreme tension, Saul turned Apostle.[25] After three days "without sight and neither did eat nor drink"[26] in the house of a certain Judas on Straight Street, he recovered, was baptized, and withdrew to "Arabia," namely to the Hawran and the territories of the Transjordan. Back in Damascus, where the Jews plotted to kill him,[27] his disciples waited until nightfall to lower him down from the ramparts hidden in a basket. His escape, generally dated around 38 C.E., kindled an ardent mission that was to provide Christianity with its cardinal tenet: witness by faith in Christ, who died and rose again for the salvation of Man. The turbulent Word tore through the empire, preaching the Gospel to Gentiles and proclaiming to all those with ears to hear that Faith was stronger than the Law, that the New Alliance depended not on ablation of the foreskin, but on purification of the heart.[28] So it was that, by coaxing Jesus' Jewish disciples out of Judaism and carrying the good news to the "Pagans," Paul made himself the true founder of

South door of the *peribolos* of the Temple of Jupiter. Detail of the moldings of the central bay architrave.

A fragmentary inscription from the *Psalms* can be seen on the lower band.

Christianity.[29] Trumpeting the hopes of Christianity to all men (the resurrection of the flesh, eternal life, and the vision of the Lord), the new doctrine also assimilated the sublunary world with the domain of Satan. The body was henceforth considered as an abject vector of spiritual death, an instrument of sin; no more was it to be a source of pleasure or "for fornication," because bodies are now "members of Christ" and the "temple of the Holy Ghost."[30] Likewise, virginity which, according to John Chrysostom—brings us closer to the angelic condition[31]—is regarded as a state of holiness, following Jesus' expression as recorded by Matthew: "There be eunuchs, which have made themselves eunuchs for the kingdom of heaven's sake."[32] Science and reason—those pernicious fomenters of pride—are also irrevocably cast out.[33] It is entirely understandable then that the tenth-century Islamic authority Mas'udi felt able to write: "When the Christian religion made its appearance among the *Rum* [Romans] it dealt a fatal blow to the structure of science. . . . Everything the Ancient Greeks had discovered was to vanish and the insights of ancient genius were clouded over."[34] For the devout, the watchwords were anaphrodisia, ignorance, and fideism. Perfection was *hypetre*—the state of reducing the body to nothingness. In political matters, the fledgling Christianity recommended absolute submission, "for there is no power but of God; the powers that be are ordained of God. Whosoever therefore resisteth the power, resisteth the ordinance of God."[35]

Anxious to ensure the survival of a sect that long had to remain on the defensive, the Early Church Fathers—Tertullian, Lactantius, and Origen—remained scrupulous in their adherence to the teachings of Christ and advocated tolerance and religious freedom.[36] All this changed when Constantine, after laying his diadem at the feet of the Lord, bound together Church and Crown in a joint plan for global domination. Abominable acts of persecution—the like of which antiquity, a model of tolerance in religious matters, had not the remotest inkling—proceeded to drench the empire in blood. Incomparable in terms of its duration, extent, and cruelty to the relatively limited numbers of Christian martyrs,[37] the vast policy of enforced conversion, unequalled at any time or place, initially affected heretics and then moved on to Jews and Samaritans, before turning in relentless pursuit of the last remaining pagans. During a massive and unparalleled campaign of vandalism, great temples, as well as great swathes of ancient literature, were laid waste by hysterical crowds egged on by crazed monks.[38] Three fateful dates in the reign of Theodosis (379–95) sounded the death knell of the ancient world: 380, the institution of Christianity as the state religion; 391, the banning of pagan worship; 394, the prohibition of the Olympic Games. In 416, pagans were excluded from military service. In 435, capital punishment was instituted for all those who persisted in the ancient cults. The coup de grace occurred in 529 under Justinian: the Platonic school of Athens, whose last director, Damascius, was born in Damascus around 480, was closed and its property sequestered.[39] With the alliance between priesthood and state, the empire degenerated into a theocracy with global designs, as testified by the title then conferred on the emperor: *Kosmocrator* or "master of the world." Obscurantist dogmas unintelligible to the common run, relating to the nature of Christ, the Incarnation, and the Trinity, sparked the famous Christological quarrels of the fifth century that heralded the final schism with Eastern Christendom and incidentally paved the way for the Islamic conquest some two hundred years later. On October 25, 451, with all due solemnity, the Council of Chalcedon defined (theologically speaking) the exact relationship between the human and divine natures of Christ.[40]

In consequence, the empire split asunder into two enemy camps: on the one hand, the Chalcedonians, champions of orthodoxy and of the Roman See; the other, grouped around bishoprics in Antioch and Alexandria, the partisans of Monophysitism, a doctrine according to which only Christ's divine nature subsisted after the Incarnation. The gulf continued to widen between the Byzantine state and the Eastern provinces, such as Syria and Egypt, where Monophysitism gained ground as an expression of political independence of mind. Determined to maintain the unity of the empire at all costs in the face of the Sassanian threat, Byzantine "Caesaropapism" embarked on a program of savage repression that prefigured the worst excesses of the Inquisition. People were burned at the stake, and everywhere "the melancholy odor of the burning flesh of martyrs, rising through the air, wafted into the nostrils of the faithful."[41] Ephrem, patriarch of Antioch, "pitilessly urged on the persecution of the entire East":[42] wretched individuals who put all the more credence in hypostases, consubstantialities, and other absurdities, as they had no clue what they meant, were forced to abjure their faith or pursued to the ends of the earth, driven into the desert, or tortured to death with a cruelty so inventive that an ecclesiastical historian, John of Asia, found it "too wanton and abominable . . . to mention."[43]

In Constantinople, the Manichaeans were herded into boats that were set ablaze on the open sea, while the emperor—ever averse to waste—"ordered their goods to be confiscated, since among them were famous women, nobles, and senators."[44] However, the worst was obviously reserved for the last few survivors of paganism who, as the Code of Justinian had it, "incited the righteous anger of the Lord."[45] Compulsory conversions were organized in every country and the law sentenced to death any apostate convert. In Constantinople, during the nineteenth year of the reign of Justinian, some pagans having been unmasked under torture, "were seized, whipped, imprisoned, and given over to the Churches so that they might learn the Christian faith as befits the pagan."[46] Under Justin II (565–78), whose policies were informed by the most Christian patriarch John Scholasticus, in Syria, Cilicia, and Cappadocia, monasteries were closed, churches demolished, bishops

deposed and arrested, and miscreants burned at the stake. The Jews were not forgotten, and, in 609 under Phocas in Jerusalem and in several other large cities, they too were forcibly baptized. As the war against the Sassanids proceeded to demonstrate the depth of disaffection in the East, a doctrinal compromise was sought under Heraclius. Called Monothelitism, it affirmed the coexistence in Jesus Christ of a single hypostatic energy and a single will, acting sometimes through his humanity and at others through his divine nature. It failed to take root, however, and once more persecution raged, with Heraclius issuing an order "that throughout the empire those who did not adhere to the Synod of Chalcedon were to have their nose and ears cut off and their house rifled."[47]

This odious regime of hatred and fanaticism was about to be swept away by the victorious horsemen of Islam. "This is why the god of vengeance," wrote Michael the Syrian, ". . . seeing the wickedness of the Romans who, everywhere they had the upper hand, were cruelly plundering our churches and monasteries and tormenting us without pity, brought to the southern regions the sons of Ismael [i.e. Muslim Arabs], to deliver us from [their] hands . . . and it was of no insignificant benefit to us to be liberated from the cruelty, spite, wrath, and zeal they showed to us, and thus find peace."[48]

In spite of the Christological disputes, Byzantine Syria—as textual sources and archaeological evidence demonstrate—enjoyed great prosperity. Its situation on both land and sea trading routes with India and the Far East ensured substantial revenues. Industry flourished—in particular that of Tyrian purple that dated from the Canaanite period, silk, established at Tyre and Beirut, and glass, for which Damascus was to become famous. Spurred on by trade and a burgeoning agricultural economy, cities thrived. In the sixth century, the historian Procopius called Antioch the greatest city of the Roman East for its wealth, size, population, beauty, and architecture.[49]

On the cultural front, the language of Demosthenes was instituted as the official lingua franca of the empire under Heraclius. The people, however, remained obstinately refractory to Greek, preferring their customary Aramaic to the extent that John Chrysostom complained that his audience at Antioch could scarcely comprehend what he was saying. Moreover, Syrian literature, which, since second-century Edessa, had been undergoing a revival, had reached its apogee by the sixth century, with historians like John of Asia and proselytizers such as Jacob Baradaeus.

During an administrative reshuffle in 381, Damascus became the chief town and religious center of Lebanese Phoenicia, an area that took in the north of the Anti-Lebanon, the valley of the Beka'a and extended eastwards to Palmyra. In the reign of Theodosius, probably shortly after the edict of 391, the cella of the temple of Jupiter was transformed into a cathedral dedicated to St. John the Baptist, whose head, brought back from Emesa, had been placed there in a special reliquary.[50] It was probably at the same juncture that a Greek inscription—inspired by the Psalms and still legible today—was carved on the architrave of the central bay of the southern gate in the peribolos: "Thy kingdom, Oh Christ, is an everlasting kingdom and your dominion endureth throughout all generations."[51] In addition to the cathedral—which, according to the testimony of Eutychius, "had not its like in the land of Sham"[52]—on the eve of the Islamic conquest, Damascus counted some fourteen churches, and there were others scattered around the green spaces and villages of the Ghuta. A host of religious communities, most famous being those of Murran, Saman, al-Nisa', and al-Hawrani, rose up on the slopes of Mount Qasiyun, where Arab sources also mention a "palace of Heraclius" that is supposed to have remained in situ until the fourteenth century. Within the city walls, at the place called al-Baris, the Arab tribe of the Ghassanid, vassals of Byzantium, also possessed a palace where, according to the poet Hasan b. Thabit, anyone who asked for something to drink received water from the Barada mixed with a delicious wine.[53]

During the Byzantine epoch, probably in the fifth century, as a consequence of the gradual replacement of cartage by portage, the Greco-Roman urban structure began to wax "Oriental."[54] The broad thoroughfares, in particular Straight Street, were slowly invaded by kiosks, around which people would meander through porches laid athwart the street or over stretches of open roadway. Successive demolition and reconstruction—all the more frequent as buildings were in the majority made out of lightweight materials, such as timber and unfired brick—both raised the level of the ground and modified the layout and width of the causeway. Little by little, the vast esplanade outside the temple of Jupiter, which had lost its purpose in a teeming city in which pagan ceremonies were banned outright, was also encroached upon. However, colonnaded passageways, erected between the gates of the peribolos and those of the enceinte protected the entrances to the Church of St. John the Baptist.

Due to its location on the *limes* of the Orient, Damascus was inevitably dragged into the perennial conflict between the Roman and Sassanian Empires. In the century preceding the arrival of the Muslim Arabs, Syria endured the devastation of sixty-four years of war. Virtually every city was besieged, only to be abandoned in partial ruin. John of Asia tells us what occurred at Antioch: "The king of Persia took it, laid it waste, brought it to its knees, burnt it to the ground," and even made off with the marble plaques built into the houses.[55]

Damascus did not escape unscathed: seized in 612 and occupied until 627, a fair proportion of its population was taken into bondage beyond the Euphrates. The following year, Jerusalem was sacked and its inhabitants put to the sword, the Church of the Holy Sepulcher of Emperor Constantine gutted, and the Holy Cross—or whatever occupied its place—

The Umayyad Mosque with its three minarets. To the west, the Qa'itbay minaret crowning the Roman tower; to the north the Minaret of the Bride; to the east the Minaret of Jesus.

packed off to Ctesiphon. This relentless struggle was concluded only in 627 with the crushing victory of Heraclius before Nineveh, leaving both empires drained and unable to offer any serious resistance to the Arabo-Muslim onslaught only seven years later.

Islamic conquest—Damascus as capital of the world's largest empire

Scarcely three years after the death of the prophet Muhammad, on February 25, 635, the Muslim armies obtained over Byzantine forces the victory of Marj al-Suffar—the "meadows with birds"—in the vicinity of Damascus. Following a six-month siege, one of its leading inhabitants—the bishop, according to certain sources; or Mansur b. Sarjun, grandfather of St. John

of Damascus, according to others—laid the keys to the city before General Khaled b. al-Walid. By paying the *kharaj*, a land rate, and agreeing to the *jiziya*, a poll tax levied on adult males able to bear arms, the Damascenes—Christians and Jews alike—were allowed to worship freely and occupy their fourteen churches and one synagogue. About fifteen years after the conquest, a Nestorian bishop paid homage to the tolerance of the conquerors: "The Tayy, to whom God has granted dominion over us, thus became our masters; yet they do not combat the Christian religion; rather they protect our faith, respect our priests and saints, and offer gifts to our churches and monasteries."[56]

Soon the first Muslim monument was to see the light of day: close to Bab Tuma, a mosque was built on the very site where Khaled b. al-Walid had prayed

during the siege. Known by the name of the conqueror, and altered repeatedly over the years, the building (today in a poor state of repair) has been absorbed into the oratories of the cemetery of Sheikh Arslan. Less than a year later, informed of the advance of a mighty Byzantine army from Antioch, the Muslims retired to the shores of the Yarmuk, not far from Lake Tiberias (the Sea of Galilee), where, on August 20, 636, they obtained an overwhelming victory over the forces of Heraclius. On reoccupying Damascus, keen to provide Muslims with a place of prayer in a more central location than that of the small mosque at Bab Tuma, Khaled b. al-Walid set up, in the southeast of the temenos of the Church of St. John the Baptist, a mosque which was known by the name of the Mosque of the Companions, until its replacement by the Great Mosque of Caliph al-Walid at the beginning of the eighth century. Immediately after his nomination by Caliph 'Umar as governor of Syria, Mu'awiya, onetime secretary to the Prophet, ordered the construction to the south of the Mosque of the Companions of a residence capped by a green cupola that gives its name to the building, *al-khadra*—"the green"—and today to the neighboring district. This was, however, probably little more than a refit of the palace that had once belonged to the Byzantine governor.

In 661, Mu'awiya, by this time caliph, having been preferred to the rival candidates, transferred the capital of an empire extending from Iran to Ifriqiya (current Tunisia) from Medina to Damascus. The first sovereign of an Umayyad dynasty whose dominance lasted until 750, Mu'awiya was the true founder of the Arabo-Muslim state. Famous for his eloquence, ruse, finesse, in short, his *hilm*—that inimitable blend of self-control, dignity, ease, and elegance—he lavished his energies on reorganizing the government, reinforcing the army, and developing agriculture and irrigation. He created a veritable finance ministry, a regular mail service between Medina and Damascus, and fostered a policy of openness and tolerance towards the Christian inhabitants. Conscious that the Mosque of the Companions could hardly be said to represent a religion whose authority strengthened with every conquest, he endeavored to obtain from the Episcopal authorities the transfer of the Church of St. John the Baptist, but to no avail. The Gaulish bishop Arculf, passing through Syria towards the end of Mu'awiya's reign, confirmed the existence of two separate places of worship. "Damascus [is] situated in a plain, surrounded by a broad and ample circuit of walls, with numerous towers and is intersected by four great rivers. On all sides beyond the walls are numerous groves of olive. The king of the Saracens has obtained possession of this city and reigns in it. The unbelieving Saracens have built themselves a large mosque here. It contains a large church of St. John Baptist frequented by the Christians."[57]

Mu'awiya passed away in Damascus in April 680 and was buried in the cemetery of Bab al-Saghir,

The supposed tomb of Caliph Mu'awiya in the cemetery of Bab al-Saghir.

where a tomb attributed to him stands today. Yazid, his son and successor, often presented by subsequent historians as a worthless and dissipated prince, in fact continued his father's labors: he completed the administrative and military reorganization of Syria, put an end to the yearly campaigns against Byzantium, reorganized the finances, and attended especially to agriculture, granting concessions on what had been up to then wasteland. In Damascus itself, he improved irrigation in the Ghuta, digging out a new channel on the flank of Mount Qasiyun above the Nahr Tawra, known in the present day by his name, the Nahr Yazid.

In the reign of 'Abd al-Malik, the mass of reforms marks a watershed in the history of the empire: whereas Arabic progressively ousted Aramaic as the written and spoken idiom, as the language of financial administration it replaced Greek and Pehlavi, while an Islamic currency, with gold dinar and silver dirhem, was minted to substitute for the Byzantine denarius. New roads were opened up, the coastal cities damaged by Byzantine raids rebuilt, and the postal service reorganized. In Jerusalem, 'Abd al-Malik built the Qubba al Sakhra, the "Dome of the Rock," and undertook construction of the al-Aqsa Mosque; yet in

Damascus, like Mu'awiya before him, he was unsuccessful in his attempts to have the cathedral ceded to him.

Ascending to the throne at the age of thirty, al-Walid, son and successor of 'Abd al-Malik, was the great builder of the dynasty: mosques were erected in Medina, at Sana'a, Jerusalem, and Fustat, while in Mecca, the Ka'ba itself was completely restored. In Damascus, meanwhile, the "cathedral affair" was coming to a head: threatened with seeing their church at Tuma converted into a mosque, the Christians were obliged to yield. According to the Damascus historian Ibn 'Asakir, the caliph himself gave the signal for its demolition with violent blows with a crowbar on the altar.[58] The cathedral was flattened and a mosque prayer-hall soon occupied the southern zone of the ancient *temenos*.

The new building was a vast rectangular hypostyle hall measuring around 446 × 121 feet (136 × 37 m), with three naves parallel to the qibla wall separated by two rows of arcades each covered with a gambrel roof. To increase the height of its members, a second blind arcade, smaller and on rectangular pillars—replaced by posts after the great

The Umayyad Mosque and Mount Qasiyun seen from the cemetery of Bab al-Saghir.

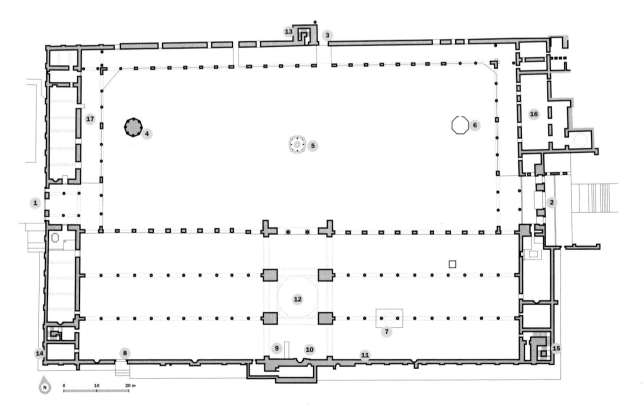

Above, top. Prayer-hall of the Umayyad Mosque.

Above, bottom. The tomb of St. John the Baptist. Plan of the Umayyad Mosque. **1** Bab al-Barid. **2** Bab Jayrun. **3** Bab al-'Amara (Bab al-Natifiyyin). **4** Bayt al-Mal. **5** Ablution pool. **6** Dome of the Clock. **7** "Tomb" of St. John the Baptist. **8** Bab al-Ziyada. **9** *Minbar*. **10** Mihrab. **11** Qibla wall. **12** Qubba al-Nasr (Dome of the Eagle). **13** Minaret of the Bride. **14** Minaret of Qa'itbay. **15** Minaret of Jesus. **16** Mashhad al-Husayn. **17** West portico.

fire of 1893—was placed above the lower arcade, visibly supporting the frame of the interior structure on corbels. A nave perpendicular to the qibla wall bisects the prayer-hall, leading to the main mihrab. Higher and broader than the longitudinal naves, it is also covered with a double-pitch roof from which there emerges a high dome on squinches above the central nave. This latter—destroyed in the fire of 1069 and rebuilt by the Seljukid sultan Malik Shah—was much admired by Muslim authors: according to Ibn Jubayr, "the mind is bewildered as to how this could be erected and assembled to such a height";[59] while for Ibn 'Asakir, "its extent beggars belief";[60] Ibn Battuta called it "the greatest mosque on earth in point of magnificence, the most perfect in architecture, the most exquisite in beauty, race and consummate achievement";[61] while Abu al-Baqa' alleged, "it rose in the air as if suspended."[62]

The principal mihrab was the richest and most ornamented part, "one of the wonders of Islam in its beauty and decorative refinement," as Ibn Jubayr assures us.[63] The prayer-hall communicated with the courtyard that occupied the rest of the ancient temenos by way of a score or so arcades which were, at the outset, closed off by no more than curtains, as attested by Ibn Shakir and the French poet Lamartine in 1833.[64] This device, common in the Byzantine period, found in the majority of early period mosques at Medina, Kufa, Basra, Fustat, Kairouan, and Samarra, and common still today in countries such as India, Pakistan, Yemen, Iran, Mali, well conveys the unity in design of the religious space: a vast compound in which the prayer-hall—the only roofed part—is sometimes termed the *zulla*, meaning "sheltered from the sun." From the outset, all around the court, in the porticos as well as on the

Above. Interior of the Dome of the Eagle as reerected between 1904 and 1910 following the fire of 1893.

Following pages. The Umayyad Mosque viewed from the northeast corner of the courtyard.

35

frontage of the prayer-hall, the tripartite arrangement alternating a pillar and two columns was already the rule.[65]

In addition to its size, cupola, and bold design, the al-Walid mosque, which was to acquire the name of the dynasty responsible, was renowned above all for the magnificence of its decoration, on which, according to Ibn 'Asakir, no less than twelve thousand marble-workers had been engaged. According to Ibn Hawqal, "it exceeded in beauty and architectural design every other mosque in Islamic territory,"[66] while, for Ibn Jubayr, it was "one of the most famous for its beauty, the solidity of its construction, the originality of its architecture, and the splendor of its ornaments and decoration."[67] The capitals were adorned with a thick layer of gold, while the walls were paneled up to the arch springings with an inlay

Above. The west portico in the courtyard of the Umayyad Mosque.
Left. Byzantine capital reused in the Dome of the Clock.
Facing page. Detail of a mosaic panel in the west porch.

of marble and colored stones, in keeping with the time-honored Romano-Byzantine tradition. Above, both in the courtyard and the prayer-hall, an exceptional mosaic extended over every wall, covering a surface area estimated at more than 48,400 square feet (4,500 sq. m). Above the mihrab, various countries were depicted to either side of the Ka'ba, since al-Walid's intention had clearly been to present an image of the immense empire which, from the Atlantic to the Indus, embraced the greater part of the known world in a *dar al-Islam*[68] organized around its mystical center—the Ka'ba at Mecca.[69] This magnificent display was to practically disappear in fires in 1069, 1401, and 1893. In 1924, however, investigations beneath some limewash on a wall of the west courtyard portico brought to light a large rectangular panel some 112 feet (34 m) long: between a pair of bandeaus adorned with rosettes, there emerged an array of architectural structures, some real, some fanciful, including multistoried pavilions, columnated rotundas, kiosks with curved façades, towers crowned with onion-turrets, etc., placed in a luxuriant natural setting in which immense trees,

Above, top and left. Details of a mosaic panel in the west porch.

Above, right. Mosaic in the Church of San Apollinare Nuovo at Ravenna showing the façade of the palace of the Ostrogoth king Theodoric (454–526), which may have been inspired by the architecture of the Umayyad Mosque (on the way the bays are closed off by curtains, see Chapter I, n. 64).

quite out of proportion with the rest of the composition, tower above the banks of a river that flows through the foreground. In addition to the extraordinary skill they demonstrate—more spontaneous than those at the Dome of the Rock— their profound feeling for nature, influenced by the Hellenistic tradition and undoubtedly fostered by views of the countryside in the outlying Ghuta, the mosaics are striking for an exceptional vivacity of hue, their genuine poetry in the transitions, and the subtlety with which the colors are arranged. Executed by Byzantine artists with tesserae transported to Damascus on orders of the caliph, they essentially continue the antique tradition. The multistoried houses, for example, in terms of composition as much

as in the treatment of perspective and shading, recall frescos at Pompeii. Under the mosaic paneling, the latticework marble transennae closing off the windows of the hall situated behind the rear wall of the portico provide the earliest example of geometric interlace in Islamic art.

In addition to its primary function as a place of prayer, the al-Walid mosque was intended to perpetuate the name of its founder and to assist him in gaining access to Paradise[70]—a less pleonastic concern than might appear, since the chronicles cite abundant instances of caliphs of distinctly nominal piety. It was also designed to proclaim the prestige of Islam and the dynasty to enemies beyond its frontiers, as well as to minority discontents within, and to

Umayyad Mosque. Openwork marble transennae fitted into the bays of the western wall of the courtyard.

vie with the beauty of Christian ecclesiastical architecture. As the center of political and administrative life, a kind of extension of the palace in the public arena, the mosque also staged the enthronements of caliphs and governors, in the course of which—if one is to believe the chronicle of Tabari— the drawing of swords was no infrequent event. It was also a place of teaching; and, in general, the mosque was to remain almost the sole focus of instruction until the arrival of a special type of establishment, the madrasa—literally "place of study"—in the twelfth century. Finally, as a sort of forum—today the

expression would be "public space"—the mosque was a place for recreation, for meeting up and promenading, with none of the awkwardness or constraint that reigns in churches. "Every evening," wrote Abu al-Baqa', "the courtyard serves as a meeting-place for the city's inhabitants and as somewhere they go for a walk. One sees them coming and going from the gate of Jayrun to that of Barid: and they stay in these places until evening draws in."[71]

As a turning point in the evolution of an architectural type, the al-Walid mosque (which the French Orientalist Jean Sauvaget considered as "one

Detail of the mosaic panel in the west portico, presumably depicting a hippodrome.

of the masterpieces of architecture from any time and in any land"[72]) imposed itself as the preeminent model to the remotest corners of the empire. When 'Abd al-Rahman I had the mosque of Cordoba built in 786, historians tell us that he did his utmost to make it resemble the one in Damascus as closely as possible. In Syria, the Great Mosque at Aleppo was little more than a replica, while in Damascus itself, the same goes for the much later example of al-Tawba.

The city possessed a *bimaristan* (hospital), which served as both care center (including for the mentally ill), and charitable institution, distributing alms to patients, lepers, the blind, and the needy in general. Its *hammams* must surely have been very numerous and splendid to look at.[73] In the south, a *musalla*—i.e., a prayer area open to the sky—had been established skirting the Hawran (Hauran) road where the al-Musalla mosque currently stands.

The reign of Caliph Hisham (724–43) ushered in the last great period of the dynasty. Muslim arms had been victorious on all fronts: in the north, the borders extended temporarily to the mouth of the Volga, in Gaul, Carcassonne, Nîmes, and Arles were occupied, and even Burgundy menaced. But within, in the peripheral provinces especially, the first serious signs of opposition to the central power were surfacing, based on ethnic, social, or religious divisions. In June 747, under the banner of the 'Abbasids, descendants of an uncle of the Prophet, al-'Abbas, a coalition rooted in diverse interests and embracing all those whom the very success of the Umayyads had excluded from power—the descendants of 'Ali as well as the *Mawali*, converted and manumitted payers of tribute, desirous of obtaining equal rights with the Muslim Arabs in the name of Koranic principles—hoisted the standard of revolt. On November 28, 749, al-'Abbas was proclaimed caliph in the Great Mosque at Kufa and, by April 28, 750, after brief resistance, Damascus capitulated. The carnage was appalling; the city was, according to Mas'udi, "awash with blood"[74] and the ramparts were pulled down. A little later, eighty Umayyads had their throats cut on the banks of the river Abu Futros.[75] On August 17, the last Umayyad caliph, Marwan II, fell, weapon in hand, in Upper Egypt, and his head was dispatched to al-'Abbas. Invited to a banquet to celebrate their reconciliation, the Umayyad princes were calmly put to the sword: "Al-'Abbas had them thrown on a carpet on which he sat, and he ate with the bodies still writhing beneath him. When he had finished, he exclaimed: 'Never have I eaten a meal that did me such good or one that tasted more delicious.'"[76]

In Damascus, the 'Abbasids busied themselves with systematically erasing the memory of their predecessors: some authorities state that the cemetery of Bab al-Saghir, where the Companions of the Prophet who had died at the time of the 635 siege and many Umayyads thereafter had been buried, was plowed up and given over to agriculture. Other historians claim that the palaces were all razed to the ground, though Ya'qubi, who for a stint sometime at the end of the ninth century was a civil servant in the 'Abbasid government, states that most houses in Damascus were former Umayyad residences or palaces, and that the palace of Mu'awiya was taken over as the governor's residence.[77]

The role of Umayyad Damascus in the growth of "religious" science had been considerable. It was there that disciplines that had already emerged at Medina—*tafsir* and *ta'wil* (commentary on and interpretation of the Koran); *hadith* (the Prophetic traditions); *fiqh* (canon law); and *kalam* (defensive apologia)—were nourished by earlier Jewish, Greek, and Christian sources, and the way paved for the great effervescence of the ninth century, which saw vast numbers of translations from Greek into Arabic, often through the intermediary of Syriac.[78] All the sciences, speculative and experimental, religious and secular, were rejuvenated, illustrating the fine words of the Prophet, so often quoted and so unlike Christian obscurantism: "Seek out knowledge from the cradle to the grave, be it in China."

The centuries of darkness–Fatimids, Crusaders, Mongols

The Turks—new masters of the orient

The new 'Abbasid state edged closer to Sassanid traditions, and the Arabs found themselves sidelined progressively, in favor first of the Iranians, then of a people originally from Central Asia, the Turks. The capital moved eastwards, initially to Kufa, then on to Baghdad, where it was established in 762 by Caliph al-Mansur, al-'Abbas's brother and successor. Syria consequently forfeited its central position within the empire, but remained a focus of the confrontation with Byzantium, and later with the Fatimids and Crusaders. On military campaigns and pleasure trips, the caliphs would frequently sojourn in a Damascus now reduced to the status of a provincial capital. In 830, back from a victorious expedition into Byzantine territory, al-Ma'mun (813–33) stayed there, obliterating al-Walid's[1] foundation inscription from the Umayyad mosque. At the summit of Mount Qasiyun, above the monastery of Dayr Murran, he had an astronomical observatory built and dug a new water channel for supplying his men. According to Mas'udi, al-Ma'mun is supposed to have built on a hill a palace that was still known in 945—the date of

Mas'udi's own stay in Damascus—by the name Qasr al-Ma'mun.[2] If Ibn 'Asakir is to be believed, the 'Abbasids would also visit the city "in a search for rest and health and for the beautiful scenery."[3] Waxing a touch nationalistic and eager to display his dietary knowledge, our Damascene author goes on to quote with glee the example of al-Ma'mun who "arrived all enfeebled," but who, managing to take in "twenty-four mouthfuls a day instead of eighteen as before, an increase of a third therefore, gained weight and put on a little muscle."[4] Al-Ma'mun, who called the trees of the Ghuta "the finest jewel anywhere on the surface of the earth,"[5] was besides the most Damascene of the 'Abbasids: "I am astonished to find people living anywhere else, he said one day, how can one live agreeably without this admirable, unequaled spectacle."[6] Ibn 'Asakir provides a striking picture of his last stay in 833, a few months before his death following a routine inspection on the Syrian–Byzantine border: "He stood on the belvedere as the snow fell. He then held out his hand towards the snow and delighted in it for a full hour."[7]

In 859, Caliph al-Mutawakkil even entertained the idea of transferring the capital to the city from

Baghdad. Palaces and splendid residences were refurbished to receive him and his entourage, scholars and scientists. Having sojourned there no more than thirty-eight days, he was forced to return to Iraq to quell disorders instigated by Turkish mercenaries.

By the end of the ninth century, the political fragmentation of the empire kindled in the Eastern provinces by the Tahirids (821–73) rippled out into more central areas. In Egypt, a Turkish officer, Ahmad b. Tulun, founded a local dynasty (independent though nominally a vassal of Baghdad); in 878 on pretext of defending its borders against the Byzantine, he extended its dominion over Syria. Against a backdrop of a declining 'Abbasid caliphate, the reign of the Tulunids in Syria (which lasted to 905) sparked off several centuries of political turbulence marked by territorial division, religious opposition, and incessant rebellion all to the benefit of various invaders—Byzantine, Fatimid, Crusader, and, not long after, Mongol. From the very start of the tenth century, with Tulunid power receding, Syria was laid waste by the Qarmat whose egalitarian and anti-urban ideology took its cue from the Bedouin tribes. Damascus itself was threatened twice, in 903 and 906. In 935, the governor of the city, Muhammad b. Tughj, made himself in turn master over Egypt and founded the Ikhshidid dynasty. He opposed the Fatimids, who had established themselves in Ifriqiya, and the Hamdanid emirs of Aleppo,[8] who were finally overcome at the battle of Qinnasrin, having succeeded in occupying Damascus during April–May 945. In 947, his successor, Kafur, a black eunuch who had reached the highest offices, signed a peace treaty with Sayf al-Dawla of Aleppo that split Syria into two: the north went to the Hamdanids and the south (including the districts of Damascus, Jordan, and Palestine) to the Ikhshidids. In Damascus, during the thirty-month interregnum between the death of Kafur in April–May 968 and the entry of the Fatimid troops, anarchy reigned and power was to change hands no fewer than eight times. Kindled by the most

diverse pretexts—such as the appointment of a qadi or an unpopular governor—riots, with their attendant plundering and arson, became a daily scourge. On several occasions, the Bedouin installed themselves as masters of the city.

On Friday, October 20, 970, following a week-long siege, Fatimid troops who had marched in from Cairo, but who originated in the Berber mountains of Ifriqiya, poured into Damascus. Forced to fall back under threat from a coalition led by the Qarmat, they reoccupied the city, without genuine opposition this time, on June 18, 974. Sheikh Ibn al-Nabulusi, well-known for his opposition to the Fatimid, was arrested, dispatched to Cairo, and publicly flayed alive, his stuffed remains left dangling from a gallows for many months . . . For this dynasty—a new rival of the 'Abbasids who considered Syria at once as a protective glacis and a base for sorties against Iraq—Damascus was a strategic linchpin: located at the crossing of two main routes of invasion, one from the east by way of Rahba and Palmyra, the other from the north via Homs, it enjoyed moreover a religious significance as it controlled the pilgrim road to Mecca.

The century of Fatimid occupation was certainly the most tumultuous in the whole history of the city. Shortly after their arrival, the Maghrebian troops had to counter endless popular revolts: whole districts were set on fire; the Bedouin tore through the farmland cutting down the fruit trees for fuel; the villages of the Ghuta were abandoned, while, with channels diverted, water became scarce, and the baths and suqs closed down one after the other. It was at this juncture, on May 14, 975, that there arrived in Damascus a Turkish officer of the name of Alp Takin, absent without leave from his master back in Baghdad. With the notables investing power in him, "he ruled wisely," as a chronicler of Damascus, Ibn al-Qalanisi, tells us: "He tamed all those who aspired to disorder and every heart quaked with fear."[9] At the end of May, the Byzantine troops of John Tzimiskes, having failed in their attack on Baghdad, traveled up

Page 46. Madrasa al-Nuriyya. Cupola of the tomb of Nur al-Din. In the foreground, the exposed archway of the northern iwan (photograph 1989).

the valley of the Orontes and approached Damascus, opening negotiations with Alp Takin. With the help of a tribute of one hundred thousand dirhem, Tzimiskes spared the city whose pleasures, as Ibn al-Qalanisi alleges, had not left him indifferent: "Having arrived and set up camp in its surrounds, the Ghuta seemed magnificent in his eyes, and he ordered his people to protect its inhabitants from harm and respect everything and anything in its district."[10]

Under constant threat from Byzantine armies, and against a backdrop of religious opposition between Shi'ites and Sunni, disorder involving Bedouin tribes, Fatimid troops, and militias remained endemic for more than a century. From the middle of the eleventh century, a serious political, military, and economic crisis that beset Cairo precipitated the fall of the Fatimid dynasty. In Damascus too, there was a constant stream of riots and uprisings. In 1068, the residence of the Fatimid governors, Qasr al-Sultana, probably situated on the heights of Rabwa, was burned down. On May 10, 1069, as skirmishes broke out between rioters and Maghrebian and Turkish contingents, the Great Mosque itself was gutted. As the sun rose, all that remained were walls fried to a crisp and smoking debris: as one chronicle reads, "the beauties of the mosque were no more and its magnificence was destroyed."[11] Shocked to the core, the population laid down its arms and indulged in a bout of public self-admonition only to join battle soon after with renewed vigor. Part of the city was plundered and torched by the Maghrebi who finally carried the field: yet the days of Fatimid Damascus were definitely numbered. On July 5, 1076, the Turkmen Emir Atsiz b. Uvaq, acting on behalf of the Seljukids, who since 1055 had been masters of Baghdad, entered the city, drove out the Fatimid governor, constructed a citadel,[12] and restored the *khutbah* to the 'Abbasids, thus putting an end to a century of Fatimid domination that was certainly the darkest in the whole history of Syria.

During the Fatimid period, as a consequence of the chronic insecurity that brought with it waves of destruction and rebuilding, the topography of the city had been altered radically. The Greco-Roman *insula* with its terraced houses had long since made way for an irregular tapestry of dwellings. Prolonging developments that started in Byzantine times, the orthogonal network of streets reserved for traffic but which also allowed access to the houses, had transformed into a skein of streets of differing statuses that not only safeguarded privacy but also improved defenses, as Aristotle had already stated[13]—main arterial roads crossing the city from one gate in the ramparts to another, lanes passing from artery to artery shut off every evening by a gate for reasons of safety, and dead ends similarly fenced off so beyond them dwellings could stand open. At the end of the tenth century, al-Muqaddasi had already observed that "the houses were not very spacious and the alleyways poorly ventilated, while space was at a premium."[14] The organic unity of the old Roman city was gradually superseded by a patchwork of more or less autonomous districts, a mosaic of cities within the city, each provided with scaled-down versions of the entire range of urban institutions: mosque, *hammam*, and bakery, with a market nearby for all staples and essential products.[15]

Damascus thus reverted to the character it had had in the Aramaean era before the introduction of a hippodamic plan. Each district, in which a population would gather according to diverse and sometimes intersecting affinities (regional, denominational, tribal, ethnic, professional, familial, etc.), often in open hostility to its neighbors, was placed under the authority of a chief—an *'arif* or sheikh who, backed up by his own militia and nightwatch, also acted as an intermediary between the government and the inhabitants. Nevertheless, elements of community did confer a semblance of unity on the city: the ramparts, rebuilt in raw brick during the second half of the tenth century;[16] the Great Mosque, both a center of religious, political, and educational life and a public arena; the suq, the focus of commercial life from

Following pages. Aerial view of the heart of the old city: Umayyad Mosque, *turba* of Saladin, Zahiriyya madrasa, 'Adiliyya madrasa, Jaqmaqiyya madrasa, Khan As'ad Pasha, 'Anbar *maktab*. Left, bottom corner, the Shi'ite mosque of Sayda Rukayya.

49

Facing page, top. Marble plaque with sixteen lines in Kufic script relating the restoration work undertaken in the Umayyad Mosque by the vizier Ahmad b. Fadl in 1082 under the Seljukid Sultan Malik Shah and Caliph al-Muqtadi. Formerly affixed to the one of the pillars supporting the Dome of the Eagle, it is today in the Museum at Damascus. 42 1/4 × 22 3/8 in. (120 × 57 cm).

which streets radiated, each devoted to its own guild. The main ones lay close by the Umayyad mosque—the booksellers and perfumers in particular—beneath the former Byzantine porticoes leading to the entrance, or else on the site of what used to be Straight Street, now a tangle of roughly rectilinear lanes covered over in places with matting, planks, or beaten earth, and lined with shops sometimes no bigger than a cupboard. It is in all probability this ensemble that al-Muqaddasi called "extremely beautiful, running the entire length of the city, open to the sky."[17] Vast commercial buildings opened on to the shopping streets: *qaysariyya*, which sold only luxury produce, and khan, sometimes called *funduq* (fonduk),[18] consisting in a courtyard flanked by four buildings with, on the ground floor, shops, workshops, warehouses, stables, a place of prayer and, on the floor above, lodging for travelers and caravaneers. Among the products that established Damascus's reputation, al-Muqaddasi mentions "olive oil, *bal'asi* [probably a fine fabric], brocade, violet pomade, copperware, nuts, figs and raisins."[19] Its abundant waters—the origin of its fertile soil and a source of delight to all—amazed visitors: "It is a land crisscrossed with watercourses, encircled by trees, where fruit abounds," was al-Muqaddasi's judgment.[20] "Water runs everywhere, in dwellings, through streets, and in baths," wrote Ibn Hawqal,[21] who listed Damascus among the most beautiful places in the world, in company with the Sughd at Samarkand and the Ubulla estuary. Beyond the city walls, market-gardening suburbs started to sprout up: in the north, al-'Uqayba, "the little slope," Shaghur to the south, and in the southwest, Qasr al-Hajjaj, after the name of an Umayyad prince who had resided there.

Of Fatimid Damascus, only a carved cenotaph, discovered in 1920 in the cemetery of Bab al-Saghir, has survived. On three of the sides of a stone slab, in a Kufic style of singular elegance, appears a verse of the Koran (2:256) and the epitaph of a certain Fatima who died in 1048, and who popular piety, with its eye for the miraculous and in spite of chronology and genealogy, persists in imagining to be the daughter of al-Husayn, granddaughter of 'Ali.

The reign of Atsiz was a calamity that exceeded in horror even the darkest days of Fatimid dominion. Chronicles report a headlong collapse in population (it is alleged down to three thousand) and record cases of famine and even cannibalism. In 1078, fearing a renewed attack by the Fatimid, Atsiz called for assistance from a brother of the Seljukid sultan Malik Shah, the emir Tutush, who, on his arrival in Damascus, had him assassinated without further ado. Occupying Aleppo in 1085, Tutush busied himself consolidating Seljukid authority in Syria. As testified by two inscriptions noted down before the 1893 fire, it was in his reign that the central part of the Umayyad mosque (dome, arches, pillars, and roof)—destroyed during the conflagration of 1069—was reerected. On his death in 1095, Tutush left two sons to fight it out—Ridwan at Aleppo and Duqaq at Damascus. The latter invested all real authority in his atabeg, Tughtakin, whose wise and disinterested policies earned accolades from the historian of Damascus, Ibn al-Qalanisi: "During his government, thanks to his political acumen, the affairs of Damascus and the provinces depending on it thrived and flourished. . . . Prices fell, grain flowed in abundance; unmolested, the people were able to turn a profit on goods both within and without the walls, a result of [Tughtakin's] excellent policy and intelligent management in which equity reigned and from which all sources of injustice were expunged."[22] In 1096, however, Ridwan, who held his brother for an impostor, assembled a force and laid siege to Damascus.

A new invader: The Franks

When the Crusader hordes appeared on the Syrian borders, the Muslim world was thus in an advanced stage of political decomposition—with two rival

Facing page, bottom. Detail of a poplar-wood openwork cloister from the mosque of the Musalla to the south of Damascus, dated 1104 according to the dedication and bearing the name of a minister, Duqaq b. Tutush. Damascus Museum.

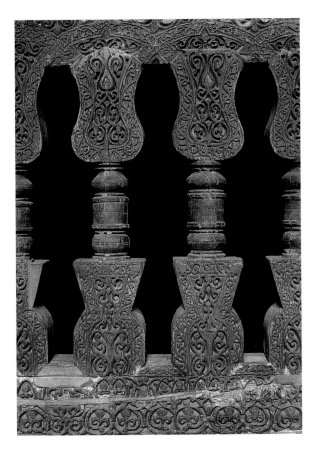

caliphates, one Shi'ite in Cairo and the other Sunnite at Baghdad; the Seljukids, the armed branch of an 'Abbasid caliphate torn to shreds by bloody quarrels over the succession, and with Aleppo and Damascus caught between two enemy brothers. "In Damascus in this year [1097]," noted Ibn al-Qalanisi, "news came of the appearance of innumerable multitudes of Frankish armies from the Sea of Marmara; reports to this effect poured in without cease and the people were much afraid on learning of it and panic set in when they heard they were widespread."[23] Claiming to want to liberate the southernmost zone of Syria that the pious call the Holy Land from the "infidel" yoke, the "disordered multitudes," as Voltaire was to dub them,[24] under the authority of the Catholic Church and European rulers, having annihilated the Turks at the battle of Dorylea, poured through Anatolia, causing destruction. In June 1098, after a seven-month siege, Antioch was stormed and the survivors cut to pieces: "One could not walk the streets without stumbling over corpses," an anonymous chronicler of the First Crusade describes.[25] Duqaq and Ridwan were not keen to intervene; instead they made separate and unfruitful forays, the first in December 1097 and the second in February 1098. Duqaq then entered into parleys with the invader, and, after receiving guarantees, proceeded to observe the progress of the Frankish armies from afar. The massacre and plunder in December at Ma'arat al Nu'man knew no bounds. The same unnamed historian writes: "Not a corner of the city was without Saracen corpses. . . . There were among our men some who did not find what they were they looking for. . . . So they sawed through the bodies, because one had found bezants hidden in their stomachs; others sliced the flesh into pieces and cooked it for food."[26]

A worse fate still befell Jerusalem, taken by storm on July 15 after a five-week siege. The account given in the anonymous chronicle is truly hellish: "There was such carnage of the Saracen that ours walked

Below. Mosque of Khaled b. al-Walid. Text carved on the door lintel. Four lines in floral Kufic: "This is the Mosque of Khaled b. al-Walid, Companion of the Messenger of God, to whom God grant His blessing and be satisfied with him as with all the Companions." (*R.C.E.A.*, vol. 8, 1937, no. 2918).

through their blood up to the ankles . . . The Crusaders soon overran the city, making off with gold, silver, horses, and mules, and plundering houses that overflowed with wealth. . . . Due to the incredible stench, an order was issued to throw all the dead Saracen out of the city, since [it] was almost awash with corpses. The Saracen left alive dragged the dead out of the city and piled them up before the gates in heaps as high as a house. None has ever heard of or seen such carnage of the pagan race: pyres were erected like milestones and no one, save God alone, knows their number."[27] The Jews were herded into a synagogue and burned alive.[28] Palestinian refugees then fled to Damascus, which was considered—thanks to the agreements negotiated by its emir—as reasonably secure.[29]

If the ancient capital of the Umayyad was to escape intact, its connections with the coastal cities—Acre, Sayda (Sidon), and Tripolis—were threatened by the establishment of the Latin States, which, moreover, controlled its vital trade routes, rich pasturelands, and grain-growing areas of two districts, the Beka'a and the Hawran. There then began a ceaseless round of diplomatic negotiation, periodically punctuated by skirmishes in which neither religious nor ideological considerations played any part, both sides being motivated solely by

the down-to-earth ambitions of princes who would go to any lengths—including collaborating with the "infidel"—to keep a hold on power.[30] The government of Damascus, which had accepted the presence of the Franks from the very beginning, saw the kingdom of Jerusalem as a rampart against the Fatimids and the principalities of Tripolis and Edessa as a bulwark against the machinations of the emirs of Mosul. Its survival thus depended on a subtle balance of power, and nothing would have been more detrimental to its welfare than a general jihad against the Franks. Thus, when, in 1104, having captured Bohemond of Antioch and Baldwin II of Edessa, the emir of Mosul, Shokurmish, held their respective states at his mercy, Damascus prudently remained above the fray. The only reaction emanated from a population outraged by the indifference of its own "elite" and by the savagery of the Franks. Survivors of the massacre of Jerusalem had pleaded for help in the Great Mosque at Baghdad as early as September 1098.

In 1106, the Damascene Sulami launched an appeal for Muslim solidarity in a treatise of jihad which, however, was heeded by very few. In February, 1111, a delegation from Aleppo once again had to travel to Baghdad, where it berated the inertia gripping the two highest authorities in the Sunni world, the 'Abbasid caliphate and the Seljukid sultan.[31]

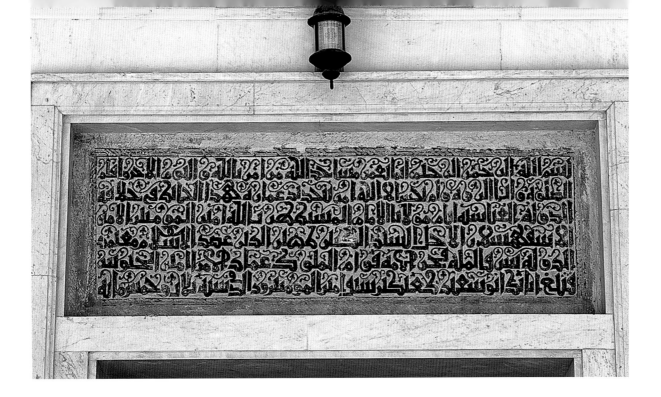

In June 1104, Duqaq died, to be succeeded by his faithful atabeg Tughtakin.

The ruler was interred west of Damascus on a hill over the Green Hippodrome in a tomb built by his mother, Safwa al-Mulk, known by the name of "Dome of the Peacocks." Until 1938, the year in which, teetering on the brink of collapse, it was demolished, this tomb that marks the introduction to Damascus of Iranian architectural traditions was the only Seljukid vestige in Damascus and the most ancient post-Umayyad monument.[32] It comprised a simple, domed square hall, extended by two roofed recesses each bearing a half-dome resting on a polygonal zone with alternating squinches and niches. Literary sources ascribe to Duqaq the construction of the first madrasa in Damascus, a *bimaristan*, and a *khanqah* (a Sufi meeting-place). The cenotaph of Sukayna, discovered in the cemetery of Bab al-Saghir, is approximately contemporary. According to most chroniclers, this daughter of al-Husayn and granddaughter of the Prophet, famous for her talent, beauty, and for her many marriages, died in Medina around 735. On the sides of the walnut case, above a Koranic verse,[33] the large letters of the epitaph, sometimes interwoven and encircled by a narrow groove, spread over a ground of floral interlace. Similarly during the Seljukid period, an emir undertook the restoration of the mosque of Khaled b. al-Walid, commemorated by a Kufic inscription carved above the main door:

"This is the Mosque of Khaled b. al-Walid, Companion of the Messenger of God, to whom God grant His blessing and be satisfied with him as with all the Companions."[34]

Following Duqaq's demise, Tughtakin reigned alone over Damascus until his own death in 1128. He was the founder of the Burid dynasty, which abided until the arrival of Nur al-Din in 1154: with the Franks, his rule was a sequence of alternating tussles and truces. In 1125, after succeeding, with the aid of the navy of Venice, in seizing Tyre, Baldwin II was equally victorious at Marj al-Suffar, about nineteen miles (30 km) to the south of Damascus; but, on the following day, probably because he did not have the means to besiege the city, he raised camp. Tughtakin passed away on February 11, 1128, after wielding power effectively for thirty-three years. He was buried in the south of Damascus near the *musalla*. Under the northern portico of the mosque of Umayyads, six lines of floral Kufic carved onto the lintel of a small door commemorate the repair of a section of wall ordered in 1109–10 by "Islam's right arm, the mainstay of the Empire, the pride of the community, the stalwart of princes, the support of emirs, the sword of the Emir of the Believers—the blessed atabeg, Abu Sa'id Tughtakin."[35] Two dignitaries from his entourage, Badr b. 'Abd Allah and Altuntash, are known by epitaphs on their tombs discovered in the cemetery of Bab al-Saghir.[36]

Above. Umayyad Mosque. Text in floral Kufic carved under the northern portico telling of the restoration of the wall by the "blessed atabeg Abu Sa'id Tughtakin in the year of 503/1109–10."

Taj al-Muluk Buri succeeded his father the year the atabeg Zenki, already master of Mosul, took possession of Aleppo: a fragile political equilibrium was about to be upset. Zenki, who derived his investiture directly from the sultan, did little to hide his ambition to extend his sway over the whole of Syria, and in particular over Damascus as a necessary first step to a jihad. As the initiator of the counter-Crusade, and regarded as "one of the most eminent Seljukid emirs,"[37] Zenki's name has lived on in Muslim history as he who begun the long-awaited resistance and reaction against the Frankish invader. "If Almighty God had not granted Muslims the grace to permit atabeg Zenki, to gain possession of Syria," wrote the historian Ibn al-Athir, "the Franks would have overrun it in its entirety."[38] The Franks with their clumsy policies also furthered his own ends. Instead of cooperating with Buri, they marched on Damascus in 1129, but, with one of their detachments that had gone to the Hawran to forage for supplies being cut to ribbons, they beat a hasty retreat. The following year, Zenki, who had bided his time during this attack, requested Damascus's assistance for a full-scale assault on the Franks. Buri thus dispatched his finest officers and five hundred horsemen under the orders of his son Sawinj, then governor of Hama. Received at the atabeg's camp with great honor, they were unexpectedly arrested and packed off to Aleppo. Zenki seized the opportunity to take the now defenseless Hama, but, making little headway with Homs, he repaired to Mosul with Sawinj and his officers in tow as hostages, demanding for their release the extortionate ransom of fifty thousand dinars.

In May 1131, Buri was assassinated in an attack financed by the Ismaelites of Alamut: "One day on the way back from the bath," as Ibn al-Qalanisi describes, "at the door of his palace in the citadel at Damascus . . . two men threw themselves on him, one striking him on the head with a saber . . . the other stabbing him in the side, wounding him between the flesh and the skin."[39] Buri died of his injuries and was replaced by

his son, Isma'il. A valorous warrior and great strategist, he succeeded in recovering Hama, Baalbek, and Baniyas, and then pushed on into Frankish territory, menacing Nazareth and Acre. In Damascus, he had the gates of the citadel restored, building a *hammam* and other buildings of which nothing subsists, but which attained, according to Ibn al-Qalanisi "the acme of beauty, delight, balance, and harmony."[40] Extremely unpopular and having already escaped one attempt on his life, in January 1135 he too was eliminated and replaced by a brother, Mahmud. In 1138, faced with the threat from Frankish-Byzantine armies besieging Shayzar, a significant fortified town of the valley of the Orontes, Mahmud and Zenki, laying their differences aside, concluded a hasty treaty by whose terms Zenki received the city of Homs and married Mahmud's mother Zumurrud Khatun, offering the hand of his daughter to Mahmud himself—a matrimonial arrangement intended to consolidate Zenki's suzerainty in Damascus.

Unur, however, who had succeeded Mahmud on his assassination in 1139, was minded to resist the ambitions of Aleppo's powerful emir. Backed with impressive material and considerable manpower, he laid siege to Damascus, encamping beneath the ramparts for six months, but, hearing rumblings from the Frankish armies of Fulk Count of Anjou with whom he had formerly come to an understanding, Unur was forced to retire. Conscious of the futility of his efforts in such conditions, Zenki instead besieged Edessa and seized it in 1144, thereby erasing from the map the first-born of the Latin States after its forty-six years of existence; it was a stinging rebuff that shocked Western Christendom to the core.

At the instigation of Pope Eugenius II, aided and abetted by the eloquent voice of the French monk, Bernard of Clairvaux, a Second Crusade marched off to Syria. No sooner had it arrived than the Frankish armies, led by Conrad III, emperor of Germany, and Louis VII, king of France, set off towards Damascus. Unur then called on Zenki's son, Nur al-Din, successor to his father, who had died two years previously at the siege of Qal'at Jabar. Beaten to and fro over the Damascus plain, breathless in the heat, and harassed by the militia and the peasantry, the Franks, as Ibn al-Qalanisi observed, "could find no way out of the net in which they were ensnared, of the chasm into which they plummeted, other than to flee in disorder at daybreak and beat a retreat, abandoned by God and vanquished."[41] Thus was the Second Crusade brought to a close.

Damascus—center of resistance to occupation under the Nur al-Din government

In 1154, after several attempts crowned by failure, and despite the Burid-Frank alliance, Nur al-Din finally managed to take Damascus. At the beginning of April, under orders from the Kurdish emir Shirkuh, uncle of Saladin, his vanguard took up its position at Marj al-Qasab to the north of Bab Tuma. In what was a watershed in the history of the "medieval" Middle East, on April 25, to the immense relief of the majority of the population, he entered the city and closed the book on the Burid dynasty. The unity of Muslim Syria from Upper Mesopotamia to the Hawran was thus established, the route to Egypt—still in Fatimid hands—lay open, and foundations were laid for encircling the territories of the Franks now cornered by the sea. Nur al-Din, however, anxious to complete the political and moral unification of Syria, instigated a policy of compromise with the Franks. He thus continued the Burid approach of entertaining good relations with Jerusalem; to the north, he attempted to stall the pretensions of the Konya Seljukids and to guarantee the neutrality of Byzantium and of the principality of Antioch; to the south, meanwhile, he tried to placate a Fatimid caliphate which was in any case subsiding into utter chaos.

Despite two centuries of ceaseless disorder, the city of which Nur al-Din took possession was far from desolate. On the contrary, a description left by the contemporary geographer al-Idrisi is that of a rich and prosperous city. "It is regarded as one of the noblest cities in all Syria," he writes.

Its situation is admirable, its climate healthy and moderate, its soil fertile, its waters abundant, its produce varied, its wealth immense, its troops numerous, its buildings superb. From this city depend a hilly piece of land and a cultivated and fertile valley called the Ghuta . . . where the villages are as large as cities . . . with populations reaching from one to two thousand. The larger part of the Ghuta is composed of orchards and gardens traversed by watercourses, so that the quantity and the goodness of the fruit this valley produces are incomparably superior to any one may imagine, to the point that the country of Damascus is one of the most delectable ever fashioned by the Creator's hand.[42]

Damascene craftsmanship also enjoyed great renown:

Various useful arts and industries congregate in that city. Much silk and floss-silk fabric is made there, particularly extremely costly brocades of inimitable perfection in their quality. . . . These cloths are the equals of the most beautiful of the Greek Empire and approach the rarest wares of manufactories in Isfahan and Nishapur. Be it fabrics of the kind in the robes of Tinnis, and in general of any sort of manufacture, it is impossible to see anything more perfect that what leaves the hands of workmen in Damascus.[43]

Agricultural production contributed to its prosperity: On the channels running within the city, a great number of mills and grinding-stones have been set up, because wheat, as well as fruits, is very abundant in Damascus. As for preserves, the quantity and the quality of what they make are above all praise and description. In sum, in terms of well-being, security, prosperity, industry, and trades, this city outstrips all others in Syria.[44]

واسکبی وشکبی وجوی وجاني ومآبي ومنابي ولالجوي نفسي ولا
تسلط علي بغير واجعليني من ادن تسلطان انصيرا اللهم اجرني بعنك وكن

واخصصني بامنك ومنك وتوليني لاختيارك وخيرك ولا تكلني الي كله غيرك
وهب لي عافيك غير عافيه وارزقني رفاهيه غير واهيه واكني هاني اللذار

as both the pilgrims themselves and the traders
accompanying them engaged in extremely profitable
"import-export" activities that transported craft
articles to the Hijaz and other goods back from
Arabia and India. It was of course precisely because
of its wealth that the caravan of the devout was so
regularly sacked by the Bedouin. Thus Ibn al-
Qalanisi describes how, in 1150, "returning from the
pilgrimage, [it] had fallen victim to pagan Arabs,
travelers, and good-for-nothings joined in a huge
swarm. Survivors arriving at Damascus related their
misfortunes: the majority had been put to death, only
a few had escaped with their lives, the women were
raped, all were stripped of everything they had and
several perished through hunger and thirst."[45]

Scattered elements of Damascus's topography of
the period shortly prior to the arrival of Nur al-Din
can be inferred from literary sources. In 1154, for
example, it possessed eleven madrasas. An
educational establishment first created at Nishapur,
Merv, and Bukhara at the time of Mahmud the
Ghaznavid (970–1030), by the time of the Seljukids
the madrasa had become a hotbed of Sunni
propaganda against Shi'ism, a genuine arm of the
state, whose prime function was to train qualified and
loyal "functionaries." Government-nominated
teachers taught every religious and legal discipline,
including reading, exegesis, Koranic commentary,
traditions, law, and jurisprudence. In general, and for
an unlimited period, it would profit from the income
generated by a waqf, that is, from goods escrowed by
donors for its benefit. The plan of a madrasa is almost
always identical: a large open-air courtyard with, on
the south side, a prayer-hall and opposite, an *iwan*, a
high arched room opening onto the court, with cells
for pupils and professors, and various other locales,
such as lecture hall, library, kitchen, and latrines.[46]
Both Seljukids and Burids also built *khanqah*, at once
both centers of Sufi activity and places where
travelers in search of spiritual nourishment might
lodge. The palaces and rich residences were almost

A crossing point for caravans from Persia,
Mesopotamia, Asia Minor, Egypt, and Arabia,
Damascus was the trading post for inner Syria, a vast
storehouse where goods from the Far East coming in
from the Persian Gulf or the Red Sea ended their
journey. The annual pilgrims' caravan—which was to
acquire supreme importance in Mameluk and
Ottoman times—did much to enhance its prosperity,

Al-Wasiti, The *Maqamat* of al-Hariri: The caravan leaves from Damascus. Baghdad, 1237 (634 H).

Bibliothèque Nationale, Paris. Ms. arabe 5847, f. 31.

all located north of Straight Street in the western part of the city. As for the mosques, according to Ibn 'Asakir, there were 241 within the city walls and 48 without—evidence of significant suburban expansion.

The long reign of Nur al-Din—whose monuments, apart from the Umayyad mosque and the Roman remains it incorporates, are the most ancient vestiges to survive—deeply affected the development of Damascus, even down to the present day. Firstly, military exigencies meant that the fortifications had to be strengthened, the northern front being pushed back to the banks of the Barada, the southernmost face of semicircular towers reinforced, new gates built, the old ones being improved with tabid-slits, machicolations, and bartizans. In the citadel itself, his place of residence in Damascus, he had two mosques built, one of which was especially for Friday prayers. Soon after taking the city, in the district of the "Golden Stone" located

between the citadel and Great Mosque, Nur al-Din built a new *bimaristan*, financed with a Frankish prince's ransom. Of Sassanid origin, this type of establishment first appeared in the Muslim world in Damascus in 707, during al-Walid's caliphate.[47]

Following on from the ancient tomb of Safwa al-Mulk, the *bimaristan* of Nur al-Din heralds the introduction in Damascus of the Iranian architectural tradition: in the center of each side of the courtyard stands a great *iwan*, with pointed vault towers above the side rooms that form the corner of the building. The hall with its square layout is domed with a *muqarnas* cupola similar to those found in the tombs of the imam Dur in Samarra, Zubayda at Baghdad, and Sheikh 'Abd al-Samad in Natanz. Opening beneath a lintel with an antique pediment, the entrance gate preserves both its leaves covered, externally, in strips of riveted iron with geometrical interlace and, internally, with splendidly carved wooden paneling. A traveler from Andalusia, Ibn Jubayr, who visited Damascus in 1184, describes the building exhaustively:

> Damascus possesses two hospitals, an old [that of Duqaq] and a new. The new one is the larger and the more important: it has a daily income of approximately fifteen dinars. There are administrators who keep by them registers recording the names of the patients and the expenditure incurred for their treatment and food, etc. The physicians do a morning round, examining patients and prescribing remedies and foodstuffs for their cure in accordance with their individual needs. . . . Firmly bound in chains, the mad too benefit from a measure of treatment. . . . Such hospitals are among Islam's greatest claims to fame.[48]

The *bimaristan*, where patients were admitted either for prolonged hospitalization or brief consultation, incorporated two separate blocks, one for women and the other for men, each equipped with everything necessary for any course of

Semicircular tower erected by Nur al-Din in 1173. The inscription commemorates repairs made in 1300
during the reign of Sultan al-Nasir Muhammad by the emir al-Afram, governor of Damascus.

treatment: surgery, ophthalmology, orthopedics, organic disease, etc. A special department was set aside for the insane, another, a little way off, for those afflicted with diarrhea. The personnel—including hospital manager, administrators, doctors, surgeons, pharmacists, male nurses, those who prepare electuaries, supervisors, servants, storekeepers, and cash clerk—was extremely numerous, and the annual budget exceeded five thousand dinars. The hospital was also an educational establishment for the exact sciences as well as for medicine, furnished for the purpose with a library including works as varied as commentaries on urine and treatises on coitus—this latter being the object in the Muslim world of much cogitation, which exceeded the confines of specialized tomes devoted to the many facets of the hankerings of the flesh.

Ibn al-Jawzi, a celebrated and much-respected jurist, in his *Sayd al-Khatir* (The Pursuit of Furtive Ideas) accords sexuality a role that is telling of the chasm that in this field separates Islam from Christianity, a religion which places virginity and anaphrodisia at the summit of godliness. First of all, pleasure is both licit and beneficial, and is not plagued by guilt: "If one marries to beget children, it is the most perfect form of devotion, and if it is to seek pleasure and enjoyment, then this too is permitted by the law."[49] Moreover—and Ibn al-Jawzi stresses this on several occasions—being a physiological need, this is ample justification for the release of sperm; in other words, nature's command in itself justifies the sex act, and abstinence can only have a deleterious effect. Those who, for one reason or another, hold themselves in check are duly

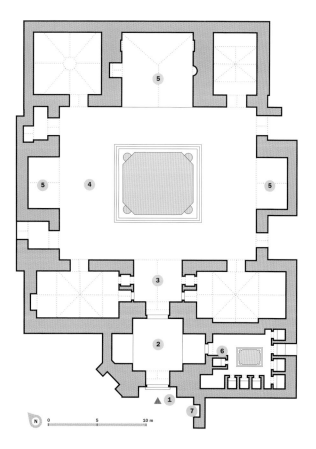

Facing page, top. Bimaristan of Nur al-Din. Doorways to the rooms standing in the northeast corner reflected in the pool in the middle.
Facing page, bottom. The courtyard to the *bimaristan.* Left, the entrance *iwan.*

warned: "Great accumulation and retention of seminal fluid may occasion serious diseases and promote the appearance of evil thoughts, as well as inducing excitement and obsessions as the vapor from the sperm goes up into the brain, causing disorders and sometimes even poisoning."[50] A reasonable stance, and, besides, our lawyer is only repeating what he learned from the wellsprings of Islamic medicine. As Abu Bakr al-Razi, a disciple of Galen, had already written in the tenth century: "Those with the greatest need to expel semen are those who, whenever they refrain from coitus, suffer heaviness of the head, darkening of the sight, anesthesia, sadness of the soul, dulling of the mind, and drowsiness, as well as those from whom all these afflictions disappear when they engage in intercourse or dream of it. Similarly, all those who

have not engaged in coitus for too long, and, due to this, whose urethra and testicles are covered with abscesses."[51] Thus no prolonged abstinence, and indeed it can be inferred from Ibn al-Jawzi that the "authorized" period is extremely brief. There follows lengthy and instructive examination of the "places" of coitus, "between the thighs, in its natural place [sic], with a virgin, with a woman who has lost her virginity, etc."—since not all possess the same "power of ejaculation"—as well as of the choice of a suitable partner, one likely to occasion "total ejaculation so that the soul [the soul, not the body, note] attains the acme of pleasure."[52] For Ibn al-Jawzi, there is no doubt: "perfect ejaculation is obtained only with a pretty woman,"[53] though, reading between the lines, he is evidently not particularly fussy on this issue. Indeed we are a

thousand miles from the lamentations of the Apostle: "O wretched man that I am! who shall deliver me from the body of this death?"[54]—and from Christianity's inherent repressions and frustrations.

If the fortifications and the *bimaristan* appeared urgent priorities for Nur al-Din, his most significant and plentiful achievements lay in the area of religious edifices. This building frenzy was motivated by a range of political goals: to bolster Sunnite fervor against Shi'ism; to reinforce the spirit of the jihad against the Franks; to breathe new life into the study of the doctrine; to make public display of the prince's Sunni zeal; to secure the collaboration of the ulemas (the conductors through which power was exercised); to expiate the sins attendant on high public office, and, finally, to

Above. The *bimaristan* of Nur al-Din. Decoration in the entrance *iwan*.
Facing page. The al-Nuriyya madrasa and the Nur al-Din *turba*. To the bottom left of the photograph the funerary madrasa of Emir al-Najibi (died 1278), governor of Damascus in the reign of the Mameluk sultan Baybars. In the background, the domes of the Khan As'ad Pasha towering over the curved sheet-metal roofs of the al-Buzuriyyeh *suq*.

vouchsafe the prayers of the pious after death. Mosques sprang up like mushrooms within the city walls near the gates in the ramparts, in the suburbs, and throughout the villages of the Ghuta, while restoration work advanced on the Umayyad mosque. A water clock was installed at Bab Jayrun borrowing its name, Bab al-Sa'at ("Gate of the Hours"), hitherto confined to a door opening in the qibla wall. To toll the hours, an ingenious device controlled by an overseer seated high up in a special chamber— according to Ibn Jubayr, it therefore "made one think it was by magic"[55]—was installed with a pair of mechanical copper falcons that dropped little lumps of metal they held in their beaks into a copper tank. At night, time was marked by a system of hydraulically powered lamps rotating behind panes of colored glass.

No less than twelve new madrasas were built in his reign, of which only two are extant: the Nuriyya and the 'Adiliyya, the construction of the latter continuing until the reign of the Ayyubids. Completed in 1172, the Nuriyya was built, according to certain authors, on the very site of the old palace of Caliph Mu'awiya. In addition to the prayer-hall, an *iwan* and various buildings set around a court centered on a pool, it also encompasses the tomb of the founder: a simple, sober chamber, square in plan, lit by two low windows open to the street and topped by an alveolar dome similar to that in the *bimaristan*. A line of text runs around the four sides of the cenotaph: "This is the tomb of Nur al-Din b. Zenki," followed by a verse pertaining to the entry of the Blessed into Paradise: "And those who are careful of (their duty to) their Lord shall be conveyed to the garden in companies; until when they come to it, and its doors shall be opened, and the keepers of it shall say to them: Peace be on you, you shall be happy; therefore enter it to abide." [56]

Facing page. Intrados of the honeycombed cupola vaulting the tomb of Nur al-Din.

Above. The courtyard of the al-Nuriyya madrasa.

Nur al-Din also initiated a new type of establishment devoted exclusively to the study of the Hadith, which in conjunction with the Holy Koran constitutes one of the principal sources of Muslim law—an eloquent testimony to the importance of this discipline in the training of jurists at this time. The Dar al-Hadith in Damascus, where the traveler Ibn Jubayr stayed in 1184, stands to the west of the Umayyad mosque and is today in total ruin.

In reaction to the sometimes over-literal, barren and pragmatic aspects of Sunni orthodoxy, as well as to the stuffy pettifoggery of the ulemas, the time witnessed the development of a current of mysticism—the *tasawwuf*—that called for the elimination of Pharisaism and a more internalized approach to worship. Dressed in simple woolen robes, the *suf*, from which they drew their name, and imbued with a deep desire for inner purification and identification with the divine,[57] the Sufi gathered under the authority of a sheikh in special establishments called *khanqah*s. Seven were built in Damascus during the rule of Nur al-Din, one of which, to the north of the Great Mosque, was reserved exclusively for women. With undisguised irony, Ibn Jubayr alleges that their delights were legion: "They are extremely well-decorated palaces, water flows in every direction and offers a spectacle as splendid as any."[58] Nothing indeed appeared too good for these mystical brotherhoods: "These Sufi are the kings of this land," Ibn Jubayr adds, "because Allah preserves them from the cares and vanities of the world, exempting their spirit from worrying about their means of subsistence and leaving them entirely to their devotions. He lodges them in palaces that offer them a foretaste of those in paradise." Men of Allah for some, supremely irreligious for others, forever on the margins of official Islam which accused them of innovation, deceit, or imposture,[59] and displaying great freedom as to their moral life and appearance, the Sufi were far from achieving unanimity as individuals. Indeed, their practices, some held,

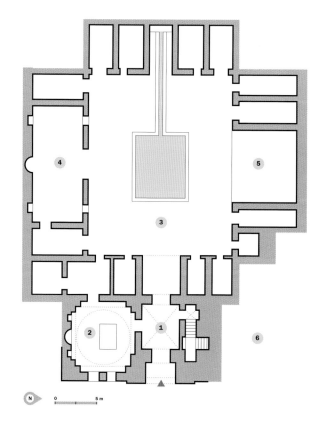

Top. Tomb of Sheikh Arslan. Portico of the Mosque of Khaled b. al-Walid, depicted in an early twentieth-century watercolor by W. S. S. Tyrwhitt. *Bottom.* Plan of the al-Nuriyya madrasa. **1** Vaulted vestibule. **2** Tomb of Nur al-Din. **3** Courtyard. **4** Prayer hall. **5** *Iwan.* **6** Site of the funerary madrasa of the Mamluk emir Aqush al-Najibi.

were not invariably pious, although practitioners considered them an integral part of the true path. Our sexologist, Ibn al-Jawzi, in whose eyes they were no better than charlatans, has harsh words for them larded with choice metaphors: "In each *khanqah*," he writes, "there is a kitchen and nights are never spent in meditation . . . the bath is always full to bursting, the singer bangs a drum hung with bells while his accomplice plays the flute, and there are girls in the songs and catamites under the candles."[60]

Concerned to pander to the piety of his people—as well as to keep them to the straight and narrow of orthodoxy—Nur al-Din refurbished many places of pilgrimage, *mashhad* and *maqam* sacred to the memory of various prophets, Companions, or mystics, ascetics, sheikhs, scholars, and men of law, whose meritorious lives had earned them the status of intercessors or dispensers of blessings. Near the

citadel, he also constructed the Dar al-'Adl, a kind of "high court" or bench of appeal, concerned with judging matters which, due to the status of the individuals implicated, were beyond the powers of ordinary qadis. Twice a week, Nur al-Din himself would sit flanked by the great qadi, the legal representatives of the four schools of Sunni Islam, and senior jurists.

The number of public baths was also on the increase. In about 1165, in the grain dealers' *suq*, Nur al-Din built a bathhouse depending on the waqf endowed for his funerary madrasa. Heir to the antique thermal bath reworked Byzantium style, the *hammam*, often associated with a mosque, fulfilled a key role in the religious and social life of the city. Contrary to Christianity—which, in its scorn of the flesh, did little to promote bodily care among its followers—Islam turned hygiene into a canonical

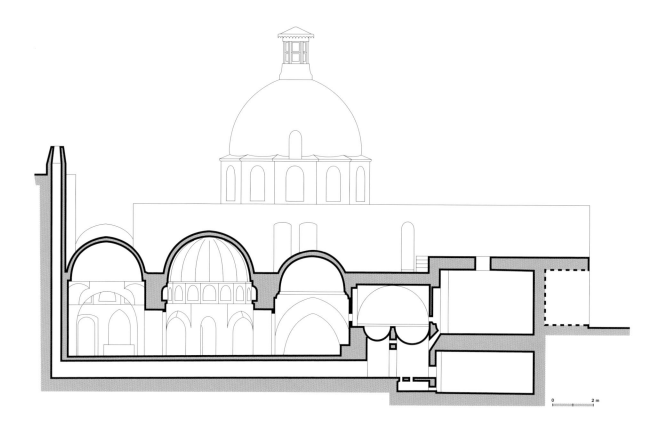

virtue: "Cleanliness belongs to the faith," proclaims a Hadith. Minor ablutions are the rule before any act of worship, while major ablutions are performed at the *hammam* before Friday prayers. The unclean pray in vain since, as another Hadith declares: "The prayer of the impure will not meet with God's approval as long as he has not performed his ablutions." Similarly, anyone who has eaten fresh onion or garlic can perhaps pray at home but certainly never at the mosque.[61] The efficaciousness of an orison is proportionate to one's degree of hygiene and one "made after cleaning one's teeth is superior to that before washing them."[62] Ritual purification after physiological activities—such as micturition, defecation, ejaculation, etc.—is obligatory, a fact addressed in countless Hadith providing the most detailed recommendations. "They are not clean," writes an anonymous Muslim, "they [the Chinese] do not wash when they have gone, but just wipe it with paper."[63]

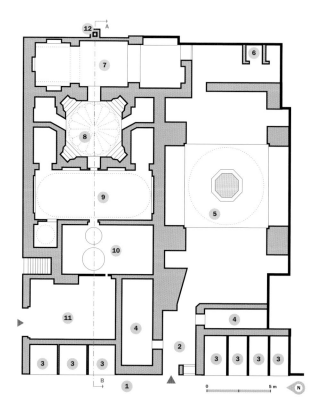

Hammam of Nur al-Din. *Top.* Cross section. *Bottom.* Plan. **1** Suq al-Buzuriyyeh. **2** Entrance. **3** Shops. **4** Water. **5** Discribing room. **6** Latrines. **7** Cold room. **8** Tepidarium. **9** Steam room. **10** Boiler room. **11** Stokers. **12** Chimney.

Legal texts are scarcely less demanding as to matters of intimate hygiene: sphincter, meatus, vulva, and the crack between the buttocks, all are treated. In the tenth century C.E., al-Qayrawani, a major exponent of the Malikite rite, wrote in his celebrated *Risala*: "This is what *istinja'* consists in: after washing one's hands, the faithful will wash the meatus, then it wipe the foulness from the anus with dry earth or something else or with the hand that he will then rub on the ground and wash again; he will then bathe the anus in water that is to run without stopping. Doing this, he will relax the anal sphincter slightly and rub it carefully by hand until it is clean."[64] Moreover, as is so often the case, a good Muslim would only have to follow the example of his Prophet who, tradition assures us, "was the cleanest and most fragrant of men."[65]

The *hammam* of Nur al-Din is the oldest active example in Damascus. It is centered on a heated room—the *tepidarium* of the Roman thermals. Octagonal in plan and with a ribbed dome, it is extended on two sides by two smaller additional rooms, the *maqsura*, reserved for body-care: washing, depilation, shaving, massage, etc. It was of course a place propitious for every kind of fantasy, since its attendant promiscuity paid little heed to the censure and prohibitions leveled against it.[66] The steamroom, the ancient *caldarium*, rectangular in plan, is roofed with a barrel vault; the cold room, the antique *frigidarium*, with a plain cupola, and the disrobing room, probably revamped in Ottoman times, with a great lantern-topped dome. Its operation called for a large staff: in addition to the superintendent, whose little office stood in general close to the entrance, this included a "heating master," a stoker, many servants, and, more especially, masseurs expert in the arts of cracking bones and relaxing the body, cup appliers, and scrubbers-down, and sometimes a barber as skillful at trimming, shaving, and dyeing beards as at rubbing, polishing, and perfuming bald pates.

The *hammam*s had first call on a water supply network that seems to have been fully operational by the twelfth century.[67] The Barada and its six derivations (the Yazid, the Tawra, the Banias, the Qanawat, the Darani, and the Mizzawi), themselves subdivided ad infinitum, formed a vast grid sixteen miles long by ten broad (25 × 15 km) which, by gravity alone, distributed water to the gardens of the Ghuta as well as to the city's houses, mosques, fountains, and *hammam*s. Nur al-Din improved it and brought running water to the public conveniences. Monitored by accredited agents, water services were public and free of charge: "It is one of the fortunate blessings there, one of the many generous gifts, one of the great distinctive merits characterizing this city, since, in most lands, water has to be paid for," observed Ibn 'Asakir.[68] As for Ibn Jubayr, he deployed all his admirable rhetorical skills in praise of the waters of Damascus: "Its ground is weary of the abundance of water, though it aspires to be thirsty. . . . The whole city is one great fountain. It is rare that a street or suq fails to possess one."[69]

Thanks to the strong-arm regime instigated by Nur al-Din, the city and the caravan routes were once again made safe, and commercial activity attained a level it had probably not experienced for centuries. "The land [of Damascus] attracts people from all the other regions of the world because of the business that can be done there," wrote Rabbi Benjamin of Tudela at the time of his stay in 1173.[70] Trade was by no means undermined by the vicinity of the Latin States, as Ibn Jubayr testifies: "The caravans plying from Egypt to Damascus through Christian territory were no more frequently interrupted than those of Muslims traveling from Damascus to Acre. No Christian merchant was ever waylaid or harried. The Christians impose a tax on Muslims in their territory that is applied in good faith. In return, Christian merchants pay on their goods in Muslim lands; the concord between them is perfect and equity is observed in every circumstance."[71] Maritime exchange with Europe was essentially in the hands of Italian republics. The first European consul in Syria came from Genoa, settling at Acre, then in the possession of the kingdom of Jerusalem, in the mid-twelfth century.

The suq which, according to Ibn Jubayr, was "among the largest in the world,"[72] and which Nur al-Din had improved substantially by paving over some of the streets, still occupied the site of the great commercial centers of Roman times: the *via recta* and the thoroughfare that connected the temple of Jupiter to the agora. The stores and crafts Ibn 'Asakir lists is impressive. In the middle of Straight Street, the Dar al-Bittikh, literally, "house of the watermelon," was a kind of fruit market with a fountain and a mosque above where all the produce from the orchards and kitchen-gardens of the Ghuta could be purchased; nearby stood the exchange (that of the money-sorters), and then markets for green vegetables, textiles, pearls, birds, fabrics, and spun wool, silk, felt, cotton, brocade.

Nearby the old agora, the Suq al-Qanadil, or "lamp market," was a vast edifice dedicated to valuable wares of all kinds, rare articles and embroidered fabrics. To the south of the Great Mosque, the Suq al-Buzuriyyin, or "market of the grain merchants," was encircled by warehouses selling wheat, barley, rice,

and sesame, from Jazira, the Homs region, or the Hawran. The flour suq possessed its own watermill powered by the Qulayt *nahr*, a tributary of the Banias. Extramurally, not far from the Bab al-Saghir, there were markets dealing in sheep, goats, and beasts of burden. "Industry" too was booming and diverse, including within the city walls a foundry, a glassworks, and two presses—one for oil, the other for sesame—while manufactures of a more noisome nature stood without the walls: on the course of the Barada, a sawyer's and other mills, with tanneries and dyers on its derivations between Bab al-Salam and Bab Tuma. A Chinese invention, papermaking had arrived in Damascus in the course of the ninth century via Samarkand and Baghdad and was widespread down the whole course of the Barada.

Craftsmen and merchants were grouped into associations that did not enjoy the same level of independence with respect to political power as did guilds in Europe. They were administered by a *ra'is*—a kind of provost—assisted by a syndic with two secretaries. His responsibilities were left rather vague and in fact depended entirely on the personality of the office-holder and the prevailing political climate. Guarantor of fair practice, responsible for protecting goods and individuals, and for ensuring equitable accounting procedures, he would also arbitrate in time

Traditional crafts live on: *Left.* Glassblower. *Right.* Textile printing.

public morality and the strict observance of religious rules. He would also inspect the markets, ensuring the exactness of weights and measures, as well as honesty in business transactions, and also supervise the imposition of town-planning regulations, the provisioning of the city, and street-cleaning, funeral services, etc. He was scarcely distinct from the *agoranomos* or *epimeletes* in a Greek city. The grand minister of the Seljukid, Nizam al-Mulk, called him "the highest expression of civilian power."[73]

In spite of Islam's egalitarian and democratic propensities, twelfth-century society had a very pronounced hierarchical structure, forming a pyramid that has survived virtually unaltered until modern times. At the top, members of the government and military "aristocracy" consisted primarily of foreigners, Turks and Kurds for the most part, with, below them, a group of privileged Muslims, descendants of the Prophet through the two sons of 'Ali and Fatima, the *Ashraf*.[74] Then came a "middle-class" made up of the chief trading families, major landowners, senior officials, physicians, and the principal merchants of the wealthy corporations: jewelers, goldsmiths, money-changers, and perfumers. As Sunni propaganda ordained, another category was in the ascendant, that of the turban-sporting clerics grouped under the umbrella term *ulemas* or "scholars in the religious sciences," and including the *fuqaha'*, qadis, *shuhud*—"witnesses"—*mufti* (that is, specialists in jurisprudence empowered to pronounce fatwas and advisers to the qadis), and the "traditionists"—faithful recorders of the traditions of the Prophet—each in his own manner implementing the revealed law in the practical domain. In theory guarantors of the Islamic character of the society and the powers that be, and enjoying immense prestige in the eyes of the people, whether they liked it or not they nearly always ended up the obliging auxiliaries of tyranny rather than spokesmen and defenders of the lowborn and humble. Then came the lower echelons, craftsmen,

of dispute, appraise and value goods, oversee the organization of public works, and, at a time of weakening central authority, enforce policing duties—or then again, as chief of a militia known in the chronicles as *ahdath*, he might also take part in wholesale banditry. Commercial activity was monitored by the *muhtasib*, a key figure in the Muslim city, who, in accordance with Koranic law, was invested with the nebulous role "of commanding good and forbidding evil." Directly appointed by the central authority (evidence of the importance of the post) and generally recruited from among lawyers trained at the madrasa, he was charged, in conjunction with the qadi and the *shurta* (i.e., the police force), with enforcing

Copper alloy chandelier with incrusted silver decoration: drinkers, musicians, banquet scenes, horsemen, courtly scenes, and animal rinceaux. First half of the thirteenth century. Probably originating in Mosul. Museum of Islamic Art, Cairo. In spite of a tentative revival, crafts of this type that contributed so much to Damascus's fame in the past are today practically defunct.

small shopkeepers, workmen, laborers, then, at the very bottom, an "underworld" rejoicing in various appellations: good-for-nothings, brigands, felons, highwaymen, all manipulated by the authorities, and who all ran the risk of the birch or the scaffold in the event of overt offence.

From around the city, the peasants of the Ghuta would come each morning—as they still do today—to sell their produce at market. From farther off in the steppe and desert, Bedouins traveled to Damascus to obtain all types of articles. Beside the Muslim population, there were *dhimmi* or "tributaries," Jews and Christians alike: they were hardly favored by Nur al-Din's severe religious stance, and their community was headed by a representative, rabbi or patriarch, responsible at the same time for collecting taxes and for furthering their interests with the prince. Continuing a trend that had started under the Fatimids, they tended to gather in the eastern section of the city, the Jews to the south of Straight Street, and the Christians to the north, as is proved by the position of the religious buildings erected under Nur al-Din, all located to the west in the vicinity of the Great Mosque. According to Benjamin of Tudela, who traveled through the East visiting synagogues and making a census of his coreligionists, in 1173 Damascus numbered approximately three thousand Jews, among whom, as he states, there were several "applied to the study of wisdom and others extremely wealthy."[75]

In the reign of Nur al-Din, then, Damascus seems to have been the most important and prosperous of all Syrian cities, a true "metropolis," as described by John of Würzburg in his *Description of the Holy Land*.[76] "It is a very large and very beautiful city girded by walls," wrote Benjamin of Tudela. "The country depending on it teems with gardens and other places of delight for up to fifteen miles around, such is the area it is believed to cover. The earth scarce contains a city more abundant in every kind of fruit than Damascus, refreshed by the water from two rivers, the Amna and the Pharphar, that descend

Mount Hermon [*sic*]."[77] The city covered a surface area of approximately 300 acres (120 ha). "It is long, drawn-out, and not excessively large," writes Ibn Jubayr. "The streets are narrow and lugubrious; the dwellings are built out of clay and reeds. . . . Everywhere the houses rise to three stories and the city thus contains a population that could fill three towns; it is the most populous city in the world. Its beauty is all external and not interior."[78] Improved security and a massive influx of immigrants furthered expansion in the suburbs. In the northwest of the city, around a *khanqah* built on the banks of the Yazid by Ahmad b. Qudama (a native of Jerusalem who had taken refuge in Damascus with his entire family), there sprang up an agglomeration of marked religious character by the name of "al-Salihiyya."

Saladin and his successors—the Ayyubids

On the death of Nur al-Din in 1174, a vast territory extending from the Tigris to the Nile and from the Diyar Bakr in the Yemen fell to his son Isma'il, whom the emirs and notables of Damascus recognized as their sovereign lord. This, however, failed to take into consideration the ambitions of Saladin, a powerful Kurdish officer, at the time master of Egypt, which he had recently shepherded back into the 'Abbasid fold, thereby curtailing the Fatimid interlude. After Damascus, which handed over its keys to him in October 1174, he went on to seize Homs, then Hama, and finally Aleppo, which capitulated in 1183 after prolonged resistance. Once he had reconstituted the empire of his predecessor—indeed enlarging it with the Yemen and the eastern Maghreb, and consolidating it with investiture by the caliph of Baghdad—Saladin turned his forces against the Franks, moving decisively. By the end of May 1187, at the head of twelve thousand horsemen, he penetrated into Galilee, invested the Tiberiad and, on July 4, gained a crushing victory on the Hattin plain.

several years, Saladin regained Damascus, for which, according to the historian Ibn Shaddad "he has a particular fondness, preferring it to any other city."[79] In February 1193, prey to a strong attack of fever, Saladin fell into a coma, while his eldest son, al-Afdal, anxious to ensure the succession for his own ends, had himself sworn in by the emirs and dispatched gifts of great price to the caliph of Baghdad. On March 3, Saladin died, aged fifty-five. According to certain historians, his standard-bearer went through the city streets with the ruler's shroud hanging from the end of a lance, crying: "Here is what Saladin, victor of the East, takes with him of his conquests."[80] Initially interred in his own residence at the citadel, his remains were transferred two years later to the funerary madrasa that his son al-Afdal had had built behind the northern wall of the Umayyad mosque.

Once Saladin had left the field free, his brother al-'Adil attempted to reconstitute the unity of the Ayyubid Empire at the expense of his nephews. In 1196, excluding al-Afdal from the fray, he took possession of Damascus and, in 1200, of Cairo, where he had himself proclaimed sultan. He passed away near Damascus in 1218, after a reign of twenty-three years, being buried in the great madrasa of 'Adiliyya.

His death sparked a series of internecine conflicts between his heirs. Temporarily shelved by the need to quash the Fifth Crusade, the fratricide led to the collapse of the Ayyubid dynasty. In 1229, Frederick II Hohenstaufen, though not the most zealous of Crusaders—entering the lists to save the tomb of Christ was never going to overly concern such an enlightened prince—signed a bilateral treaty with al-Afdal's eldest son, Sultan al-Kamil, under the terms of which he recovered Jerusalem, Bethlehem, Nazareth, Acre, Jaffa, and Sayda, thereby reversing Saladin's efforts at a stroke. The shock and condemnation in the Muslim world knew no bounds: "When news came that Jerusalem had been handed over to the Franks," wrote Sibt Ibn al-Jawzi, "an outcry arose in all the countries of Islam. The event appeared so

Thus Frankish power was laid low: Acre ('Akka), Nazareth, Caesarea, Nablus, Sayda, Beirut, Jubayl, and Ashqualon (Ascalon) were all occupied. After a twelve-day siege, Jerusalem fell on October 2, 1187. In the region of Tripoli and the principality of Antioch, many fortresses once considered impregnable were taken by assault. By the beginning of 1189, crammed into a handful of coastal enclaves with no hinterland and a few citadels held by the Hospitalers and Templars, including the famous Krak des Chevaliers, the situation facing the Latin States had become desperate. In November 1192, after an absence of

The turba *of Saladin in a late nineteenth-century engraving.*

grievous that ceremonies of public mourning took place. . . . While poets composed many verses to the glory of Jerusalem."[81] In 1238, al-Kamil died in Damascus, leaving the ambitious Ayyubid princes to tear themselves apart. In May 1250, just as the king of France, Louis IX, had been taken prisoner at Mansura together with his military leaders, a group of Turkish mercenaries, the Mameluks, put the Ayyubid sultan of Egypt, Turan Shah, to the sword, and seized power. Al-Nasir Yusuf, an Ayyubid prince of Aleppo and Saladin's great-grandson, headed a coalition that took Damascus and went on to Egypt. Beaten back by the Mameluks at al-Kura', in October 1250 he was forced to beat a retreat.

Meanwhile, the Mongols, who had been masters of Central Asia and Iran since 1220, were progressing westwards. On January 27, 1258, Hulagu, brother of the Great Khan Möngke and grandson of Genghis Khan, availed himself of Baghdad, set fire to the city, put the entire population to the sword, and cut down the last 'Abbasid caliph, al-Musta'sim billah. An auxiliary army, commanded by Kitbugha, a Nestorian officer, set off for Damascus, while the bulk of the troops, reinforced by Armenian and Frankish contingents under the command of Hulaga, seized Aleppo, whose people were either massacred or enslaved. "The inhabitants of Damascus," Maqrizi relates, "learning that the Tatar had already crossed the Euphrates, were transfixed with fear. A great number sold their worldly goods for next to nothing and headed off for Egypt, but since it was then wintertime many of the fugitives perished along the way, while most of the others were robbed of all they took with them."[82] Abandoned by part of his army, al-Nasir Yusuf also fled to Egypt where Emir Qutuz, "on the pretext that events called for a harsh regime,"[83] had himself proclaimed sultan.

In March 1260, Kitbugha entered a desolate, defenseless Damascus. Government was in the main handed over to the Persian Shi'ites and the Umayyad mosque converted into a church in the presence of Hethum (Hayton), king of Armenia, and his son-in-law, Bohemond IV, prince of Antioch and Tripolis. Supported by their new masters, the Christians indulged in horrendous provocations: "They now began to lord it over the Muslims," wrote Maqrizi.

In the month of Ramadan, they would publicly drink wine and pour it over the clothes of Muslims in the street and onto the doors of mosques. When they walked wearing the cross, they would force merchants to get up, abusing all those who refused: they would go forth into the streets with their cross to the Church of Mary where they pronounced sermons praising their religion and they declared openly: "The one true faith, the faith of the Messiah, is today triumphant." He [Hulagu] covered the Christian priests with honor, attended their churches, and protected their religion to the hilt.[84]

Masters of Damascus, the Mongols promptly proceeded to Egypt. At the head of a considerable force that joined troops from Egypt and Syria with Arab and Turkmen auxiliaries, Qutuz set off for Palestine, where, on September 3, 1260, he crushed the Mongols at 'Ayn Jalut or the "well of Goliath." In Damascus, reprisals were at hand: "As soon as victory was announced, the inhabitants threw themselves on Christian houses, plundering and destroying all they could. They demolished the church of the Jacobites, as well as that of Mary, setting the latter on fire, so that only a heap of ruins remained. They cut the throats of a huge number of Christians, taking the others into slavery."[85] Neither Jews nor Muslim "collaborators" were spared: "At the same time, they attacked several Muslims who had embraced the party of Tatar and massacred them . . . slitting the gizzards of a great number of Mongols. The city presented a grizzly spectacle."[86] A week after the victory, Qutuz marched into Damascus before leaving to subdue all the towns of Syria "from the banks of the Euphrates to Egypt,"[87] restoring Ayyubid princes here and there, conferring "fiefdoms" on emirs, and appointing governors and functionaries. For the first time since Saladin, Egypt and Syria were united under a single authority.

The century of the Ayyubid was certainly one of the most opulent in Syrian history. In Damascus, the suburbs that had burgeoned in the reign of Nur al-Din increased in size. According to a contemporary, Yaqut (1179–1229), author of one of the largest geographical encyclopedias of his time, they surrounded the entire city, except to the east, and their surface area equaled that of the districts within the walls.[88] To the north of the ramparts, by the end of the twelfth century, the district of 'Uqayba featured five mosques and two bathhouses. At the foot of Mount Qasiyun the suburb of al-Salihiyya, which had amounted to a handful of houses in the middle of the twelfth century, gradually extended along the Nahr Yazid until the increase in population was such that, at the dawn of the following century, it warranted the construction of the first Great Mosque outside the walls—the al-Muzaffari or Hanbalite mosque. With its many mausoleums, mosques, madrasas, and civic buildings (suq, khan, *hammam*, and even, from the mid-thirteenth century, a *bimaristan*), it looked increasingly like an autonomous urban entity. To the east, there arose a colony of Kurds who had come to Damascus in company of their compatriot, Saladin. Indeed, the district is still known today by the name of the "district of the Kurds," Hara al-Akrad.

On the commercial level, in spite of—or, perhaps, thanks to—the holy war, and in disregard of Pope Innocent III's vow to excommunicate any Christian involved in business with Muslims, trade boomed. Benjamin of Tudela maintained that twenty-eight European countries, regions, or towns traded with Alexandria. In 1207, Venice concluded with Ghiath al-Din Ghazi, sultan of Aleppo and one of Saladin's sons, an economic agreement that stipulated the enjoyment of a bathhouse, a church, and a *fondaco* in the city, as well as dwellings for the merchants and storage for their commodities. As Ibn Jubayr deplored, exchange between the Latin States and the Syrian hinterland were far from halted.

In Damascus, the suq was growing, south of the Umayyad mosque in particular. To the west of the citadel, Marj al-'Ashariyyin ("of the Asharites"), the current Merjeh concourse, became a hub of urban life and many a suq sprang up there. The Dar al-Bittikh, a fruit and vegetable market, was transferred without the city walls to the north, where it is still held today.

The Ayyubid period was one of frenetic architectural construction: several hundred buildings—civic, commercial, and, especially, conventual—saw the light of day, of which nearly a hundred are still extant (the others are known through texts), making present-day Damascus the city with the most Ayyubid monuments. In 1259, shortly before the Mongol invasion, Ibn Shaddad counted eighty-nine intramural baths—more than twice the number Ibn 'Asakir had quoted less than a century earlier. As for madrasas, nine were built under Saladin and about

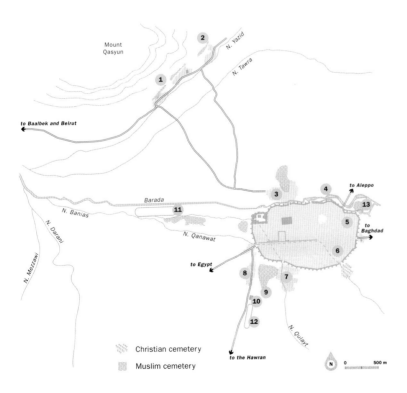

Christian cemetery
Muslim cemetery

Damascus in the mid-13th century. **1** Al-Salihiyya. **2** Kurdish quarter. **3** Al-'Uqayba. **4** Papermakers and tanneries. **5** Christian quarter. **6** Jewish quarter. **7** Shaghur. **8** Qasr al-Hajjaj. **9** Cemetery of Bab al-Saghir. **10** Musalla. **11** Green Hippodrome. **12** Hippodrome of the Stones. **13** Cemetery of Sheikh Arslan.

sixty under his successors, the majority between 1120 and 1260, the most prosperous period of Ayyubid rule. Initially a princely concern, they were soon being erected by members of the reigning family, high-ranking dignitaries, emirs, and other notables, in the main within the city walls in the western area, with others north of the Green Hippodrome, or in the faubourg of al-Salihiyya. A characteristic feature of the time, almost all were funerary madrasas, incorporating the tomb of the founder who thus benefited post-mortem from the merits attached to the study of the religious sciences and the intoning of the Koran. Such pious foundations also provided a ready way of securing an estate against expropriation.

Military architecture was of course promoted by the conflict with the Franks and made considerable advances. Several gates in the enceinte were overhauled, and virtually every time this was accompanied by a consolidation of the rampart and the moat, at Bab Tuma (1227), Bab al-Faraj (1239), and Bab al-Salam (1243), as well as Bab al-Jabiya and Bab al-Faradis during the thirteenth century. Pivotal to the city's defenses, the citadel was above all the cynosure of political power, and, at least since Burid times, the chief residence of emirs and sultans. In addition to the private residence of the prince and its outbuildings, it also housed the throne room (namely, an *iwan* where solemn audiences and feasts were held), the offices of the civil and military administration, a dovecote for the pigeon post, a barracks for the guard, an arsenal, a treasury, a mint, a garden, the state prison, and even a provisional burial-ground for members of the ruling family. Like a city within the city, it also possessed a suq, a bathhouse, and a congregational mosque in which all

View of a vegetable market in the neighborhood of the former Suq al-Khayl.

those residing in the citadel could perform Friday prayers without venturing into the bustling city. In 1203, it became the subject of a genuine rebuilding program inaugurated by al-'Adil, a brother of Saladin's, more concerned with protecting himself from attack by his nephews than by the Franks.

Rebuilding is commemorated in six inscriptions dating from 1208 to 1217. The construction—one of the largest and best preserved of all larger Syrian fortresses from the time of the Crusades—owes its main lines today to this refurbishment: a perfectly regular enclosure—except in the northwestern corner due to the course of the Barada—it covers a vast rectangle of 656 × 492 feet (200 × 150 m) flanked by thirteen towers of which six remain in their original state. A moat that could be flooded at will (now obstructed with rubble) encircled the building, whose outer walls were faced and rusticated.

Top. Bab Tuma (photograph 1989). *Bottom.* Bab Tuma in an engraving from the end of the nineteenth century.

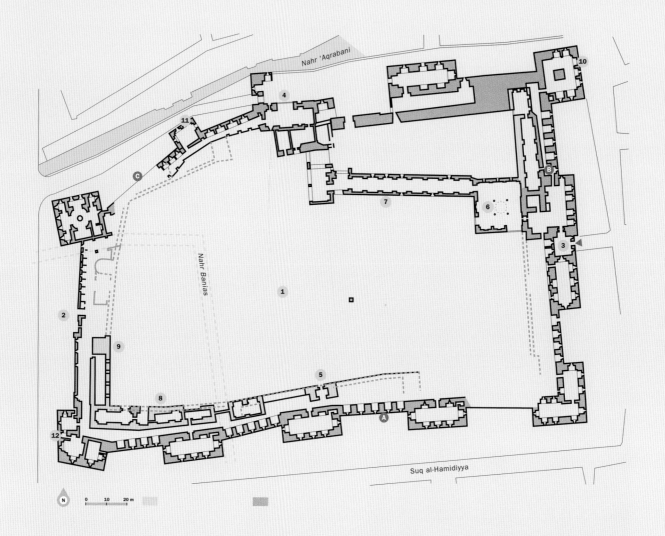

Top. Plan of the Citadel after H. Hanisch. **1** Concourse. **2** West gate. **3** East gate. (1213). **4** North gate (Bab al-Hadid). **5** South gate.

6 Columnated hall. **7** Long gallery. **8** Building known as the "Ayyubid Palace". **9** Tower of the earliest enceinte ("Seljuk" period) bearing an inscription dated 1085-1086.

10 Northeastern tower (1209). The east front has an inscription ringed by a trefoil moulding. **11** Tower reconstructed in 1508. **12** Tower reconstructed in 1986.

A Inscription of Baybars. **B** Inscription of Qalawun. **C** Inscription of Nawruz al-Hafizi.

Facing page, bottom left. The east gate to the Citadel, perhaps built by an architect from Aleppo. It is linked to the columnar hall down a "hairpin" bend.

Facing page, bottom right. Inscription ringed with trefoil molding adorning the east front of the northeast tower. Above the frame two rows of *muqarnas* with (right) a lion passant. Six lines of Ayyubid *naskh* commemorate the construction of this "blessed tower" by Sultan al-Malik al-'Adil in 1209. R.C.E.A., no. 3650.

Above. The northeast tower of the Citadel in a late nineteenth-century engraving.

Following pages. Aerial view of the old intramural city. Left, in the foreground, the Citadel cut off from the Hariqa quarter by the *suq* al-Hamidiyya rebuilt after French bombing in 1925 (see fig. p. 281). In the bottom right hand corner is the Bab al-Saghir cemetary.

On the southern front, still excellently conserved, towers about ninety-eight feet (30 m) apart (a distance dictated by the range of a crossbow) are linked by a curtain wall four and a half feet (1.40 m) thick, complete with arrow-slits, loopholes, and battlements. Rectangular in plan, the massive towers, whose walls are some eleven feet (3.40 m) thick in places, project from the curtain and incorporate three levels of halls with groin or barrel vaults. The tower on the northeastern corner, the most solid of all, might have served for a last-ditch defense, rather like a keep. The foundation inscription appears in a trefoil frame on the east front: "The construction of this blessed tower was ordered by our Master, sultan al-Malik al-'Adil . . . and that in the year 606/1209."[89] On the northern front, a tower—now much dilapidated——was afforded natural protection by the Barada and once sheltered an entrance that dog-legged no less than five times, extended by a bridge straddling the river. There rose on its terrace a *tarima*, a kind of rotunda from where the sultan and his suite might watch the military parades held on a vast stretch of land below. In a tower on the east front erected in 1213, a second entrance opens into a splendid gateway, the oldest example in Damascus with *muqarnas*, following the architectural tradition of northern Syria. The entryway emerged into a large hall set around an octagonal pool capped with a since-collapsed central dome and with eight groined side vaults carried on four sturdy antique columns. This is undoubtedly the dome referred to by the Chevalier d'Arvieux in 1660: "a rather vast and totally open dome supported on four pillars of such disproportionate size that I am convinced they would bear the dome of St. Peter's in Rome."[90]

As in the approximately contemporary 'Adiliyya madrasa, many architectonic features—the size and cut of the stones, the type of groined vaulting, etc.— betray the participation of architects from Aleppo. We know that al-'Adil had requested financial assistance from members of his family and it is not impossible that his nephew al-Zahir Ghazi, the emir of Aleppo, dispatched architects together with his teams of workmen.

There remain very few Ayyubid monuments contemporary with Saladin. These are largely *turbas*, i.e., mausoleums, almost always associated with madrasas, built by princes, princesses, or emirs concerned to perpetuate their earthly memory. Nonetheless they testify to great advances in building technology: the lightweight materials of the preceding period (hardcore, brick, and timber) make way for splendid ashlar carefully laid according to the northern Syrian tradition, with brickwork appearing solely in the cupolas. Smooth or ribbed, the domes generally repose on two superposed drums ensuring the transition from the square plan of the funerary hall: an upper sixteen-sided drum over a lower octagonal one.

The *turba* of al-Mansur Hasan with its ribbed dome; center, that of 'Ala al-Din; right, the far wall of the al-Shamiyya madrasa.

The mausoleum of the Turkman emir 'Ala al-Din, whose construction was commanded by his mother between July and August 1173, lies to the northwest of the citadel, in what is now the district of Suq Saruja. Here, the two superposed drums are octagonal, blind, and totally plain. In the middle on the southern side, opens out a large, pointed-arched bay whose neatly laid course is larger in size than that of the walls. Above the arch, a foundation text describes 'Ala al-Din as a "youth" and a "martyr," the implication being that he died young in the field against the Franks. Issuing from the Aleppine tradition, this mausoleum is the earliest of a long series that was to be perfected under the Ayyubids, and which includes some of the greatest achievements in all Damascus.

To the west of this, a mausoleum with a ribbed dome on two drums houses the burial places of three of Saladin's close relations: al-Mansur Hasan, his son, who died prematurely on October 4, 1179; Shahansha, his brother; and Fath al-Din, a first cousin, son of Shirkuh. In the immediate vicinity towers the Shamiyya madrasa, probably erected before 1186 by Zumurrud Khatun, a sister of Saladin, nicknamed Sitt al-Sham, the "Lady of Syria." Of the original building only the *turba* and the basin in front of it are still standing. According to an approach unprecedented at the time, the funerary hall is a vast square of approximately thirty-three feet (10 m) along each side, covered with a majestic groined vault springing from four angular masses only four feet (1.20 m) from the ground. It also contains one of the finest and most complete ensembles of carved plaster in the city: bas-relief moldings picked out with blue paint underscore the main lines of the structure, particularly the curved intersection of the

Interior of the al-Shamiyya madrasa. Left, the tomb of Husam al-Din; center, that of Nasir al-Din; right, that of Turan Shah.

webs. The floral-interlace stringcourse on the north face and the medallions of the eastern and western walls are exceptional. In the center of the hall, splendid inscriptions identify the pointed, ogival shells of three tombs. To the south stands that of Turan Shah, Saladin's elder brother and right-hand man, the artisan of the conquest of Nubia and the Yemen that Saladin—then all-powerful in Egypt— wished to annex in order to control the Red Sea trade and thus swell his revenues. In the center rises that of the emir Nasir al-Din, son of Shirkuh, and first cousin of Saladin, who died in Cairo in 1186, while that of the emir Husam al-Din, son of Sitt al-Sham, who died in 1191, lies in the north. Sitt al-Sham herself, who passed away on January 23, 1220, was laid to rest near her son.

Several hundred feet to the west of the aforementioned complex, on a hillock over the River Barada, stands the madrasa of Farrukhshah, son of Saladin's brother Shahanshah. Governor of Damascus when Saladin returned temporarily to Egypt after occupying the city, he played a paramount role in the jihad. In 1181, he fought the Franks at the castle of Kerak, preventing Renaud de Châtillon from occupying Tayma, a locality in the north of Arabia. In 1182, he devastated the area of Tiberiad, bringing valuable booty back to Damascus, including a thousand prisoners and twenty thousand head of cattle. He died on September 20, 1183, and was buried in a *turba* whose construction had been commissioned by his mother. The building conforms to the Ayyubid type of domed tomb: a square room with a large pointed-arch recess on each side surmounted by a dome over two superposed drums and four cul-de-four squinches. The interior walls and extrados of the cupola are stuccoed, though the ornamentation is restrained. The lower octagonal drum has small twinned bays on its inner median sides, while the upper, taller drum presents alternating bays and niches. Flat, faintly projecting bands underscore the chief features of the structure,

Top. Al-Shamiyya madrasa. Detail of the carved plasterwork following recent restoration.
Bottom. Al-Shamiyya madrasa. Fragment of the carved decor as brought to light by J. Sauvaget, *Les monuments historiques de Damascus*, Beirut, 1932, p. 56.

framing the walls, edging the arrises in the recesses and opening out into fleurons at the summit of the arches. A sizable floral interlace medallion, painted cobalt blue on a white ground, adorned the undersurface of the squinches. The door, whose frame is set in large, perfectly pointed dressed stone, is surmounted by a lintel carved with a text commemorating its foundation and a relieving arch fixed with a black false-keystone in the middle. A second *turba* of more modest size abuts the southern flank of the preceding. This belongs to the son of Farrukhshah, Bahramshah, emir of Baalbek for forty-eight years before his assassination in Damascus in 1229–30 by one of his Mameluks, whom he had suspected of stealing a belt and inkstand.

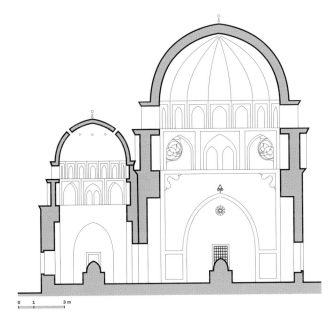

Top. The *turba* of Farrukhshah (right) and of Bahramshah (left).

Bottom. Cross section through the *turba* of Farrukhshah and of Bahramshah.

85

To the north of the Great Mosque, in the district of al-Kallasa, rises the *turba* of Saladin himself, in which he was finally buried on December 15, 1195, having been provisionally interred at the citadel on March 4, 1193. The following year, after appropriating Damascus from his brother al-Afdal, al-'Aziz built, to the east of the *turba*, a madrasa, the 'Aziziyya madrasa, of which today only the arch atop the great *iwan* survives. Saladin's *turba* is in the style of other contemporary monuments: a square chamber covered by a cupola with sixteen fluted ribs borne on two drums of eight and sixteen sides resting one on top of the other. Beside "the ghastly white marble tomb"[91]—a gift from Emperor Wilhelm II placed at the center of the room in 1903—stands the splendid carved wood cenotaph that dates, partially at least (only two sides are original), from the end of the twelfth century. Above horizontal epigraphic banding (Koran, 2:256), the field is divided by a polygonal molding with a star motif inscribed within octagons in panels containing vigorously chiseled floral motifs. At each corner vertical bands sport a decor of alternating cornucopias, fleurons, and bunches of grapes. Jean Sauvaget, who placed these pieces among the finest to survive from twelfth-century Syria, saw the interlace pattern as one of the masterpieces of decorative art from any era.[92] The plaster tracery in the windows and the ceramic cladding date from restoration work carried out in 1627 by an Ottoman pasha eager to express his gratitude to Saladin for delivering Jerusalem from "the stain of the Infidel."[93]

The *turba* known by the name Ibn al-Muqaddam, in which Emir Fakhr al-Din Ibrahim (died c. 1200) was buried, displays some points in common with that of 'Ala al-Din. A funerary chamber of square plan, open to the outside through four high ogival bays pierced to the center of each side, shelters beneath a cupola with twelve fluted ribs borne on two dodecagonal drums connected to the square below by curvilinear spandrels. The inner face of each drum is decorated with a floral interlace and foliate pattern in stucco that is both the most remarkable and the best preserved of any from the Ayyubid epoch.

Slightly to the west of the *turba* of Saladin, rises a madrasa that, in the absence of epigraphy, has had to be identified through literary material. The construction of this edifice started under Nur al-Din, but was halted following his death, only to be continued by the brother and successor of Saladin, al-'Adil, and completed by the latter's son, al-Mu'azzam, who ruled in Damascus from 1218 to 1227. Dying on August 31, 1218, and initially interred in accordance with custom in the citadel, al-'Adil's remains were transferred in 1222 to the *turba* of this madrasa, which henceforth bore his name (the 'Adiliyya madrasa). The way the stone is dressed and bonded here bears the traces of this two-stage construction program: smooth, finely jointed facings for the first ten courses of the *turba*, while elsewhere the ashlar, less carefully laid, is bush-hammered. In terms of plan—identical to that of the madrasa of Nur al-Din— as well as of building technique, the structure stems from the Aleppine architectural tradition. Various ranges are distributed around a large square court furnished with a central pool for ablutions: a prayer-hall, accessible through five bays, a funerary hall, a large and another smaller *iwan*, various other rooms, latrines and, on the floor above, quarters for students. Contrary to the usual practice in Damascus, the cupola of the funerary chamber does not rest on two layers of drums but on four alveolar pendentives that form a single octagonal drum on the outside. The most remarkable section of the building is the gate, a masterpiece of stereotomy and bonding: the recess is covered by two accolated domes, while a gigantic dropped keystone with two trefoil arches bestrides the topmost visible arch. According to an age-old Ayyubid tradition, great care was lavished over relieving the load from the window lintels, with a segment of semicircular arch to the height of two courses, and, above this, a horizontal slit in the masonry.

The tomb of Saladin.

Above, left. Interior of the drums and the intrados of the cupola of the *turba* of Saladin. *Above, right. Turba* of Ibn al-Muqaddam.
Facing page. Intrados of the cupola of the *turba* of Ibn al-Muqaddam. The finest example of carved plasterwork in Damascus.

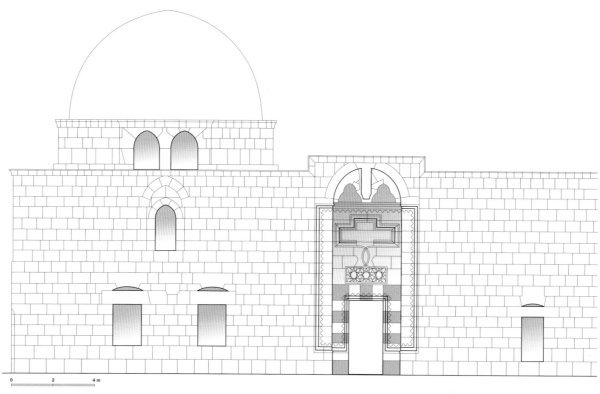

Top. The domes of the tombs of al-Malik al-'Adil (right) and of Baybars (left). In the background, the Qa'itbay minaret and the Dome of the Eagle, together with the domes of the Khan As'ad Pasha.

Bottom. Elevation of the east façade of the al-'Adiliyya madrasa.

High above the Barada and the ancient Sufi cemetery, a domed *turba* and a gate are the only vestiges of a funerary madrasa of al-Mu'azzam's chamberlain, the emir Aybak, endowed as waqf in 1224, as indicated by a text carved on the door lintel commemorating its foundation. Governor of Salkhad for many years, Aybak, under suspicion of treason, was thrown into prison in Cairo where he expired in 1248. Eight years after his death, his remains were transferred to Damascus to be buried in the *turba*. In the early twentieth century, this building remained the only one of its period to preserve traces of painted decoration on the underside of the cupola: a vermilion-tinged coating in the upper reaches, with, below, a row of fleurons in the same color picked out on a broad white field. As in all contemporary monuments, stained glass with plaster cames fills the windows opening into the drums beneath the cupola.

The highest concentration of *turbas* and funerary madrasas is to be found in the al-Salihiyya quarter:

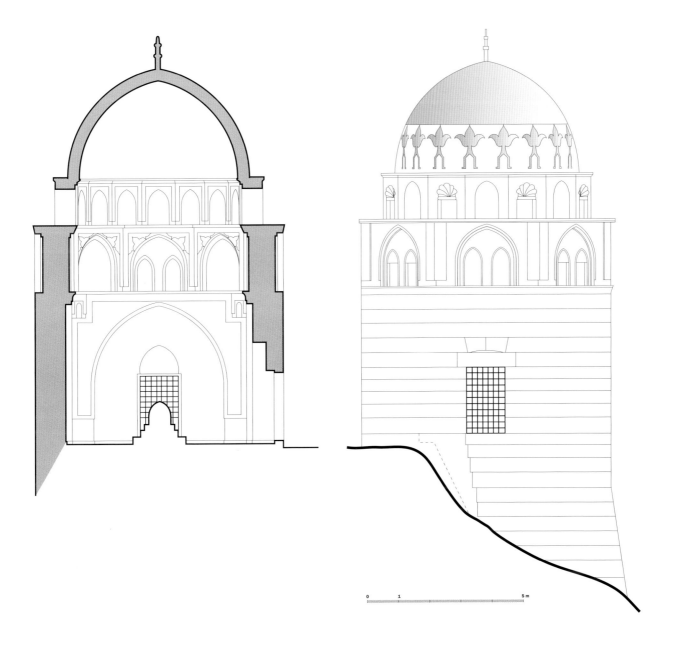

Turba of the al-'Izziyya madrasa (of Emir 'Izz al-Din Aybak). Left, north–south section; right, elevation of the west front

the 'Umariyya madrasa, constructed in the final decades of the twelfth century on the site of the *khanqah* built by Ahmad b. Qudama; the *turba* of Ismat al-Din Khatun, daughter of Unur and Nur al-Din's wife, erected in 1182; the Badriyya madrasa founded at the end of the twelfth century by Badr al-Din Hasan, one of Nur al-Din's most important emirs; the funerary madrasa of Emir Jaharkas b. 'Abd Allah, initially commander of Saladin's Mameluks before becoming an officer in the army of al-'Adil, constructed in the first half of the thirteenth century; the *turba* of Emir Mithqal, who occupied an exalted position during the reigns of both Saladin and al-Mu'azzam, inaugurated in May 1224, the *turba* of Sheikh 'Ali al-Farnathi; the funerary madrasa of Emir Rukn al-Din Mankuwirish, governor of Damascus under al-'Adil; the *turba* of Shibl al-Dawla Kafur, a black eunuch belonging to Husam al-Din, son of Sitt al-Sham; the Maridaniyya madrasa, erected in 1226–27 by the spouse of al-Mu'azzam; the Atabekiyya madrasa, funerary madrasa of Princess Tarkan Khatun, granddaughter of Zenki and wife to al-Ashraf Musa who reigned in Damascus from 1228 until 1237; the Sahibiyya madrasa, the funerary madrasa for a sister of Saladin's Rabi'a Katun; the madrasa of Arghun al-Hafiziya, a manumitted slave of al-Adil who died in 1250; the Murshidiyya madrasa, funerary madrasa belonging to Khadija Khatun, daughter of al-Mu'azzam; and the *turba* of Emir Sayf al-Din Qaymari, renowned for his bravery and his equestrian knowledge, who died in Nablus on August 26, 1256.

Known for its *turbas* and madrasas (Yaqut declared: "The foot of this holy mountain [the Qasiyun] which on judgment day will alone be spared in the universal tumult, conserves the most pious Muslims, the most venerated emirs"[94]), Salihiyya also included many civil monuments—suq, khan, *hammam*, luxurious residences, a *bimaristan*, as well as a Great Mosque—making it a veritable museum of Ayyubid architecture without peer in Egypt or elsewhere in Syria. According to a text carved above

the west door, the Great Mosque, whose construction began in 1203, was the work of Muzaffar al-din Gokburi, husband of Rabi'a Khatun, and Saladin's brother-in-law. The basic composition of the mosque, sometimes called al-Muzaffari and elsewhere "of the Hanbalites," takes its cue from its venerable Umayyad predecessor, with the prayer-hall with three naves parallel to the qibla wall, a courtyard with a central pool encircled by porticoes, and a minaret of square section adjoining the north wall. The prayer-hall is covered with curb roofs whose frame is borne on two porches on columns alternating with two consecutive pillars. The *minbar*—according to the text carved above the door, ordered by Gokburi, "fervent slave of God's mercies"[95]—has kept much of its magnificent carved decoration, disfigured, alas, as is the entire hall, by later daubing of the most dreadful kitsch. The seven doors of the prayer-hall open beneath carved wooden lintels; two of these are still surmounted by openwork plaster transennae that feature lively compositions, combining exceptionally well-carved palmettes with foliate elements. Several windows even conserve their original stained glass intact.

The Salihiyya *bimaristan* is the best preserved and perhaps the finest Ayyubid monument in Damascus. Several inscriptions appearing on the gate give a date (August 1248) for the beginning of construction, as well as the identity of the founder (Emir Sayf al-din Qaymari), and list the property comprising the waqf, including "villages of the Marj, portions of other villages, mills, a *qaysariyya*, about thirty shops, two khans."[96] The plan of the building, inspired by Nur al-Din's *bimaristan*, displays perfect symmetry along the north–south axis: a vaulted gateway with *muqarnas*, a vestibule, a square court with central basin, a large *iwan* in the middle on the southern side, two smaller *iwans* in the center to the east and west quarters, and a dozen or so rooms open onto the court. Its clarity of plan, majesty of volume, and almost austere sobriety, is tempered by an unobtrusive decor that emphasizes

Facing page. Turba of the al-Rukniyya madrasa.

92   *Page 94. Top, left. Turba* of Ibn Salama. *Top, right.* Amat al-Latif and Raihan *turba. Bottom.* Remains of the al-Shibliyya madrasa.

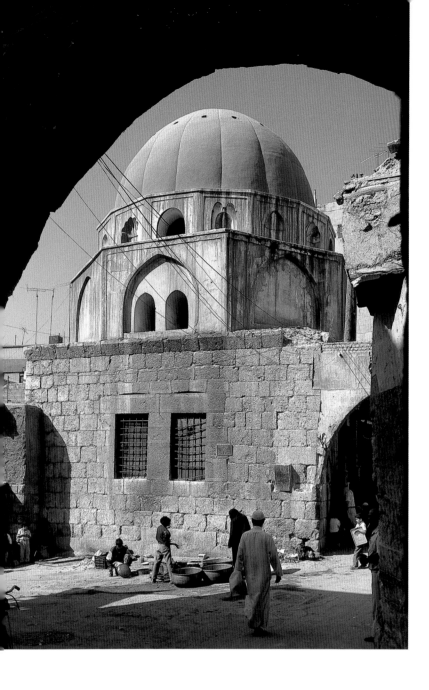

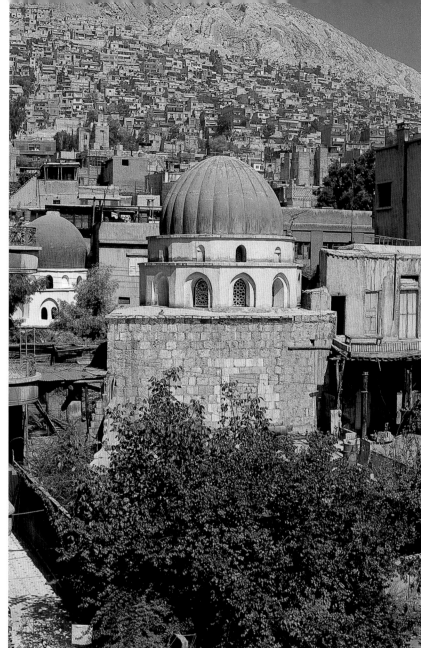

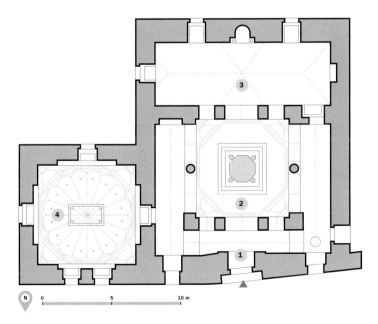

a few chosen points in the structure: on the plaster-coated vault of the larger *iwan*, two very fine medallions adorned with palmettes bordered by acanthus leaves; at the springing, a long inscription in red on green repeats the profession of faith: "There is no God but God and Muhammad is his Prophet." Adjoining the center of the north front, the gate prefigures the early Mameluk style as it is to appear at the Zahiriyya madrasa, the funerary madrasa of Sultan Baybars: corner colonnettes, epigraphic stringcourses running over three sides, half-cupolas with three rows of *muqarnas* topped by a squinch, arch summit with two-color multifoil arch stones.

In addition to the mosque of the Hanbalites, the increase in population and the extension of the

Top, left. Al-Maridaniyya madrasa. *Top, right.* Al-Murshidiyya and al-Atabikiyya madrasas.
Bottom. Plan of the Rukniyya madrasa. **1** Entrance. **2** Roofed vestibule with central pool. **3** Prayer hall. **4** Tomb.

Top. Al-Hafiziyya madrasa. *Bottom*. Al-Qaymari *bimaristan*. Stucco medallion adorning the southern *iwan* vault.

Above. Mosque of the Hanbalites. Interior of the prayer-hall. Note the abuse of varnish and paint daubing over the woodwork throughout.

Page 98. Detail of *muqarnas* on the vault of the gateway to the al-Qaymari *bimasistan*.

Page 99. Mosque of the Hanbalites. Carved plaster transennae above one of the entrance doors to the prayer-hall.

97

suburbs precipitated the creation of new congregational mosques: that of al-Tawba at al-'Uqayba, that of al-Jarrah outside Bab al-Saghir close to the sheep market, and that of al-Musalla, further to the south, in the district of Midan. The circumstances surrounding the foundation of the al-Tawba mosque preserved in a written account cast some light on an aspect in the history of attitudes in the first half of the thirteenth century: having made himself master of Damascus in 1228, Musa al-Ashraf, son of al-'Adil, a pious and austere prince, made up his mind to devote his energies to moral reform in order to curry favor with the more pious factions. "He was a man of great continence," reveals a seemingly well-informed author, "and the only wives he knew were his own."[97] Clearly root and branch reforms were in store and his sights were set shortly after coming to power: "He let it be known that jurisconsults were to deal with tradition,

the interpretation of the Koran, and jurisprudence, and nothing else."[98] If one is to believe the chronicles of the time, such measures were no easy task to enforce and they beg the question as to what else jurisconsults had become involved in. . . . None of this prevented the logic and science of the ancients from "also being banned from the city."[99] These sound like the words of a Father of the Church; a retreat to religious science sensu stricto was soon underway. Nevertheless, in the suburb of al-'Uqayba, there stood a khan, known by the name of al-Zinjari, where, besides the commercial activities for which this type of establishment was in theory intended, the Umayyad traditions of the good life still thrived, where wine ran in torrents and where "people of loose living disported themselves in the most reprehensible acts."[100] This khan—indeed, like many a hotel in the modern world—often doubled as a bawdy house whose

Above. Al-Tawba Mosque. Courtyard, ablution pool, façade of the prayer-hall.

Facing page. Minaret of the Mosque al-Jarrah.

manager acted as a regular "pander," charging fees on services, a substantial proportion of which made their way into the public purse. In 1232, al-Ashraf, in pursuance of his "clean-up" policy, had the khan-cum-hostelry demolished, erecting in its place a mosque suitably dubbed, al-Tawba—"Repentance." The edifice was completed only in 1251, fourteen years after the death of its founder. Its design is in all points congruent with that of the Umayyad mosque: a courtyard ringed by a simple portico, a prayer-hall covered with oblong gambrel roofs, a broader and taller orthogonal nave, with pediment and dome. The prayer-hall, however, comprises only two vessels instead of three, separated by a pillared portico.

In addition to the construction of several hundred new buildings, many others were periodically restored, or refurbished, or even entirely rebuilt after flood, fire, or earthquake.[101] The al-Kallasa madrasa and the minaret close to al-'Arus ("of the betrothed"), which fell prey to flames in August 1174, were restored in 1185 by Saladin. As may be expected, the Great Mosque was the focus of the scrupulous attentions of the princes of the dynasty. In 1179, Saladin himself had the marble cladding on two of the pillars in the cupola refitted. In 1183, a disciple of Sheikh Arslan restored the mosque of Khaled b. al-Walid. Almost entirely in ruins today, the building has nonetheless preserved its glorious mihrab (restored in 1984) in two-color bond with a vault on small squinches, radiating monoliths, and corner posts.

In 1202, the whole of Syria was shattered by a tremor so violent that, according to the physician 'Abd al-Latif, "everyone believed it to be the earthquake that would herald the Last Judgment."[102] Most of the town of Acre fell like a pack of cards, and a third of Tyre and Safita was literally engulfed. Many houses collapsed in Damascus, and the al-Kallasa madrasa was obliterated; the walls, cupola, and a minaret of the Great Mosque cracked, while another minaret and sixteen battlements collapsed. Restoration work began immediately, followed by an accelerating policy of further improvements: in 1208, came the courtyard paving; in 1211, the leaves of the western gate were restored; in 1214, the paving in the prayer-hall; in 1216, the framework of the dome was repaired; in 1238, a window giving on the al-Kamil mausoleum was opened under the northern portico; in 1249, the southeast minaret, destroyed by fire two years earlier, was rebuilt.

Anxious to pursue the policy of the Seljukids and of Nur al-din, the authorities also attended to many burial places belonging to famous men in general venerated for their piety, as well as various places regarded as sacred due to their role in myth. The popularity of such sites is amply demonstrated by the appearance of what amount to guides for pilgrims, the oldest of which is that by al-Harawi (died 1215), as well as by the countless pages devoted to them in travelers' accounts. In Damascus particularly, Mount Qasiyun—which Ibn 'Asakir had already called "one of the four mountains of Paradise"[103]—was much vaunted. In one cave, the "cave of hunger," seventy prophets were supposed to have perished, having found themselves with but one loaf of bread between them. According to the testimony of Ibn Jubayr, this was lit night and day and also housed an oratory. On the western slopes of Mount Qasiyun rose the "blessed hill" (the former hill of Nayrab that became simply al-Rabwa, "the hill") where Jesus is supposed to have stayed with his mother, as is apparently made clear in the verse: "And we gave them a shelter on a lofty ground having meadows and springs."[104] There too stood an oratory, "one of the most splendid sights in this world," as Ibn Jubayr put it, citing its "beauty, splendor, elevation, solidity of construction, refinement of ornament, [and] perfection of style."[105] In the cave in which Jesus is supposed to have rested and to which the faithful hastened to pray, had been set a fountain ("none more beautiful could be seen") , together with basins with plashing water for ablutions.[106] Another much-contested tradition had it that this hill was also the site of the tomb of the Virgin Mary.

It is again on Mount Qasiyun that Elijah is supposed to have sought refuge from the kings of his tribe,[107] and that figures such as St. John the Baptist, Abraham, Lot, and Job came to pray. It was at the foot of the same venerable mountain, in the village of Barza, that Muslim tradition locates the birthplace of Abraham, in a cave above which Ibn Jubayr describes "a large and lofty mosque provided with a tall minaret and divided into many oratories like high rooms dominating the country around."[108] Its reputation, however, was based on a pre-Islamic legend, since Flavius Josephus already mentions "the village in the surroundings of Damascus that bears the name Abramu *oikesis*, dwelling of Abraham."[109] To the south of Damascus, in the village of Qadam, the Mosque of the Foot contains a rock bearing an imprint that some claim to be the foot of Moses and others that of Muhammad.[110]

In addition to the graves of the prophets, among which Ibn Jubayr has no hesitation in including that of Moses, and whose number seems to swell over time—in the fourteenth century Ibn Battuta reported a tradition according to which there were seventy thousand[111]—the "blessed monuments" also included the tombs of the Umayyad caliphs, of the descendants of 'Ali, of the Companions of the Prophet, and even of one of Muhammad's wives, Umm Habiba, sister of Mu'awiya. They were also the object of ongoing maintenance and periodic restoration work. In 1228, for example, the tomb of Bilal, the muezzin of the Prophet, was subject to refurbishment commemorated in an inscription. Moreover, there were tombs of pious and much-revered contemporaries such as Ibn 'Asakir, a celebrated "traditionist" and author of a vast biographical history of Damascus, who died in February 1176 and was buried a little to the east of the tomb of Mu'awiya, in the cemetery of Bab al-Saghir; the Andalusian Sufi Ibn 'Arabi, who passed away in 1240 and was interred at the foot of Mount Qasiyun; and Sheikh Arslan, who died some time between 1160

and 1165, and who was laid to rest close to the mosque of Khaled b. al-Walid.

As for the Damascenes, in contradistinction to conventional biographical accounts and chronicles that paint them as virtually unthinking pawns of world events and disasters such as plague, fire, flooding, swarms of locusts, drought, earthquake, siege, rioting, brutal foreign soldiery, or the goodwill of a prince, etc., Ibn Jubayr—a sagacious if unforgiving observer—describes them as beings of flesh and blood who breathe, eat, and enjoy their lives to the full. . . . The first thing that strikes him is their manner of treating strangers. All here enjoy "innumerable advantages" he proclaims, before adding however that, still more than in any other land of the Orient, esteem, honor, and civility are lavished on "those who know the Koran by heart or who aspire to learn it."[112] Their attitude towards pilgrims returning from the hajj literally astounded him: "They go as a body to greet them, men and women alike taking them by the hand to rub it against them . . . while the women offer them bread which, as soon as they have bitten into it, they tear from their hands and swallow down so as to get the *baraka* [good luck] the pilgrim gave it when he ate of it."[113] This is followed by a skit on "How to be a Damascene"—a series of droll observations on local attitudes and customs. The Maghrebi characterize their manner of greeting as "a kind of inclination or prostration. One stares as necks alternately rise and fall, crane forward and backwards—a process that can last an age: one bows, the other stands erect, while in front of them the turbans nod."[114] This is indeed a far cry from accepted good manners in North Africa, where incessant bowing and scraping is something only lower-class women, female slaves, and "earring wearers" do.[115] As reprobation gives way to scorn, our traveler concludes: "Damascenes waste their souls in gestures for which proud souls can feel only disdain."[116]

The Bab al-Saghir cemetery.

Government
by the Turks

The end of the Latin states,
and the Mongol offensive

After a brief sojourn in Damascus, where he busied himself extending and consolidating his control over Syria, Qutuz once again set out for Cairo. Stopping off at al-Qusayr, he was assassinated at a shooting party on October 22, 1260, by a group of conspirators, led by the Turkish emir Baybars, unhappy at being muscled out of the Aleppo government. Elevated to the sultanate, Baybars made his solemn entry into Cairo, chose it as his capital, took possession of the Citadel of the Mountain, and began his rule over Egypt and Syria, "from the territories of the Euphrates to the Sudan."[1] It was he who provided the foundation for the new Mameluk State—one of most solidly established in the whole history of Islam—that was to endure until the arrival of the Ottoman in 1517. He swiftly set about unifying Syria, subjugating

the autonomous "principalities" one by one: after 1268, the only independent entity was Hama, where an Ayyubid prince bent over backwards to accommodate every demand. Backed by an army of twelve thousand men split equally over two fields of operation, in Cairo, and in Aleppo and Damascus, he led a merciless campaign against the Mongols who still harried the borders north of Syria. Taking a string of cities and fortified towns, he pursued with tireless ardor Saladin's jihad against the Franks. A lion-hearted warrior, a fine strategist, crafty, vicious, cynical, violent, indefatigable, unscrupulous, and pitiless, gifted with unparalleled political acumen and boundless energy, an incomparable puppet-master, who acceded to power by overcoming two reigning sovereigns—Turan Shah and Qutuz— Islam's new strong man well deserved his nickname of Baybars (the "panther"). A legend in his own lifetime, the account of his campaigns makes the head spin: he spent his whole seventeen-year reign in the saddle, crisscrossing states from Cairo to Cilicia in all weathers, forever in camps, sieges, and battles. In November 1260, according to a process repeated almost systematically at each change of reign, he had to deal with a rebellion by the governor of Damascus appointed by Qutuz, Sanjar al-Halabi; making the troops swear him the oath, he had himself proclaimed sultan and smartly got to work reinforcing the citadel: "Even the women," Maqrizi records, "engaged in the task."[2] Following al-Nasir, Hulagu, and Qutuz, he was no less than the fourth lord of Damascus that year. Yet his chance in the limelight was short-lived—two months later, Sanjar al-Halabi was captured in Baalbek, dispatched in chains to Cairo, and hurled into a dungeon.

Baybars could finally focus on reinforcing the Mameluk state, modernizing the arsenal and the fleet by building a staggering number of galleys in the ports of Damietta and Alexandria. At enormous financial cost, he also made improvements to the postal service, setting up new staging posts thanks to which news from Damascus arrived in Cairo in four days. Concerned to secure Syria against fresh attack from the Mongols and to prepare for battle against the Franks, he rebuilt a great number of fortresses (Ajlun, Salkhad, Bosra, Baalbek, etc.), setting up garrisons and stockpiling significant reserves of ammunition and food. In Damascus, which served as his base for the many wars he waged in Syria and where, after each victory, he would make his entry "preceded by prisoners and by men brandishing the heads of his enemies impaled on spears,"[3] he had the Dar al-'Adl ("law courts") built, and made repairs to the citadel where the battlements and the upper reaches of the towers had been dismantled by the Mongols.

Keen to legitimize a power founded on a brace of assassinations, he had a certain Abu al-Qasim proclaimed caliph. This young boy who, it was mooted, was the son of the 'Abbassid caliph Zahir Abu Nasr, claimed to have escaped a violent death

at the hands of the Mongols at the time of the sack of Baghdad. A ceremony of enthronement was arranged, during which the new Emir of the Believers, Mustansirbillah Abu al-Qasim, offered Baybars the robes of honor, an insignia of investiture that conceded him not only regions already under Islamic control, but also all those he might wrestle from the Infidel, repeating the ritual formula vouchsafing the separation of temporal and spiritual power: "I entrust the entirety of the governance of the Muslims to you and invest you with all the authority with which I am invested with respect to matters of the faith." Caliph, sultan, and the whole army then set off to Damascus where, in the presence of the city dignitaries, a great ceremony was held in the Umayyad mosque. The caliphal fiction stumbled on, but the heir to Harun al-Rashid and al-Ma'mun was a paper tiger (he could not even leave his residence without authorization), whom a successor of Baybars, Sultan Qalawun, was not above throwing into prison.

On the military front, Baybars fought without quarter against the Ismaelites, the Mongols, the Franks, and the Armenians. From the first of these, he wrenched fortress after fortress: Maynaka, Qadmus, and Kahf. He gained many victories against the Mongols, whom he excluded totally from Syria. Once that threat was had been neutralized with the death of Hulagu, he went on to inflict decisive blows on the Franks, reducing their states to a cordon of land along the coast. In 1265, he made Caesarea, Haifa, Arsuf, and Tibnin his own. In 1268, having harried Acre and taken Beaufort and Jaffa, he materialized before Tripoli—but, halted by the snow blanketing Mount Lebanon, he returned by way of Hama and set about taking Antioch by storm, plundering and burning the city. The churches of St. Paul and SS. Cosmas and Damian were destroyed—depending on the authority, the number of fatalities ranged between seventeen and forty thousand. What had been one of the most beautiful and admired cities in antiquity never recovered and become the drab overgrown village that it remains. With Antioch taken, the strongholds of the Orontes—Darkush, Kafardubbin, and Belmis—fell like dominoes; the Templars surrendered Baghras, Hajar Shughlan, and Arsuz without a fight. At the beginning of 1271, Baybars seized Safita, then, in March, the Krak des Chevaliers, the celebrated fortress of the Hospitalers hitherto considered impregnable. Two years later, the submission of the Ismaelites was complete.

In 1266, during a stay in Damascus following the taking of Safad, Baybars ordered the building of the Green Hippodrome on the right bank of the Barada, at Maydan al-Akhdar, on the site of the current Sulaymaniyya *takiyya*, a palace known as Qasr al-Ablaq. Faced entirely in an alternating black and white bond, it became the model for the palace of the same name Sultan Qalawun had built in Cairo a few years later. The sheer size of the building, as well as its richness and artistry impressed all: "The lofty roofs touch the clouds," enthused al-'Umari,

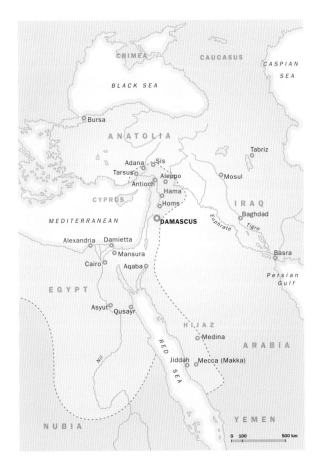

"dominating the city and the Ghuta to all four points of the horizon."[4] Various outbuildings, royal pavilions, stables, a *hammam*, etc., stood about the gardens amid flowing waters. Opposite on the left bank, an *iwan* dominating the hippodrome was built for receptions. Perhaps the palace was damaged in the flash floods of summer 1270, which "carried off a great number of people, uprooted trees, broke river banks, and knocked down houses."[5] Having for more than a century served as the residence of sultans when they passed through Damascus, it was to be destroyed in 1400 at the time of the sack of Timur.

In June 1277, returning from an expedition to Anatolia, Baybars stopped off at Qasr al-Ablaq, where, having mistakenly sipped from a cup of poison intended for an emir he wanted to eliminate, he died, wracked by fever and diarrhea. Certain less than generous authors describe him as dying from an arrow wound in the anus: "His soul is said to have departed when, after several days, the surgeon finally succeeded in extracting the arrowhead."[6] Back in Cairo, his son al-Sa'id who, Maqrizi alleges, leapt for joy on learning of the death of his sire, now ascended to the throne. In Damascus, the deceased's body was temporarily buried in the citadel, while the governor of the city, Emir Aydamur, on the orders of al-Sa'id, requisitioned a residence opposite the 'Adiliyya madrasa so as to erect a *turba* and a madrasa as speedily as possible. The walls scarcely dry, Baybars's remains were borne to the Umayyad mosque for the prayer for the dead and then buried beneath the dome where reciters of the Koran gathered to intone the holy writ.

The best-preserved zones of the complex are the gateway and the *turba*, a simple square hall covered with a cupola on squinches resting on a pair of octagonal drums. The funerary hall, lit by low windows pierced in the southern and western walls, is faced with panels in an arrangement of marble marquetry and colored stones surmounted by a broad mosaic band on a gold field. Less well crafted than

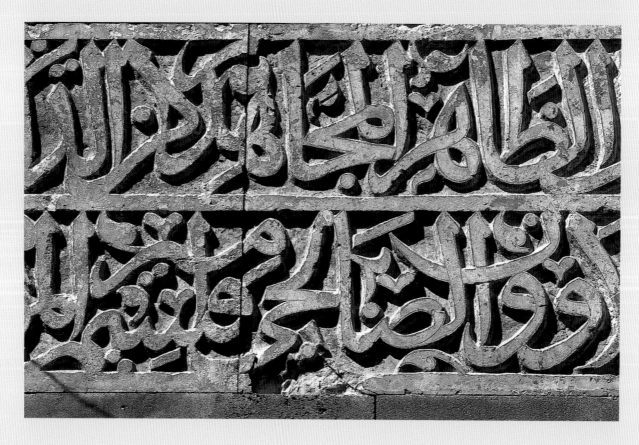

Top. Al-Zahiriyya madrasa. Detail of the mosaic frieze of the Baybars *turba*.

Bottom. Al-Zahiriyya madrasa. Detail of the epigraphic band on the gateway.

Top. Left, Cupola of the al-'Adiliyya madrasa; center, that of the al-Zahiriyya madrasa; right, that of the *turba* of Saladin and the Minaret of the Bride of the Umayyad Mosque. *Bottom.* Al-Zahiriyya madrasa: Detail of the *muqarnas* vaulting on the gateway.

those in the Umayyad mosque, these mosaics bedecked with trees and palaces attest to the persistence of Byzantine mosaic techniques in thirteenth-century Damascus. The mihrab curves between two small columns in the middle of a polychrome marquetry panel presenting geometric and foliated motifs. The most interesting part of the building is the gateway, one of the most accomplished in Islamic Syria. Ensconced in a deep oblong recess, it bears two epigraphic bands, masterpieces of Mameluk calligraphy. Two lines of text on the upper strip list the goods comprising the waqf that endows the madrasa: villages, cantons, orchards, a mill, two khans, a store, and the ground floor of a qaysariyya; the lower band provides the date of construction: 1277. In the left corner in the rear of a cell appears the signature of the architect, Ibrahim

b. Ghanaim, also the builder of Qasr al-Ablaq. By its proportions, clarity of line, depth of relief and the precision of its stone-carving, the vaulted gate with its four rows of *muqarnas* surmounted by a conch is of exceptional quality.

After a short-lived interregnum by two sons of Baybars, a new iron man, the emir Qalawun, ascended to the throne with the title al-Malik al-Mansur. In Damascus, the troops uttered the oath of fidelity to the new sultan, and for a week the city was splendidly decked out. But in April 1280 the governor of Syria, Sunqur al-Ashqar, just as Sanjar al-Halabi had done before him under Baybars, openly instigated rebellion with the support of the great Shafiite qadi, Ibn Khallikan, author of a renowned biographical dictionary. Initially beaten back at Gaza, and a second time beneath the walls of Damascus,

Above, left. Mihrab of the *turba* of Sultan Baybars. *Above, right.* Interior of the vault of the *turba* of Baybars.
Facing page. The Minaret of the Bride, the *turbas* of al-Malik al-'Adil, of Baybars, and of Saladin, as seen from the Citadel.

the rebel nonetheless avoided capture, immuring himself in the castle of Sahyun whence he harangued the Mongols to invade Syria. In October, the latter did indeed carry out a raid on Aleppo, during which the city was partially gutted. At the head of an army fifty thousand strong, Qalawun took the Damascus road, where he joined quotas of Turkmen and tribal Arabs "helmeted, sporting swords across their shoulders and wielding spears, followed by women and the baggage train, and accompanied by a musician who sang in praise of the warriors' composure as they went to face death."[7]

While his forces were descending the Orontes, in Damascus all those who had not yet fled to Egypt were stricken with panic and placed themselves in God's hands. Maqrizi describes the scene: "The entire population gathered in the Great Mosque and addressed supplications to God accompanied by cries and tears. The 'Uthman Koran was carried aloft. Then the whole crowd surged out of the mosque and made for the *musalla* outside the city, all beseeching God to grant the Muslims victory over their enemy."[8] As day broke on October 29, 1281, on the plain of Homs, faced with the fifty thousand Mongols and thirty thousand motley Georgians, Greeks, Armenians, and Franks commanded by Mangu-Timur, Qalawun deployed his army for battle: on the right wing, the tribal Arabs, on the left, the Turkmen, in the center, the emir Turuntay, vice-sultan of Egypt, and Qalawun himself, flanked by eight hundred Mameluks and four thousand riders of his personal guard, the *halqa*. Though at the outset the result seemed in doubt, the Mameluks finished masters of the field. A carrier pigeon was released to fly news of the victory to Damascus where it was celebrated with music in the citadel. A week later, Qalawun entered the city for a solemn feast day that poets acclaimed in myriad verses. After the customary nominations and dismissals, and having ordered a tower of the citadel and the *bimaristan* of Nur al-Din to be restored, the sultan set off once again for Cairo.

The Mongol menace temporarily marginalized, the jihad against the Franks was to be given an extra turn of the screw: on May 25, 1286, after a thirty-eight day siege, a powerful Hospitalier fortress, Marqab, capitulated. On April 20 the following year, it was the turn of Latakia. Northern Syria was now emptied of Frankish presence. Christian theologians reasoned—in the manner of theological explanation—that this catastrophe was a punishment from God inflicted on the Franks for their divisiveness and shortcomings. In February 1289, Qalawun assembled his forces in Damascus and departed to besiege Tripoli, which was taken by storm on April 26. According to an eyewitness, Abu'l Fida, after the Muslims "had finished killing and ransacking"[9] the city that John

Above. Rare wood cenotaph presented in 1265 by Sultan Baybars to the mausoleum of Khaled b. al-Walid in Homs to commemorate a victory over the Armenians of Cilicia. Detail of the decoration. Damascus Museum.

Facing page. Detail of the epigraphic bandeau running around the cenotaph.

Phocas had called "worthy of admiration for the height of its ramparts and the beauty of its buildings,"[10] and whose ramparts, according to Maqrizi, "were so broad that three mounted horsemen could pass through them abreast,"[11] and whose inhabitants "possessed great wealth, amongst other things, four thousand looms," the place was "demolished and razed to the ground"[12] by order of the sultan. Amid general rejoicing the latter entered Damascus, where he had a covered gallery linking two doors in the citadel restored. Back in Cairo, while preparing to attack Acre, he died on November 10, 1290, at the term of an eleven-year reign "to a glorious and propitious end."[13]

Impressive ceremonies were organized in Damascus. "The qadis," writes al-Jazari, "all the reciters of the Koran, the *fuqaha*, the imams, the Sufis, the emirs, the commanders, and the greater part of the inhabitants gathered together in the Green Hippodrome [lit by candles and covered in rugs] opposite the Qasr al-Ablaq outside the city on the evening of November 11 on the orders of the *na'ib*. . . . On Sunday from midday to sunset, the complete

Koran was read out, after which a feast was prepared and the people ate, everything served being consumed. Then they began to intone the Koran until the middle of the night. . . . After which, the *na'ib* commanded the preachers to ascend the *minbar* and to pronounce sermons on the late sultan. . . . That night, the gates of Damascus were left unshut."[14]

Al-Ashraf Khalil mounted the throne and soon resumed his father's work. On April 5, 1291, he appeared with an impressive artillery battery beneath the city walls of Acre, where Templars, Hospitalers, Knights of the Holy Land and of Cyprus, and Crusaders recently arrived from Europe, as well as Italian traders and all the inhabitants took part in the defense. On May 18 at dawn, after beating the drum on the backs of three hundred camels, he launched the final attack. The carnage was appalling, with any Frank who failed to escape by sea being slain on the spot. The ramparts were dismantled and the churches and all other buildings delivered to the flames. The good news was announced in Damascus by pigeon post: "The whole town arrayed in its finery and military music resounded through the citadel and to the gates of the emirs."[15] Festivities lasted an entire month with al-Ashraf being hailed as liberator of Syria. In the following months, Tyre, Beirut, Sayda, Athlit, and Tartus surrendered or were evacuated without a stand: Latin Syria was effectively erased from the map. Abu'l Fida summed up the achievement: "Thus were all Syria and the coastal zones purified from the Franks who had been on the brink of conquering Egypt and seizing Damascus."[16] Only the enclave of Arwad opposite Tartus still remained in the hands of the Templars.

The very next month, Damascus found itself undergoing a refurbishment program. In the citadel, the palace of the sultan, the *tarima*, and a dome known as al-Qubba al-Zarka', "the blue dome" were rebuilt. Marble was in demand throughout Syria and, in Damascus, as al-Jazari describes, "great Roman columns were torn down."[17] Bathing places were set

up along the canals, the small Green Hippodrome was extended as far as the banks of the Barada, the work (as al-Jazari further states) being undertaken by emirs, commanders, troops, and most of the population of the city.

In putting a stop to the Crusades after a conflict lasting two centuries, al-Ashraf's victory had indeed "purified" Syria of the Franks, but an inventory drawn up by Abu'l Fida at the turn of the fourteenth century portrays a bleeding, devastated land, beset by regressions in urban life and a declining population—an image in marked contrast with the one we have of the eleventh century. "Once flourishing" al-Rastan "lies in ruins";[18] Caesarea, "formerly a large metropolis, is today just ruins";[19] Arsuf, "today is in ruins and deserted";[20] Acre, "today, it is in ruins";[21] Tiberias, "ruined since Saladin regained it from the Franks";[22] Tyre, "ruined, today lies deserted";[23] Edessa, "formerly a large city . . . that contained more than three hundred Christian monasteries. Today, it is in ruins";[24] Harran, "today it is in ruins";[25] Manbij, "partly ruined";[26] Raqqa, "today, in ruins and deserted";[27] Mosul, "nowadays, hardly two thirds of the city stands."[28] And, if descriptions by successive travelers in following centuries are to be credited, the country, especially the southern zone, was hardly to rise from its ashes before the modern era.

If the Franks were indeed cut off—at least until the return of Westerners in the first half of the twentieth century—on the northern flank the threat from the freshly Islamized Mongols installed in Iran had not evaporated. According to what was a now well-rehearsed script, on December 13, 1293, on the way back from a shooting-party, al-Ashraf was assassinated by a band of conspirators led by one of his own principal lieutenants, the emir Baydara. The portrait Maqrizi gives of the victim diverges rather from that of most Mameluk sultans. In contrast to Qalawun, whose Arabic was rudimentary, and to so many others who were almost to a man uncultured

and coarse, "al-Ashraf was characterized by charm in conversation and he displayed in discussions with men of letters a superior mind and a talent blessed with extraordinary finesse."[29]

The death of al-Ashraf heralded a series of bloody palace revolutions that witnessed the rise and fall of four sultans in a matter of five years: the emir Baydara; a son of Qalawun, hardly nine years old, al-Nasir Muhammad; the emir Kitbugha of Mongolian origin; and the emir Lajin, one of al-Ashraf's murderers. On January 15, 1299, after a reign of two years, as another Mongol attack loomed on the northern border, this last succumbed in his turn, victim of a plot fomented by emirs jealous of the influence of his Mameluk favorite, Mankutimur. Al-Nasir Muhammad, then seventeen, was elevated to the throne. While the Mongols led by Ghazan had already swept past Aleppo, the new sultan arrived in Damascus at the head of an army of his own at the end of November 1299. Battle was joined north of Homs; the Mameluk force was beaten and fell back to Damascus where panic was endemic. "The women left their houses with faces uncovered, men abandoned their shops and goods, and fled from the city. The crowds were so vast that many people were suffocated at the gates. Some inhabitants ran off to the mountaintops and villages. Others, in great number, made off to Egypt."[30]

While al-Nasir and those close to him repaired to Cairo at full tilt, the inhabitants of Damascus sent a delegation to Ghazan headed by the great qadi and composed of notables, lawyers, and reciters of the Koran. Five days later, the Mongols swept into the city, where the surrender conditions were announced to the populace gathered in the Great Mosque. Initially came the "ideological" justifications: "Inspired by religious zeal and Islamic fervor," the Mongols had undertaken the war against the Mameluk sultans because the latter "had departed from the true religion" and their victory, which "brings a reign of justice," would be gratifying to God.[31] Plundering was prohibited and the troops commanded to abstain from "harming any of those who follow various religions, Jews, Christians or Sabeans . . . since the protection granted to them is an obligation prescribed by religious law."[32] However, having refused to yield, the commander of the citadel, Emir Arjawash, organized resistance and responded to Mongol bombardments by setting fire to everything to hand: "Fire consumed quantities of buildings located outside the city," wrote Maqrizi, "among others the mosque of al-Tawba . . . and an infinite number of palaces, houses, and gardens."[33] The Mongols then compelled the city fathers to negotiate with Arjawash, threatening to plunder the city and massacre the population if he refused to halt engagements. The battle became fiercer, barricades sprang up and the insurrectionists essayed sorties against the soldiers manning the Mongol mangonels erected in the courtyard of the Umayyad mosque. Aided and abetted by Christian auxiliaries—Georgians and Armenians—the Mongols then fell on Salihiyya, sacking it and putting the population to the sword. The carpets and lamps that once decorated the mosque of the Hanbalites were carried off, numerous monuments destroyed or burned down, and many inhabitants had their throats slit or were taken into captivity. According to Maqrizi, the number of fatalities and prisoners amounted to 9,900.[34]

In Damascus, the Great Mosque "was transformed into a den of iniquity where Mongols drank wine and indulged in prostitution and pederasty,"[35] while a hefty levy was imposed in the most brutal manner. "The belt-makers market was taxed to one hundred and thirty thousand dirhem, the spearmakers to one hundred thousand, and the copperworkers to sixty thousand. The principal citizens had to disburse four hundred thousand dirhem. In dealing with every echelon of the population, the Mongols supervising collection struck people,

tortured them, and forced them to endure every kind of insult and humiliation. . . . The sum of what entered the treasury of Ghazan alone . . . amounted to three hundred million, six hundred thousand dirhem, excluding weapons, cloths, beasts of burden, and grain, and then there was the plunder. . . . More than twenty thousand camels and horses were removed from the city."[36] According to Maqrizi, in the city and its surroundings, one hundred thousand people had their throats cut. It was at this point that, faced with a rebellion by one of his circle, Ghazan entrusted authority over Syria to Emir Qutlushah and repaired to Persia. This only proved a signal for a fresh outbreak of pillage that extended to the whole of the city, whence a sum about equal to the first contribution was exacted, and many buildings (among which the 'Adiliyya madrasa, the *bimaristan*, and Nur al-Din's Dar al-Hadith) suffered fire damage. Yet, in April 1300, losing hope of ever taking the citadel and informed that a powerful Mameluk contingent had left Cairo, the Mongols evacuated Damascus. Arjawash at once restored prayers in the sultan's name, halted "the criminal practices introduced by the enemy, had the taverns closed, the wine poured away, and the vessels containing it smashed."[37]

As in 1260, retribution was at hand: "Informers and perverts," Maqrizi observes, "who, during Ghazan's dominion, had been appointed to raise levies, were systematically rooted out." There follows a Dantesque inventory of the exactions inflicted on them: "Some had nails driven through them, others were strangled, several had their feet and hands severed, others, with their tongues ripped out and blinded, expired the very same day."[38] Damascus now experienced one of the darkest days in its history. In the beginning of October 1300, as the rumor of a new Mongolian offensive arrived, the authorities demanded fresh funds. "The inhabitants cut down fruit trees and sold the wood. . . . The Ghuta was emptied of its population and a substantial proportion of the inhabitants fled to Egypt . . . filled with fugitives escaping from Syria."[39] But with driving rain and heavy snowfalls having killed off many of his army's camels and horses, Ghazan ordered a retreat. Respite was brief, and in March 1303 the Mongolian chieftain was again at the Euphrates whence he dispatched to Syria eighty thousand men under the command of Qutlushah. Trembling with terror, the population of Damascus "spent the night in the Great Mosque, beseeching Allah's help with great cries."[40] Battle joined near the city in Shaqhab, where the Mameluk troops had taken up position accompanied by reciters of the Koran "who extolled the Muslims to fight and promised them paradise."[41] In spite of their squadrons, who "approached like the darkness of the night,"[42] on April 22, 1303, the Mongols were annihilated.

The denizens of Damascus strode out to al-Nasir who advanced at the head of an immense procession "of horsemen, common people, distinguished men, women, children. . . . Tears flowed in abundance . . . and the day presented a spectacle the like of which had never been seen."[43] The city was magnificently arrayed and the sultan lodged at the Qasr al-Ablaq. A few weeks later, in the midst of a jubilant crowd, he made his entry into Cairo, "preceded by Tatar prisoners in chains with the heads of companions who had died in combat hanging round their necks . . . and with a thousand heads stuck on a like number of spears."[44] After Ghazan's death on May 19, 1304, and with peace agreed between his brother Oldjaytu and al-Nasir, the Mongol menace was momentarily checked. After a brief interval for the fleeting rule of the emir Baybars II between March 1309 and March

North gate of the Umayyad Mosque (Bab al-'Amara, formerly Bab al-Natifiyyin): repoussé bronze cladding of one of the door leaves dating from restoration undertaken in 1406. (On the cup, emblem of the Mameluk sultans, see p. 182.)

1310, the reign of al-Nasir—the longest and indeed one of most tranquil in all Mameluk history—lasted until his death in June 1341. He was followed on the throne by a succession of eight sons, the majority under the tutelage of emirs who were, logically enough, rivals in power.

The century of Tankiz

If Damascus had twice escaped from attacks from the Franks, it was harshly affected by the Mongolian occupations of 1260 and 1300. It needed the peace and security afforded by the reign of al-Nasir and the enlightened authority of his governor, Tankiz, for it to regain the prosperity it had enjoyed during the first half of the fourteenth century. Purchased young at the Cairo slave market by the emir Lajin, Tankiz entered the service of al-Nasir following the death of his master. Named emir, he took part in the battle of Shaqhab against the Mongols and was elevated shortly afterwards to the post of governor of Damascus, into which he made ceremonial entrance on April 24, 1312. "During his reign, the population was safe from the tyranny of the emirs and the powerful, so much so that, fearing his wrath, none so much as dared commit an injustice, not only against Muslims, but even against the dhimmi."[45] Such were his popularity and prestige that after his death his tomb became a place of pilgrimage. The Damascene chronicler Ibn Tulun, generally less than laudatory with regard to such personages, drowns Tankiz in a deluge of eulogizing epithets: "great," "just," "knowledgeable," "excellent," "religious," "intelligent," "endowed with great authority;" while another describes him as being "born under happy auspices and endowed with virile qualities."[46] The famous Maghrebian traveler, Ibn Battuta, who sojourned in Damascus in 1326 during Tankiz's reign, portrays him as "a governor of the good and upright kind."[47] He was at once son-in-law, father-in-law, and chief political adviser to al-Nasir, "who would do nothing in Cairo without asking his advice from Damascus."[48]

While Tankiz appears to have been more humane than some of his counterparts, his love of lucre cannot be gainsaid. As his power strengthened, his "fiefs," herds, and income also increased. Like all parvenus, he had a penchant for showy luxury: "On his horse," writes Ibn Sasra, "everything was made of gold, even his hunting drum."[49] After the death of al-Nasir in 1341, probably grown too rich for his own good, Tankiz was arrested and marched off to Alexandria, where he was fatally poisoned. In his residence were found eight hundred camel loads of gold, money, and cloth, and horses, mules, and slaves in quantity. In addition to the famous "House of Gold" (Dar al-Dhahab), estimated at six hundred thousand dirhem, and the Emerald House, his estate included many dwellings complete with out-buildings, bathhouses, khans, qaysariyyas, gardens, orchards, fields, vineyards, entire villages as well as quarters, halves, and other fractions thereof—scattered throughout Syria.

His reign in Damascus had nonetheless been a period of unequaled magnificence and prosperity. Concentrating primarily on economic infra-structure, he had the water-supply channels dug out and restored, undertook significant road improve-ments, in particular in the northern and western suburbs, built bridges, and tried to confine the growth of the city to northwest of the ramparts. In November 1333, he restored Bab Tuma, his endeavors being commemorated on an inscription carved into the lintel over the bay. Naturally, the greatest care was lavished on the Umayyad mosque: the qibla wall was rebuilt, the mihrabs assigned to various rites fixed in place, and the marble facing in the prayer-hall repaired. This architectural mania did not stop at the gates of his province, however: he had a ribat built in Jerusalem, completed significant

works in Mecca, erected a *bimaristan*, a khan, and several other buildings in Safad, as well as a house, a *hammam*, and various shops in Cairo. During his reign in Damascus, where competitive generosity among the great emirs, the ulemas, and the wealthier traders was rife, nearly forty establishments were either erected or restored. He bought the Dar al-Fulus ("the House of Copper Coins") on the site of the current 'Azm palace, transforming it into a sumptuous residence to which he gave the evocative name of Dar al-Dhahab—or "House of Gold." Nearby, in the area around the basket-makers' suq, he had a madrasa built of which only the gate with alveolar vaulting subsists. He also erected a *turba* for his wife, Sotayta, and a mosque to the west of the citadel with two *muqarnas* gateways and a minaret

characteristic of the Mameluk style: square base, octagonal shaft, niches with a polygonal front arch, engaged colonnettes, twisted or fluted, epigraphic bands, honeycombed balconies, a gallery on a corbel with *muqarnas*, latticework balustrade, twinned bays, and turquoise faience disks that mark the first appearance of such pottery in Damascus. The *turba* in which he was interred in 1344 adjoins the east gate. Certain details aside, with respect to the proportions in particular, its square hall, two drums, and cupola remain in line with Ayyubid archetypes. The interior decor, on the other hand, is much more colorful, with fine, geometrical interlace marble marquetry on the cenotaph and molten glass mosaic over a gold ground on the vault of the mihrab. All the commercial buildings erected during his reign have

Mausoleum of Arak: decor of the upper reaches of the gateway.

disappeared, though the name and location of some are known from the written tradition, epigraphs, and even the inventory of the goods confiscated following his dismissal, such as the al-'Arasa ("of the arena") khan, located outside Bab al-Jabiya, and the al-Jawar khan located to the north of Straight Street and dedicated to the slave trade.

The image of the city bequeathed by historians and travelers of first half of the fourteenth century testifies to unheard-of wealth and prosperity. Immediately after the fall of Acre, the four greatest places of trade of the time—Venice, Genoa, Pisa, and Barcelona—had transferred their colonies from Syria to Cyprus, though trade continued unabated, in spite of papal injunctions prohibiting commerce with the Infidel. Moreover, the Venetians were selling quantities of weaponry made in their arsenal, the most powerful in all Europe. In 1302, scarcely eleven years after the destruction of the Latin States, the Venetian ambassador Guido de Canali requested the renewal of historic privileges from the Mameluk sultan. After withdrawing to Lesser Armenia for a brief period, flocks of Western magnates were once again landing in the Syrian ports of Beirut, Tripoli, and Latakia linked to the two great cities of Damascus and Aleppo, where trade with the Levant was concentrated. In 1332, the pilgrim William of Boldensele of the Order of the Predicant Friars described Damascus as what nowadays would be called a hub of world trade: "The most delightful, well-watered, and populous city of Damascus is very beautiful and prosperous, abundant in wares and in all manner of foodstuffs: spices, precious stones, silks, and all species of valuable things are brought to it and thence carried off by merchants to other parts of the world."[50] According to James of Verona, who, at the time of a short stay in summer 1335, tells of the existence of a khan set aside specifically for Christian traders, "in the matter of wealth, the city of Damascus is supreme by its wares and goods. From Assyria,

Façade of the mausoleum of Arak.

India, and many other lands there arrive an infinity of camels bearing pepper, ginger, cinnamon, and other spices in huge quantities."[51] As for the pilgrim Ludolph von Sudheim, who visited the city in 1340, Damascus was "so pleasant and so rich, so noble and so beautiful that it would be hard to find another city on earth superior to it . . . it teems with all the delicacies of the world and is blessed with every delight human ingenuity can devise . . . populous and inhabited by various nations, Christians, Saracens, and other schismatics . . . one finds there goldwork, silverware, precious stones, vases, furs, garments embroidered with gold, silks, woolens, and every kind of valuable fabric in vast amounts."[52] Our pilgrim also observed that, in the last year of Tankiz's government, "such great peace reigns that there is never any sedition and, although various nations live cheek by jowl, internecine quarrels are infrequent"[53]—a situation rare enough in the city's history to be worthy of note.

There survives a description of singular accuracy penned by al-'Umari, who occupied the post of "Secretary of State" to Damascus following the death of Tankiz. It first deals with the territory Tankiz ruled: it was remarkable in extent, going from al-'Arish in the south to Salamiyya in the north, from the coast in the west up to al-Rahba in the east—a substantial source of tax revenue, in other words. Other observations might also apply to the city today:

Its monuments are for the most part in stone, its houses smaller than those in Cairo, but more richly decorated; however, marble is used less, though its varieties are more beautiful . . . Aleppo is probably more superbly constructed, because recourse to stone is more frequent there, but Damascus possesses more charm and splendor, as water is supplied to the whole city and is common everywhere. The houses are furnished in poplar wood, *hawar*, instead of palm, but it is not painted white, the beauty of its natural appearance being sufficient. . . . The most

densely populated districts are those to the west and north, while the most opulent residences, those with gilt ceilings and marble floors, lie close to the Great Mosque. The suqs are admirably laid out and the *qaysariyya*s solidly built. Craftsmen, building workers, arms manufacturers, jewelers, embroiderers, etc., are skilled in every trade and produce all manner of excellent products and are proud of their superiority over all others in the rest of the kingdom.[54]

Al-'Umari goes on to list among the most sought-after produce, bows, objects in damascened copper, gilded glassware, and lambskin tanned with *qarath*, whose quality, he states, was proverbial.[55]

In spite of its beautiful buildings, profitable businesses, and luxury crafts, Damascus seemed still more remarkable for its amenities and gardens, and for the lifestyle enjoyed there: the profusion of water and greenery in such a harsh, near-desert climate was literally astonishing and any narrator worth his salt felt compelled to employ the most high-flown language. "Outside the city of

Turba of Emir Sayf al-Din Ji'an/*Wali* al-Shaybani. The interior is adorned with a carved plaster vine-leaf design.

Damascus," enthuses James of Verona, "there are many gardens or orchards irrigated by rivers or running waters of great limpidity that delight the eye. These gardens or orchards are estimated at more than thirty thousand, and one can find there oranges, lemons, apples of paradise, very fine pomegranates, vines, figs, vegetables, and much other produce for the delectation of the human body."[56] Similarly al-'Umari, otherwise more inclined to the administrative style, waxes lyrical for the occasion:

> Damascus and Salihiyya possess splendid gardens where a skein of little brooks envelops a broad swathe of trees and where branches bow to the twittering birds. The pleasure gardens contain constructions of considerable size, lofty summerhouses, deep pools, immense orchards in which stand pavilions and reception halls symmetrically arranged. Around them extend the plantations, interwoven rows of bushy cypress and the slim outlines of poplar trees, with wafting scents of fragrant plants, and ripening fruit and mouthwatering berries—a thousand exquisite things so famous that it is pointless to describe them.[57]

All this bounty is, of course, due to the Barada and its seven offshoots, in particular the Nahr Tawra, the "true Nile of Damascus on the banks of which stand the main buildings, as well as the majority of the pleasure pavilions, and where the people promenade."[58] Besides, thanks to some sophisticated hydraulics, water was not only beneficial to the gardens, but also to the city as a whole:

> In the same way, the Qanawat flows through the city . . . its waters traverse underground conduits up to the dwellings and other places from which it has been ordained to distribute it. The water surpluses and reserves, and the waste products are discharged into arched subterranean drains that meet to form in their turn a river that,

especially outside the city, waters the gardens.[59]

Yet the acme was the wonder of the upper valley of the Barada River. Here, al-'Umari's prose turns to poetry:

> It offers one of the most admirable spectacles one can hope to see, here water from the sky and on earth is plentiful, the sun and air are heavy with dew; the two mountains bordering it are carpeted in violets shaded by the intertwined boughs of willow; between them, plump cheeks of roses shed their fragrance, the jasmine half opens into a smile, lilies dart out their tongues, the murmuring water answers the cooing doves, the wind gathers like a winged steed, the northern gales scud over beds of artemisia, and the noonday breeze wafts over scented fields.[60]

Under the early Mameluks, urban expansion beyond the ramparts had much accelerated. "There are sizable suburbs all around the city," noted al-'Umari, "the most considerable being those west and north. At the foot of the citadel, that to the west leads to a vast square on the river bank, the Suq al-Khayl, which serves as a parade ground for the cavalry."[61] As for the northern one, "called al-'Uqayba, it is an independent city in itself, with vast estates of housing and major buildings, inhabited by many emirs and military men."[62] To Ibn Battuta's way of thinking, the most impressive thing in Tankiz's Damascus was the Great Mosque: the edifice itself, of course (in his eyes, nothing less than "the most sublime mosque in the world"[63]), but still more its bustling activity and manifest religious fervor. He counts seventy muezzins and thirteen imams; the prayers and readings from the Koran continue unceasing from daybreak until two-thirds of the way through the night; the audiences for lessons in every religious science are huge and the voices intoning the holy text splendid; teachers leaning against the columns elucidate the word of God for children; a throng of *mujawirun* are busy praying, reading the scriptures, and praising God unstintingly.[64]

Timur's occupation

After the death of Tankiz, Damascus entered a period of relative decline from which its northern "rival," Aleppo, was the chief beneficiary. The city suffered first and foremost from its distance from the field of military operations: after the last campaign in 1322, the quelling of the Frankish danger and the persistence of the Mongolian threat on the Euphrates resulted in military command being switched from the capital to northern Syria. Thus, between 1334 and 1348, no less than eight expeditions against Armenia were launched from Aleppo, all made (with one exception) in the absence of participation of armies from Damascus and Egypt. In addition, in the ten years following the death of al-Nasir, disorder was endemic throughout the country. In their turn, the emirs of Aleppo voiced claims to the sultanate, while the debilitated central authority fanned the flames of Bedouin indiscipline. After 1330, and then with only rare intervals until the beginning of the twentieth century, disruption by local tribesmen was a thorn in Syria's flesh. Attacks on caravans hit trade, while raids on villages damaged harvests, sometimes resulting in the abandonment of arable land and the ruin of the irrigation system.[65]

In addition to embezzlement perpetrated by Damascus's own governors, the court of Cairo itself was not above making requisitions from the city: in 1373, as well as materials for building work he was engaged in at Cairo, the sultan demanded embroidery and brocade for his harem, gold and silver chains, embroidered covers for she-camels, and silver-incrusted camel saddles. Damascene tradesmen were compelled to pay for the gold and silver necessary and were summoned to execute without delay seven hundred pieces of brocade, two thousand gold pins with pearl heads, three thousand silver pins with gold heads, hundreds of covers, a number of short-haired pack-saddles, three hundred palanquins incrusted with gold and silver, dozens of

pairs of gold and silver stirrups, etc. The chronicler Ibn Tulun alleges that there was an unbroken line of caravans to Cairo.[66] The recession obviously had an effect on the public purse: in Damascus, between the death of Tankiz and the end of the century, there were fewer than thirty construction and restoration projects.

In the final decades of the century, bloody rivalry between different Mameluk factions plunged the empire into chaos. On November 26, 1382, the emir Barquq, a one-time slave bought in the Crimea, dethroned the last descendant of Qalawun and had himself proclaimed sultan. Anarchy was still at large, however, and was to precipitate the return of the Mongols. During the violent conflict that opposed Barquq and the rebellious emir of Aleppo, Damascus was again besieged in 1391, and the entire district located northwest of the ramparts devastated by firing from the citadel: "The artillery roared night and day," wrote Ibn Sasra, "while mangonels hurled enormous stones; people were killed or drowned, while others cried for help in extinguishing the fire . . . or begged Allah to succor them in their hour of distress."[67] Without the city walls, battle raged on for days and the mosque of Tankiz fell prey to the flames. The whole population was mobilized, "even the Christians and Jews were forced to fight. All with an ounce of strength left were mustered by religion, profession, and district, with bows and arrows, weapons and provisions, each according to his ability, while a great crowd gathered outside the city."[68] In the end, Barquq carried the day and set to punishing the rebels: a score of emirs were crucified beneath the walls of the citadel, paraded on camel-back through the city, and then "cut in two one after the other."[69]

Peace and security appeared to have been restored when, at the end of 1393 there arrived news of the capture of Baghdad by the armies of Timur. In December 1400, having already occupied Aleppo, Hama, Homs, and Baalbek, Timur's forces sheltering behind a veritable wall of elephants, besieged a Damascus that the Mameluks had already placed on a defensive footing. Barquq's son and successor, Sultan Faraj, however, more concerned to quell a rebellion brewing in Cairo, had scurried off to Egypt. Many emirs and a proportion of the troops promptly defected, leaving Damascus at the mercy of Timur's onslaught. A delegation of dignitaries lead by the notable historian Ibn Khaldun, who at that time occupied the post of great Malikite qadi in the Egyptian army, negotiated the conditions of surrender in the tent of the Mongol chieftain. A written proclamation, guaranteeing the safety of the inhabitants, was read aloud in the Umayyad mosque: then Bab al-Saghir was thrown open to the besiegers. The following Friday, the *khutba* was pronounced in Timur's name. Yet unfortunately the classic turn of events unfolded, and the governor of the citadel refused to capitulate. In response, Timur imposed a heavy tribute on the city. "The distress resulting from these measures was indescribable," observed Ibn Iyas, "especially as prices had risen during the siege, a bushel of corn fetching forty Syrian dirhems."[70] The stronghold was then besieged: onagers, balistas, naphtha launchers, and catapults were drawn up all around, more particularly in the courtyard of the Umayyad mosque. The moat was drained, high towers were heaved up against the ramparts, and, while those inside rained down stones, Greek fire, arrows, and pots of naphtha, engineers and sappers set to undermining the fortified curtain. A breach having opened, the governor yielded up the keys of the citadel, treasury, and stores. The Mongols seized a great quantity of riches, jewels, and choice fabrics, "rarities that had been conserved for several centuries,"[71] as well as a "famous" granary filled with corn equivalent to the joint income of the Holy Cities of Mecca and Medina.[72]

If the citadel was not razed to the ground as Ibn Khaldun claims (the ramparts stand as proof to the contrary), the interior structure was seriously mauled. Then, in order to quicken payment of the tribute, the violence redoubled:

Each householder was made to stand in his rags before the door to his house, and bidden to pay the sum allotted to him; when he replied that he had nothing left, he would be violently beaten, his house entered, all the furniture and copper utensils would be taken away, and his wives and daughters would be violated before his eyes. . . . Ingenious forms of torture were devised: hempen cord would be tied round a man's head and tightened till it sank in. . . . Men were suspended by their great toes [*sic*] and fires lighted under them till they either died of the agony or fell into the blaze. Timur's soldiers did things as it whitens the hair to hear of.[73]

And this was only the prelude: on March 4, 1400, a ferocious horde of infantrymen tore through the city, waving scimitars and "committing every sort of carnage, violence, and pillage imaginable."[74] They enslaved the men and women and seized all their property and finery, which consisted in an unimaginable quantity of gold, precious stones, luxury fabrics, valuables, and all kinds of rarities. Such was the quantity of treasure amassed that the horses, mules, and camels requisitioned from Sebaste (Sivas) to Damascus were not enough to carry them. Many soldiers had to abandon the cloths of silver and gold and the precious belts from Egypt, Cyprus, and Russia they had plundered at the beginning of the campaign to make room for the loads of precious stones, money, and silver and gold vases they had purloined during the more recent spate of pillaging. Worse was to come, when, on March 17, a great fire broke out in the city. In spite of Ibn Khaldun's denials, it seems that the order was indeed given by the Mongol chief himself. According to the Bavarian traveler Schiltberger, at that time held captive by the Mongols, Timur had wood deliberately piled up around the Great Mosque in which more than thirty thousand people had sought refuge and had it set alight.[75] "All Damascus was burned, and a huge amount of property within ransacked, as was the rest of Syria," wrote Sharaf al-Din.[76]

In point of fact, the conflagration did not reach farther than the Qilijiyya madrasa to the south; nonetheless it was a long time before Damascus recovered from the conqueror's presence. At the end of March 1401, after setting the Qasr al-Ablaq ablaze, Timur, intent on countering the Ottoman menace, set off back to Baghdad, leaving behind him a drained, emaciated city. The damage report drawn up by Ibn Iyas is frightening:

> Thus, Damascus, that had been so prosperous, so happy, so luxurious, so magnificent, was turned into a heap of ruins, of desolate remains, destitute of its beauty and all its art. Not a living being was moving except carcasses partly burnt, and figures disfigured with dust, covered with a cloak of flies, and become the prey and spoil of dogs. Even a sagacious man could not find the way to his house, nor distinguish between a stranger's dwelling and his own.[77]

In spite of restoration work undertaken as early as summer 1403 by the new governor (covering the Dar al-Sa'ada, the Umayyad mosque, the *bimaristan* of Nur al-Din and several madrasas), Ghillebert de Lannoy was to note at the time of his stay in 1422 that Damascus, "razed at the time of Timur, was now beginning to restore and rebuild in earnest."[78] Ten years later, traces of the catastrophe were still visible, as testified by Bertrandon de La Broquière: "Damascus had been burned and destroyed it is said by Tamburline [Timur] about the year 1400; for, one still sees signs of it as appear in a district of the city not yet rebuilt near a gate called the Gate of St. Paul [Bab Kaysan]."[79]

If trade was not long in recovering its former vigor, the same could not be said of the crafts, since all the artisans had been frog-marched off to Samarkand. In 1449, the pilgrim Stephan von Grumppenberg, desirous of acquiring some famous Damascene silk, was advised that they now "came from Venice because all the master craftsmen had been removed by Timur."[80] Indeed, the manufacture of luxury goods never regained its luster, particularly as it had been severely hit by a fall in income from the emirs linked to the decline in agriculture. If, in 1432, Bertrandon de La Broquière could still sing the praises of Damascus swords, "the finest and best in all Surye [Syria],"[81] the damascened copper, gilt glass, and once celebrated fabrics—silk, brocade, velvet, and satin—were now less expertly made. Certain trades seemed to have simply vanished into thin air: to restore the roof of the Umayyad mosque destroyed in a fire in 1401, roofers specialized in laying lead had to be fetched in from Anatolia. From the fifteenth century, no traveler would maintain, as the Florentine Gucci had fifteen years before the advent of Timur: "[In Damascus], more work of whatever kind, little or great value, is done than in any other part of the world, as silk cloth, cotton cloth, linen cloth, and gold and silver work, copper and brass work of every kind, and every kind of glass. In that place they excel both there and here and very great masters they are in every art."[82]

Damascus's supremacy in craft industry, which had contributed so much to the enduring fame of the city, was well and truly over. Moreover, the increasing—indeed ongoing—competition from European products began to make its impact. Italian-made brocade, damask, and gilded glass were exported to the East, and an author like Maqrizi (died 1442) was soon regretting the disastrous effects of Italian cloth imports and complaining about the preference granted to European wares, more competitively priced and of superior quality. As can be seen, trade with Europe was once again intense. In spite of violent outbursts by sultans and emirs, the insolence of low-grade civil servants, the insults, misappropriations, exactions, affronts, blackmail, and even blows they endured, European traders, beguiled by the profits

France.[83] In Damascus, European traders possessed their own khan, which bore the name of its founder, Sultan Barquq, and in which they were able to safely store their stock.

The economic reversal this foreshadowed was in fact merely one aspect of a more general shift in favor of the Occident that had already been underway for some time. Ibn Khaldun (died 1406) was all too aware of this deterioration and deplored it in texts that, if in general relatively positive with respect to the Mameluk regime, are haunted by the theme of decadence. Noting a decline in science, medicine, grammar, and education in the Muslim world, he observes "an abundance of the arts in non-Arab countries such as China, India, the Turkish territories, and the Christian nations, which are their wellsprings now."[84] It is more especially the intellectual ascendant of the West that he presents as a novelty: "I have recently learned," he writes, "that the philosophical sciences are much approved of in the land of Rome and on the northern shores close to the country of the Franks. I have been assured that they are being studied once more and taught in many classes. There are supposed to be a large number of treatises on these sciences, many people who know them well, and numerous students learning about them."[85] The time when an author like Mas'udi (died 956), confident of the intellectual and cultural superiority of the Islamic world, could expatiate ironically on the decline of Greek science in the West—which moreover he perceptively placed at the door of Christianity—was a distant memory.[86]

By 1468, when, against a backdrop of economic, political, and social decline, Sultan Qa'itbay began a reign that was to last until 1496, the major threat was no longer the Mongols, but a power now dominant in Anatolia: the Ottoman Turks. Initially prosecuted through intermediary "vassals," direct conflict between the two protagonists was not long in coming, culminating in the annihilation of the Mameluks by the second decade of the seventeenth century.

to be made, were again numerous in the cities of the Levant. In 1395, the Seigneur d'Anglure already noted the presence in Cairo of *funduqs* for merchants from France, Venice, Genoa, Catalonia, Cyprus, Naples, Ancona, Marseilles, Crete, and Narbonne. In 1432, Bertrandon de La Broquière met in Damascus Venetians, Genoese, Florentines, Catalans, and French, among whom a certain Jacques Coeur, then a mere merchant from Bourges, who, like so many others, had come to seek his fortune in the East and who was to acquire fame as *grand argentier* or "Chancellor of the Exchequer" to Charles VII, king of

Following pages. Audience granted to a group of Frankish traders by the governor of Damascus at the end of the Mameluk period. The scene takes place in an edifice close to where the 'Azm palace has stood since the eighteenth century. The *hammam* of Nur al-Din and the Umayyad Mosque with the Mameluk minaret, the Dome of the Eagle, and the Minaret of Jesus are all clearly visible. School of Gentile Bellini, late fifteenth century. Musée du Louvre, Paris. (This picture is almost always wrongly given as a view of Cairo.)

Stagnation and demise of the Mameluk state

In 1486, the Ottoman armies invaded Cilicia, occupying Tarsus and Adana, but they were beaten back in 1490 at Kaysariyya. A peace was signed, but this did little to decrease the tax levies necessary for equipping the troops and settling their back pay. In Damascus, five months' rent on all buildings was imposed, including the waqfs the *bimaristan*, mosques, madrasas, and mausoleums, while the principal worthies and wealthier traders were, once again, "invited" to make stiff contributions. The rapacity of the provincial governors, who sought compensation from those under their sway for the annual sums they disbursed to Cairo, ruined agriculture and reduced income from farm rents. On Qa'itbay's death, the Ottoman danger was temporarily stalled, but recent military campaigns—the cost of which had exceeded seven million dinars—had drained the collective coffers.

On April 20, 1501, the emir Qansuh, a former slave freed by Qa'itbay, was, rather against his better judgment, raised to the sultanate. The situation was dire: in Iran, Shah Isma'il was building the foundations of the Safavid dynasty, and international trade—in particular in spices—with the Far East had been in recession since Vasco da Gama's discovery of a sea route to the Indies in 1498. The fall of Grenada and the policy of enforced conversion to Christianity that followed had exacerbated religious feeling in Muslim lands to the extent that the sovereigns of Morocco and Tunis called for the expulsion from the Levant of all merchants from Christendom and the closing of the Holy Places to pilgrims. Domestically, the undisciplined Mameluks (who had by now, as Ibn Iyas observes, lost all respect for the sultan) auctioned off their obedience to the highest bidder, while the tribal Arabs, taking full advantage of an enfeebled central authority, ran riot, holding villages to ransom and plundering caravans—even

that accompanying the pilgrimage, which was canceled or ransacked almost yearly.

In Syria, the Ghuta and the Hawran were devastated, while the number of settlements on the plain of the Beka'a plunged from three hundred to forty. In Damascus, unpopular measures introduced by the governor Qansuh al-Burj and exactions committed by the troops plunged the city into turmoil. According to Ibn Iyas, the damage caused by what were now pitched battles between the Mameluks and the people's militias was such that there was fear of the whole city being engulfed.[87]

The Damascus chronicler Ibn Tulun, writing of the governorship of the emir Siba'i that began in April 1506, speaks of little but the economic crisis, the high cost of living, the shortage of bread, and the dire predicament of the common folk: "The situation grew worse and worse: the local people were burdened with taxes, the *muhtasib* imposed levies on shops and on craftsmen, stores were subjected to regular extortion by the *zu'ar* [people's militias], and tradesmen could sell not a thing in their suqs without these ruffians taking their cut."[88] Moreover, Mameluks of Circassian origin—new recruits of unconscionable greed—showed up in the city: "They carried off provisions, clothes, and anything they needed; they stopped passersby in the street and robbed them of their turbans or veils; they stole merchandise and sold on the products of their larceny . . . many shops and suqs had to close."[89]

In terms of foreign policy, the situation was also becoming more critical with each passing day. Conscious, like Venice, of the danger posed by a European presence in the Indian Ocean, the Mameluks undertook several maritime expeditions, but, following victories in 1508, they were utterly defeated in February of the following year. "The audacity of the Europeans," then noted Ibn Iyas, "knew no bounds, for now, after the defeat of the Egyptian expeditionary force, they dreamed of establishing themselves in India."[90] Indeed, in 1510, the Portuguese, already masters of the Persian Gulf and the Red Sea, seized Goa, thus laying the foundations for their overseas empire.

On land, the Ottomans marched on relentless: in 1514, Selim I occupied Tabriz, Qashan, and most of Safavid Iran. There was general consternation in Cairo: "On learning the news, the sultan did not sound the drum, while his officers kept a weather eye on the Ottoman power,"[91] observed Ibn Iyas. It was thus in a calamitous atmosphere on every front that, in autumn 1515, the curtain rose on the last act of the Mameluk tragedy: an Ottoman flotilla around four hundred strong made for Damietta and Alexandria, while an immense army stood on the point of crossing Syria's northern border; in Cairo, mobilization was to exhaust the few surviving resources of the empire. Officers were bought off to the tune of thousands of dinar: five thousand alone for the chief of staff, Sudun Ajami, and one hundred—four months pay and the price of a camel—for each Mameluk. The emir Tumanbay being installed as leader of the government in the absence of the sultan, at the end of May 1516, the Mameluk force left Cairo. On June 18, "in the midst of a procession such as had never been seen before,"[92] and accompanied by the emir Siba'i, governor of Damascus, who bore the parasol and the crescent, Sultan Qansuh al-Ghuri made his entrance into the ancient Umayyad capital. The city was festooned for the occasion and drum rolls resounded from the citadel; at a sumptuous feast, Siba'i received a robe of honor, the sultan fourteen trays laden with silver dirhem and precious fabrics, ten horses and the same number of Mameluks "chosen among the most attractive and who belonged to people of the Book."[93]

On July 10, the army arrived at Aleppo where Qansuh al-Ghuri put his treasure in the citadel for safekeeping. The officers swore the oath on a copy of the Koran and, in the presence of the caliph, the four qadis, and the sheikhs of the principal brotherhoods, the army, marshaled in its entirety at the Great Hippodrome, listened all night to a complete reading of the sacred text by torchlight. The encounter with the Ottoman forces took place on August 25, at Marj Dabiq, a few miles north of Aleppo. Just as victory seemed to be within the Mameluks' grasp, the emir Khayrbak defected and confusion gripped the Syro-Egyptian ranks; Sudun Ajami, Siba'i, and the sultan himself all perished on the field of battle. Marj Dabiq proved the Mameluks' Agincourt: many officers were slain, while the rump of the army—a horde of wretched soldiers without uniforms, the majority mounted on asses, some stark naked, others draped in a Bedouin tunic or a simple blanket—fell back on Damascus in disorder. Back in Cairo, power was invested in Tumanbay, while in Damascus the emir Janbirdi—recently appointed governor—convinced that Ottoman firepower rendered all resistance futile, made his escape, trailing the city's worthies after him.

On October 3, the governor of the citadel having laid down his arms, Selim I, flanked by a great crowd of soldiers, made a brief appearance in the city, and had his beard shaved at the al-Hamawi bathhouse. The very next day, he attended Friday prayers in the Umayyad mosque, where he was extolled as the "victorious Servant of the two holy cities, Mecca and Medina" by the great qadi Ibn Farfur. On December 15, after dispatching to Cairo an emissary empowered to invite Tumanbay to submit, Selim left Damascus by Bab al-Jabiya and made his way to Egypt, where the sultan endeavored to prepare a defense. Popular militias were mustered and artillery pieces were thrown together capable of holding their own against the Ottomans: guns fixed on wooden carriages drawn by oxen and buffalo. But, on April 2, 1517, on the left bank of the Guiza, "deafened by the cannonade,"[94] the last square of soldiers Tumanbay had formed was routed. Captured by a Bedouin chief, the last Mameluk sultan was delivered up to Selim, who had him promptly strangled and strung up at Bab Zuwayla "until his corpse gave off a fetid odor."[95] Thus, amidst the most dreadful carnage, the regime of the Mameluks, who had held sway over the fates of Syria and Egypt for 257 years, came to a brutal end.

For the society of the time, governed everywhere by Shari'a law, however, it amounted to hardly more than a spot of local difficulty: Turks succeeded other Turks, clean-shaven Janissaries replaced bearded Mameluks, and the capital was transferred from Cairo to Istanbul. In mid-September 1517, having first purloined al-Mutawakkil's sources of revenue (according to some authorities, the caliph is supposed to have ceded him the title), Selim I once again made his way to Syria, carrying off, like Timur before him, an immense train of booty: rare articles of all kinds, copper work, weapons, horses, mules, camels, marble ripped from monuments, a thousand camels laden with gold and silver, hundreds of craftsmen of every trade, thousands of dignitaries—emirs, qadis, ulemas, senior officials, magnates, eunuchs, etc. "Egypt had not witnessed such a pitiable catastrophe since the time of Nebuchadnezzar the Babylonian, who set fire to the country and so ruined it that it took it forty years to recover," lamented Ibn Iyas.[96] In October 1517, Selim arrived back in Damascus, where he stayed for more than four months before regaining Istanbul in February 1518. Above the great central gate of the Umayyad mosque, the red standard of the Ottoman replaced the yellow silk banner of the Mameluk: until the end of World War I, the venerable city of the Umayyads was to be little more than a provincial capital of the Ottoman Empire.

A city of wealth and prosperity

Mameluk Syria was divided administratively into six *niyaba* or "governorships," each headed by a *na'ib* with capitals at Damascus, Aleppo, Tripoli, Hama, Safad, and al-Karak. At the top of the hierarchy—and the largest—stood Damascus, whose jurisdiction extended from Homs to al-Karak and from Tyre to Palmyra. Acting as a kind of ersatz sultan, the city's

na'ib was a figure of importance, the opulence of whose court might vie with that of Cairo. "The *admiral* [emir] of Damascus is rich and extremely powerful, and first among *admirals*," wrote Jean Thénaud in 1512.[97] He was deluged in titles and honors granted to none other, and official correspondence—in which he was referred to by the title "responsible for exercising the noble power in Damascus the well-guarded"—was written to him on red paper, a color ostensibly reserved for the sultan. Representing a weighty responsibility in view of the size of the waqfs attached to them, both the *bimaristan* of Nur al-Din and the Umayyad mosque came under his direct control. Lavish ceremonies marked his coming to power, and, while they served to remind everyone (indeed himself included) from the nominee downwards, of their own rank, they were above all devised to make a show for the rabble, whose eyes, as Khalil al-Zahiri—that Machiavelli of Mameluk literature—so rightly observed, "are in constant need of being dazzled with pomp and circumstance."[98]

Nonetheless, so as to limit his ambition—the importance of his office being of itself something of an incitement to rebellion—he wielded no authority over the commander of the citadel, who was appointed directly by Cairo. History shows that even this shrewd precaution was only partially effective: out of the eighty-four governors of Damascus whose biographies have been examined by Gaston Wiet, twenty-nine rebelled, of whom two attained the sultanate, fourteen were executed, five pardoned, five imprisoned, while two succeeded in fleeing abroad. As if to demonstrate its importance in the eyes of the authorities, the nomination of the commander began with a eulogy of the citadel itself. Lauded as "sister to the one in Cairo" (which was nothing less, it should be recalled, than the "sultan's betrothed"), it was always the vastest, the strongest, but more especially the highest—so much so that its towers "scaled the signs of the zodiac."[99] However, it was also where

Facing page, top. Leather military carry-case decorated in leather and fabric appliqué (the latter has disappeared), with a loop on the back so it can be carried around the waist. Fifteenth century. Recently discovered by the Franco-Syrian Mission in a light well in a building southwest of the Citadel.

capital punishments were meted out and one of the empire's most important political prisons, where, at night, to prevent escapes, the sentinels were kept awake by drumbeats rattled out every four minutes. Water was provided not only by the Banias *nahr*, but also by wells to ensure security of supply. In addition to the Mint, it incorporated a significant arms depot, packed with sabers, bows and arrows, spears, coats of mail, sheet-iron body-armor covered in brocade, axes, mangonels, and other materiel, as well as a quartermaster stores and warehouses crammed with biscuits, flour, butter, honey, fodder, and cattle, all stockpiled in case of siege.

The resistance Damascus had offered to the Mongols on several occasions won the city undying glory, and, thanks to its ramparts, its nickname "well-guarded" was fitting: geographers, historians, travelers and observers generally were justified in seeing them as the most significant construction after the Great Mosque. "One of the beauties of Damascus is its citadel, the excellence of its structure, and its sheer extent. Indeed, it is as big as a city," declared Abu al-Baqa'.[100] "Inside the city, the *rex Damasci*, the king of Damascus, dwells in the mightily reinforced citadel of the sultan," observed von Sudheim,[101] while Bertrandon de La Broquière related: "There is also a fine castle large and strong, on level terrain, ringed by splendid large and deep moats which are cleaned."[102]

Damascus performed another task crucial to the court at Cairo: the gathering and transport of snow to keep the sultan's beverages cool. This was such an elevated responsibility that Maqrizi keeps a record in his chronicle of all the years "when no snow fell in Damascus."[103] Collected in the mountains of Lebanon, loaded at Beirut or Sayda and conveyed by sea to Damietta and along the Nile to Bulaq, the port of Cairo, it was carried on mule-back to the palace of the sultan where it was stored in cisterns. As soon as khans had been built along postal routes making them passable to caravan traffic, the snow was transported overland. Every couple of days between

Above, bottom. Cloth fleur-de-lis made to be stitched to a support (equestrian ornament?). Second half of the fifteenth century. Discovered in the same light well as the leather military carry-case.

the beginning of June and the end of November, five camels laden with the precious cargo started out from Damascus, "led by a man skilled in the art of preserving it and escorted by a courier bearing orders for each staging-post."[104] This singular habit aroused the curiosity of European travelers. The Franciscan friar Poggibonsi wrote in 1348: "Damascus is very cold and in the mountains round about the snow lasts till June; and this snow is carried down on camels for sale in Damascus where it is sold in May and June; and also they keep it in the caves and eat it in their beverages."[105] According to the Florentine Sigoli, it was used to refresh not only drinks but also fruits, which are "so well-chilled that their taste is all the more delicious."[106] There was, however, snow and *snow*: al-Jazari tells how, in 1297, there being a shortage of snow in Damascus, it was fetched from old snow stores in the Tripoli mountains that had not been opened for twenty years; nevertheless it was "not as refreshing as the snow usually employed in Damascus," and people opted to cool their beer instead by leaving it outside at night.[107]

As the second biggest city of the empire after Cairo, in spite of the sieges, revolts, riots, Mongol incursions, and natural disasters, the Mameluk era was one of prosperity and expansion for Damascus. From von Sudheim to Jean Thénaud, and from Dimashqi to Khalil al-Zahiri, authors, travelers, geographers, and chroniclers alike are unanimous in its praise, seeing the city, as the epitome of grace and bounty thanks to its gardens and plentiful water. For Dimashqi, it was like "a white bird settling in a vast meadow and drinking of the waters that flow up to it from every side."[108] For Ibn Battuta, it is "the city which surpasses all other cities in beauty and takes precedence of them in loveliness." [109] For Ludovico di Varthema, "it would not be possible to describe the beauty and the excellence of this Damascus."[110] Shortly before the final defeat, as a debilitated regime frittered away its last hours, Jean Thénaud could still write: "The city of Damascus, into which I was

permitted to enter, is the finest in all Souldan [the Sudan, after Cayre [Cairo], so beautiful, so pleasant and fecund that its fertility outstrips all belief and reckoning. There are two rivers formerly named Abana and Farfar that drain a land most productive in wheat and vines on which grapes grow all year round, and meadows, olive, orange, and pomegranate trees and all kinds of trees besides."[111]

In the Mameluk era, the prosperity and swelling population of Damascus, which Europeans, in all probability with some exaggeration, estimated at some one hundred thousand,[112] occasioned significant expansion in the outskirts: "It is said by experienced men that that Damascus with the suburbs has a population three times that of Florence,"[113] wrote an Italian, Gucci. In spite of the assertions of some travelers, the suburbs were not uniformly distributed around the ramparts, as is proved by the position of the congregational mosques, which were only erected when a district became large enough to make one necessary. There were no suburbs beyond Bab al-Sharqi to the east. Even today, no clear line of demarcation exists in the area between the intramural city and the Ghuta. To the edge of the northern flank, however, there lay a belt of developments, each with its own mosque: al-Saqifa, al-Aqsa, al-Jawza, al-Mu'allaq; to the northwest, the mosques of al-Mu'ayyad, Yalbugha, and al-Ward; to the west the mosques of Sandjaqdar and Tankiz; to the southwest, on the road to Egypt, the Tawrizi mosque; to the south, on the route to the Hawran and the Hijaz, in the Midan quarter, the Manjak, al-Karimi, and al-Taynabiyya mosques. On the foothills of Mount Qasiyun, the district of al-Salihiyya—to which James of Verona was surely alluding when he wrote that "more than a thousand of the city's houses were built on the mountainside"[114]—included, by the end of the Mameluk period, several hundred mosques, a hundred or so madrasas, ten khans, twenty or so bathhouses and several suqs, one of which (though he does not supply a name) Ibn Battuta held to be of

Minaret of the al-Aqsab Mosque. (The Ottoman-style conical crownpiece is later in date than the minaret.)

unparalleled beauty.[115] Within the ramparts, the density of occupancy was already such that, compared to the preceding period, Mameluk constructions could be but few in number: the main ones include the Dar al-Hadith of Tankiz, his wife's mausoleum, the madrasas of al-Jawhariyya, al-Jaqmaqiyya, and al-Khaydariyya, the minarets of Hisham and al-Qal'i, and the Sabil al-Khazna—or "fountain of the treasure."

If in Mameluk times the beating heart of the city was still the section located within the walls—encompassing the citadel, Umayyad mosque, the wealthier residences and the majority of the khans and suqs—there was an increasing tendency (accentuated in the Ottoman and contemporary period) for activities to move out. At the foot of the northern front of the citadel, on the left bank of the Barada, at a locality named Tahat al-Qal'a, "under the citadel," was held the Suq al-Khayl, the "horse-market." Essential to an army composed almost exclusively of horsemen, it was the great center of military life where, twice a week on Monday and Friday, prior to the solemn audience, the governor would review the whole body of his troops. Gradually, the guilds attendant on this military clientele—arms manufacturers, tailors, innkeepers, saddlers, straw and barley merchants, etc.—as well as the brothels, purveyors of alcohol and hashish, and diverse dens of iniquity, moved out from the intramural area to set up on the fringes of the Suq al-Khayl, where one can still find edge-tool makers, blacksmiths, copper-beaters, saddlers, harnessers, and manufacturers of skin-bottles today. Moreover, as the mischievous description by Abu al-Baqa' attests, the Suq al-Khayl was soon to become one of Damascus's favorite haunts, a place for promenading and all manner of entertainment:

> One of the beauties of Damascus is the lower parts of the citadel as it serves for the foreigner as a watering hole. It consists in an open-air esplanade that is used as a meeting place. It is

Facing page, top. Upper section of the gateway to the al-Ward Mosque (restored, photograph 2003). *Facing page, bottom.* Al-Taynabiyya madrasa. Detail of the decoration of the façade (before restoration, photograph 1989).

bordered with houses and castles tower over it; it places before one's eyes everything a man could wish, everything lip and tongue might desire. . . . There one finds the "house of the water melons" where all the fruits of the city are sold. . . . Beneath the citadel, there is a market for cloth sold by the cubit; a market for sewn cloth, one for men, the other for women; a market for furs, the market for vendors of bric-a-brac, the market for ironmongers, the market for knives, the market for merchants of goatskin bottles, the leather-workers' market, the market for cloth and harnesses, the markets for horses, mules, beasts, and cattle, and the markets for camels, and ewes. One finds there the market of the ragpickers, the market for camel-litter makers, joiners, and turners. It contains the market for dry-fruit merchants, the "house of oil" dealing in all sorts of goods, the market for sieve-makers and for glasswork traders. As for the concourse, one cannot even see the ground because of the throng of eateries. Among them mingle wrestlers, buffoons, impresarios, storytellers, and night talkers. One finds there everything to bewitch the ear and fill the soul with desire.[116]

From the Suq al-Khayl, these promenades and amusements continued along the Barada and its channels and, beneath shaded avenues of poplar to deep within the Ghuta, a veritable garden of delights where the inhabitants of Damascus—and not solely the least devout—would relax from the strictures of Islamic observance. The remarks of the Florentine Sigoli in this connection are unambiguous: "Outside of Damascus," he writes, "are very beautiful gardens well planted with every kind of fruit you can dream of, and when they are in leaf they are so dense and the sun cannot penetrate, and in this the men and women there take great delight."[117] Khalil al-Zahiri too lists among the "delightful walks" (he was, he confesses, spoiled for choice) that "of the Lover," 'Ashiq, and "of the Beloved," *Ma'shuq.*

Right. Al-Taynabiyya madrasa. Entrance gateway (photograph 1989).

Like any Muslim city, Damascus consisted of a patchwork of districts called *hara* or sometimes *mahalla* or *akhtat*. At the beginning of the sixteenth century, they numbered approximately seventy within the city walls and about thirty in the great suburb of al-Salihiyya. Beyond the commercial areas in which the suqs, khans, and shops congregated, there stretched residential districts, each with its own mosque, bathhouse, and local stores, and occasionally including craftsmen, weavers for the most part. If the Jewish and Christian districts were evidently cemented by religious factors, in Muslim areas they were much more complex in nature, a combination of ethnic or tribal origin, economic level, nature of commercial activity, or denomination—Shi'ism or one of the four legal schools of Sunnite Islam. Thus, the suburb of al-Salihiyya, one of whose districts was almost exclusively populated by families of Kurdish origin, was affiliated to the Hanbalite school, while the remainder of the city was Shafiite. For the majority, the wealthier echelons appear to have occupied the western part of the intramural city and the west and northwest suburbs, but it does not appear that economic standing was, as in the Occident, the determining factor in social segregation.

In certain districts—those of the tanners, dyers, copper workers, grain dealers, etc.—even in the absence of actual corporations, people clearly gathered together according to trade. In any case, the chronicles show that the districts possessed a real sense of community reinforced by the social, administrative, and penal duties imposed on them by the government. One of the city's principal dignitaries, invested with the nebulous title of sheikh or *'arif*, and appointed and dismissed at the governor's behest, was at once community leader, administrator, and local representative to the powers that be. In addition to his primary task of allocating and collecting taxes, in particular exceptional levies, he was, with the assistance of other notables (emirs, ulemas, and magnates), also charged with maintaining public buildings, transport routes, channels, etc. His functions also extended to policing, and he was responsible for preventing crime, capturing criminals and tracking down escaped prisoners, after-dark security, enforcing public health regulations, ensuring that shops observed proper opening hours, and, if ever the need were felt, with clamping down on prostitution or wine and hashish consumption.

In the penal domain, collective responsibility of the district (inherited from tribal solidarity among the Arabs) was the rule—to the distress of the inhabitants who vainly pleaded that punishment be visited on the guilty parties alone. If one is to believe some often far-fetched "local news" items, culprits were seldom identified: one night in 1295, for instance, a group of forty or so, pretending to walk down the streets in a candlelit cortege, suddenly drew sabers and cudgels, smashed into a shop, killed a bystander, assaulted others who had mistaken them for a bridal procession, and made off with the spoils: all, according to al-Jazari, "took to their heels unmolested."[118]

In the Christian quarter, the duties of the sheikh were performed by a patriarch who was in addition charged with applying the various onerous measures meted out on the dhimmi from time to time, generally under pressure from the Islamic population during periods of international tension: these included prohibitions against riding horses or mules, carrying weapons, erecting buildings taller than those of the Muslims, ringing bells, purchasing Muslim slaves, etc., and the imposition of the blue turban. According to von Sudheim, in 1340, there were nearly sixteen thousand Christian houses in Damascus.[119] Jacobites, Melkites, Orthodox, etc., all claimed to be "more authentic Christians than the Franks," who in their turn scorned them as unbelievers and vile schismatics, hardly better than the "pagans," namely the Muslims.

The humble Franciscan Poggibonsi deplored that among all the Christian churches in Damascus, there was none for the Latin rite.[120] In the Jewish community, the sheikh's functions were generally fulfilled by a rabbi. In 1481, Meshullam ben R. Menahem counted four hundred and fifty Jewish heads of family in Damascus, "all wealthy and honorable merchants," led by "a wise, respected, and pious Jew, the physician R. Joseph."[121]

In spite of many trades and crafts moving to the foot of the citadel, the main "business district" remained south of the Umayyad mosque. In addition to evidence left by travelers—telling enough in itself—the extensive program of commercial building also attests to the commercial prosperity of Mameluk Damascus. From the oldest, inaugurated in 1260–61 by the na'ib al-Waziri, to that built in the "lane of the fullers" outside Bab al-Jabiya by the emir Siba'i, the last Mameluk na'ib, sources mention one hundred and forty-nine khans or qaysariyyas, against twenty-four for the Ayyubid era, and only eighty-four under the Ottoman. The part of the emirs, possessors of vast capital funds accruing from land concessions, was preponderant in the execution of these projects. Of the forty-one buildings whose developers can be identified, the sultan financed five, and emirs—who would often transfer the most lucrative crafts and trades there for their own benefit—twenty-eight. Only three poorly-preserved examples survive, however: the al-Jawar khan dedicated to the slave trade, already converted into a dye-works in Ottoman times, which now houses a printer's; the Jaqmaq khan, built by the emir Jaqmaq, na'ib of Damascus between 1419 and 1421, comprising eighteen makhzan ("stores") on the ground floor and twenty-two rooms above, with a splendid entrance gate comprising two wooden doors covered with nailed iron plates; and the much-altered al-Shaghur khan, whose upper floors on the east and west sides are presently occupied by dwellings.

As a major regional center, Damascus imported goods from all over Syria: fruit from the immediate area, as well as cereals from the Hawran, rice from the Hula region, oil from Nablus, and milk and cereals from the Beka'a. In return, it exported craft products and skilled labor (stoneworkers, monumental masons, mosaicists, for example) to all four corners of the kingdom, as well as natural produce, including timber. Ibn al-Shihna informs us that wood was imported from the Damascus region for work on

Mameluk decree carved on a column of the west vestibule of the Umayyad Mosque. Set up in busy areas, these decrees in general covered the abolition of illegal taxation, but proved to be of limited effect.

the citadel of Aleppo.[122] As for international trade, the city received by caravan goods from all the countries of the Orient. In Jedda, Bertrandon de La Broquière witnessed spices being unloaded from boats and put on camels bound for Damascus.[123] From Central Asia, the Caucasus and Africa, there arrived slaves for domestic employment, and more importantly fresh recruits not only for the "elite" corps, but also the Mameluk cavalry. Bertrandon de La Broquière alludes to the special khan set aside for this trade: "In Damascus, I saw them sell a black girl of fifteen or sixteen. She was taken totally naked, except for the belly and the behind and a bit above, and paraded through the streets."[124]

By way of the ports of Sayda, Tripoli, and Beirut, Damascus sent on vast quantities of goods, foremost among them the spices Menahem saw in Beirut brought in from Damascus and loaded for Venice,[125] but also products of its renowned craftsmanship: glass, metal, ceramics, jewelry filigreed in gold, silver and copper, and especially sumptuous textiles—silks, brocade, damask, embroidered and braided garments, etc. It was the Venetians who appropriated the lion's share of this trade, leaving the other "nationalities"—Genoese, Catalans, Florentines, etc.—to make do with the crumbs. A treaty signed right in the middle of the Crusades, in 1207, provided for a permanent trading post to be established at Aleppo—the first European outpost of its kind in the Levant. Venetian domination was still attested in 1482 by Felix Fabri: "The Venetians have more sway among the Saracens than other Christians; not only do they not fear them, they even punish them"[126]—no small boast when one recalls how the Mameluk were wont to behave. Venetian activities extended throughout Europe: in the first half of the fifteenth century, for instance, they exercised a near total monopoly over trade between Bruges and Damascus.[127] Moreover the first European consul to set up in Damascus was the Venetian, Francesco Dandello, in 1384.

At the time, French trade was virtually negligible: thanks, however, to the efforts of Jacques Coeur, future *grand argentier* or Chancellor of the Exchequer under King Charles VII, the chronicler Georges Chastelain could write: "He plied the entire Levant with his ship and the only masts [to be seen] in Orient seas were hoist with the fleur-de-lis."[128] There were exports of silk from Lyon, fabric from Burgundy, broadcloth from Bourges, cheese-cloth from Arras, cotton from Provence, and imports of granulated sugar from Cyprus, cassia from Egypt, cloves, spices, ginger, pepper (both fresh and crystallized), cinnamon, silk and stuff from Damascus, velvet from Alexandria, satin and taffeta from Cairo, gold thread from Cyprus, Persian rugs, marten and ermine fur, Aleppo and Hama cotton, aloe wood, incense, musk, cochineal, madder, indigo, amber, and balsam. The picture painted by travelers of life in the city among its craftsmen and merchants—especially before Timur's sack and the enforced exodus of its artisans—is literally dazzling: "This city is stocked with every precious thing and with every jewel," wrote Poggibonsi in the mid-fourteenth century, "so that you could not ask anything but is there found [*sic*]; and there things are better worked than in any other part of the world."[129] A little later the Florentine, Sigoli, reported that, "it is said by Christians who are acquainted that really all Christendom could be supplied for a year with all the merchandise of Damascus."[130]

Although lack of accurate records makes it difficult to gauge the precise commercial impact of the pilgrimage to Mecca, in Mameluk times it undoubtedly amounted to a significant factor in the Damascus economy. Each time in effect, thousands of people had to be mounted, fitted out from head to foot, and provided with a viaticum sufficient for a journey across the desert lasting several weeks; numerous pilgrims would also return with precious cargo from Arabia and the Far East. Ibn Jubayr was already describing the commercial side-effects of the hajj in the twelfth century: "[Mecca] is the place best supplied in foodstuffs, fruits, delights, commodities, merchandise, were it to exist at no other time but that of the pilgrimage. . . . In a single day (never mind the following) they sell precious jewels, pearls, jacinth, and other stones, perfumes of all kinds, musk, camphor, aloes, Indian essences. . . . There are no valuable wares or goods that cannot be found in the city at the time of the pilgrimage."[151] The hajj was in any case an annual event of the greatest importance, during which immense crowds would gather in what were almost always harsh conditions: in winter torrential rain and in summer heat and lack of water—then, come rain or shine, the Bedouin. Portrayed by Ibn Iyas as "crueler than Timur,"[152] they had little hesitation in attacking the caravan in spite of the armed detachment that protected it and the tribute (approximately ten thousand dirhem) generally paid them. In the chronicles, one can scarcely keep count of the number of hajjs that had to be cancelled for security reasons.

The number of participants obviously varied greatly. Al-Jazari estimates the Syrians and Iraqis in 1279, a year of exceptionally high turnout, at approximately forty thousand.[153] In 1503, thanks to the good offices of a Mameluk officer of Italian origin, Ludovico di Varthema managed to join the caravan escort "clothed . . . like a Mameluk" under the assumed name of Yunis. That year, in the cortege "there were thirty-five thousand camels, about forty thousand pilgrims, and were sixty Mameluks in guard of the caravan. One third of the Mameluks went in advance of the caravan with the standard, another third in the center, and the other third marching in the rear."[154] Obviously, the return to Damascus after so many hardships was the occasion for festivities, as recorded by Bertrandon de La Broquière, an eyewitness in 1432:

> I saw the caravan from Mecca enter and it was said that there were three thousand camels and that it took nearly two days and nights to get into Damascus and was an event of grand solemnity, in their manner. For, the lord and all the city's worthies went before it in welcome owing to the Alkoran [Koran] they were carrying. This is thetestament that Machommet [sic] has given them and it is borne on a camel draped with a silken cloth with the aforementioned Koran on top and covered over by another piece of silk, painted and inscribed with Moresque lettering. And there came in front of this four minstrels and plenty of drums and nakebs to make a great din. And there was in front the said camel and surrounding him as many as thirty men, some bearing crossbows and others with their swords drawn and others with small cannons they fired off several times. And after the said camel, eight elders mounted each on a fleet-footed camel. And after them, others led on horses bedecked with rich saddles, as is the custom in this land. And afterwards, there came a lady of Turkey, a member of the Great Turk's family.[155]

New-style architecture

Returning to the urban fabric, it seems initially that streets in the suburbs, as Ibn Battuta and James of Verona noted, were broader than those within the city walls.[156] Perhaps this hints at efforts to regulate city growth, a tendency already implied by certain diktats of Tankiz. Many thoroughfares were roofed with vaulting with skylights for ventilation and daylight, and were fitted with night lighting. This is confirmed by Sigoli: "The greater part of the streets in Damascus are covered with roofs or vaulted, with openings that admit enough light when needed, and when night comes they light many glass lamps in every street. They say that more than thirty thousand lamps are lighted every evening in all the streets."[157]

With their courtyards and their supply of refreshing running water, the dwellings (a topic of much comment in Ottoman times) already constituted one of the principal curiosities of the city: "The houses are very high," observed Poggibonsi, "made of wood, but it does not appear . . . the floors [are covered with] mosaic; and, few are the houses that have not their own sculptured fountain which is a marvel to see."[158] Gucci provides more information:

> Almost every house has a fountain in the center of the courtyard, and so from house to house by an underground conduit the . . . water goes: and the conduits are marvelous and well arranged. Then at the foot of the said fountains, everything necessary for the house is washed, and that water then dirty [sic] flows off through another conduit, and so through the whole city there are conduits for good water and there are conduits for bad water. Then all this bad water collects together, and it is so great a quantity that it forms a good mill-dam and that it works several mills; and then the said water flows out of Damascus, they make great use of it so that they water with it a great deal of land.[159]

Ludovico di Varthema lays stress on the contrast between the inside and outside of these dwellings—a characteristic of Oriental towns, and of Damascus in particular—returned to countless times in subsequent centuries: "The houses are very ugly outside," he writes, "but within they are very beautiful, adorned with many works of marble and porphyry."[140] Among its monuments, only the Umayyad mosque ("la principale mesquitte")[141] is mentioned, most of the time to recall that it housed the resting-place of the body of St. John the Baptist (or even, according to some, St. Zachariah), and more especially to stress the flagrant, but long-lived, misconception that it was in reality a Christian church that al-Walid had reassigned to Muslim worship.[142] Nevertheless, some observers were impressed by the building and James of Verona for one, if he deplored the fact that prayers were held there in accordance with "the infamous law of Mahomet,"[143] went as far as to confess that he had never seen "any church, in any region of Italy which, in size and beauty, equaled this mosque."[144] Naturally enough, the venerated places relating to the epic journey of St. Paul were the most frequently visited, especially the site of his conversion located three miles to the east of Bab al-Sharqi on a hill on which there stood an Orthodox church[145] and his place of baptism, occupied at the time by a mosque. There is no mention of other buildings. And yet, with Cairo, Damascus was one of the cities with the greatest number of Islamic monuments.

In the Mameluk period, this heritage was enriched with several hundreds more, financed for the majority by the emirs and na'ibs. Whereas the earliest Mameluk monuments of Damascus, such as the Zahiriyya madrasa, followed straight on from Ayyubid architectural traditions, by the end of thirteenth century the first signs of deterioration began to surface: substandard materials, a strain for symmetry betrayed by the appearance of twin domes, and less harmonious proportions. Owing to the growing influence of the art of Cairo—some na'ibs even had teams of craftsmen sent up from the capital—from the very early fourteenth century these tendencies were exacerbated: timber and brick reappear; the masonry and stone-cutting are less well finished; plans lose their clarity and logic; ornamentation becomes fiddly; polychrome invades façades now dressed in red, white, gray, etc., marble, with turquoise faience, niches, plaited colonnettes, oculi, festoons, flat-arches with two-color multifoil voussoirs, merlons with crops; the gateway muqarnas are laden with spindly and ever more numerous projecting needles; the vault above them contracts into a tiny, shallow-looking conch; minarets grow narrower, their square plans waxing polygonal,

The minaret of the al-Siba'iyya madrasa.

and are weighed down with corbels, balconets covered in a more and more obtrusive polychrome; windows are now ensconced in recesses topped by honeycomb work; polychrome gradually creeps over the interior, the walls being clad in a marquetry of marble and colored stone (less commonly ceramics); and the roofing elements and ceilings are overrun by painted motifs. By the end of the Mameluk period (as testified by the minaret of the Sibaiya madrasa), inlay is no longer executed in stone but, following a technique widespread by Ottoman times, a predetermined pattern of colored stucco fills a slight recess in the facing. Whereas in Mameluk Egypt, mosque architecture derived its models from glorious precedents of the Fatimid era, in Syria the prototype remained the Umayyad mosque: a rectangular courtyard surrounded by porches, a prayer-hall with vessels parallel to the qibla wall, and a gambrel roof. Out of the two hundred and fifty-three Mameluk buildings inventoried in literary sources, only about fifty are extant.

In Salihiyya stands the *turba* of Taqi al-Din al-Takriti, who died in Damascus in 1299. "Man of eminent merit,"[146] formerly one of Qalawun's Mameluks, he acted as vizier to five sultans. Anepigraphic, and identified by literary tradition, the building, datable only by comparison, well reflects the Mameluk style of the end of the thirteenth century, still imbued with the unpretentious vigor of Ayyubid constructions. The main entryway in the southern front opens on to an oblong vestibule with two groined vaults. To the right, this latter leads to a funerary chamber covered with a dome on twin drums with eight and sixteen sides, and to the left to a groined prayer-hall. On the façade, the lintels and the relieving arches of the bays are laid in the best Ayyubid tradition. The stucco decoration in the prayer-hall—an epigraphic band with interlace blossoms over a ground of foliate pattern—was probably executed in the fourteenth century after the

141

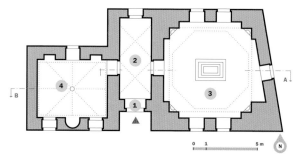

Left. Façade of the al-Takritiyya madrasa.

Below, top. Plan and cross section. **1** Entrance. **2** Vaulted vestibule. **3** Tomb. **4** Prayer hall.

Below, bottom. Al-Takritiyya madrasa: Stucco in the prayer-hall probably executed by an artist from Andalusia.

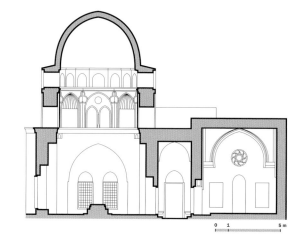

sacking and burning of Salihiyya by Ghazan's Mongols in 1300. The sole example of this type extant at Damascus, it is similar in every respect to the Andalusian tradition as it adorns the walls of the Alhambra at Grenada.

In the district of al-Suwayqa bordering the route from Palestine and Egypt, the emir Khalil al-Tawrizi, grand chamberlain of Damascus from 1415, built a substantial architectural complex including a mosque, his own *turba*, and a *hammam*. The first to be erected, the *turba* was completed when work started on the mosque in 1420. This was inaugurated a short time before or after the death of its founder in June 1423. A square room of small size accessible from within the mosque, the *turba* is capped by a stilted dome borne on a brace of twelve-sided drums, the lower pierced by eight windows and the upper by twelve. Opening onto the street through a door beneath a trefoil arch, the mosque, whose front is coursed throughout in black and white, consists of a covered hall with a basin in the middle replacing the courtyard—an arrangement frequent in Cairo, though unusual in Damascus—and a prayer-hall with three parallel naves whose frame is borne on a pair of three-bayed arcades. The minaret, independent from the mosque across the street, is similar to that of the al-Aqsa mosque built in 1408 in the district of Bab al-Salam. As in the

The funerary mosque of Khalil al-Tawrizi. Behind the tomb's dome one can see that of the *hammam*.

time-honored Syrian practice, it is square in section, and an inscription gives its date as 1423; originally it bore rich ceramic decoration of a white foliate pattern over a blue ground of which, however, only scattered fragments remain. The prayer-hall and *turba* on the other hand still contain superb ceramics, making the Tawrizi complex a peerless example of Islamic art. Hexagonal tiles painted under a colorless transparent glaze line the walls within the *turba* to a height of almost ten feet (3 m) and cover the base of the qibla wall and of the east wall of the prayer-hall to a height of some five feet (1.5 m). The tiles in the *turba*, where floral and star motifs stand out cobalt blue against the white field, are precisely jointed at their summits with the interstices being filled with turquoise triangles of smaller size. Those in the prayer-hall, ostensibly laid side by side, appear to have been thrown up every which way—some even with the look of recycled oddments. Of a singular spontaneity of execution and teeming variety, their motifs, similarly cobalt blue over a white ground, betray the influence of Chinese iconographical repertory:

flowers with fifteen or thirty petals with straight or spiral stalks, motifs in the shape of algae or parts of some fantastical plant, vases, ewers, birds, geometrical forms, generally in six-pointed stars and sometimes associated with a floral or vegetal pattern. Manufactured in Damascus workshops re-established for restoration work on the Umayyad mosque following the sack of Timur, this highly original creation, so unlike the standard product, is assumed to be the work of a certain 'Amal Ghaybi al-Tawrizi (that is, "from Tabriz"), as indicated by a signature traced in small characters on one of the panels on the qibla wall. This ensemble, the most substantial of the period (the number of tiles exceeds 1,300) and preserved in situ, forms part of a truly "international" style that reoccurs in several buildings of the time: in the mausoleum of 'Ali Najm at Cairo, the exact date of which is not known but whose style is patently Mameluk; at Jerusalem, in the al-Aqsa mosque; at Sayda, in the Qutaysh mosque;[147] at Damascus, in the al-Aqsab mosque, in the minaret of the al-Buzuri mosque, and in the mosque of Bab al-Faraj; in central Anatolia, at Kazimkarabekir, where there survive eight hexagonal tiles with blue floral motifs over a white field; and, especially, in the mosque at Edirne, built in 1435–36 by the Ottoman sultan Murad II, where hexagonal tiles are conjoined at the top with turquoise triangles fitted in the intervening spaces, just as in Tawrizi's *turba*.

In addition to panels or fragments in situ, at the end of the nineteenth century many detached tiles—very close in facture and pattern to those in the Tawrizi mosque—entered museums in London, New York, Berlin, and Copenhagen.[148] Their provenance is not known with certainty, but they might have be employed for the great restoration of the Umayyad mosque under Sultan al-Mu'ayyad in 1419 before finding their way onto the art market after the conflagration in 1893 that left the building in a bad state.

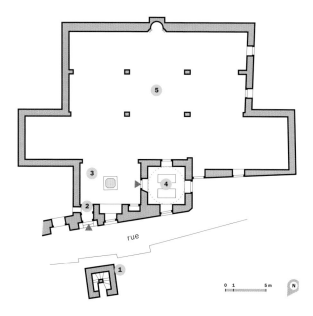

Left. Plan of the al-Tawrizi Mosque. **1** Minaret. **2** Entryway. **3** Roofed vestibule with central pool. **4** Tomb of the emir. **5** Prayer hall.

Facing page. Ceramics lining the walls in the *turba* of Khalil al-Tawrizi.

Ceramic tiles along the base of the qibla wall
in the al-Tawrizi Mosque.

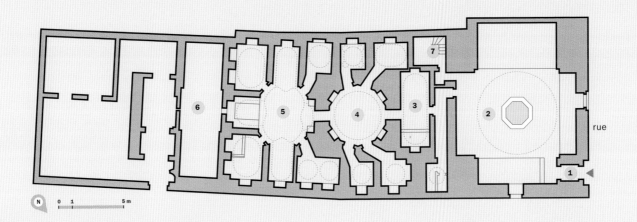

Facing page. Al-Tawrizi *hammam*. A bather in the hot-room getting soaped (page 244 describes the process).

Above, top left. Al-Tawrizi *hammam*. The *tepidarium* with the masseur seated in a niche. *Above, top right*. The cupolas of the al-Tawrizi *hammam*.

Above. Plan of the al-Tawrizi *hammam*. **1** Entrance. **2** Disrobing room. **3** Cold room. **4** *Tepidarium*. **5** Steamroom. **6** Boiler-room. **7** Stairway to the terrace.

The *hammam* near the mosque was only completed in 1441–42. Still active and perfectly conserved (having so far escaped—a rare thing in Syria—misguided attempts at restoration, except for a partial replacement of the paving), it is highly characteristic of Mameluk period baths, the only one to date from the fifteenth century and, in my opinion, one of the finest Islamic monuments in all Syria. Aligned with the mosque and coursed in polychrome, its frontage is pierced with a simple low window and a doorway that leads to the changing room down a dogleg passageway. Spanned with a dome on pendentives capped with a small lantern, the latter possesses a central basin with a water jet and, on three sides, *mastabas*—a sort of rostrum beneath which open little niches for the bathers' footwear. The disposition and relative sizes of the rooms here is a good reflection of the evolution of this type of building in the Mameluk era. The cold room is now very small and is the only one to keep to the rectangular plan that was also adopted for the hot rooms in the bathhouses of Nur al-Din's time. As in earlier periods, the *tepidarium*, covered by a dome to a dodecagonal plan, has four *maqsuras* separated by four intercalary niches. With regard to surface area, the treatment of volumes, the annexes, and the decoration (polychrome paving, niches capped with conches, *muqarnas* transiting from vault to plan), the hot room is now clearly the most important. It consists of a central zone on an octagonal plan extending on three sides into exedra, of which two—those to the east and west—are very deep; one of the five remaining sides leads to the *tepidarium*, while the four others give on to *maqsuras* furnished with hot and cold water and some small stone tanks.

Decor on the gateway to the al-Yunusiyya *khanqah*.

The emir Jaqmaq, *na'ib* of Damascus in the reign of Sultan al-Mu'ayyad, chose to build his funerary madrasa in the vicinity of the northern door of the Umayyad mosque on the site of a former *khanqah* destroyed by fire during the sack of Timur. Arriving in Damascus in 1418, Jaqmaq entered into overt revolt against Cairo in January 1421 and seized the citadel, but, driven out by loyalist forces, he fled to Salkhad. Arrested shortly afterwards, under torture he revealed the extent of his fortune before being put to death in August 1421 and interred in his *turba*. Nearby, he had had a madrasa built for orphans and a *khanqah* for the Sufi, but only the funerary madrasa remains. Completed in 1419–20, as much as in terms of plan as of decoration, it is characteristic of architectural trends in the capital: a recessed gateway roofed by a conch on *muqarnas*, a hall with a central basin spanned by a richly ornamented wooden ceiling over broad arches borne on columns, a prayer-hall on a raised floor, and a *turba*. The Mameluk decorative repertory is here fully and painstakingly deployed, with all the care, precision, and delicacy that distinguishes Syrian monuments from all periods, complete with epigraphic band; multifoil platband; black, white, and pink courses; crown and merlons with fleurons; tall, rather shallow niches; stucco transoms set with colored glass; oculi; conches; *muqarnas* dais; and interlace ribands, etc. The walls inside are clad with tall marble marquetry plinthing, surmounted by an epigraphic stringcourse framing an extremely delicately decorated mihrab whose rounded vault swells into a polychrome arabesque pattern.

Three fifteenth-century minarets (those of Hisham, al-Qal'i and Qa'itbay) are equally representative of developments in decoration. With its octagonal barrel, the first, built in 1427 at the wool suq by the head of the chancellery of Damascus, remains rather close to the minaret of the mosque of Tankiz. Poorly coursed and divided into layers by slightly salient alveolar bands, it is surmounted by a

Detail of the decoration of the mihrab in the al-Jaqmaqiyya madrasa. Mother-of-pearl and colored stone.

gallery covered with an awning borne by a corbel with three rows of *muqarnas*. On the sides of the shaft, the busy ornamentation conveys a muddled impression: basalt stringcourses, chevron patterns, balconets, discs with a central ceramic cabochon, engaged colonnettes, blind niches, bays with polylobe arches, etc. Although unfinished, the al-Qal'i minaret, erected around 1470, is the most heavily ornamented instance in Damascus. Beneath a gallery with a twelve-sided base transiting to the drum through five rings of *muqarnas* corbelling, the decoration spreads over two zones separated by a flat arch set in black and white multifoil arch-stones. Over the upper level on each face, a ribbon molding forms into a square, entwines around four turquoise earthenware cabochons, and curves into a circle inside which three concentric crowns enclose a small oculus. The black geometrical interlace pattern over a white ground adorning the spandrels was completed on only one side. The lower level reads like a glossary of Mameluk decorative art: chevron colonnettes, rounded dais with stalactites, balconets on *muqarnas*, shallow

Above. The *muqarnas* vault of the gateway to the al-Siba'iyya madrasa.

Facing page. The al-Qal'i minaret.

niches, trefoil arches, lambrequin cornices, voussoirs with *muqarnas*, conches, oculi, black-on-white geometrical inlay, cabochons, ceramic discs and tiles.

The western minaret of the Umayyad mosque, destroyed in the fire of October 13, 1479, was rebuilt in 1488 on the orders of Sultan Qa'itbay. In style rather close to its counterparts in Cairo—though of more sturdy proportions—it is divided by two galleries with openwork stone railings on *muqarnas* into three stories of decreasing section. Its ornamentation is more sober and better composed than that of the al-Qal'i minaret: niches with colonnettes and trefoil arches, an oculus surrounded by medallions with calligraphy or multifoil voussoirs, and black stone stringcourses.

The ultimate Mameluk constructions of any note were erected by the last governor, the emir Siba'i. In 1509, outside Bab al-Jabiya, he built a structure that combined the functions of Great Mosque, madrasa, and *zawiya*, and incorporated, naturally enough, his own *turba*. In his zeal to complete a construction finished only in February 1515, Siba'i does not seem to have been overburdened with scruple: "He did not leave a single abandoned mosque or well-preserved burial-place in Damascus without making off with stones, materials, marble, and columns ... performing these depredations most punctiliously. Things came to such a pass that the Damascus ulemas dubbed the building *al-jami' al-jawami'*, 'the mosque of mosques.'"[149] Though his mother and daughter were indeed buried in the *turba*, the founder himself was killed and disappeared during the battle of Marj Dabiq, never to reappear in Damascus.[150] Bereft of architectural qualities, awkward and squat, the building bears witness to a period when, even more than usual, the resources of the empire were being funneled into the army—the regime's last bastion against the machinations of the Portuguese and the rapacious Ottoman appetite for conquest.

Damascus, provincial capital of the Ottoman empire

The century of Süleyman the Magnificent

On his return from Cairo on October 7, 1517, following his final victory over the Mameluks, the Ottoman sultan Selim I overwintered in Damascus. He set up a mosque at Salihiyya near the tomb of the great Andalusian mystic Ibn 'Arabi, approving the plans himself, had a mosque and a bathhouse demolished, and, eager to see the work completed as quickly as possible, entrusted its management to an Ottoman administrator to whom the sum of ten thousand dinars was remitted. He also had built a *takiyya*—a meeting-place for the Sufi—as well as a mausoleum for the tomb of Ibn 'Arabi, and earmarked the income from seven villages for the expenses incurred in maintaining and operating the buildings. For tax purposes, a census of the population was carried out, as well as a land registry drawn up, covering residences, shops, khans, etc. Four months later, on Friday, February 5, 1518, and flanked by the principal civil and military dignitaries, he celebrated prayers in his shining new mosque. Syria was divided into three provinces, now called *wilaya*—Aleppo, Tripoli, and Damascus—each directed by a wali possessing the rank of vizier and the title of pasha. The largest of these was that of

Damascus, extending from Ma'arat al-Nu'man in the north to al-'Arish in the south. On February 8, 1518, Selim I set off for Istanbul, leaving at the head of the *wilaya* the former Mameluk emir Janbirdi al-Ghazali and endowing him with the power to nominate civil servants and the responsibility of farming taxes evaluated at 230,000 dinars.

In September 1520, on the death of the sultan, Janbirdi refused to recognize his son and successor Soliman (Sulayman)—our Süleyman the Magnificent—and triggered a revolt. Seizing the citadel, he struck currency emblazoned with his name, and, at the head of an army made up of Mameluk, Turkmen, and tribal Arabs, occupied Hama, Homs, Tripoli, and marched on Aleppo. But, being apprized of two armies on the horizon—one from Anatolia and the other from Egypt—he fell back to Damascus where he had himself proclaimed sultan in the Umayyad mosque. Raising a popular militia and enrolling villagers from the Ghuta, on February 6, 1521, at Qabun, before a much larger Ottoman contingent supported by artillery numbering around one hundred eighty guns, he suffered a crushing defeat. Several of his lieutenants and three thousand men perished on the battlefield. He himself was taken prisoner and put to death; his corpse was decapitated and, to proclaim the victory, his head, together with "a thousand ears removed from the bodies of his soldiers,"[1] was sent to Istanbul.

Janbirdi's ill-fated escapade constituted an ultimate bid for Mameluk restoration. The Ottoman army rabble fanned out through the city, giving free rein to its basest instincts: "They did not hesitate," Ibn Jum'a writes, "to strip the women and lost all respect for the virtue of men, neither Sufi, nor jurisconsult, nor notable found grace before them."[2] Everything was plundered, including the suqs, the shops, and the khans. It reached the point that, as Ibn Jum'a informs us, "people considered the disaster that had just befallen Damascus comparable to that of Tamburlane or even to the disasters that will signal the resurrection."[3] By February 7, Farhad Pasha, the Ottoman chief of general staff, had restored order in the city. All the posts occupied to that point by former Mameluks were handed over to Ottoman functionaries, and the administrative organization of Syria was placed on a new footing, which remained largely in place until the middle of the seventeenth century. The *wilaya* of Damascus then saw its importance reduced and was now solely comprised of the *sandjak*s of Damascus, Safad, Jerusalem, Nablus, Ajlun, Lajjun, Tadmor, Sayda, and al-Karak. His wali was personally appointed to head the troops placed under his authority, to maintain public buildings, to enforce law and order, to keep the Bedouins, the Druzes, and other turbulent "minorities" in check, to keep the Hijaz road open, to ensure the safety of the hajj, and to oversee supplies of cereals and staples to the cities. He was assisted by an armed force made up of paid infantrymen, including the celebrated Janissary corps, and horsemen, the *sipahi*. Commanded by an *agha* and recruited by *devshirme*s, i.e. "levies" of youths from the Christian populations of the empire, the Janissaries' heaviest responsibility was for maintaining law and order in conurbations. Under the command of an *alay-beg* and garrisoned in recently built fortresses along the roads to the Hijaz and Egypt, the *sipahi* were in principle affected to guarantee the safety of the pilgrimage.

Pursuing a prestige-building policy, Süleyman (1520–66) took the power of the empire to its zenith. His allegedly invincible army, which made Europe tremble, could be increased from 300,000 men in times of peace to 600,000 on the eve of war, to which should be added 300 galleys, as well as other ships, such as galleons, galliots, *carmouses*, and frigates. His artillery was redoubtable and his infantry well drilled: "The weapons of the Janissaries," wrote the French traveler Jacques de Villamont, "all foot-soldiers, are bows, scimitars, and blunderbusses . . . [they] are valiant and steadfast, have no fear of

Page 154. At the foot of Mount Qasiyun, the mosque and mausoleum of Muhyi al-Din b. 'Arabi. Behind, the twin domes of the *takiyya* constructed by Selim I.

death, nor any type of suffering, such as work, hunger, thirst, or sleeping in the open, and the infinitude of travails they have to endure."[4] Against the Christian West, Süleyman first took Belgrade in 1521, then Rhodes in 1522, crushing the Hungarians at Mohács in 1526, and finally besieging Vienna in 1529. Hostilities against the Shi'ite Iran of the Safavids flared up again in 1534 and, on November 30, Süleyman made his solemn entrance into Baghdad, where he restored the tomb of Abu Hanifa, the founder of the official legal school of the state.

Although relegated by the Ottoman conquest to the rank of a capital of a modest pashalik, and despite Aleppo's acquiring commercial supremacy in Syria, Damascus still profited from a regular flow of interchange, as the principle meeting place before the annual pilgrimage caravan and thanks to its situation on many of the camel routes of a vast empire, where, from the Maghreb to Persia, the Black

Sea to the Red Sea, transport was covered by the same administrative regulations. About the middle of the century, it could boast approximately thirty-seven districts or *mahalla*s, about two-thirds of which were extra mural, including 7,500 Muslim homes, 600 Christian, and 520 Jewish, making a total population of some 55,000. The description left by the earliest European traveler of the Ottoman period, the rabbi of Ancona, Moses Bassola, is that of a prosperous, busy, exuberant, open city, where good food was to be had, where it appeared easy to acquire wealth, and where, in spite of Islamic injunctions, lending with interest was rife: a kind of free enterprise paradise where trade and all kinds of deals were booming, practically unscarred by recent events—a town in any case that could bear favorable comparison with any large city in the West:

> Damascus is a great town twice the size of Bologna. It is surrounded by walls and fortifications of great strength and by a moat. There is also a very strong citadel. There are many very beautiful markets, those where trade is carried on being covered on top. . . . There are to be found all kinds of trades and crafts, to an even greater extent than in Venice. In particular the silk manufacture and trade are on a large scale. Women also earn a lot, and, in general, whoever wishes to exert himself in trade can keep his family there in plenty, even if he has but little capital, for there is profit in everything. . . . The wealthy acquire large stocks when things are cheap and put them in storage until prices rise . . . This land has been blessed with an abundance of foods and fruits and of all kinds of royal dishes and a man can find every kind of pleasure in it. . . . The houses are beautiful inside with gardens and fountains and in the markets also there are fountains in plenty. . . . They [the Jews] have three synagogues, well built and beautiful, for the Sefardim, one of native Jews of Damascus, and one for Sicilians.[5]

Plan of 16th-century Damascus. **1** Potteries. **2** Al-Salihiyya. **3** Kurdish quarter. **4** Saruja Suq. **5** Al-'Uqayba. **6** Green Hippodrome. **7** Sufi cemetery. **8** Sultan's palace. **9** Al-Suwayqa. **10** Qasr al-Hajjaj. **11** Shaghur. **12** Tanneries. **13** Al-Qubaybat. **14** Hippodrome of the Stones. **15** Potters' district. **16** Christian cemetery.

157

A few years later, the French naturalist Pierre Belon du Mans was dazzled by the beauty of its markets "covered over;" by the khans, "built like large markets where all wayfarers, foreign as well as those of the country, can lodge free of charge, or else for very little;" by the *bazistan*, "a famous place where the most expensive and finest merchandise in the city is sold, such as silks of all colors, goldwork, silverware, Oriental stones, scimitars, saddles, bridles, and other wares of great price, and also male and female slaves;" by the Ghuta, "a plain more fruitful than any other we have ever seen . . . whose denizens take great pains to make fertile . . . and whose wine is very strong;" and by dwellings whose system of thermal regulation he is the first to describe: "They are extremely well adapted to take in fresh air. And, just as in northern climes they install steam-rooms to keep them warm, so in Damascus they have a manner

of porch with rather low windows to both sides so that, placed against the ground they can have the air coming in rather low so they remain cool."[6]

Following the death of Süleyman in 1566, the empire entered a prolonged decline under a procession of incompetent sultans. The defeat at Lepanto during the reign of Selim II (1566–74), who had placed affairs in the hands of his grand vizier so as to give himself over totally to his taste for vice and wine, tolled the death-knell for Ottoman supremacy in the Eastern Mediterranean. Moreover, an aggravated economic crisis led to illicit taxation and tax-farming. Whole areas were riddled with insecurity and/or permanent rebellion, while Bedouin raids ruined agriculture and curtailed trade; many sources attest to the corruption of functionaries, governors, and even of qadis, such the infamous Ibn al-Farfur, the great Shafiite qadi of Damascus under the Mameluk, one of Selim I's

Bayt Saqqa' Amini. Façade giving onto the court. This dwelling—which has a checkered past—incorporates the oldest vernacular stonework in Damascus. Due to lack of maintenance, many houses of this type are in an advanced state of dilapidation (photograph 1990).

protégés, who was accused—among other mal-feasance—of purloining goods belonging to orphans and to the partisans of Janbirdi. Military institutions were not immune to the decline. Many a *sipahi*, who found the income from land concessions insufficient, attempted to garner some more lucrative administrative or civil office, while others sold their weapons to the peasantry; still others, finding rapine more diverting and more profitable than war proper, went over, complete with arms and equipment, to the Bedouin. As for the Janissaries, intent on making up for the erosion of their wages in this inflationary climate, some embarked on careers as craftsmen or traders. In addition, Europe had begun a period of accelerating expansion characterized by brutality: she too was saber-rattling and striving by every means possible to meddle in the affairs of the empire.[7]

The Europeans, and the papacy in particular, had never resigned themselves to the loss of the portion of southern Syria Christians call the Holy Land. Shortly after the fall of 'Akka (the Acre of the Crusaders), and in spite of widespread disaffection with these types of adventure, Pope Nicolas IV exhorted the Genoese and the Venetians to settle their disagreements and for all Christian princes to call for a Crusade. Chivalric ambition burned bright even among upper-crust *matrone* of Genoa who, to cover the new Crusade's expenses, were to sell off their most valuable jewels. At the instigation of various crowned heads—Henry VII, Philip IV the Fair (Philippe le Bel), and Edward III of England—and with the primary purpose of wheedling subsidies out of the clergy, sporadic expeditions were made ready, but each time they came to naught. In 1421, the duke of Burgundy, Philip the Good (Philippe le Bon), then the most powerful monarch in Europe, galvanized by the idea of the Crusade, sent Ghillebert de Lannoy on a mission to reconnoiter the shores of Egypt and Syria. To similar purpose, in 1430, he also dispatched his esquire trenchant, Bertrandon de La Broquière. Pope Calixtus III made serious preparations and, in autumn 1456, a

flotilla of sixteen galleys, commanded by the famous Jacques Coeur—at the time persona non grata at the court of France and promoted for the occasion "captain general of the Church against the Infidel"—sailed off for the island of Rhodes. Pius II (1458–64) continued to preach the crusade incessantly, taking up the Cross himself, only to die of exhaustion at Ancona in 1464 before he could embark. Christopher Columbus, a wide-eyed enthusiast who believed himself an instrument of Providence chosen by God, spurred on by the idea of the universal triumph of Christianity, left in search of the Indies to find gold to fund the recapture of Jerusalem.[8] In 1526, the Treaty of Madrid signed on January 14 between Charles V and Francis I stipulated in article 26: "That the Emperor and the King will write in concert to the Pope to urge him to commence a general Crusade against the Turk and the heretics."[9] In reality, the suppression of the Order of the Templars, the redoubtable might of the Mameluks followed by that of the all-triumphant Ottoman, intellectual developments, and especially the fratricidal conflicts in which Europe's national monarchies were engaged, had extinguished all hope of ever regaining Palestine.

However, things were about to take a decisive turn at the instigation of Pope Clement V: substituting military conquest for the conversion of the "Infidel," the sword was ousted by the wafer—temporarily at any rate—and a new species of Crusade took shape. Its theorist was the mid-seventeenth-century Father Besson, of the Society of Jesus: "The mission," he wrote, "is to accomplish the conquest and it should be all the more precious to us since the words of God which are luminous weapons are preferable to the arms of the conquerors that are only steel and iron." And furthermore: "Our mission is a perpetual Crusade and all Syria for us is a Holy Land. . . . Our weapons are prayers and tears."[10]

In France, it was Richelieu's renowned éminence grise, Father Joseph, of the Order of the Capuchins, who, in 1625, planned the first systematic mission to

Syria so as to continue, more peaceably, the task interrupted by the Crusaders. Such enterprises did much to open the door to commercial advantages and colonial expansion.[11] Egged on by the papacy and by France—the latter regarding the Christian minorities as a beachhead for its policy in the Orient—Catholic Orders took the road east. Already in 1217, in mid-Crusade, the Franciscans in the *custodia* of the Holy Land, with the support of the Holy See, had been granted rights over the guard of the Sepulcher. In 1333, the same Franciscans, after protracted negotiations with the Mameluks, became "proprietors" of the holy sites. In the mid-sixteenth century, a Cordeliers' convent set up in Beirut. In 1578, Pope Gregory XIII dispatched to the Maronites of Mount Lebanon two priests from the Society of Jesus, which, by the beginning of the seventeenth century, had succeeded in establishing a permanent mission in Istanbul, from where it set about spreading to Syria.[12]

If the missions were well aware that their moral impact paved the way for economic gain and political dominion, the decisive stage of European interference in the interior politics of the Ottoman Empire was the signing of commercial treaties known as the Capitulations. The first was ratified in due form on October 18, 1569, and encompassed two sections: a treaty of establishment and a commercial agreement. The first guaranteed individual, religious, and commercial freedoms to subjects of the king of France, and, in subjecting them to a specific legislation enacted for them by the king, largely sheltered them from Ottoman law. The second specified which products could be legally traded and fixed the level of customs duties. A particular privilege was granted to France: any vessel of a nation not endowed with Capitulations (only the Venetians and Genoese possessed them) were authorized to sail under her protection.[13] These Capitulations, which in principle amounted to a unilateral act, a "gracious concession" valid for the lifetime of the signatory sultan and renegotiable at beginning of each reign, were

renewed in 1597, 1603, and 1673. The watershed came in 1740, when they were no longer limited to the life of a particular sultan and became instead perpetual and irrevocable. Moreover, the French kings, who regarded themselves as "advocates" for the Holy See, using the pretext of rivalry between the Greek, Latin, and Armenian communities to "take possession" of the holy sites, extended their protection not only to all Europeans, but to Catholics generally, and gradually to all Christians subject to the sultan. Whereas, in Mameluk times, European interference had been piecemeal and within diplomatic norms, in the Ottoman period, as soon as the empire betrayed signs of wavering, the European Powers—France, England, Austria, and Russia—could turn to the Capitulations to assert their "right" to intervene militarily.

Ceramic panel on the walls of the mausoleum of Muhyi al-Din b. 'Arabi. Above and along the base of the arches appear the names of Allah, Muhammad and the first four caliphs; in the center: "Glory is God's alone."

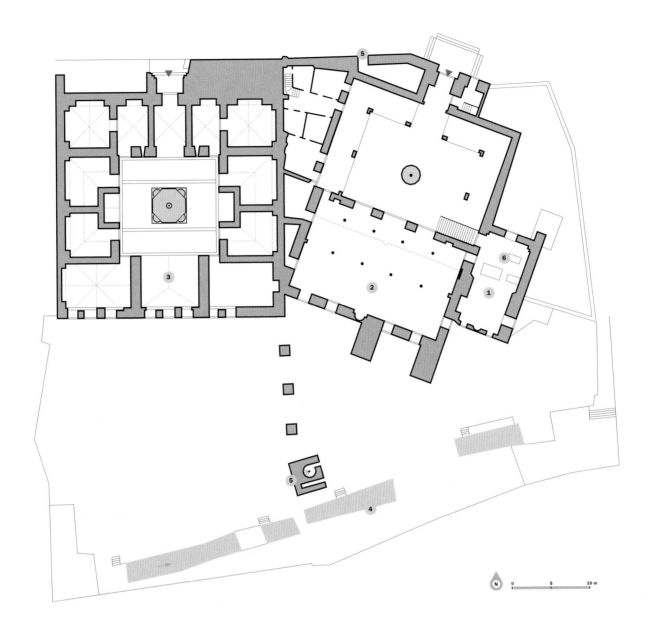

Architecture in the Istanbul style

In the sixteenth century, Damascus experienced one final architectural boom. Even if at a lower rate than in Mameluk times, construction and restoration accelerated, almost always on the initiative of some high-ranking Ottoman. Thus it was that, shortly after the conquest, Selim I himself issued an order to build, in memory of the famous Andalusian mystic Ibn 'Arabi, the first Ottoman buildings in Damascus, comprising a mosque, *turba*, and *takiyya*: this religious complex soon eclipsed all earlier pious foundations and remained the most important religious center in Salihiyya until our own time. With its courtyard surrounded by porticoes, its prayer-hall covered by a terrace, the mosque is absolutely in keeping with the Damascene architectural tradition. In spite of a typical Ottoman conical crown, the minaret——with its niches, polychrome, and its two galleries on *muqarnas*—remains largely in conformity with the Mameluk style. The *takiyya*, rebuilt after the fire of 1554, consists in a large covered rectangular hall with twinned cupolas and various technical areas. Erected above the tomb of Ibn 'Arabi, the *turba* abutting the eastern side of the mosque is domed on a single drum and attracts the eye with ceramic tiles lining the walls inside to a height of over sixteen feet (5 m).[14] In spite of the presence of cypresses, characteristic of the Ottoman decorative repertory,

Plan of the Muhyi al-din b. 'Arabi mosque and mausoleum, with the al-Qaymari *bimaristan*. **1** Tomb of Ibn 'Arabi. **2** Mosque of Ibn 'Arabi. **3** Al-Qaymari *bimaristan*.
4 Nahr Yazid. **5** Noria and aqueduct supplying the two edifices with water. **6** Site of the tomb of Emir 'Abd al-Qadir.

these tiles, in technique and palette—white for the ground, cobalt blue and olive green in the motifs—derive from Syrian traditions and were doubtless manufactured in local workshops.

In 1554, Sultan Süleyman had built, on the very site of the onetime palace of Baybars, the Qasr al-Ablaq to the west of Damascus on the right bank of the Barada, a monumental complex intended for paupers, Sufis, and pilgrims starting off for Mecca, and including a mosque, madrasa, and *takiyya*. Completed in 1560 under the directions of a Persian architect following plans of the celebrated Turkish architect Sinan, the *takiyya* marks the introduction into Damascus of the Istanbul imperial style, as much in terms of overall concept as in certain ornamental details. Preceded by a double portico with keel-arches and granite columns, the mosque, coursed in black and white—the sole concession to the local manner—consists in a square room beneath a dome on pendentives in the Ottoman tradition. The only ornament on the two polygonal minarets with plain shafts and conical tops is *muqarnas* corbelling supporting a gallery with a latticework balustrade. Aligned along the sides of the large courtyard before the mosque, the cells for the Sufis are square in plan, domed, and furnished with a fireplace and preceded

by a portico with keel-arches. Above the doors and windows, a relieving arch incorporates a panel of floral ceramic tiles with motifs borrowed from the Ottoman repertory but presented in a range of colors—turquoise, cobalt blue, purple, olive green, and white—that remains typically Damascene. Located east of the *takiyya* and bordered on the northern side with a suq probably intended for pilgrims, the madrasa was completed only in 1566, the year of Süleyman's demise. Composed of a small mosque on a dome with cubicles for the students laid out around a court with a central basin, it is tighter in design and more modest in scale than the *takiyya*, but its ornamentation is richer and more colorful: courses in black and white, platbands with multifoil arch stones, encrusted medallions, marble marquetry, and floral ceramic tiles of a predominantly blue pattern.

This new complex of constructions built to the right of the route from Beirut early on attracted attention from European travelers. Jacques de Villamont visited it in August 1590, describing it as follows:

A quarter of mile from Damascus lies a very beautiful khan named Tacheyé [*takiyya*], built by Süleyman Sultan, father of the Great Turk who now reigns, to lodge all the Muslim pilgrims who travel to Mecca to visit the sepulcher of Mahomet [*sic*] and to feed them, and likewise their horses and camels for a space of three days without them paying a penny, though if one stays longer, one has to pay one's own board. These lodgings are well built and very pleasant owing to their beautiful garden and the fine arched galleries surrounding it. . . . In the middle of the yard, there is a fountain with excellent water, of which each drinks as he will, and all these buildings are made in a square shape and are all roofed in lead, as too is the adjoining mosque. . . . In this khan, Christians are as well received and nourished for three days like Turks, since Turkish charity extends to all, irrespective of religion.[15]

Facing page. The mosque of the al-Sulaymaniyya *takiyya*.

Above. The al-Sulaymaniyya *takiyya* and the Barada River seen from the west in a late nineteenth-century print.

Above. The gateway to the al-Sulaymaniyya *takiyya* mosque.

Facing page, top. Details of the ceramic paneling inside the mosque of the al-Sulaymaniyya *takiyya*.

Facing page, bottom. Ceramic panels placed above the doors to the cells of the al-Sulaymaniyya *takiyya*.

Above. Detail of a ceramic panel inside the al-Sulaymaniyya madrasa.

Facing page. Darwish Pasha Mosque. Ceramic tiling reemployed over the west wall of the courtyard.
The head of the bird has been subjected to the attentions of an overenthusiastic iconoclast's hammer.

Page 168. Darwish Pasha Mosque. Ceramics lining the interior of the prayer-hall.
Since antiquity, vine-plants have been a very frequent ornamental motif in Syria.

Page 169. Darwish Pasha Mosque. Ceramic tiling reemployed over the west wall of the courtyard.

The other sixteenth-century monuments all owe their existence to the "generosity" of governors, concerned at once to inveigle themselves with the pious citizenry, to grow rich, and, by the means of waqfs, to make their fortunes immune from confiscation and the rapacity of the Revenue. In 1563, the very year he took up his post, Lala Mustapha Pasha had built, near the Suq al-Khayl, a khan, the Khan al-Bittikh, which, according to certain authors, "was unlike any other."[16] Demolished in 1936 during the construction of the main city market, the building incorporated 170 stores, many boutiques, a bakery, a

mosque, a room for ablutions, and latrines. Moreover, he had a suq constructed, with several *takiyya*s and a *hammam*. In 1568, in the Suwayqa district, the new governor, Murad Pasha, had a mosque built, which, in spite of the cupola, remains shot through with Mameluk influence, and a *turba*, whose interior walls are lined in earthenware tiling.

Assuming his functions in 1571, the great vizier, Darwish Pasha, soon set to building. In addition to a bridge, a suq, a *qaysariyya*, a khan, a *hammam*, and several *sabil*s, he also had erected, close to the Sibaiya madrasa, a mosque and a *turba* in which he

Above, left. Darwish Pasha Mosque. Ceramic panels within the prayer-hall.
Above, right. Darwish Pasha Mosque. Ceramic tiles beneath the courtyard porch. Right, top, in medallion the word "Allah"; left "Muhammad," and between: "Hasten to pray before it is too late and repent before you die."

Top. Darwish Pasha Mosque. Panels of ceramics lining the northern wall of the court. Stylized fruits and volatiles stand out
in white on the panel borders. In the center, two lines of inscription: "Our Lord, you who hark to and know all things, accept our repentance,
for you are the Merciful." *Bottom.* Courtyard in the Darwish Pasha Mosque.

171

spontaneity of execution, delicacy of coloring, and especially for the presence of a bird whose head has attracted the attentions of the hammer of a punctilious iconoclast.

The *qaysariyya* located southwest of the Umayyad mosque was endowed as a waqf in favor of its mosque. At one time designated by the name of its founder, it is known today by the name of Khan al-Harir, the "silk caravansary," and is composed of a rectangular court with a central basin surrounded by four ranges of buildings including a ground floor coursed in basalt including stores and a story above laid in limestone for the merchants' chambers. Relatively well preserved, and not substantially altered over time, the Khan al-Harir is occupied today by various warehouses and workshops, producing such items as socks, babouches, shoes, clogs, belts, and embroidery.

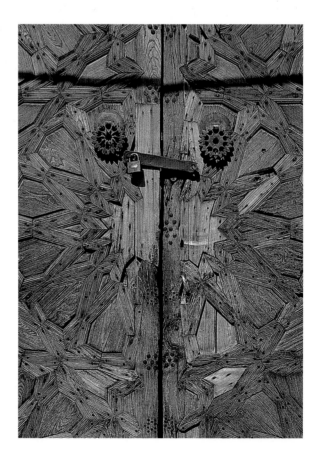

was buried in 1580. Very much after the Istanbul style, the mosque finds space for underglaze-painted ceramic panels: if the floral repertory patently derives from the Ottoman style, the white, green, blue, and mauve color scheme, technique and vine-branch motifs are influenced by the Syrian tradition. At the base of the western wall of the courtyard, to the center of a panel composed rather haphazardly out of recycled fragments, one hexagonal tile stands out for its remarkable naturalism, exquisite

Above, top. The Darwish Pasha *turba. Above, bottom.* Detail of the entryway to the Darwish Pasha Mosque.

Facing page. The gateway to the al-Sinaniyya Mosque.

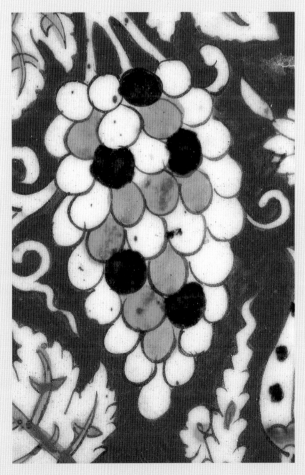

Facing page. The al-Sinaniyya Mosque courtyard.

Top. Al-Sinaniyya Mosque. Panels of ceramics adorning the courtyard front in the prayer-hall.

Bottom, left. Sinaniyya Mosque. Pourer at the ablution pool. *Bottom, right*. Sinaniyya Mosque. Detail of a ceramic panel inside the prayer hall.

Though governing for no more than eighteen months, the grand vizier Sinan Pasha was just as active on the architectural front: in addition to building roads in Palestine, Damascus, and the outlying areas, he built *hammam*s, khans, shops, suqs and a host of religious buildings: mosques, madrasa*s*, *maktab*s (schools), ribats and '*imara*s, for whose maintenance he drew up many waqfs. Early in 1587, soon after taking up his position, on an exceptional site outside Bab al-Jabiya, located at the junction between Straight Street, the artery skirting the western rampart, and two streets that run out into the western suburbs, he built the Great Mosque that bears his name—the Sinaniyya. With an octagonal basin in its center and accessible through three doors, the court is bordered on its south side by an elegant, keel-arched portico covered by seven domes. Superbly delicate, its ornamentation is particularly rich: black and white courses on the external walls, polychrome on the back wall of the portico, black and white arch stones, barley-sugar columns, marble marquetry panels, colored stained glass, carved plaster on the pendentives of the cupola, green-glazed bricks on the shaft of the minaret, vault *muqarnas* at the gate, and panels of ceramic over which sprout cypresses, bunches of grapes, and various floral motifs. Isabel Burton, who stayed in Damascus in 1870, regarded this mosque as most beautiful in the city.[17] Nearby, up against the rampart, Sinan Pasha also had a *maktab* erected—a simple square hall domed on pendentives, intended for about fifty students, half of whom were to be orphans. He also ordered the construction of a suq comprising at least seventy-four shops on the ground floor and thirty-four rooms on the first, and another intramural mosque of more modest dimensions—perhaps in the district known currently as Hariqa. In terms of the size of the estate, as well as for its large personnel, Sinan Pasha's foundation became one of most important in the province of Damascus, probably second in significance only to the Umayyad mosque.

In the sixteenth century, a new type of establishment sprang up in Damascus, the *khammara*, a kind of hostelry intended primarily— even if its etymology evokes alcoholic beverages—for serving coffee. Introduced for the first time in 1534 and prohibited in 1546 at the instigation of the devout and certain muftis, it was finally authorized and *khammara*s multiplied. They reached Istanbul in 1555 on the initiative of a "wag called Shams," an inhabitant of Damascus who is meant to have returned to Syria three years after having amassed a fortune worth five thousand gold pieces.[18] These novel establishments— unparalleled in the West where coffee was to be introduced only in the mid-seventeenth century— were a source of much curiosity for European travelers. Balthasar de Monconys, passing through Damascus in December 1647, left a short description: "They are all covered over, with panes of glass in the middle; there is a beautiful fountain with several jets of water falling into a large square basin; all the benches are covered with rugs and there are theaters where divert drinkers are entertained by cantors and players of instruments."[19] During his two years as governor, between 1593 and 1596, near the Khan al-Harir of Darwish Pasha, Murad Pasha[20] built an ensemble of commercial buildings, including a *khammara*, suq, khan, and *bazistan*. The *bazistan*, reserved for the sale of luxury textiles, was a

pilgrims from Anatolia, the Balkans, Istanbul, Upper Mesopotamia, Kurdistan, the Caucasus, Azerbaijan, and Persia. The majority assembled in the east of the Sulaymaniyya madrasa, while others lodged in the Khan al-Haramayn located in the district of Bab al-Barid, and the Shi'ites in the district of Kharab, the great Shi'ite center of Damascus. After devotions performed at the tombs of saintly personages and in religious buildings, on the 15th of the month of *shawwal*, with great pomp and protected by an escort of approximately hundred *sipahi* and two hundred Janissaries, the caravan left Damascus, accompanied to the village of al-Kiswa by the governor, the great qadi, city worthies, and a jubilant crowd. At Muzayrib, the last gathering place, it paused for a week, fine-tuned its preparations, and paid to the Bedouin chiefs whose territories it was about to cross the various "tributes" designed, as Pierre Belon neatly puts it, to forestall the pious pilgrims being "fleeced en route by the Arabs of the desert."[23]

Even if, in European eyes, the Damascus of this era was no longer the dazzling trading metropolis of Mameluk times, it was still an attraction for its amenities, its natural backdrop, and for its lifestyle. As Jacques de Villamont wrote in 1590:

> It is a very large and very powerful city, built on a very beautiful and very rich plain, through which run two rivers . . . that subdivide into an infinity of brooks that water delightful gardens. . . . The streets are for the majority covered and arcaded, so that one can walk without fear of the heat of the sun nor the inconvenience of the rain; a beautiful and remarkable thing, indeed, as is the lighting which is not absent a single night. As for the houses, they are rather high and lofty, and not very beautiful outside since some are built out of earth, but inside they are magnificent and superb, enriched with paintings in mosaic, which is a gilded thing of the greatest value. Apart from that, practically all have fountains and extremely beautiful and delectable gardens, where all kinds

quadrangular edifice with a central basin and, preempting a famous eighteenth-century khan—that of As'ad Pasha—was covered with nine domes borne on sturdy pillars. Its location is said to be the site of a construction known since the nineteenth century as the Khan al-Jumruk—the "customs caravansary."[21]

At the end of the century, Damascus seemed to have regained its prosperity. The appearance of two new districts in the census of 1596–97 proves at any rate that the city was expanding. The concentration of dhimmi—Jewish and Christian alike—in the eastern part of the intramural city, supported by the large measure of autonomy accorded them by the Ottoman administration, was ever more clearly apparent, contradicting Pierre Belon's observation that only the Jews were "locked up separately, as in Avignon."[22] Although only the fifth city of the empire and the second in Syria behind Aleppo, it enjoyed an immense cultural and religious prestige in the eyes of all Muslims. It remained, moreover, the point of departure for one of the two pilgrimage caravans— the other, for pilgrims from the Maghreb, left from Cairo—for which each year there gathered, under the direction of the *amir al-hajj*, several thousand

Facing page. A coffeehouse in Damascus on the banks of the Barada in a print from the first half of the nineteenth century.

Above. Damascus as pictured by late sixteenth-century European geographers. G. Braun and F. Hogenberg, *Civitatis orbis terrarum. . .* Cologne, 1572–98, f. 114.

of excellent fruit grow for eating. . . . And certainly, people here delight greatly in the beauty of their gardens, the waters from which, and from the fountains too, flow through the majority of the streets of Damascus, thereby cleaning the said streets and bearing away detritus. . . . Whosoever considers the beauty, situation, and richness of this city well would judge it paradise on earth, not for the appearance of the city's buildings, but for the bounty of the land alone.[24]

The decadence of Ottoman power— missions and capitulations, instruments of European interference

In the seventeenth century, the decline of the empire accelerated. Consular dossiers, statistical data, imperial firman, chronicles, collections of biographies, accounts by travelers—all testify to the impoverishment and depopulation of the countryside, to the dilapidation of the cities, to the indiscipline of the nomads, to the insecurity of communications, to the corruption of civil servants, to the arbitrariness of the government, to the dissatisfaction of the people, and to the diminution of central authority. Taking advantage of the situation and the wars the empire was waging against Persia and Hungary, petty local dynasts, individual emirates, Bedouin sheikhs, Kurdish, Turkmen, or Arab emirs rattled their Ottoman overlords and did much to the benefit of their own power at the expense of the Sublime Porte and their neighbors. In Syria, a minor Druze emir, Fakhr al-Din Ibn Ma'n, whom the governor of Damascus, Murad Pasha, had promoted *sandjakbey*, backed by the Maronites, succeeded in extending his hegemony over Ajlun and Safad. At the head of an army some forty thousand strong, he sought support from European Powers (the Medici in particular), promoted trade with Europeans so as to increase revenues, and encouraged the building of churches and monasteries. According to the Recollect friar Eugène Roger, who became closely associated with him during a stay between 1629 and 1634, his power was such that "the pashas of Damascus and Tripoli had power only in their cities whence they could no longer extract sufficient income to pay the Grand Seignior."[25]

Murad IV decided to bring events to a head: the governor of Damascus, Kujak Ahmad Pasha, a man with an iron fist who had earned his spurs with the vigorous repression of banditry, marched on Beirut at the head of a considerable force, while the Ottoman fleet plied the coast. Betrayed by those close to him, Fakhr al-Din had no choice but to make way. Conducted in chains to Istanbul, he was garroted on March 14, 1635, in spite of the "fourteen mules laden with gold and silver coin and other riches he had presented to the Grand Seignior."[26] The authority of the Porte was restored and, to facilitate the supervising of the Druze regions, the *sandjak*s of Sayda, Beirut, and Safad, hitherto dependent on Damascus, were amalgamated into a single province: the province of Sayda.

Woefully deleterious to trade, the insecurity of transportation routes was pervasive. In the Mediterranean, among Christians and Muslims, Turks, Barbary, Maltese, Italians, French, Majorcans, and Spaniards, piracy was rife. On land, the Druzes, and more especially the tribal Arabs, enjoying impressive military resources—worthy competitors at any rate with those of the Porte—waylaid travelers, holding caravans to ransom and levying "tributes of fraternity" from sedentary populations. Their law held sway up to the approaches to the cities, and the pashas of Damascus and Aleppo, incapable of marshalling a force sufficient to oppose them, often saw themselves constrained to pay them off. Not even the holy caravan of the hajj, its pilgrims loaded down with merchandise, was safe from their clutches. In 1603–04, it was attacked and plundered, with only a few pilgrims escaping. In 1660, Laurent d'Arvieux notes that the French consulate was removed from Damascus to Sayda, due to "the risk of transferring money over three days of perilous and often impassable roads because of raids by Arabs and Druzes."[27]

In 1674, Colbert's envoy, the Marquis de Nointel, observed that, between Aleppo and Tripoli, "the dangers of the journey came from posts of Turkish soldiers dotted along the roads and stationed there to ensure safety for the caravans in exchange for a fee, [as] for them, levying this toll served as a pretext for extortion and spoliation; they waylaid travelers, when they did not slaughter them; of all the brigands with which this country swarmed, these Turkish gendarmes were the most feared."[28] Many towns in Syria thus presented an impression of desolation, particularly in the southernmost part. Tyre, Jubayl, Jaffa, Caesarea, Sayda, Acre, Tiberias, Safad, Lydda, Ascalon, and Ramla were, according to various expressions used by travelers, sometimes completely ruined, and sometimes reduced to the state of villages. A great number were deserted through fear of the nomads, such as the town of Homs which, according to the Italian Pietro Della Valle, "was only very sparsely inhabited because of the violence perpetrated at that time by Arabs of the desert, who from time to time coerced larges sums of money from these poor people."[29]

Travelers and chronicles provide fulsome reports of the high-handedness of the government— apparently no longer observant of Islamic law, even if, as a whole, it appears to have been less ruthless than the Mameluks. The Reverend Coppin observed that the pasha of Cairo was a law unto himself, that he could confiscate the goods of whomever he liked, and "put to death anyone with no need of any other trial, save the order he [gave] for it."[30] As d'Arvieux comments, in their eagerness to profit from the year of their mandate to recuperate with interest the sums that, in exchange for their function, they had advanced to the sultan's treasury and to their patrons

and protectors, pashas and qadis alike wielded their exactions and tyranny to reduce "the people to despair and force them to abandon their homes and property."[31] The miserable condition of the lower orders was stressed on many occasions. "The majority of the great cities," wrote a Cordelier, Father Jacques Goujon, "were teeming with a throng of all kinds of folk of the utmost poverty who survived solely on rice, lentils, oven-cooked or boiled peas and ash-baked bread an *écu* [coin] thick."[32]And, as Eugène Roger informs us, even in Damascus so celebrated for its richness, "most of the children, to eight or ten years old, go around without a stitch on."[33]

By means of tools such as Capitulations and missions, the European Powers made the most of the opportunity to gain ever greater influence in the internal affairs of the empire. As an ethical component of political action, the missions entered the fray in seventeenth century. First came the Jesuits, who, at the instigation of Pope Urban VIII and with French support, soon turned their eyes towards Syria from Istanbul, where they had been established since the beginning of the century. In 1627, they were in Aleppo, reaching Damascus, Sayda, and Tripoli by 1644 and 'Ayn Tura in 1657. The Capuchins ran a hospice in Damascus, with a church and a monastery at Tripoli. The Recollects were in Jerusalem, where they took possession of the Holy Places in 1628, while the Cordeliers of the Holy Land were in Damascus by 1660. Wholly prohibited from proselytizing Muslims, by Ottoman as much as by Papal law, they exercised their apostolate on the Eastern Christians, Copts, Monophysites, Armenians, Orthodox, etc., all held, in varying degrees, to be heretics, so that "on this land sprinkled by the blood of Christ . . . and today profaned, for it is like the sewer containing so great number of Muslims, Arabs, Moors, Negroes [*sic*], and the meeting place for schismatics, heretics, and Jews. . . . the Western Church dispenses its enlightenment on the Eastern."[34] These are the words of the good

Jesuit Besson, imbued, as can be seen, with Christian charity. This policy of conversion, shadowed by a propaganda campaign in praise of France, aroused indignation and sometimes revolt. Catholic sources report that in 1692 the "heretics," led by their patriarch, came to protest before the seraglio of Aleppo, crying "they want to make us into Franks, but this we do not want to be. We are faithful subjects of the Grand Seignior."[35] Moreover, as Eugène Roger attests, it was in the Holy Land that Orthodox opposition to the Catholic presence was at its most intransigent.[36] Nevertheless, missionary activity bore fruit, and Eastern Christians, separating from their own Churches, subjected themselves to the Roman: in 1662, a Syrian Catholic Church split from the Jacobite Church, and there appeared an Armenian Catholic Church in 1740, followed by a Catholic Coptic Church in 1742.

In the seventeenth century, the Capitulations were renewed and the privileges thereby granted enlarged, making the consul and his "nation"—that is, all those lodged in a khan enjoying genuine extraterritorial status—into a kind of state within the state. Those of 1603, signed between Ahmad I and Henri IV of France, expressly granted to the king "protection" over the Holy Places whose "possession" by the Latin monks was recognized. These were confirmed in 1673 by negotiations by Nointel that also stipulated that the passage through Suez and the Red Sea be opened to French trade. In 1674, Louis XIV granted his protection to the Jesuits and to the Franciscans by letters patent. From the middle of the century, projects for intervention multiplied. In 1672, Leibniz drafted plans to be presented before Louis XIV for taking Egypt, while, in 1686, for the first time in a French document, the possibility was mooted of opening a canal between the Red Sea and the Mediterranean. All the elements of the Great Game, which was to conclude (provisionally) at the end of World War I, were already in place. Nointel who, with d'Arvieux,

surpassed the other travelers of his time in terms of finesse and sagacity, encapsulated it marvelously in a letter addressed to the king: "Turkey is hardly more than a phantom of power. . . . It is up to the maritime powers, and in particular to France, to complete its ruin, to deal the decisive blow, to achieve the liberation of Chrisendom."[37]

The Ottoman Empire was soon to be known as "the sick man of Europe," whose demise was delayed only by squabbling among the Western Powers. To provide purchase for this policy of interference, every breach in the empire became ripe for exploitation. For instance, before the Maronites were dubbed descendants of the Phoenicians, the Druzes were turned into heirs to the Crusaders: the honest Cordelier Jacques Goujon, relying on a simplistic homophony, would even refer to them as "descendants of the Druids, ancient sacrificers of the Gaul."[38] If the idea of "liberating" the Christians from Muslim domination recurred as a leitmotiv, the notion of freeing the Arabs from the yoke of the Turks (destined for long life) made progress too, as remarks by d'Arvieux attest: "It is certain that, if the Christian princes were to join forces to drive them [the Turks] out, the Arabs too would stand up and be counted, and prove very helpful in this worthy task."[39] It would be nearly a quarter of a millennium before history was to bear out d'Arvieux's vision—thanks to the help of the lies propagated by Western diplomacy—with the outbreak of World War I, preceded by the diffusion into the East of nationalist ideologies.

The industrial production of seventeenth-century Damascus was no longer, above all in terms of quantity, what it had been in the time of the Mameluk, and its commercial preeminence seemed at an end. As early as 1612, Jean Mocquet was writing about it in the past tense: "Formerly, there was the greatest trade [there] from the Indies, Persia, Chaldea, Armenia, and other places."[40] The French consulate, still there in 1634 at the time of the Eugène Roger's visit, was shortly afterwards transferred to Sayda, mostly due to the insecure communications. In the second half of the century, no more European residents are mentioned, and the city increasingly takes on the appearance of a closed, even "fanatical" place. Its reputation was further enhanced by steel-quenching, damascening, the manufacture of blunderbuss bores and sabers, and by textiles, an industry famous for the variety, quality, and richness of its fabrics: silk, velvet, taffeta, and damask, brocade, rugs, mohair, and cotton cloths. The trade in "ashes" produced by the calcination of grasses from the Anti-Lebanon or the Ghuta and used in the manufacture of soap and crystal was of such crucial importance that a decree shared them equally between Europeans, officials, and soap makers. Although still in direct communication with the ports of 'Akka, Sayda, Beirut, and Tripoli, for exchange with Europe and the East, Damascus now depended primarily on Aleppo. It imported such items as bolts of silk, paper, bonnets, cochineal, indigo, and sugar, as well as pepper, the movement of which was now entirely in European hands. It exported various craft products, except for swords whose sale to Europeans was, in theory at least, prohibited, and for the "ashes," bought up by Venice for the manufacture of crystal and by Marseille for soapmaking. Its trade with Europe was, however, far less extensive than that with the East. Via Aleppo—and to a lesser extent directly from Baghdad—it imported dates, cotton, wool, silk, spices, and gallnuts. From Persia, India and Arabia, each year it received by way of the pilgrimage caravan precious stones, silk, various drugs, ginger, indigo, gums, camphor, coffee, as well as slaves from the Sudan and Abyssinia. It sent textiles, gallnuts, soap, olive oil and dried fruit to Cairo, importing rice, beans, lentils, and, in bad years, wheat.

If few new significant buildings were built in Damascus in the seventeenth century, the distance to the empire's borders rendered fortifications unnecessary and fostered the extension of the suburbs. The moats were gradually filled in and dwellings invaded the ramparts, which, moreover, had long ceased to be maintained. "The wall," wrote Fermanel in 1632, "is almost completely ruined and has collapsed in several places, so that one can walk out of the city over its debris."[41] To the west, urbanization intensified in the vicinity of the *takiyya* and the Sulaymaniyya madrasa, as well as in the district of Qanawat, where many Ottoman officials, civil and military, had residences built. The most outstanding developments occurred in the south along the pilgrim road. In Bab al-Jabiya, around the mosque of Sinan Pasha, a new suq appeared, providing necessary articles—harnesses, saddles, packs, tents woven out of hemp from the Ghuta, etc.—for pilgrims departing for Mecca, as well as for peasants of the Hawran and nomads of the desert. Then, over approximately two miles (3 km), from Bab al-Jabiya to Bab Allah, came a mix of crafts shops and corn stores, forming a genuine suburb that took the name Midan, after the ancient Maydan al-Hasa, the "hippodrome of stones," located nearby. The village of al-Qubbaybat ("of the small domes") was little by little overrun, but its domes, similar to those one can see today in villages in northern Syria, are referred to by Monconys in 1647: "It is one of the most beautiful things in the city, though all the houses are only made of earth, and likewise their sugar-loaf domes."[42] The camel market was, naturally enough, sited on the approaches to this recent suburb, while the Suq al-Khayl—the celebrated horse market of Mameluk times—was slowly taken over by adjacent suqs. In the north, the quarter of Salihiyya, where many Kurdish emigrants settled as the century progressed, looked increasingly like a resort: "The majority of people in Damascus," wrote d'Arvieux, "have a home for recreation, both beautiful and agreeable, as much for the eye as for the gardens that go with them, and the beautiful waters that run everywhere from this hill."[43] In 1675, Governor Kur Husayn Pasha had the thoroughfare linking it to Damascus paved.

In the cityscape sketched by travelers, certain features deserve special mention. The ramparts sowed confusion: many said they were double, some even triple; almost all underline their state of decay, except d'Arvieux who calls them modern, "except on the side where St. Paul was lowered in a basket."[44] As a whole, the streets found little favor "because the buildings are muddled, low-set, and from the outside lack proportion."[45] However, and in the suqs especially, they presented a characteristic that proved surprising to European observers, who were as yet unacquainted with roadsides dedicated to pedestrian use, now known as "sidewalks": "The sides have elevated embankments serving for people on foot," writes d'Arvieux, "the middle, which is lower, being used by carts and animals. This precaution means that the way for people on foot is always kept clean."[46] As far as the houses are concerned, Maundrell is the only one to express great astonishment that they are built in sun-dried brick, whereas the neighboring mountainsides abound in stone "suitable for raising beautiful buildings."[47]

If the places linked to memories of St. Paul or to alleged Biblical episodes seem to have been the primary reason for a "pilgrimage" to Damascus, some Muslim monuments too began to attract attention—in particular the Zahiriyya madrasa, the tomb of Saladin, the *bimaristan* of Nur al-Din, the Sulaymaniyya *takiyya*, and the mosque of Sinan Pasha, often mentioned by the name of the Green Mosque (so-called thanks to its glazed-brick minaret). As for the Umayyad mosque, all regret that, as Christians, none are permitted to enter "under pain," as Jean Coppin puts it, "of being impaled or turning Turk."[48] It is inevitably referred to as the onetime church of Zachariah or of St. John the Baptist, complete with observations which can sometimes raise a smile: Fermanel managed to make out several Holy Fathers represented in the mosaics, while the goblets appearing on the bronze cladding of the doors—which are none other than the insignia of the Mameluk sultans—are seen by the irrepressible Jesuit Besson (according to the Jesuitical manner of interpretation) as "the divine hallmark of Christian sacrifice, which is a chalice."[49] The citadel was also out of bounds to foreigners, but d'Arvieux—because he had friends in Damascus and wore Turkish clothes—was one of the first Europeans to enter it. Some travelers mention the lazar-house built outside the walls, near Bab al-Sharqi, on the site of the house of Na'aman where the prophet Elisha cured leprosy.[50] It was a vast enclosure with a garden where Fermanel, in August 1630, saw "five or six lepers cruelly scarred by disease, with some whose jaw had fallen out monstrously rotted."[51]

The al-Qal'i minaret viewed from the south.

The century of the 'Azm

The signature in 1699 of the catastrophic Treaty of Karlowitz, by means of which, vanquished by the Holy Alliance, the empire ceded great tracts of land to Poland, Russia, and Venice, combined with the end of the Köprülü dynasty of grand viziers at the beginning of the following century, further weakened the central authority, while the degradation of the system of land concession accelerated the decline of the military. During the eighteenth century, in a Damascus already rudely affected by natural disasters—plague, famine, and swarms of locusts—conflicts between the imperial Janissaries, the *kapikulu*, and local entities, the *yerliyya*, reached a degree of ferocity unknown in the previous century. Outside the cities, Ottoman authority was everywhere run ragged by "feudatories" backed by religious minorities—Druzes, Maronites, *mutawali*s, and *nusayri*s—and by sheikhs of Arab tribes, who thus extended their "jurisdiction" over ever-vaster stretches of territory. Profiting from these circumstances, Catholic missionaries redoubled their efforts, and, in the eighteenth century, European forces—initially the Russian navy and afterwards the French army—resurfaced in Syria for the first time since the Crusades.

Damascus at the end of the seventeenth century (early eighteenth century?) seen by an anonymous artist. 'Azm Palace, Damascus.

The safety of the pilgrimage in respect of the Bedouin remained a constant source of concern for the Ottoman government because, in addition to its considerable economic importance for Damascus and the surrouding area, for the sultan himself, caliph and guard of the two Holy Cities, it was above all of major political import which could have repercussions on his prestige throughout the Muslim world. Sums paid to the Bedouins had continued to soar during the last decades of the seventeenth century: in 1678, 24,000 piasters were enough to obtain "rights of passage"; at the beginning of the eighteenth century the cost had risen to more than 100,000. Moreover, some pashas concerned to rein in their expenses simply reduced the military escort or diverted part of the sums allotted into their pocket, thus aggravating Bedouin belligerence. Traveler Carsten Niebuhr is one of the few to mention this effect: "Plundering caravans should not invariably be ascribed to the Arab passion for brigandage," he wrote. "If the Bedouin do sometimes ransack these caravans, the haughty and perfidious conduct of the Turkish officers is always the primary cause. These vainglorious Turks look on all Arabs as rebels, that is to say . . . as weaklings who have the insolence not to bend the knee to the stronger party. This splendid piece of reasoning means that they break their word and the Arabs exact revenge by plundering the caravans."[52]

Keen to improve safety for the pilgrimage, the Porte, breaking with its earlier policy, now frequently named the wali of Damascus *amir al-hajj*, while the pashas of Tripoli and Sayda took charge of the *jarda*, namely the convoy that went to meet the hajj about halfway to provide it with provisions and an additional escort on the route back to Damascus. Nevertheless, both hajj and *jarda* were attacked on several occasions in the first decades of the eighteenth century. The insubordination of the Bedouin was no less harmful to commercial caravans, all the more since their military escorts often refused point blank to engage with them in combat. Thus, in 1722, the caravan within which the Englishman Thomas Shaw was journeying was attacked between Ramla and Jerusalem and "the Turkish infantry . . . were not able, or durst not at least" protect it from the Bedouins.[53] The latter, moreover, did not just rampage along caravan tracks, but over entire *sandjaks* around the desert's edge, in particular the area of Hama, Transjordan, and Palestine, where villages and harvests were regularly pillaged. These circumstances furthered the reinforcement of local authorities, whose struggles with the representatives of the Porte were to persist through the eighteenth century. From Dayr al-Qamar, which he had made into his "capital," the emir Haydar Shihab (1707–32) reverted to the policy of Fakhr al-Din and succeeded in extending control over a vast area, including the near totality of the *wilaya* of Sayda, Tripoli, and a considerable part of Damascus. Conscious of the gravity of the situation, in March 1725 the Porte appointed the pasha of Tripoli and commander of the *jarda*, Isma'il al-'Azm, governor of the province of Damascus with the title *amir al-hajj*. This conferred on him authority over the *sandjaks* of Jerusalem, Gaza, Nablus, and Ajlun, while his brother Süleyman was elevated to chief of the province of Tripoli. This marked the beginning of the rise of the powerful family of the 'Azm [or Azem] that was to dominate Syrian political life for most of the century.

So as to butter up the inhabitants and the ulemas, Isma'il erected many buildings: a madrasa, two *hammam*s, a coffeehouse, suqs, a mosque, a library, and a new palace. He fostered trade and the Catholic missions, and displayed noteworthy evenhandedness in the clashes between the various Christian denominations. His repeated success in controlling the hajj earned him great regard in religious milieus, added to his luster in Istanbul, and was probably the main reason for the renewal of his appointment for six consecutive years. At the same time, his close relations attained key positions in Syria. His son, Ibrahim Pasha, was appointed in Tripoli, while Süleyman obtained the *wilaya* of Sayda. As'ad Pasha, another of his sons, was placed at the head of the *sandjak* of Hama, one of richest in the *wilaya* of Damascus. From al-'Arish to the borders of the province of Aleppo—and contrary to the sacrosanct principle of the balance of power—Syria was for the first time almost entirely in the hands of a single family. In the eyes of the Porte, this new situation furthered three priorities: the collection of taxes, the maintenance of law and order, and the security of the pilgrimage. Yet this approach was quite at odds with customary practice, according to which, in order to avoid the establishment of dynasties and any stirrings of "national" solidarity, the wali— always "foreigners" with respect to the provinces they controlled—were, as a rule, replaced every year.

In October 1730, the sultan, Ahmad III, was overthrown and succeeded by his nephew, Mahmud I. Accused of abuses of power and illegal money-making activities, the members of the 'Azm family were arrested, imprisoned, and their property confiscated. Their eclipse was of short duration: in 1734, Süleyman returned to Damascus, which, as absolute master, he was to govern (except for a three-year interlude) until his death on August 26, 1743. Looking to increase his revenues, he favored trade, in particular with the Franks, thereby shifting the focus of their activity from Sayda to Damascus. Moreover, he tried to calm rivalry between Orthodox and Catholic, as well as that between the different Latin Orders. He also built a madrasa, two *hammam*s, and a khan. Six of the seven pilgrimages he conducted returned to Damascus without mishap; during the seventh, in spring 1743, many pilgrims were killed, though the cause was torrential rain. Backed by a mercenary militia of Bosnians, Maghrebi, and Turks, he pursued a firm policy and

succeeded in restoring order. He repealed many illegal taxes, stimulated the craft industries, and refurbished the Nahr Qanawat, thus improving water supplies to the city. Nevertheless, famine, food shortages, and plague, as well as price rises fanned by speculation and tax increases due to the resumption of hostilities with Persia sparked regular revolts among the underprivileged. In order to extend his authority over southern Syria, Süleyman named in Sayda his nephew As'ad Pasha who was to go down in history as the most famous governor of eighteenth-century Syria. Within his own jurisdiction, Süleyman possessed a rival in the person of the *defterdar* al-Falaqinsi who, assured of powerful backing in Istanbul, founded his ambition on the *yerliyya* and the *a'yan*, that is to say the great landowners. Thanks to the immense financial leverage his function earned him, he promoted a policy of public works which in principle was solely in the hands of the wali: rebuilding two minarets of the Sulaymaniyya mosque in 1737–38; improving the road to Salihiyya in 1742–43; various restoration projects in the Umayyad mosque in 1743–44; the construction of a madrasa in the Qaymariyya district, and in the Midan suburb, the "stronghold" of the *yerliyya*, a *hammam*, and a coffeehouse. His lifestyle and expenditure befitted a sultan: for his daughter's wedding, he threw a sumptuous feast with each day being reserved for a particular category of guest: Süleyman and his entourage, ulemas, officers, major traders, Christians and Jews, peasants and, on the last day, prostitutes.

The main threat to the authority of the Porte, however, lay in Galilee where Sheikh Zahir, son of 'Umar, of the tribe of the Banu Zaydan, was growing in power. Master of the Tiberiad, which he busied himself fortifying and which he made his capital, he presided over a strategic point where the Damascus-Gaza road, vital for the control of the southern *sandjak*s, crossed the Jordan. In 1743, an expedition

combining the forces of the *wilaya* of Damascus, Tripoli, and Sayda was setting off to Galilee when Süleyman's sudden demise put a halt to operations. Now unafraid to show his hand, al-Falaqinsi immediately took the reins of the city, arrested several relations of the deceased, and made strenuous efforts to garner the *wilaya* of Damascus. Thwarting his expectations, however, the Porte named As'ad Pasha, Süleyman's nephew. Rivalry between the two men continued unabated for nearly three years, until on July 5, 1746, while the *defterdar* was on a visit to the seraglio, As'ad Pasha flourished a firman ordering his execution. The felon was immediately decapitated, his head dispatched to Istanbul, and his body dragged for three full days through the streets. His property and that belonging

Fathi Mosque (al-Qaymariyya madrasa), built by the *defterdar* al-Falaqinsi in 1743: Porch giving onto the prayer-hall.

to several members of his family were confiscated. Any partisans unable to flee in time were arrested and put to death. Others joined forces hostile to Ottoman power: Sheikh Zahir, the Bedouin, and the Druzes, bolstered by whom they were to launch a series of attacks on the city.

The elimination of al-Falaqinsi was far from curtailing the mayhem occasioned by the bad blood between *kapikulu*s and Ashraf, various military groups, Greek Orthodox and Greek Catholic, but also by enemies from the "exterior." In September 1748, having laid the southern suburbs to waste, former supporters of al-Falaqinsi, joining forces with the Druzes, surged through the city in an attempt to free their fellows under lock and key in the citadel. The districts that fell into the hands of the insurrectionists were the theater of one of the most ferocious battles in Damascus's history: from al-Suwayqa to Midan, all was reduced to a heap of rubble. The violence was worsened by the indiscipline of the troops, who molested the population, plundering and raping throughout the *wilaya*. The efforts of As'ad Pasha failed to restore Ottoman authority over the rebels. In the Lebanese mountains, Emir Mulhim, son and successor of Haydar Shihab, threatened the plain of the Beka'a and annexed Beirut, which was soon to become one of the most important ports in Syria. As for Zahir, strongly supported by the Porte, his ambition grew boundless. He grabbed the port of 'Akka, which he needed for trade, fomented insubordination among the tribes, and encouraged Maltese pirates, whose booty was readily turned into cash in his own territories. Only tribes in the southernmost areas were more or less subdued. Almost every year, expeditions struck out for the Hawran or the desert to contain turbulent tribes of Bedouins and Turkmen, who threatened supplies to Damascus and the pilgrim road. Their power was, however, hardly affected and they continued to loom large on the Syrian political chessboard.

The situation among the lower echelons of the population remained precarious. In addition to natural disasters—in particular drought and plagues of locusts that could wipe out agriculture—shortage of food was manipulated by speculators, while the qadis and *muhtasib*, roundly bribed, turned a blind eye to illicit activities. The greatest speculator was inevitably As'ad Pasha himself, who lent at interest and traded in all and sundry. Using traducement and extortion, and confiscating the property of his adversaries and of pilgrims who died en route, he amassed an immense fortune and an impressive portfolio of real estate virtually all endowed as waqf for his children and grandchildren, including land, houses, orchards, khans and even mills—the latter enabling him to control bread prices. In spite of violent repression, torture, and death sentences, there was still periodic rioting. In July 1746, a starving mob marched on the seraglio and stormed several public buildings, which were sacked and set ablaze. Faced with the dissatisfaction of the majority, As'ad Pasha sought support from the Jewish and Christian "minorities." To secure their backing, he even suspended clothing restrictions. A Greek Orthodox annalist, Mikha'il Burayk, stated in his *History of Damascus* that, though he had consulted histories of the city from the Muslim conquest to his own day, none he found alleged that the Christians enjoyed more influence and honor than they did during the ten last years of the government of As'ad Pasha al-'Azm.[54]

His one undeniable achievement was without question the security of the hajj. Conscious that failure would entail immediate revocation, he lavished attentions on the enterprise, and in his fourteen-year reign there was not one mishap. The first, which he conducted shortly after his entrance to Damascus, in winter 1743–44, went down in history—Ibn Jum'a declared it a splendid hajj[55]—thus consolidating his reputation and standing with the Porte. Others too were successful, and the number of participants, attracted by the improved safety record, swelled yearly. Water cisterns were placed along the trails and a citadel built at the stage of al-Mada'in. Apart from isolated incidents that can be laid at the door of natural events—floods in winter and blazing heat in summer—only one actual attack is mentioned, that by the Harb tribe in

November 1752. There is no doubt that this oft-repeated triumph was the primary reason for the exceptional length of his mandate, a record in the annals of the *wilaya* of Damascus. Sultan Mahmud I sent him the kinds of sumptuous gifts usually reserved for victorious grand viziers, thereby demonstrating the immense value the Porte placed in a satisfactory hajj.

The 'Azm Palace. The haremlik courtyard. Reflections in the basin in front of the *iwan*.

Deploying his immense fortune, Asʿad Pasha carried out substantial restorations and built several edifices that redound to his fame today. In 1749, he had the madrasa that his father had set up in the Suq al-Khayyatin restored, adjoining a mosque. The same year, on the site of the old Dar al-Dhahab of the Mameluk governor Tankiz, he had a new seraglio built, on which all the craftsmen of Damascus and more than eight hundred workmen toiled for two years. The building was regarded as one of the finest, and al-Budayri bore witness that there was nothing like it in the Ottoman empire, not even the sultan's palace.[56] He had mosques and madrasas restored, overhauled the water supply, paved the Midan road between Bab Musalla and Bab Allah, enlarged the al-Kiswa bridge, and built a *hammam* in the district of Shagur. Keen to curry favor with the Shiʿites, he had a mausoleum erected above the tomb of Sayyida Zaynab. In May 1751, he started acquiring houses and shops in the Suq al-Buzuriyyin, on the site of which he planned an immense khan: begun in 1753, and costing the moderate sum of 1,100 piasters a day, it was completed in less than fourteen months and earned the admiration of the inhabitants. Al-Budayri once again observed that nothing like it had ever been built anywhere in the Muslim world.[57]

In December 1754, Sultan Mahmud I stood down in favor of his brother ʿUthman III. Envy and back-stabbings were soon to get the better of the powerful governor of Damascus, and, on January 20, 1757, he was deposed, appointed to Aleppo, and replaced by Husayn Pasha. The whole city was promptly gripped by pandemonium, with *kapikulu*s, *yerliyya*s, Druzes, Kurds, Maghrebis, Ashraf, every party, every faction, pouring into the streets armed to the teeth. Pleas from the ulemas, the *aʿyan*, and the notables were of no effect, and Damascus soon looked like a city at war, with several districts being ransacked, and monuments burned—not even mosques were spared. The disorder also extended to the villages of the Ghuta. At the beginning of September, Husayn Pasha

having refused to pay the Bedouin their usual tribute, the hajj was attacked by the Banu Sakhr and the Harb on its return journey. This was the most dreadful episode in its history: among the dead—estimated at some twenty thousand—were the sister of the sultan and many imperial dignitaries. Those who escaped the carnage wandered half-naked in the desert, without water or food. Many of those who had survived until a rescue party arrived were to die of exhaustion on their return to Damascus. The whole empire was in a state of shock and the dead were mourned in cities throughout the Muslim world. Heads rolled in Istanbul too, while a rumor spread alleging that Asʿad Pasha himself had bankrolled the attack, eager to entertain the notion that his presence at the head of the hajj was essential. The new sultan, Mustapha III, was all the more readily convinced to eliminate him as he had urgent need of fresh revenues. Asʿad Pasha was condemned to exile and, on April 14, 1758, was strangled when performing his ablutions at a *hammam* in Ankara. His fortune, estimated at more than fifty million piasters, was soon expropriated and it represented a substantial contribution to the imperial coffers. It took more than six months to unearth and to amass property, including gold, jewels, horses, weapons, textiles, and slaves, in the city and throughout the *wilaya*. Then, to ensure that nothing had been forgotten, Damascus's beautiful seraglio was completely rifled. It seemed that this time the ʿAzm had been definitively eradicated from the political scene.

The Porte then named in Damascus a veteran from the Persian wars, ʿAbd Allah Pasha. All the rebellious factions were subdued at the conclusion of pitched battles that left a substantial proportion of the city in ruin, but civil peace was at last restored: "We could sleep with our doors unlocked, said the inhabitants of Damascus."[58] During his first pilgrimage, "which he led," as Volney put it, "saber in hand, without paying a single piaster to the Arabs,"[59] ʿAbd Allah Pasha obliterated the Harb and the Banu

Sakhr, beheading their captured sheikhs. His successor, 'Uthman Pasha, made his entry into Damascus in December 1760, occupying the post for a full eleven years. He managed to moderate the price of bread and other staples, abolished many illicit taxes, restored various public buildings, had the channels refurbished, and, in 1769–70, installed in the courtyard of the Umayyad mosque a pool fed by the waters of the Barada. He even guaranteed the safety of the hajj for the entire duration of his governorship. In the provinces, 'Uthman Pasha followed a much more offensive policy than that of his predecessor, concentrating his forces against Zahir, increasingly powerful in Galilee, and attempted to counter 'Ali Bey, a Circassian Mameluk who had succeeded in making himself independent in Egypt. At the beginning of June 1771, however, as the latter's troops commanded by the emir Abu Dhahab penetrated into the district of Midan, 'Uthman Pasha in the company of senior officials, military chiefs, and many ulemas, made his escape. On June 9, Damascus was again occupied, and once again the commander of the citadel refused to yield. But, less than ten days later, to universal amazement, Abu Dhahab, whom more pressing business recalled to Cairo, withdrew from the city. After a brief return by 'Uthman Pasha, the Porte named Muhammad Pasha, grandson of Isma'il al-'Azm on his mother's side, who entered Damascus in November 1771. The situation in the provinces, however, had reached boiling point.

Determined to increase his dominion, Zahir, now in cahoots with 'Ali Bey, who had been overthrown in Cairo by Abu Dhahab, extended his control to the Hawran, while a Russian fleet, which had had the better of the Ottoman at Tshesmé in July 1770, plied the Eastern Mediterranean. On June 18, 1772, at the request of Zahir and 'Ali Bey, Russian vessels bombarded Beirut, unloaded troops, plundered the city, and, almost immediately afterwards, re-embarked. At this point in time a daring Bosnian adventurer, a certain Ahmad, whose sanguinary actions and talents as a torturer in the service of 'Ali Bey had earned him the nickname al-Jazzar, "the butcher," embarked on a brilliant career that was not long in making him the most powerful man in eighteenth-century Syria and the eventual adversary of Bonaparte; it was he who, by his resistance at Acre, was to cut off the French general's route to Damascus. After the July 1774 treaty of Kuçuk Kaynarca had put a halt to the war with Russia, the Porte decided to get rid of Zahir. In August 1775, the Ottoman fleet rode before 'Akka, where Zahir had taken refuge, while Muhammad Pasha advanced at the head of a considerable force, combining troops of his own with those of the pasha of Jerusalem, the pasha of Adana, and of Jazzar, who had recently returned from Istanbul with the rank of pasha and the indeterminate title, "*muhafiz* of the Syrian coast." The old sheikh refused the surrender conditions offered and was duly assassinated. In accordance with custom, his head was packed off to Istanbul "to be displayed to the sultan and to the people."[60] Jazzar's moment had finally arrived: busying himself with filling the power vacuum in southern Syria left by Zahir's elimination, in March 1776 he obtained the *wilaya* of Sayda with the title of vizier. Succeeding where so many wali before him had failed, he eventually managed to quell the rebels. Zahir's son, 'Ali, was slain, and his brothers and their children had their throats cut. Jazzar then occupied Mount Lebanon and the plain of the Beka'a, subduing the Druzes and the *mutawali*. His pitiless extortions and skill in stimulating trade gained him substantial financial rewards that allowed him transform his bands—Bosnian and Albanian horsemen and Maghrebi infantry—into the most powerful army in all Syria. He transferred the headquarters of the *wilaya* of Sayda to 'Akka, whose defenses he bolstered, while he strived his utmost to obtain that of Damascus. On January 19, 1785, with the dual threat of a new war with Russia in the north and of a

Wahhabi invasion from the south creating ideal conditions for a strong hand on the Syrian tiller, he finally secured the much-coveted *wilaya*, while two of his relations were named at Sayda and Tripoli. His authority thus extended over the whole of central and southern Syria, including—something inestimable in the eyes of the Porte—the mountains of Lebanon, hotbeds of agitation and insurgency. From his first nomination at Sayda in 1776 to his death in 1804, the intrepid Bosnian exercised his power for a total of more than a quarter century—a record in the annals of Ottoman Syria. In Damascus, complaints from those he governed brought about his transfer on three occasions, but each time he managed to have himself reinstated. His tyrannical absolutism recalled the worst days of the Mameluk era. Of limitless greed, he procured ownership of all the harvests, made himself contractor of all farm-rents, and extended his monopoly over virtually every major trading business. An expert torturer, his cruelty was unbelievable. According to Volney, in Tyre in 1784, he disemboweled a mason with an axe.[61] During the siege of Beirut, he had every prisoner who fell into his hands walled up alive, leaving only the head exposed to enemy fire. He impaled, hanged, drowned, and quartered; he slit throats and severed noses, hands, ears, and other organs: the French Consul to 'Akka, Renaudot, dubbed him the "most ferocious, bloodthirsty, and insatiable tyrant."[62] This was the man Bonaparte was about to find barring his path.

Margaret Thomas, The hajj returning to Damascus. (Painted at the beginning of the twentieth century.)

191

The return of the Franks—Bonaparte in Syria

Before the end of the century, the most serious threat to the territorial integrity of the empire was going to come, not from Russia, but against all expectations, from France. Departing from the ancien régime's policy of conciliation, which had been practiced since Francis I, in 1798, revolutionary secular France set out on the conquest of Egypt. The plans that Leibniz had put before Louis XIV, and which Baron de Tott had in turn revived in 1778, were finally to be put into execution. It was no more a question—as it had been with earlier colonial enterprises—of promulgating or imposing Christianity, or, leaning on Biblical antecedents,[63] of exterminating idolaters in order to purloin immense territories emptied of their population, but instead, as faithful disciples of Saint-Simon and Condorcet, of forcing on a people considered as "backward" what is commonly termed "civilization." Though thinly veiling the true goals of the expedition, this ambition is well conveyed by the foreword to that compendium of European colonial hypocrisy entitled *The Description of Egypt*: "To punish the oppressors of our trade . . . to abolish the tyranny of the Mameluks, to extend irrigation and agriculture, to provide permanent communications between the Mediterranean and the Arabian Gulf, to set up trading concerns, to present the instructive example of European industry before the Orient, and, finally, to palliate the condition of the inhabitants and offer them all the benefits of developed civilization."[64]

In July 24, 1798, after overcoming the Mameluks at the Battle of the Pyramids, Bonaparte made his entry into Cairo. In Syria, after an initial period of astonishment and disquiet occasioned by the overwhelming military superiority of the French, Jazzar reinforced the fortifications of 'Akka and placed the other cities on a defensive posture, establishing garrisons at Jaffa and al-'Arish. Then, in order to prevent intelligence being passed from the Christians to the invader, he had them expelled from the harbors in which, attracted by trade and protected by their consuls, they had settled in droves. The troops gathered to drive the French out of Egypt were concentrated in Damascus. On February 10, 1799, six months after the naval disaster at Aboukir, and convinced that his arrival in Syria would be sure to ignite a popular uprising against Jazzar, Bonaparte left Cairo at the head of an army of twelve thousand men. In mid-March, the siege of 'Akka began, but, in spite of the defeat of the army from Damascus at the battle of Mount Tabor on April 16, operations stagnated. Jazzar received constant reinforcements; neither mortar nor mine breached the ramparts; there was a dearth of ammunition and supplies; the troops lost discipline; and plague, typhus, and dysentery accounted for dozens of soldiers a day. On May 10, after one final fling had come to naught, Bonaparte halted engagements and, on May 17, issued the order to retreat. On June 14, what remained of the French task force arrived back in Cairo. In the night of August 22 to 23, leaving his army in the command of Kléber, Bonaparte boarded the frigate *La Muiron* and clandestinely sailed off to France, recalled by the *Directoire* concerned at reverses suffered in Italy and on the Rhine front. Encircled in Alexandria by British and Ottoman troops, the last French forces, after problematic negotiations, evacuated Egypt in November 1801. For France, the much-vaunted expedition had resulted—in addition to considerable loss of life—in total fiasco.

Damascus, "jewel of the empire"—
the last architectural masterworks

After all the destruction and slaughter, Syria ended the eighteenth century bled dry. The disastrous effects of internecine rebellion compounded the general decline of the empire, the impoverishment caused by external wars, the tyranny, corruption, exactions, insults, and diverse abuses. This was even before the scorched earth policy employed by the French Army in its retreat following its failure at 'Akka, and southern Syria had been literally devastated by the wars prosecuted against Zahir and 'Ali Bey. The report Volney drew up in 1785 makes for dire reading: Palestine was one of the most devastated provinces in all Syria, Ludd [Lydda] was no more than hovels and debris, Jaffa was as nothing, Ramla was almost as devastated as Ludd and in the enceinte one walked through debris, Gaza was a defenseless fort, populated by two thousand souls at most.[65] As for the peasants—ruined by the greed of the pashas and their agents, by usury, degradation, and insecurity—their condition was utterly wretched. Throughout a country crippled by shortages, they were reduced to eating barley bread, onions, ash-cooked or boiled acorn mash, lentils, and water. Depopulation in the countryside consequently accelerated, as the traveler W. G. Browne, who stayed in the Middle East in the last decade of the century, remarked: "The villages are in general are so much deserted, that, in the neighborhood of Aleppo, where, within the present century, stood three hundred villages, there now

remain no more than ten or twelve."[66] Yet among all the wreckage, a few Syrian towns—especially in the northern sector—managed to enjoy relative prosperity: on the coast, Tripoli, Latakia, Beirut, and, in the interior, Aleppo and Damascus. It was Beirut that benefited most from the prevailing circumstances. Thanks to the good governance and tolerance of the Druze, to the promotion of commerce, the silk industry, and European traders, it had become "the richest and most populated city on the entire coast . . . a storehouse for flourishing trade."[67] Profiting from the decline of Sayda, it was soon to become, in spite of problematic communications through the Lebanese mountains, the principal port for Damascus. Aleppo, meanwhile, even if it could no longer be called the first port of the Levant, remained late in the century the most active focus for trade in Syria.

As for Damascus, this was probably the city that traversed the century the least scathed. Venture de Paradis esteemed it populous and extremely wealthy,[68] and its *wilaya*, according to Volney, was the least ruined in Syria, thanks to the good management and lengthy mandate of the 'Azm.[69] It remained the quintessential city of pleasure, "one of the most beautiful and richest cities of the empire," Charles de Sainte-Maure declared.[70] Among its monuments, it was the Umayyad mosque—still forbidden to Christians and considered by them a church—that awakened the greatest curiosity. In this respect, the English Orientalist Richard Pococke was the first—and only one of his century—to show genuine archeological awareness. Although he still considered the building as a onetime church, he was the first to observe the rather untoward nature of its composition; more especially, he was the first to report that, according to observers relying on texts by Arab historians, the mosque would have been erected by Caliph al-Walid.[71] If the city's craft and commercial activities were no more the source of wonder they had once been, its fine bazaars—

The Umayyad Mosque as viewed by the Russian traveler Barsky in the eighteenth century. Convinced that the mosque was in reality a church, the artist had no hesitation in adding crosses to the minarets and the Dome of the Eagle.

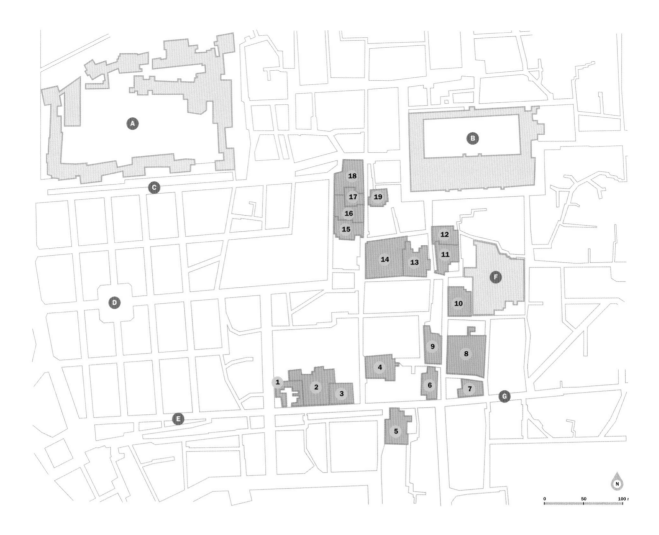

well-covered and whose width contrasted with the narrowness of the other streets—was almost always remarked upon. Its artisans still enjoyed a higher reputation than those of other towns in the Turkish Empire, and even if once-renowned trades, such as the manufacture of saber blades, were in patent decline, it still produced, "in large quantities and quite artfully," cotton and silk fabrics, as well as such items as dried fruit, sweetmeats, roses, apricots, and peaches.[72]

The peace and relative security the city enjoyed in the eighteenth century under the government of the 'Azm favored the construction of new buildings: madrasas, khans, palaces, and residences. Nurtured over the previous two centuries, the fondness for commercial buildings on a grand scale continued, and several khans saw the light of day to the south

of the Umayyad mosque in a district that had attained its definitive layout by the end of the century. Yet, whereas earlier edifices—apart from the *bazistan* constructed by Murad Pasha before 1608—had all been hypaethral, henceforth, in accordance with the Ottoman tradition, the central space was domed over: the Khan Süleyman Pasha (1732) possessed two cupolas, the Khan al-Safarjalaniyya (before 1757) three, the Khan al-Sidraniyya (before 1757) two, and the Khan As'ad Pasha (1753) boasted nine.

Begun in 1732 and completed in 1736, the Khan Süleyman Pasha is entirely coursed in alternating black and white, in keeping with Mameluk tradition. It opens to the southern side of Straight Street through a door surmounted by a foundation inscription and two small windows of the guardian's

The khans of Damascus. **A** Citadel. **B** Umayyad Mosque. **C** Al-Hamidiyya suq. **D** Hariqa quarter. **E** Midhat Pasha suq. **F** 'Azm Palace. **G** Straight Street.

1 Khan al-Dikka (19th century?). **2** Khan al-Zayt (16th century?). **3** Khan Jaqmaq (1420). **4** Khan al-Jukhiyya (c. 1560). **5** Khan Sulayman Pasha (1732–1733). **6** Khan al-Fauqani (18th century?).

7 Khan al-Ruzz (18th century?). **8** Khan As'ad Pasha (1752–1753). **9** Khan al-'Amud (17th century?). **10** Khan al-Sawwaf (19th century?). **11** Khan al-Sadraniyya (mid-18th century).

12 Khan al-Safarjalani (mid-18th century). **13** Khan al-Tutun (18th–19th century). **14** Khan al-Harir/Darwish Pasha (1573–1574). **15** Khan al Za'faranjiyya (19th century).

194   **16** Khan al-Jumruq/Bazistan Murad Pasha (1608–1609). **17** Khan Shayk Qatana (18th–19th century). **18** Khan al-Muradiyya (16th–19th century). **19** Khan al-Haramayn (19th century).

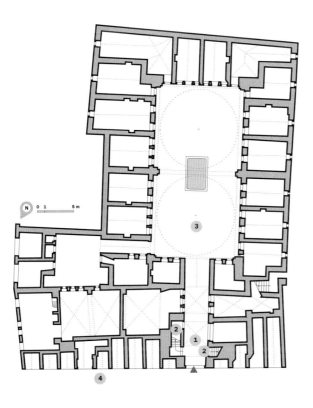

room located on a floor above. A vestibule covered with two groined vaults and flanked on either side by a staircase and a store gave onto a rectangular yard of approximately 36 × 79 feet (11 × 24 m), centered on a large basin and roofed by two cupolas on pendentives (today collapsed) borne on seven large pointed arches. On the ground floor, seventeen stores with barrel vaults open through a door with lintel and transom. On the floor above, a gallery gives access to nineteen rooms, also barrel-arched. In 1906, according to the Baedeker Guide, these were devoted primarily to silks and Persian carpets.[73] Not long ago, the ground floor was still used as a warehouse for grain, coffee, aniseed, olive oil, and jute, while the floor above was occupied by tailors' workshops and import-export offices. It was closed in May 2003; soon to be restored, it will perhaps be reopened as a hotel.

Top. The Khan Süleyman Pasha in 1989. The edifice is today threatened by conversion into a tourist hotel.
Bottom. Plan of the Khan Süleyman Pasha. **1** Vestibule at the entrance. **2** Stairs to the floor above. **3** Courtyard with central pool. **4** Suq Midhat Pasha (Straight Street).

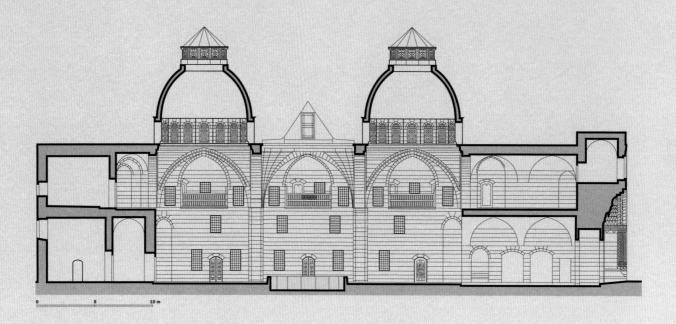

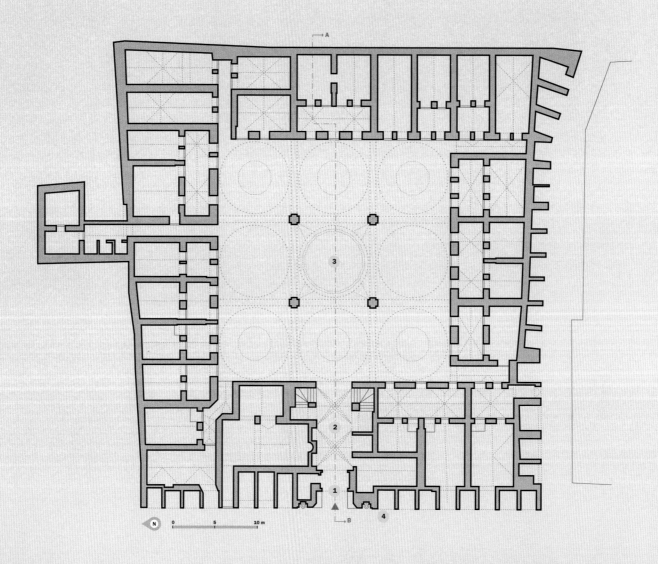

Khan As'ad Pasha. *Top*. Cross section east–west through A–B (the section pre-dates the rebuilding of the domes).

Bottom. Plan of the ground floor **1** Entrance and monumental gate. **2** Vestibule with side staircases going up to the first floor.

3 Courtyard with central pool. **4** Suq al- Buzuriyyeh.

Located at the Suq al-Buzuriyya, on the site of two *qaysariyya*s, several houses and shops that were demolished for the occasion, the Khan As'ad Pasha was erected between February and November 1753. It is the largest commercial building in the city and one of its most famous monuments, an object of tireless admiration on the part of travelers of all origins. In 1833, the French poet Lamartine, who considered it the "finest khan in the Orient," ventured to write: "a people whose architects are able to design and whose workmen are able to carry out such a monument . . . cannot be dead to the arts."[74] Alternatively coursed in black and white, it consists of four ranges surrounding a courtyard centered on a basin and covered with cupolas resting on pillars. Lamartine considered its entryway, which opens in the center of the west front, as "one of the pieces of Moresque architecture with the richest detailing and of the most imposing effect one could hope to see anywhere in the world."[75] Four cruciform columns divide the court into nine equal sections, each roofed with a dome on pendentives borne on mildly pointed arches, a system that possessed antecedents in Damascus in the columnated hall of the citadel. The cupolas, which had collapsed at the time of the 1759 earthquake, have recently been re-erected. Built in bricks and mortar, and surmounted by skylights to a height of over seventy-two feet (22 m), the domes are supported on sixteen-sided drums, each with small apertures. Two preserve on their undersurface a layer of stucco decorated with stars, rosettes, and floral or geometric motifs. A groin-arched gallery on the floor above runs around the courtyard and provides access to rooms that are all barrel-arched and furnished with two windows—one giving on to the gallery, the other to the exterior. Strongly marked by Ottoman tradition, this vast commercial structure is without precedent or equivalent, neither in Damascus nor in the rest of Syria. Much more than an indication of Damascus's prosperity in the eighteenth century, it appears above

Top. Charles Robertson (1844–1891), A caravan arrives in the Khan As'ad Pasha. Watercolor. Private collection.

Bottom. The gateway to the Khan As'ad Pasha. Late nineteenth-century engraving.

197

all to have been a prestige development, devised on the one hand to display the power of its promoter, and, on the other, to insure the significant revenue from the many waqfs constituted for the benefit of his descendants. Recently, it was still being used as warehouse for traders in gunny bags, spices, household utensils, etc. On April 5, 1973, it was listed as a historic building and the occupants relocated. Today restoration is complete, though its function is yet to be decided.

The Fathi *hammam*, the best conserved of the eighteenth-century baths with those in the 'Azm palace, was built in 1745 on the main street of Midan by the celebrated *defterdar* al-Falaqinsi. It is one of the few baths in Damascus blessed with a genuinely monumental frontage. Coursed in polychrome, in the middle it opens through four windows with grilles flanked by two large recesses with trefoil arches, one

Khan As'ad Pasha. *Top*. Arches and domes. *Bottom*. Vault of the entrance vestibule.

Top. General view of the interior of the Khan As'ad Pasha.

Bottom. Gallery on the first floor of the Khan As'ad Pasha.

199

set back to the north sheltering the entrance door, and another to the south, a *sabil*, namely, a public fountain. Betraying no subsequent alteration, its plan follows that of the eighteenth-century public *hammam* in which the hot-room became predominant. After long serving as a granary and warehouse, it has just been refurbished.

In addition to its khans, madrasas and *hammam*s, the eighteenth century has also left us the oldest houses in Damascus. Of those from the end of the Mameluk era and the early centuries of Ottoman rule there remains, in effect, little more than windows, stretches of wall, or doorframes integrated here or there into a contemporary fabric. According to the antique Mediterranean and Near East tradition, dictated in particular by the demands of the climate, houses turn inwards, with all the rooms opening onto an inner courtyard. The contrast between the appearance of the façades—sober, austere, and even shabby—and the opulence within has been pointed out many times. "For the most part, the houses are only of earth," wrote d'Arvieux in 1660. "They do not look much from the outside, but the insides are quite different. The apartments are large and well presented; they are clean, well furnished, with paneling and ceilings, and are painted in the manner of the country. They spare neither gold nor lapis lazuli. Very few of these houses fail to possess a fountain for adornment and convenience."[76] This discrepancy is often encapsulated in a well-turned phrase: "A nugget of gold in a husk of clay,"[77] or "Hovel without, delectable palace within."[78]

Smooth and without ornament, the wall on the ground floor—laid in stone to provide added protection from damp—seldom betrays the limit between adjoining housing units. It is pierced by a single main door, the generally sash windows being always placed on the floor above. Built in studwork, this floor, with a roofed terrace, almost invariably juts out from the frontage to offer shade and freshness on the street-side: it has a timber frame in poplar from the Ghuta, with raw brick filling the spaces, the whole rendered with a mix of earth and straw. The appearance is earthy, sometimes rural, sometimes weather-beaten, and was hardly to the taste of the most travelers: "The outsides of the houses are just sun-dried brick," wrote Maundrell in 1696. "Or else a kind of mire as coarse as seen in the vilest hamlet. These kinds of buildings present several inconveniences, one of them being that, in heavy rain, the muck becomes soft and turns the streets into a sort of swamp."[79]

Contrary to Cairo, characterized by verticality and density, the habitat in Damascus developed horizontally around interior courtyards that can occupy between 25 and 48 percent of the built area, the courtyards growing in size in proportion to the wealth of the residence.[80] An essential component of family life, the primary function of the courtyard is to regulate the temperature: in summer it forms a reservoir in which the cool night air accumulates; in winter it helps to heat the rooms to the north. This function is aided by the vegetation, a further source of shade and freshness, and especially by the constant presence of water, which, on evaporating, lowers the temperature and releases moisture into the air. The center of the courtyard is occupied by a large pool located in line with the *iwan* and known as a *bahra*. In the standard arrangement, the *iwan*, a vast feature over two floors, is in the main covered by a vault opening broadly onto the court, and stands to the southern side in the shade to keep as cool as possible. It is flanked by two rooms: one called the *qa'a*, as a rule richly decorated, and another, in general accessible from the entrance corridor that is designed—especially in Muslim families—for the reception of male guests. Protected from the sun, the southern side is used for the most part during the hottest times of the summer day. Various elaborately adorned reception rooms, including the winter hall, occupy the north side. Occasionally slightly raised above a basement, this latter hall consists in a lower

Page 202, top left. Bayt al-Siba'i. Façade giving onto the haremlik court in the ceremonial hall shown p. 201. In the 1950s, Bayt al-Siba'i served as the residence of the Belgian consul. *Page 202, top right.* Bayt al-Siba'i. Ornamental detail on an arched doorway. *Page 202, bottom. Selamlik* courtyard.

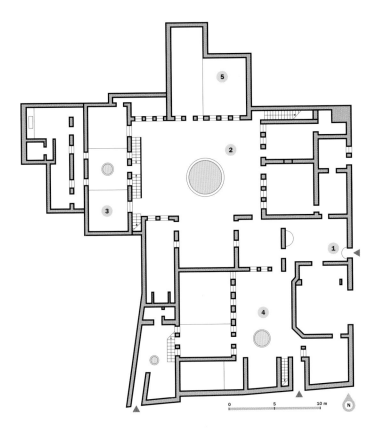

section, the *'ataba*, separated from an upper section, the *mastaba*, by a low marble or cedar-wood balustrade. Centered on a *fisqiyya* (a small ornamental fountain), the *'ataba* was where servants and slaves congregated and where shoes were removed before proceeding to the *mastaba*, bordered on three sides by cushions, chairs, and couches of all kinds. The east and west sides of the courtyard are occupied by staircases and various locales serving as a library or offices. On the floor above, almost always accessible through a gallery opening to the court, are the reception rooms and bedrooms, those to the north being used in the winter and those to the south in summer.

Variations on this basic organization appear that reflect for the majority the owners' wealth and, to a lesser extent, religious affiliation. The most humble houses, around 1,000 square feet (100 sq. m) in area, have only one relatively small courtyard, sometimes without a central pool. The most luxurious, with an average surface area of 12,000 square feet (1,100 sq. m), possess two or even three intercommunicating

courts. In Islamic residences, preserving the privacy of the family assigns a specific function to each courtyard: the largest, the haremlik, is reserved for women and family members; the smallest, most often directly linked to the preceding, leads to the domestic areas: kitchen, *hammam*, storeroom, servants' lodgings, etc. A third, the *selamlik*, is allocated to guests and is generally provided with private sanitation, a well, and a small kitchen for making tea, coffee, "sweets," or sorbets. This radical separation between private and public spheres is also apparent in the treatment of the entrances: whereas the *selamlik* is directly accessible from the entrance, one can reach the haremlik only down a dogleg passageway—replaced in more modest houses by a curtain or folding-screen—so that visitors do not lose their way and also to prevent unintentionally wandering or wantonly prying eyes from violating the privacy of the home.[81] If the Jewish house often resembles the Muslim one—with the proviso that there the southern *iwan* can act as a domestic synagogue—the Christian house generally presents a single, very large court, accessible directly from the street, and is often provided on the western side with a second *iwan* preceded by a porch protecting it from the rays of the rising sun.

Several eighteenth-century houses remain, scattered about the various quarters of the city. In the Muslim districts are to be found the Ahmad al-Siba'i house, dated, according to two inscriptions, to 1769–70 and to 1773–74; the al-Nabulusi house dating from 1780; the al-Quwatli house dating from 1797; the 'Abd al-Qadir al-Jaza'iri house, the oldest part of which dates from the end of the eighteenth century; and the al-Safarjalani house. In the Christian quarter there is the house of Antun Franjiya; in the Jewish quarter, the Lisbuna, Dahdah, and Mu'allim houses. In 1807, according to the Spanish traveler Badia y Leyblich, *alias* 'Ali Bey, Damascus possessed more than five hundred magnificent houses of large size worthy of the name "palace."[82]

Page 203. Bayt al-Siba'i. Ceremonial room of the haremlik.

Pages 204–205. Detail of the ceiling of the great *iwan* of Bayt Dahdah.

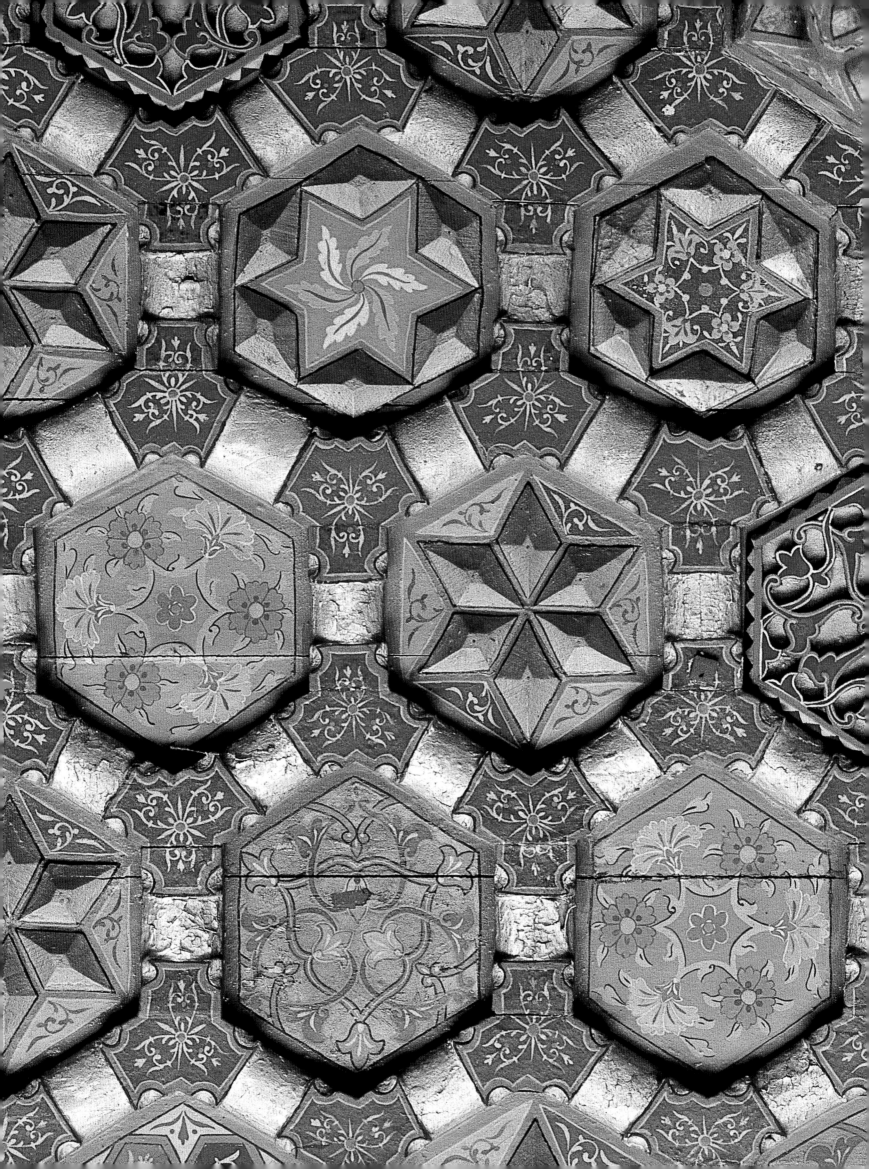

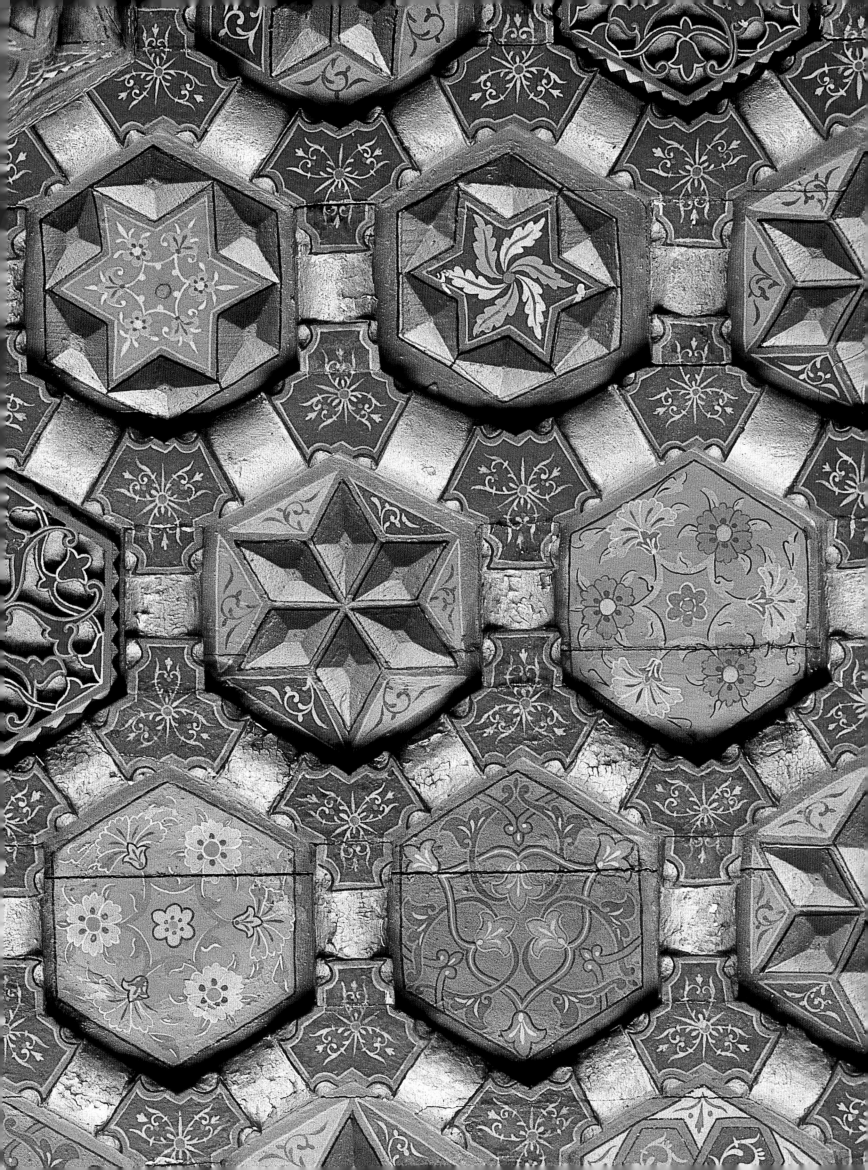

Plan of the 'Azm Palace. **1** Entrance hall. **2** Porter's lodge. **3** Twisting corridor leading to haremlik. **4** Bedrooms. **5** Terrace stairways. **6** Kitchen for preparing coffee. **7** Iwan. **8** Main reception (*qa'a*), damaged in 1925 and since rebuilt. **9** Chamber. **10** Room with painted-wood paneling. **11** Columnated portico with *mastaba* at each end. **12** Chamber. **13** Small reception room. **14** Iwan. **15** Hall with painted-wood paneling. **16** Bath with changing- and rest-room, *tepidarium*, steam-room, sweat-room, massage parlors and boiler with under-floor heating. **17** Service entrance to the bathhouse and fuel store. **18** Vaulted storerooms placed above a cellar accessible by way of a staircase. **19** Chambers. **20** Kitchen with chimney. **21** Stairway to the terraces. **22** Stables.

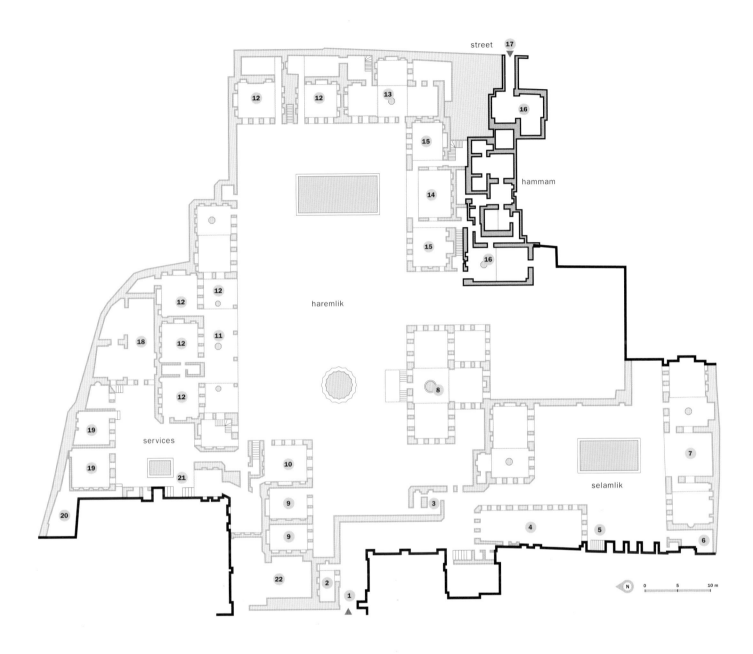

The most celebrated and luxurious of all eighteenth-century residences is obviously the palace that As'ad Pasha al-'Azm had built from 1749 on, south of the Umayyad mosque. The means deployed were impressive: all workmen and craftsmen in Damascus were commandeered; the suqs were ransacked, and stones and joinery removed; the antique monuments of the Hawran were dismantled; the ancient columns of Dera'a and Bosra were dragged off to Damascus on oxcarts; the course of the Banias was diverted to extract stone blocks, so that the residents had no water for ten days. As'ad Pasha himself criss-crossed the city in a ceaseless quest for precious materials, seizing—by honeyed words or by coercion—a cypress here, a basin, or marble

Facing page, top. Bayt al-Siba'i. Detail of the ceiling.
Facing page, bottom. Bayt Dahdah. Reception room opening onto the main *iwan.*

207

plaque, there, some basalt or timber. . . . The work was undertaken in double-quick time: three days before leaving on his eighth pilgrimage, As'ad Pasha set up his wives in the harem; on his return, all was finished and great festivals celebrated the event, also commemorated by inscriptions painted on the woodwork. "This is the house of felicity, smiling and well lit, raised with the assistance of He who helps, the Almighty. The sun of grandeur shines in its sky; it has no equal. Happiness lives within forever . . . glory is its handmaiden . . . power its confidante."[83]

Little affected by the many alterations made over the intervening centuries, the plan is in all points in conformity with that of substantial Muslim residences of the time. Accessible from the street

through a bent passageway, the *selamlik* includes an *iwan* and several reception rooms surrounding a court planted with orange trees and cooled by a rectangular central pool. From the *selamlik*, another dogleg corridor, closed off by three successive doors, leads to the haremlik—the largest and richest in the palace—the dwelling place of the pasha and his family. Paved with colored stone, the court is adorned with two basins, one rectangular, the other polygonal and a garden with orange and lemon trees, jasmine, and myrtle. On the northern side, the rooms are sheltered from the harsh rays of the sun by a portico whose attractive five pointed arches rest on recarved ancient columns and reused capitals. To the south, a large *iwan* opens out in line with the rectangular basin, while near the entrance stands the *qa'a*, a particularly luxurious ceremonial room.

Accessible by a double staircase and slightly raised, it consists of four areas conforming to a T-shaped plan: a lower zone centered on a basin with water jets and three higher sections opening into large pointed arches with black and white marble arch stones falling onto consoles with *muqarnas*. Still imbued by Mameluk tradition, the decor, with a frontage coursed in alternating ocher and black and white, is extremely neat. The door, topped by an inscription commemorating its foundation in 1749, is framed by a decor in marble, mosaic, and mother-of-pearl. The walls are paneled to halfway in polychrome marble surmounted by a timber cornice forming cells, each decorated with a painted bouquet of flowers. Set on fire at the time of the events that shook Damascus in 1925, the *qa'a* was entirely reerected in 1934. The haremlik includes, moreover, a series of rooms opening onto the court, all of the same type: a low room, sometimes cooled by a small fountain, and an upper one elevated by about twelve inches (30 cm). To halfway up, joinery decorated in relief with paintings ringed by an old-gold fillet wraps the

'Azm Palace. The rear of the great *iwan* of the haremlik.

walls, whose upper reaches—sometimes pierced by openwork plaster windows set with stained glass—are simply whitewashed. The sumptuous ceilings are profusely decorated: painted beams with floral motifs, high-relief geometric interlace, octagonal coffers, etc. In certain specific areas—in particular on the facing of the arches over the doors—there appears a decorative technique peculiar to Damascus, where the motif, generally a bunch of flowers, is initially incised then filled in with stained cement. In 1922, the 'Azm palace, then jointly owned by sixty-eight descendants of As'ad Pasha, was bought by the French government to house the French Institute of Archaeology and Islamic Art.

Doorframe in the 'Azm Palace. Colored stone-paste decor.

Above. Qa'a northwest of Bayt Khalid al-'Azm: the *qa'a* derives its name *mataha* (labyrinth) from the marble *fisqiyya* and was restored between 1970 and 1983 (the residence itself is named after the 1962 prime minister Khalid al-'Azm).
Facing page, top. 'Azm Palace: The *qa'a* of the haremlik. *Facing page, bottom.* Bayt Khalid al-'Azm: The *qa'a* of the haremlik.

Page 212, top. 'Azm Palace: Façade on the court of the *qa'a* of the haremlik. *Page 212, bottom.* Bayt Khalid al-'Azm. Façade giving onto the court of the *qa'a* of the haremlik. *Page 213.* Bayt Khalid al-'Azm: Door to a room giving onto a little yard. *Pages 214–215.* 'Azm Palace: The main haremlik *iwan.*

Top. Carved decoration of the side of a *sunduq* (wooden coffer). Late nineteenth or early twentieth century. 'Azm Palace. *Bottom.* Bayt Khalid al-'Azm: Detail of woodwork. *Facing page.* 'Azm Palace, *qa'a* of the haremlik. Detail of the ceiling of the central *mastaba. Top.* The center. *Bottom.* The edges.

216

Egyptian conquest, European interference,
and religious strife

Jazzar died at 'Akka on April 23, 1804, shortly after obtaining the *wilaya* of Damascus for the third time. Now rid of a troublesome master, Bashir II (1788–1840) could consolidate his position in the Lebanese mountains. Although a Maronite, he was always regarded as the "sovereign prince of the Druzes and all the mountains in the Lebanon,"[84] and instituted a policy of reconciliation with representatives of the Porte. As soon as quarrels broke out among the pashas following the death of Jazzar, Bashir II put his weight behind the official candidate. The Wahhabi threat afforded him a fresh opportunity of showing his allegiance to the Ottoman authority. Followers of a "fundamentalist" movement founded in the eighteenth century by Muhammad b. 'Abd al-Wahhab (1703–1792), and driven by both political and religious ambitions, the Wahhabi preached the restoration of Islam in its original purity, as well as the gathering of the Arab nations into a single great Sunni state. After unifying the Nadj, with the support of the Sa'ud family, they turned their eyes beyond the Peninsula. In 1802, they seized Kerbala, massacred its inhabitants and ransacked the mausoleum of the Husayn imam. Occupying Medina, Mecca, and Jeddah, they later blocked the pilgrimage train. In 1810, they penetrated into Syria and threatened Damascus, but were forced to retire before a force combining the city's wali, Yusuf Pasha, Bashir II, and Süleyman Pasha, the wali of 'Akka. Compelled to restore safety to pilgrimage road and authority over the Holy Cities, Sultan Mahmud II appointed Muhammad 'Ali pasha of Egypt to carry the fight to the Wahhabi. A powerful army commanded by his son Ibrahim Pasha marched through Arabia and, seizing the oasis of Dar'iyya, put an end to the dissenting kingdom, whose king 'Abd Allah b. Sa'ud was decapitated in Istanbul on December 17, 1818.

This victory, which gained him authority over the Holy Cities, increased both the prestige and the ambitions of Muhammad 'Ali. He availed himself of a "national" army made up of Egyptian peasants recruited by conscription; this was a well-trained, well-equipped army, organized on the European model, and stiffened by French officers who had come to Egypt at the Restoration. On March 1, 1811, massacring the Mameluks in the citadel at Cairo, he broke down the resistance of the beys supported by the English. He then set to modernizing the government and education, developing the exploitation of Egyptian resources, creating new agriculture and industries, and opening up Egyptian society to the outside world. In Syria, he played a mediating role in internal rivalries, maintaining excellent relations with Bashir II and 'Abdallah, the pasha of 'Akka. In 1824, Mahmud II once again requested his assistance—this time to subdue a Greek insurrection. Ibrahim Pasha seized Crete before disembarking in Morea, but was constrained to retreat after intervention by England, Russia, and France and the destruction of the Turkish and Egyptian fleets in the Bay of Navarin on October 20, 1827. Signed on September 14, 1829, the Treaty of Andrinople, which recognized the independence of Greece and the autonomy of Serbia, Moldavia, and Valachia, heralded the dismemberment of the Ottoman Empire. The imperialism of the Great Powers now extended throughout the Mediterranean. On June 14, 1830, French troops landed in Algeria. Bogged down in Syria, the Porte could not intervene, and in Orania resistance organized around the figure of the emir 'Abd al-Qadir. These events had great repercussions in Syria, as Joseph Michaud observed in 1831: "The indefinable fear of a French expeditionary force circulates among the Muslim population of Damascus; here, much more than in other cities of the Orient, the news of the taking of Algiers has resounded like a roll of thunder."[85]

Failing to obtain Crete and Morea, which had been promised to him in exchange for his intervention in Greece, Muhammad 'Ali demanded from Mahmud II the government of Syria. Faced with the sultan's refusal, he prepared a military offensive under what seemed like favorable auspices. For so long on the defensive, the empire was tottering; the Janissaries—that solid bulwark of the throne—had been put to the sword in Damascus five years previously, the wali Salim Pasha had just been assassinated during a popular uprising, and Aleppo's troops were bogged down in Mesopotamia. To France, which granted him its support and hastened to interpret his actions as a renaissance of Arab "nationalism" against Turkish "tyranny," 'Ali

Ibrah'm marche a pied à la tête de ses troupes

presented himself as continuing the work of Bonaparte by introducing "civilization" to Syria and regenerating the Ottoman Empire. To the Syrian peoples, he postured as a defender of justice and of Islam, acting in the name of the one true caliph, the sharif of Mecca, who happened to have been dependent on him since the conquest of the Hijaz. At the end of November 1831, 'Akka was besieged by a task force of thirty-five thousand men commanded by Ibrahim Pasha and Süleyman Pasha (the onetime Captain Sèves, toughened in the Napoleonic wars, Grouchy's aide-de-camp demobilized after Waterloo). Breaking with his policy of loyalty towards the Porte, Bashir II joined the assailants and placed the coastal cities on the defensive. Succeeding where Bonaparte had failed, Ibrahim Pasha took 'Akka on May 27, 1832, after a six-month siege, occupying Damascus shortly afterwards. Mahmud II, having first had Muhammad 'Ali branded as a traitor and rebel by the ulemas, dispatched an army under the orders of Husayn Pasha. That army overcome, Ibrahim Pasha penetrated into Anatolia, crushed a second Ottoman army at Konya, advancing on to Kütahya, and menacing Istanbul. Turning undaunted to a former enemy, Mahmud II called for assistance from Russia, which sent to the Bosphorus a powerful squadron whose immediate withdrawal was demanded by France and England. This the Russians accepted in exchange for Egyptian forces evacuating Anatolia. An agreement was finally signed at Kütahya between the Ottomans and Muhammad 'Ali on March 29, 1833: Ibrahim Pasha withdrew from Anatolia but kept Syria, Cilicia, and the Hijaz, while his father, confirmed as leader of Egypt, was presented with Crete. For the first time, the fate of Syria had been sealed in Western chancelleries; the intervention of the Great Powers was subsequently going to prove a constant factor in Ottoman political life.

Ibrahim Pasha divided Syria into five pashaliks—Aleppo, Damascus, Tripoli, Acre, and Gaza—and set up a new administration centered at Damascus, whose

Ibrahim Pasha marching at the head of his troops. Watercolor print after an original by M. J.-A. Beaucé (before 1847).

governorship was offered to a member of his family, Sharif Pasha. Inspired by the West, his hastily implemented reforms turned traditional life upside-down. Dignitaries saw their authority usurped by functionaries, the police force and mechanisms of justice were overhauled on the French model, and the ulemas were confined to dealing with personal matters. Representative councils were instituted, composed of both Jews and Christians. The Bedouin and all forms of highway robbery were violently opposed, corruption was severely repressed, while agriculture and industry were encouraged. However, many reforms occasioned deep dissatisfaction among Muslims: the mushrooming of European consulates, the abuses of consular protection, the extension of personal taxation—hitherto imposed only on dhimmi—and of conscription, the increased wealth of a new class of Christians and the political equality granted to the Christians, who were from now able to enter government and build churches as they liked. For their part, the Maronites, and their religious hierarchy in particular, viewed this policy of centralization as an intolerable aggression, as well as eroding their autonomy and privileges. The cavalierly imposed construction of an allegedly "modern" state thus met with almost universal dissatisfaction. Events naturally reinforced community consciousness and tensions worsened between Christian and Muslim, Druze and Maronite. This disastrous policy—during which Syrian society experienced its first contacts with "Western modernity"—was to herald an uninterrupted stream of crises which, exacerbated if not catalyzed by shameless intervention by the European Powers, continue today to have grave repercussions on the unity of the Middle East.

Traveling through Syria less than a year after the Egyptian invasion, Lamartine attests to the unpopularity of Ibrahim Pasha's regime:

> The officers and soldiers of the pasha of Egypt . . . are on their guard at Damascus. . . . News of the slightest setback in Syria for Ibrahim would be the signal for a general uprising and ferocious fighting in Damascus. The thirty thousand Armenian Christians who live in the city are terrified and are sure to be massacred if ever the Turks gain the upper hand. The Muslims are irritated by the equality that Ibrahim Pasha has introduced between them and the Christians. At the moment, some of these misuse their tolerance and insult their enemies by violating their customs, succeeding only in embittering their fanaticism.[86]

Naturally enough this "fanaticism" was exacerbated every time Christian provocation went unpunished. Fanned by the Porte and repressed viciously with the assistance of a faithful ally—the Maronite emir, Bashir II—the first rebellions broke out in 1834 in southern Syria, at Nablus, gaining Tripoli, and later the region of Latakia. In 1838, all the Druze "fiefs"—the Hawran, the Chouf and the Wadi al-Taym—boiled over, and Damascus found itself under threat. In early summer, the combined forces of Ibrahim and Bashir II finally succeeded in crushing the rebellion. Ibrahim Pasha, whose resources had been hemorrhaged by the need to maintain the occupying force, had recourse to exceptional taxation, almost always levied with the utmost brutality. Édouard Blondel records echoes of this in 1838:

> Tirelessly, the Egyptian despot toils to the ruin of his country; he will soon leave these wretched people with nothing but the memory of his wealth and his lavishness. The exorbitant taxes he imposes on the inhabitants under a thousand ever-changing pretexts are not enough for him. Lately, he has devised for the Damascenes a compulsory loan scheme. To this purpose, he has sent each trader, without due process, an order to pay to his treasurer five, ten, fifteen, even twenty thousand piasters, according to whatever he sees fit to assign. Those forced to advance money are under no illusions; they know they will never recover a *para* of it.[87]

The majority of observers and travelers—even those who, like J.-J. Ampère, persisted in seeing Muhammad 'Ali as a continuator of "the civilizing task begun by France"[88]— considered the policy of Ibrahim Pasha as a veritable economic catastrophe, laying the impoverishment of Syria at his door. "This government is envious of all and any economic prosperity," wrote Joseph Michaud, "it has meddled in every industry with any prospect of rich pickings, and everything is collapsing, decaying, because of monopoly privileges and the burdensome prohibitions of the Revenue."[89]

Egged on by the Porte and by British agents aided and abetted by Protestant missionaries, Syrian restlessness encouraged Mahmud II—who had never resigned himself to the loss of Syria—to speed up preparations for taking it back. On April 21, 1839, commanded by Generalissimo Hafiz Pasha and officered by Russian, English, and Prussian instructors, the Ottoman army crossed the Euphrates, but, on June 24, was soundly beaten by the better-disciplined and better-trained troops of Ibrahim Pasha. The sultan, 'Abd al-Majid, son and successor of Mahmud II, saw himself forced to open negotiations with Muhammad 'Ali who, in exchange for keeping the peace, demanded no less than hereditary rule over Egypt and Syria. At this point, the Powers decided to impose arbitration. On July 15, 1840, in defiance of France, which backed Muhammad 'Ali, the United Kingdom, Austria, Russia, and Prussia signed with the Porte the London Convention: an ultimatum stipulated the evacuation of Syria in ten days and, in reciprocation, granted Muhammad 'Ali hereditary rule over Egypt, with the title of *khedive*, and the government of the pashalik of 'Akka for as long as he lived. Presented with the rejection of Muhammad 'Ali, British and Austrian ships bombarded Beirut, while Turkish, British, and Austrian troops took possession of the larger coastal cities. The Egyptian army having been overcome at Bharsaf on October 10, Bashir II went into exile, and Ibrahim Pasha retired to Damascus. Muhammad 'Ali then negotiated an accord with Commodore Sir Charles Napier that acknowledged his hereditary rule over Egypt in exchange for the evacuation of Syria. Recalled to Egypt, Ibrahim Pasha ordered a retreat. Following desertions and in inclement weather, however, less than a third of his army made it back to Cairo.

If European intervention saved the empire, it had also placed it under the tutelage of the Powers: the fate of the East was destined increasingly to depend on European mediation. "For nearly twenty-five years," Saint-Marc Girardin was to write around 1860, "it is Europe that governs in Constantinople; but it governs solely by leverage and through the aid of intermediaries."[90] When the Egyptian question was settled, France immediately insisted on guarantees for the Christians, and voices were raised demanding military intervention. Thus, in the *Revue du Lyonnais* dated December 25, 1840, a certain Pierre Lortet wrote: "What was done for the Greeks when they labored beneath the Turkish scimitar could be done for the Christian tribes [*sic*] of Syria. . . . They want neither Egyptian despotism nor Anglo-Turkish despotism. These people could provide the framework for a Christian state in the Orient."[91] Following the example of France, which turned its position as "protector" of the Catholics to such good advantage, each power wanted to have its own "protected" community. The Russians made noises in favor of the Orthodox, while the British, in the absence of a "natural" candidate, looked to the Protestants, Druzes, and Jews. As early as 1839, the London press ran with an idea aired by certain UK officials who, preempting Zionism, saw the establishment of Jews in Syria as a means of firming up British influence in the Middle East. The following year, the British government attempted to convince the Ottoman authorities of the benefits of placing Jews in southern Syria: with their capital, business acumen, and industriousness, they would provide a barrier against any moves to Egyptian expansion, and, as Lord Palmerston glibly put it, "would promote the progress of civilization therein."[92] All these were arguments in favor of the kind of sanitized colonialism which had already been tried and tested in both continents of America with an all too familiar outcome and which the official founder of Zionism, Theodor Herzl, was to take up at a later date.[93] Faced with the Porte's reservations, the British were content to ask for a protectorate over the Jews in the empire, to which the Porte objected that the dhimmi enjoyed sufficient guarantees and that European "protection" was unnecessary.

Following Ibrahim Pasha's departure, the situation quickly worsened in the Lebanese uplands. The interminable reign of Bashir II and eight years of Egyptian domination had bequeathed an intractable legacy of antagonism that saw Druzes and Maronites backed by contending Powers. From October 1841, denominational disorder burst out, bringing burning, massacre, and plundering in its wake. The Europeans weighed in, with France and Austria clamoring for the reinstatement of a principality led by a Christian emir. The Porte proposed a compromise known under the name of the dual *qaymaqamat*: the northern part of the mountain was to be ruled by a Maronite *qaymaqam,* and the south by a Druze counterpart. But with government in the mixed districts proving more delicate, in 1845, the arrangements were redrafted. By the end of 1857, bad feeling between Druzes and Christians was becoming acute. Other factors relating to the international situation, however, redoubled these local rivalries and precipitated the events of 1860 that were to plunge Syria in blood, with pressure from the Western Powers being first in line. In compensation for having assisted the Porte during the Crimean War, France and Great Britain, keen to extend their spheres of influence, demanded reforms that alienated virtually the entire population. The *khatt-i-humayun* (imperial charter) of February 18, 1856,

allotted full equality in terms of taxation to all Ottoman subjects, introduced universal conscription, and removed obstacles to public office for all, regardless of religious denomination. This constituted a radical break with the *dhimma,* a statute of Koranic inspiration which had governed the status of the People of the Book within the *umma*—the Community of Believers—since the inception of Islam.[94] The Treaty of Paris on March 30, 1856, on the face of it favorable to the empire, had in fact increased the right of intervention of the Great Powers.[95] In addition, in spite of requests from the Porte—which justifiably observed that recent reforms had erased its raison d'être—it also renewed the system of Capitulations, transforming what used to be privileges into fully fledged rights.[96]

The Christians benefited from these "rights" to grow rich and gain "emancipation," thus upsetting traditional community balances. Muslim milieus were simmering and could boil over into open revolt at any moment: before the end of 1856, anti-Christian riots exploded in Aleppo and Nablus. In India, the revolt of the *sipahi* against the British, followed by the proclamation of the end of the Mughal empire, the devastations of the conquest and occupation in Algeria in combination with the defeat of 'Ab al-Qadir, rekindled anti-Christian feeling throughout the Muslim world. Finally, European economic penetration, favorable to the Christians and Jews, and promoted by increasingly enterprising missions, further exasperated denominational strife.[97] In 1858, for the first time, French capital made inroads into the empire: work was begun on the Damascus–Beirut road, confirming the preeminence of the latter city over 'Akka, Sayda, and Tripoli.[98] In October of the same year, a quarrel within the Maronite community extended to the mixed sectors and at once took on a religious character. In May and June 1860, the Chouf, the Wadi al-Taym, the Beka'a, the cities of Hasbaya, Rashaya, Zahle, and Dayr al-Qamar were engulfed

in fire and blood. Eleven thousand Christians were slaughtered and four thousand reduced to virtual destitution.[99] The number of refugees was estimated at about two hundred thousand. In July, the disorder reached Damascus. From midday on July 9, a furious mob, wielding "sabers, enormous blunderbusses, and brand-new axes,"[100] tore through the Christian quarter, ransacking, killing, and raping. The following day, the Russian consulate was stormed, and the dragoman and all the employees massacred. Plundering and arson extended to the Bab Tuma district, while those fleeing to the French consulate were ruthlessly cut down. At this juncture, the emir 'Abd al-Qadir, assisted by his family and by all the Algerians in exile, redoubled their efforts to save lives, by sheltering hundreds of families, as well as the French, Russian, and Greek consuls, and Sisters of Charity and Lazarists, in his own house or in the citadel. Nevertheless, on Wednesday July 11, the Christian district, where the ground was strewn with corpses, had the appearance of a huge furnace. "In the stricken district of Hara al-Nasara," wrote Joseph Poujoulat in a letter of November 27, 1860, "I saw hundreds of dogs who had died of a surfeit of human flesh."[101]

The death toll reached approximately six thousand, and thousands of dazed survivors fled toward Beirut or Alexandria. As Abbé Lavigerie,

Aerial view of the Christian quarter. Maronite church, Franciscan church and monastery, Armenian Catholic church, and convent of the Sisters of the Sacred Heart.

223

future Archbishop of Algiers, noted when passing through Damascus shortly after the events, within the city walls, the Christian district, with its three thousand eight hundred houses, languished utterly devastated. "Of the houses in which they had once lived, not one remained standing. They were all destroyed, razed so that not even the rubble could be occupied."[102] Three religious communities had been demolished stone by stone, including the Franciscan monastery founded in 1664; eleven churches had been gutted, and the palace of the Greek patriarch ransacked from top to bottom. Symbols of European interference, all the consulates, except that of the United Kingdom, had been consigned to the flames. On the other hand, Christians in the extramural districts escaped the massacre, as the French paper *Le Monde* reported: "The two thousand Christians who lived in Midan, the most ill-famed Muslim district of the city, suffered relatively little. The riffraff defended them and gave them asylum in their own houses, vigorously repelling assailants who tried to take the life, honor, or property of any Christian."[103]

Damascus was to bear traces of these wounds for a long time: in 1893, the traveler Charles Lallemand could see in the Christian district "the ruins of houses still blackened by the fire that had consumed them [and] not yet rebuilt because the families who had lived there had vanished."[104] In France, the press was unanimous in calling for intervention. In a lengthy article in *Le Correspondant* of August 1860, Melchior de Vogüé, presenting events as spawned by a "vast Muslim conspiracy whose center is in Mecca and whose goal is the extermination of the Eastern Christians," called for "a new Crusade of Christendom and civilization," the occupation of Damascus, and the creation of an independent Christian state encompassing "Mount Lebanon, the plain of Baalbek, the Christian cities of Hasbaya and Rashaya, and the entire coastline from Tripoli to Tyre," enriched—he points out—by European capital attracted by the silk trade.

Few observers apportioned to European, and more specifically to French policies, any share of responsibility in the situation. Around 1875, Doctor Lortet, Dean of the Faculty of Medicine at Lyon—whom one can hardly suspect of sympathy towards Islam—having noted that the Maronites were sponsored by France "in a deplorably partial manner," went on to add with rare clear-sightedness: "It is these exclusive, petty, and regrettable policies that have blown up trifling tribal squabbles into major issues, and on several occasions led to the massacre of our unfortunate clients in the Lebanon and elsewhere."[105] In order to obviate the intervention of the Great Powers and to reimpose its authority over Syria, the Porte resorted to draconian measures. On July 17, as European vessels rode off the coast, the Foreign Minister, Fuad Pasha, arrived in Beirut, invested with full powers to restore order. In spite of opposition from the Porte and British misgivings, the Powers nevertheless decided to send a task force to Syria to, in Napoleon III's own words, "help the sultan to restore obedience among subjects blinded by the fanaticism of an earlier age."[106] On August 16, General Beaufort d'Hautpoul landed in Beirut with six thousand men, but, concerned to deprive him of any pretext for intervening in the Syrian hinterland, Fuad Pasha had wasted no time in

Emir 'Abd al-Qadir. Print published in June 1883 in *Le Journal illustré*, p. 185.

Damascus and had been punishing the guilty parties with the utmost severity for several weeks. A hundred Ottoman soldiers and officers were summarily tried and shot. On September 8, in the enclosure of the citadel, the governor of Damascus met with the same fate, while fifty-six further culprits, civilians and functionaries, were hanged. Qanawat, almost exclusively inhabited by Turks, saw its occupants expelled and the district given over to the stricken Christians.

The Muslims had to pay heavy compensation, and, finally, three thousand five hundred men suspected of participating in the massacres were dragooned into the Ottoman army. On September 11, Fuad Pasha returned to Beirut, whose governor, Khurshid Pasha, and other senior officials were imprisoned, while two hundred and fifty Druzes were exiled to Tripolitania. As for the French troops, they contented themselves with humanitarian actions in the Chouf, from where the Druzes, with the complicity of the Ottomans, had succeeded in fleeing into the Hawran. "The only benefit to have come from this intervention," wrote Richard Edwards, "is that the scales dropped from six thousand French

Massacre of Christians in Damascus, July 9, 1860. Print (after a sketch by M. Belbèz) published in the weekly *L'Univers illustré*, no. 116, Thursday, August 2, 1860. Oddly, the scene is shown taking place in an architectural setting that is more like Cairo than Damascus.

eyes and that they saw things as clearly as we do in this unhappy question of Syria. They came to defend the Christians, and they left feeling, instead of pity, very different sentiments towards their coreligionists."[107]

In Paris, the hawks expressed regret—through their mouthpiece, Melchior de Vogüé, in particular—that "the task of repression, hamstrung by intrigues of every kind, makes no progress," and called for "French honor" to be upheld.[108] At the beginning of October, a European commission arrived in Beirut to reorganize the administration of the Lebanese uplands. This resulted in the Organic Law, which turned the country into an autonomous province divided into seven districts, each controlled by a *mutasarrif* appointed by the Porte, being endorsed by, and answerable to, the Powers. Later modifications were progressively to annul the terms of the Organic Law. Towards the end of the century, Syria was

divided into six governorships, which remained in force until 1918: three *sandjak*s formed the *wilaya* of Aleppo, and five that of Beirut; the *wilaya* of "Syria," with Damascus as its capital, was divided into four *sandjak*s—Hama, Damascus, the Hawran, and al-Kerak; finally, three autonomous *sandjak*s were placed under direct Istanbul control—Dayr al-Zor, Jerusalem, and the Lebanese mountains, extending from south of Tripoli to north of Sayda.

The final decades of the century were marked by increasingly far-reaching interference by the Powers, and in all fields—military, political, administrative, financial, economic, and cultural—by the creeping loss of the Porte's sovereignty, and by the growing exasperation of the Muslim population. Awaiting final dismemberment, there first came the appropriation by European states of various territories, which—nominally at least—still depended on the authority of the Ottoman state. In 1878, Cyprus

The Barada as it flows into Damascus, with pilgrims camping out on its banks before setting off for Mecca.
Right, the al-Sulaymaniyya *takiyya*; left, on the heights, the al-'Izziyya madrasa. Print by W. H. Bartlett, nineteenth century.

was relinquished to the UK in exchange for military support against Russia. In 1881, the Republican France of Jules Ferry occupied Tunisia so as, as the founder of state schooling put it unblinkingly, "to deal a death blow to the renaissance of Muslim fanaticism [and to render] a new and capital service to the cause of civilization."[109] In Egypt, in 1882, a revolution led by some officers having ousted the dynasty of the Khedives considered too obliging towards European interests, the Powers—all the more disquieted since Egypt, on the brink of ruin, might have endangered their financial interests—decided to intervene, and the country was soon occupied by Britain.[110]

At the same time, cultural and religious penetration that, under cover of "good works," paved the way for the commercial treaties, intensified as never before. Missions multiplied: Lazarists, American missionaries, Jesuits, Ladies of Nazareth, Sisters of St. Joseph, Little Franciscans of Mary, Brothers of the Christian Doctrine, Marists, Daughters of Charity all opened day- or boarding-schools and dispensaries—all institutions that a secular and radical France, anxious to preserve the

advantages it accrued, continued to subsidize in accord with Gambetta's glorious formulation: "Anticlericalism is not an export article."[111] The point was no longer simply to convert schismatics, but to create "elites" that would be receptive and docile to Western objectives—in a word, as Maurice Barrès formulated it so well, "to execute the moral conquest of the Levant."[112] According to a report published shortly before the war, fifty-two thousand pupils—more than half the school population of the country—had studied in French institutions. Many Muslim intellectuals, including Sheikh Muhammad Abduh, loudly denounced this insidious aspect of European interference, all too aware of the aims and perils of the phenomenon.[113]

Economic and financial infiltration developed in parallel. From 1860 on, deprived of capital, machines, and factories—one would speak today of an underdeveloped country—the Ottoman empire appeared to European financiers as virgin territory into which manufactured goods and capital might be poured and turn a brisk profit. The 1878 bankruptcy resulted in significant sources of public revenue—

Damascus from the slopes of Mount Qasiyun. In the foreground, the suburb of Salihiyya. Nineteenth-century print.

Umayyad Mosque. Muezzin calling the faithful to prayer from the top of the Minaret of Jesus.
Nineteenth-century print (prior to the fire of 1893).

the salt monopoly, duties on alcohol, incomes from tobacco, etc.—falling under the control of a cosmopolitan organization dominated by France and England, the "Administration of National Debt." This had saved the empire from the fate of Tunisia and Egypt, occupied following insolvency, but amputated the state of yet a further facet of its sovereignty. In 1863, the Beirut–Damascus toll road, built by a French company, opened to traffic. In 1875, the Crédit Lyonnais bank set up a branch in Istanbul. In January 1890, a company of Ottoman nationality, but whose capital was mainly French, was formed to develop and manage a tram system in Damascus, as well as a railway line connecting Beirut, Damascus, and the Hawran. In Beirut in 1894, a new port, also built by a French concern, entered service. In 1903, a railway line between Damascus and Dera'a—the first section of the main line that was to connect the Syrian capital with Mecca—started operation. At the same time, commercial competition and technological progress

in the West condemned many sectors of Ottoman industry to extinction. Statistical data and information provided by travelers also attest to the extent of the phenomenon: between 1820 and 1840, the number of workmen in silk-weaving workshops dropped from ten thousand to one thousand in Aleppo, and from eight thousand to two thousand in Damascus. From 1830 on, the market was flooded with English-made cotton. In the same year, Baron Taylor noted that the main source of income in the Tripoli region—the trade in raw silk—lay in the hands of a small number of Europeans, and that both furniture and clothing for the more affluent Turks were imported from Europe.[114] Ibrahim Pasha's open-door policy accelerated this process: in 1839, Édouard Blondel, noticing a reduction in the number of weaving looms, foresaw the total destruction of the Damascus silk industry in the near future.[115] In 1849, the Comte de Pardieu noted: "Everything of quality is fetched in from Europe, stitched silks come from

Damascus from the slopes of Mount Qasiyun. In the foreground, the extramural al-'Adiliyya *turba* that today lies in the Muhajirin district; the mausoleum of al-Malik al-'Adil Kitbugha, who was sultan of Egypt (1294–96). Nineteenth-century print.

Lyon, whence they are ordered expressly for the East, and the muslin, percale, and broadcloth from Switzerland, France, or England."[116] Around the middle of the century, the American missionary W. McC. Thomson could report that European manufactories had virtually wiped out all the branches of local arts and crafts that had formerly flourished in Damascus.[117] In May 1860, the Comte de Paris observed that "the ruin of trade and industry has made Syria dependent on Europe."[118] Fifteen years later, Doctor Lortet observed that silk-weaving was declining in Damascus because of competition from Beirut and massive imports from Nîmes and Lyon, that cotton fabrics—"dreadful imitations of old local cloth," to boot—were nearly all American and English imports, and that even the dyes, with some exceptions, were brought in from Europe.[119] In 1922, a report by the office of the French High Commission affirmed that "the silk industry survives only because of its links with France," and that between 1890 and 1905, due directly to foreign competition, the number of silk- and cotton-weaving looms had fallen by a third and the number of workmen employed by half. [120]

Even imperial domestic policy was subjected to interference from European states. It was under pressure from them that major reforms known as Tanzimats, sparked in 1826 by the massacre of the Janissaries, were adopted. On November 3, 1839, the sultan, 'Abd al-Majid I, promulgated a *khatt-i humayun*—the so-called Edict of Gulhäne—which turned the legal, financial, and governmental sectors upside-down. Civil, criminal, and commercial courts were created, and new penal and commercial codes came into effect. The *khatt-i humayun* of February 18, 1856, confirmed the preceding. At the end of 1876, following pressure by a movement called the Young Ottomans supported by the Powers, a representative regime was born. A constitution, including plans for ministers, an appointed senate, and an elected chamber of deputies, was promulgated by 'Abd al-Hamid II. The experiment was transitory: less than a year later, parliament was dissolved, the constitution suspended, and its author, Midhat Pasha, taken under house arrest to the Hijaz. This sounded the end of the Tanzimats and the beginning of an

The courtyard in the Umayyad Mosque. Nineteenth-century print (before 1893).

autocratic reign lasting more than thirty years that was marked by a backlash against earlier policies of imposed "Europeanization," by a return to Islam as a leaven for "national" solidarity, and by a rapprochement with Germany as a counterweight to French and British ambitions. In October 1898, in a statement made in Damascus, Emperor Wilhelm II, guest of Sultan 'Abd al-Hamid, assured the three hundred million Muslims living in the world of his protection. Contrary to France and Great Britain, whose "protection" was offered at the cost of territorial and political concessions, the new German "friend" endeavored to present itself as disinterested, requesting only the concession for the Baghdad railroad.

The birth of a new threat: Zionism

The Capitulations, as well as various legislative innovations undertaken in the wake of the Tanzimats, fostered the settlement in southern Syria of Jewish immigrants fleeing from European anti-Semitism. This is explicitly accepted in the words of Eliezer Ben-Yehuda, who was living in Jerusalem in about 1880:

> The most concrete, most powerful, indeed almost unlimited protection against this [Ottoman] government and its oppression was afforded by the status of *himaya*, i.e., foreign national. Neither junior nor senior officials, nor the central government, nor even the sultan in person, could do anything against the *himaya*. The power of European nations in Turkey was then very great under the terms of the "special rights" the French call *capitulation*. . . . This characteristic of the Turkish government . . . was our salvation in our actions for national resurrection. . . . The status of *himaya* amounted to paradise for a foreigner.[121]

Concerning legislative provision, it was primarily the law of June 16, 1867, which, by opening rights of ownership of property to aliens, allowed for the implantation of Jewish colonies in Syria. Throughout history, Jews had emigrated to Syria, in greater or lesser numbers, and—always for religious motives—particularly to Safad, where they awaited the advent of the Messiah.[122] In 1860, in a climate of national revival, various currents, breaking with the traditional passivity of Messianism, preached genuine national reconstitution. Palestinophile societies of a philanthropic nature multiplied, including the Amants de Sion and Hebraic societies for the colonization of the Holy Land, in London. In 1870, after promptings by one of its founders, Charles Netter, the Alliance Israélite Universelle founded close to Jaffa on a terrain of some six hundred acres (240 ha)—and with a ten-year tax exemption—a school of agriculture, Mikveh Israel

Detail of a mauve velvet robe embroidered with golden thread (of the *sarma* type), late nineteenth century. 'Azm Palace.

("Hope of Israel"). After the pogroms perpetrated at the beginning of the 1880s in Berlin, in Brandenburg, Pomerania, and Russia, the idea gained favor that the only possible response to the failure of assimilation was the reconstitution of a Jewish "nation" on "its" own territory. After three to four thousand immigrants arrived in Palestine from Russia, in 1882 the Porte, which already had enough on its plate with secessionist movements and interference from the Powers, prohibited immigration and the sale of land to foreign Jews—that is, those not subjects of the empire.

Nothing, however, could prevent clandestine immigration, or indeed purchases of land aided and abetted by corrupt local civil servants, venal feudal landowners, and an impoverished peasantry.[123] In 1891, thanks to the financial support of Baron Edmond de Rothschild, a score of Jewish hamlets had already been set up in Palestine. Nevertheless, it was not until the end of the nineteenth century that Zionism,[124] hitherto of essentially philanthropic nature, would take on a truly political character under the influence of Theodor Herzl: modern technologies were to make massive systematic emigration possible, leading to the formation of a state on territory whose acquisition would be underwritten by international treaty and where the Jews would be sovereign. Faced with the Porte's opposition, other territories were proposed: Argentina, Uganda, Cyprus, and even the al-'Arish area, which was under British authority after the conquest of Egypt in 1882. In the case, however, of it becoming possible to acquire Palestine, certain Zionist currents were not above protesting that a Jewish State should extend "from the Nile to the Euphrates."[125] Unflaggingly, Herzl crisscrossed Europe, traveling to Istanbul five times. Deliberately positioning his plans in the context of European colonial expansion, he underlined to Western interlocutors that Zionism "in Palestine [was] the

advanced guard of culture against Asian barbarity [sic],"[126] and that it would reinforce their influence in the Eastern Mediterranean, while to the Ottomans he observed it would bring prosperity to the empire and "greater happiness and culture to many human beings."[127] Furthermore Herzl had little doubt that the Arabs whose "displacement" he was already envisaging would, in keeping with a hackneyed colonialist argument, welcome "the civilizing benefits" of Jewish immigration with open arms. In 1896, to an envoy of Herzl who came offering financial assistance in exchange for an official support for Zionism, 'Abd al-Hamid II offered this premonitory reply: "Let the Jews save their billions. Perhaps, one day, when the empire is divided, they will have Palestine for nothing. But it is our corpse that will have to be divided. I cannot accept vivisection."[128]

Nevertheless, in spite of opposition from the Porte, the Jewish population of Palestine continued to increase, passing from twenty-five thousand in 1880—approximately 5 percent of the total population—to sixty-five thousand by 1920. On the ground, the "civilizing benefits" had patently no effect on the peasants expelled from their property. By 1886, four years after the arrival of the first wave of immigrants, they attacked recently implanted Jewish colonies, protesting against being dispossessed of their villages. In June 1891, dignitaries from Jerusalem, fully conscious of the dangers pursuant on Zionist political aspirations, delivered a petition to the grand vizier asking "that the Jews of Russia be forbidden to enter into Palestine and purchase land there."[129] Gradually, opposition to Zionism extended to broad swathes of the population and took a more political twist. A direct threat for the local farming community, it also appeared simultaneously as a danger to the empire, to fledgling Arab nationalism, to the integrity of Syria, and to the Muslim community as a whole.[130]

In April 1909, the Turkish journalist Yunus Nadi issued the following warning: "[they] dream of an Israelite kingdom comprising the ancient states of Babel and Nineveh with Jerusalem at its center."[131] Opposition reached its zenith shortly before World War I. Anti-Zionist associations were established in Istanbul, Jerusalem, Cairo, Beirut, and Haifa. In spring 1914, senior figures in Jerusalem, Jaffa, and Gaza launched an appeal in an Istanbul newspaper: "If sincere men fail to come to the aid of the Palestinians, their fate will be that of the Indians of America. Zionism, a state within the Ottoman state, threatens the very existence of the Arabs in Palestine."[132] In 1908, the revolution of the Young Turks wrested from the sultan the reestablishment of the 1876 Constitution and a promise to reconvene Parliament. Inspired by the Jacobinism of the French Revolution and anxious to preserve the unity of the empire, the Young Turks pursued a vigorous policy of centralization and Turkization, which served to rekindle the aspirations of Arab separatists. Secret societies mushroomed—in Beirut, in Cairo, and in Damascus—launching appeals for secession and the union of Arabs of all denominations—Muslims, Christians, and Jews. Nationalist ideology was imported from Europe, where it was about to give rise to the bloodiest conflict in the history of humanity, bore fruit, shattering the unity of the *umma* which, since the state of Medina, had—after a fashion, and overriding ethnic or linguistic criteria—created bonds of solidarity and a sense of identity on a religious basis. "By misfortune," the sultan, 'Abd al-Hamid, was to say, "England, through its perfidious policy, has managed to light the fires of the national idea in various regions of my empire."[133]

From the European imperialist viewpoint, the opposition between Turks and Arabs, already perceived by d'Arvieux and Nointel as a factor of political action, was finally fulfilling its promise. With virtually one voice, the French press

proclaimed the rights of France in Syria; in March 1913, in the periodical *Questions diplomatiques et coloniales*, George Poignant expanded the idea according to which "French Syria [*sic*] formed an intrinsic part of the French heritage."[134] At the end of January 1913, in the middle of the Balkan wars, a group of officers headed by Enver Pasha seized power. On September 9, 1914, Turkey denounced the Capitulations and put an end to the regime of autonomy in the Lebanese mountains which—as the very text of a dispatch sent to Germany recalled—"had been imposed on the imperial government under French pressure."[135]

On October 29, in spite of British promises, recent failures in the Balkans, and "empty coffers, inadequately dressed troops equipped with obsolete weapons,"[136] Turkey entered World War I on the side of the central empires after much procrastination. In November, Sultan Muhammad V launched an appeal for a jihad against the Allies that had little effect on the Arab subjects of the empire, as General Liman von Sanders, head of the German military mission, perceived: "Among the Muslim Arabs subject to Turkish domination the proclamation of a holy war is not enough to outweigh the deep-rooted antagonism that exists between Turks and Arabs, and the general discontentment which for generations Turkish governments have done little but breed and exacerbate."[137] Jamal Pasha, the commander in chief of the Turkish army in Syria, repressed the Arab nationalists with great brutality: thousands were exiled and dozens executed, including the grandson of Emir 'Abd al-Qadir, in whose company Maurice Barrès had visited Damascus. When the time came, Great Britain had but little to do (gold and promises—unfulfilled—overcame any lingering reservations) in order to convince the sharif of Mecca to raise the standard of rebellion against the Turks.

The end of the "pink city"—
Damascus through travelers' eyes

In the first half of the nineteenth century, Damascus had all the appearance of a bastion of resistance against European penetration. This characteristic is almost always labeled as "fanatic," even by the few observers who admit the deep-rooted tolerance of Islam. This characteristic—when not blithely regarded as congenital to the Muslim or Oriental—is often laid at the door of its isolation, its lack of intercourse with Europe, and the great annual caravans that attracted thousands of pious Muslims on their way to Mecca.[138] Recalcitrant Damascus was then patently unreceptive to the superiority of Western civilization and to its values which, from the New World to Algeria, were ostensibly importing bliss

and prosperity at the cost of blood, saber, and compulsory conversion. In this, the city's inhabitants presented similarities with the "natives" François Charles-Roux mentions in an account of the Egyptians living under Bonaparte's iron rule: "[they] cannot be aware of the potential for progress brought about by the foreign domination imposed on them; and even if they were aware, the vast majority of them would not understand a thing about it."[139]

In 1807, the Spanish traveler Badia y Leyblich, who had converted to Islam for the purposes of espionage, observed that "the fanaticism of the people of Damascus surpasses that of the inhabitants of Egypt, since a European cannot without danger present himself in the streets in the dress of his country, but is obliged to assume the costume of the East."[140] In 1831, Joseph Michaud noted that the city

Above. A European traveler in Damascus at the end of the nineteenth century. Engraving after Gustave Bauerfeind, *L'illustré. Soleil du dimanche*, October 10, 1897, p. 6.

Facing page. The Umayyad Mosque shortly after the 1893 fire.

of Damascus in its endeavors to remain holy strove "to prevent the profane spirit of Europe ever blowing through it."[141] "Nowhere else," observed Baron Taylor, "are the forms of Muslim fanaticism more repulsive or more savage."[142] Indeed, Lamartine himself was careful "to finish off" his Turkish costume before entering the city, because, "alone among Orientals, Damascenes feel mounting religious loathing and horror for the name and costume of Europeans. . . . Damascus is a holy city, fanatical and independent; nothing must soil it."[143]

From the reign of Ibrahim Pasha on, however, there were more and more signs that the city was opening up. "Here," wrote Charles de Pardieu in 1849, "one sees the results of the energetic measures of Ibrahim Pasha, who has drilled respect for foreigners so well into these savage Muslims that, even a long time after he has gone, a Frank in European costume can walk abroad in complete safety."[144] In 1850, Gustave Flaubert vaunted the courtesy and good manners of the people of Damascus, "much less fanatical and more tolerant than previously."[145] The 1906 edition of the Baedeker Guide stated clearly:

"However, one cannot claim that Muslims are more fanatical here than followers of other religions; indeed, they distinguish themselves from the indigenous Christians by much greater honesty."[146]

The mosques remained closed to Westerners during the first half of the century.[147] In 1830, Baron Taylor lamented that he was only able to penetrate into the hall of the Umayyad mosque. A little later, Lamartine, convinced that "any Christian daring to profane the mosque by entering it would risk death," had to be satisfied with a glimpse of the great courtyard "through the door that gives on the bazaar."[148] The prohibition seems to have been lifted only after Fuad Pasha's repression following the massacres of 1860. Since this time, Lycklama a Nijeholt affirmed, "provided one is accompanied by a dragoman or by one of the consulate's *cawas* and makes liberal use of baksheesh, one can, as long as one does not tarry, traverse various parts of this mosque."[149] Photography, on the other hand, seems to have been prohibited for longer, as John Kelman averred. Having informed us that, in 1906, he had himself been able to take photographs unhindered, he adds that "less than ten years ago, a Damascene was almost killed by the mob for attempting to photograph the ruins of the mosque after the fire [of 1893]."[150]

For longer than Istanbul, Cairo, or Baghdad, Damascus seems to have conserved the "Oriental" flavor that so many travelers craving local color and the picturesque reveled in. In 1831, Robinson stressed its wholly Oriental character,[151] while, shortly after, Lamartine added that it seemed "quite unlike Europe."[152] In 1835, the excellent observer Charles Greenstreet Addison wrote: "Damascus is a true Oriental city and possesses much more character than Constantinople. Here, everything is eastern; there are no Frank quarters and shabby beings in black hats and pea-green jackets wandering around, no fantastic aping of European dress by the command of some innovating sultan. . . . Damascus is, I think, superior in interest to any other oriental town

I have seen."[153] Isabel Burton viewed it as the most Oriental and picturesque city in the world. [154] At the end of the 1870s, Dr. Lortet, who hardly met more than twenty or so Frenchmen and Englishmen there, observed that it was "considerably more interesting to visit than Cairo or Constantinople, which have both today become almost European cities."[155]

At the beginning of the twentieth century still, Roland Dorgelès thought that there he had reached "the legendary Orient."[156] Yet, in spite of reticence and rejection, Europe had long dwelt there. As early as 1850, Gustave Flaubert was one of the first to observe the process: in a coffeehouse in the perfumers' bazaar, he writes, it suddenly seemed like "Europe in Asia"—Turks in European costume, and in some of the residences Venetian glass chandeliers, and in an ornamental style, "so tortuous, that it sometimes attained Louis XV."[157] At the same time, Major Fridolin observed this influence gaining the very center of that stronghold of conservatism, the holy pilgrimage caravan, whose infantry regiment, "in almost European costume, performed Rossini and Meyerbeer" to the singular amazement of the bourgeois of Samarkand, the dervishes, and the bankers of Teheran.[158] In 1872, Eugène Melchior de Vogüé deplored "the invasion of European furniture that has dealt a fatal blow to [its] old houses."[159]

After costume and furniture came architecture: in about 1881, Alcide Leroux saw villas built in an Oriental style, but "adulterated by contact with Europeans," and adds that the district most affected was the promenade along the banks of the Barada.[160] In 1894, Pierre Loti was delighted to find in Damascus "the merry Orient, a laughing and open Muslim city," but lamented "these atrocious imports, clocks in imitation bronze, oil- or hanging-lamps in the dining rooms." "What," he wondered, "will it be like next year when the railway is finished and everyday the tawdriness of the West will spew out over Damascus?"[161]

During the early twentieth century this process of "Europeanization" accelerated. The Baedeker Guide records that Western clothing was frequently worn, especially by Christians.[162] On the eve of World War I, arriving in Damascus by train from Beirut,

Maurice Barrès saw "European houses"[163] along the Barada. If it remained a quintessentially "Oriental" city, Damascus was no less, at the end of the nineteenth century, as Loti put it so well, "*à son grand soir*"[164]—in her twilight years. Indeed, the time was long gone when wide-eyed travelers would confess, as Poggibonsi had done in 1348, that they could not write about everything they saw lest no one believe them. . . .[165]

In the nineteenth century, the predominant theme was that of decline. Material decline, initially. For Dr. M. Busch, who made his visit little before 1860, "Today, Damascus has lost much of its luster . . . [and] the beautiful buildings of the Saracen yearly deteriorate more and more."[166] For Eugène Melchior de Vogüé, "it has nothing of its former brilliance, and

none of its past splendor remains. . . . It is hardly more than a wretched village . . . a cluster of mud and chopped-straw houses, squat, hunched, peeling, lost in a maze of hideous alleyways and huddled around mosques three-quarters ruined."[167] A further sign of decrepitude: the nocturnal lighting that so charmed visitors to the medieval city had vanished and this "City of Light" was no more: on the contrary, now people were astonished to see that, unlike in contemporary Western cities, streetlights were conspicuous by their absence. "The streets of Damascus are not only not lighted at night but all circulation in them is, in a manner, interdicted at that hour, there being at the head and end of each, a wooden barrier drawn across it, apparently with a view to prevent insurrectionary movement; so that,

Bayt Nizam. *Facing page*. The *selamlik*. The property is today owned by the Syrian state.
Above. Façade giving onto the haremlik courtyard.

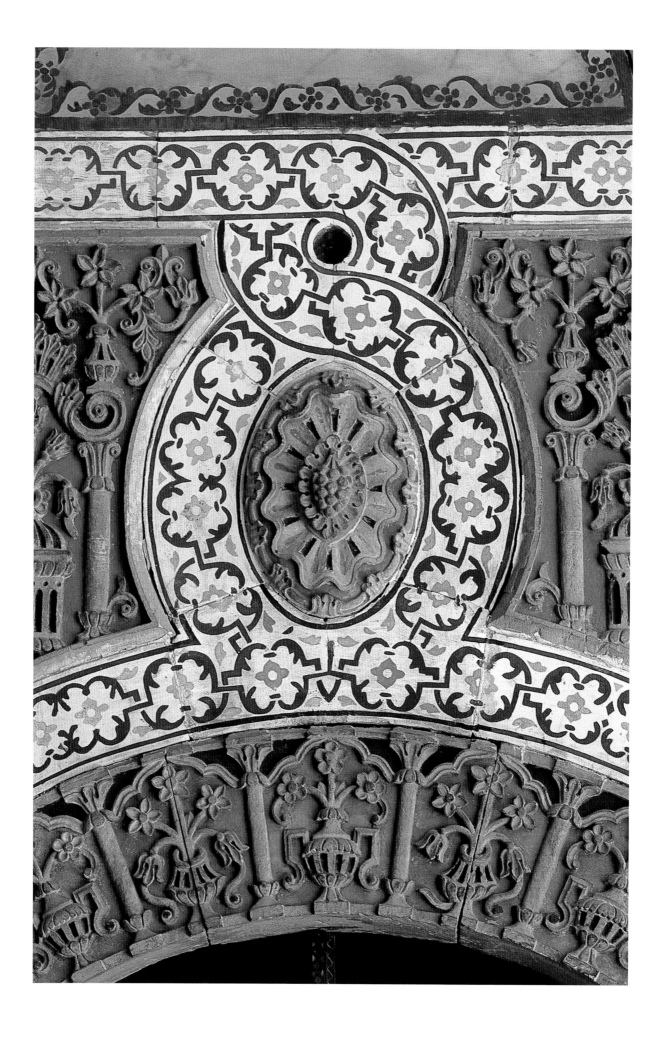

238   Bayt Nizam/Sawan. Detail of decorated doorframe opening onto the *iwan*.

to visit a friend in the immediate neighbourhood, one is obliged to be accompanied by a person carrying a paper lanthorn and armed with a stick, to demand admittance at several gates."[168]

Then there was economic recession: hard hit by competition with Beirut and by European produce, cruelly undermined by Ibrahim Pasha's policies, signs of industrial recession in Damascus, in terms of quantity as well as in quality, had long been plentiful.[169] These were exacerbated after the massacres of 1860 and the Christian exodus that followed.

Bayt Nizam. *Top*. The *qa'a* of the haremlik.
Bottom. Detail of gilt woodwork decoration in the *qa'a*.

Bayt Nizam. Colored stone-paste decoration on the entrance door to the *qa'a*.

Note the stylized ducks' heads around a central flower.

Facing page, top. Decor of a door archway. *Facing page, bottom.* Detail of the decoration in the *qa'a*.

In a city condemned as senile and decrepit, only the suqs, the coffeehouses, the baths, the interiors of the wealthier residences, and—because they were more recent and had something of a European air—the western districts of the city were spared. Reservoirs of "local color"—"folksy" to European eyes accustomed to gray uniformity—the multifaceted suq seemed like an escapist paradise, the quintessence of an idealized Orient. Each experienced there some form of enchantment: for Lamartine, a crowd as numerous as that under the arcades of the Palais Royal in Paris, but infinitely more picturesque; for Isabel Burton, the most characteristic suqs of the Orient; for Goupil Fesquet, a dazzling diversity of types and costumes; for Greenstreet Addison, the rough and ready Arabs of the desert and the merchants of Baghdad, Persia, Egypt, and distant India all very different in appearance, and all sporting a vast range of costumes.[170] Flaubert has left us a colorful description of characteristic clairvoyance which, moreover, gives the lie to some entrenched prejudices:

> Life in Damascus is entirely concentrated in the bazaars which are as lively and seething with people as the streets are deserted and quiet; the robes of the men, pink, green, or blue, and the mass of silks, the whole illumined from above by soft sunlight, makes for a gaudy burst of color of special charm. . . . Here and there, in the midst of the bazaars, a bathhouse; the *fellah* passes naked with just a towel around his body off to buy sugar at the grocer's for some *cawadja* back at the bath . . . a fakir walks through stark naked . . . barren women come and kiss his member; some time back, one of them was soiling them right in the middle of the bazaar and some pious Turks at once surrounded the group and hid him from the public gaze with their robes.[171]

As for the coffeehouses, Joseph Michaud sees them as encapsulating "the whole poetry of Damascus."[172] As the English traveler Charles Greenstreet Addison recalls, the city was renowned for the number and elegance of these cafés which, to his way of thinking, made it seem like Paris in the Orient.[173] If the "Two Roses Coffeehouse" and the "Coffeehouse of the River" were among the busiest and liveliest, Damascus's pride and joy was that of Bab al-Salam, in the midst of three rivers and shaded by great willow trees. Every day, in the shade of the trees or of hanging mats and listening to the sound of running water, more than two hundred people would gather there to smoke a nargileh, drink the bitter liquor (coffee), or play chess on a dais or a raised bench.[174] The 1906 edition of the Baedeker Guide hands the coffeehouses of Damascus the palm as the largest in all the Orient. The *hammam*s, which, according to Joseph Michaud, "exceeded in convenience and elegance those of Smyrna and Constantinople . . . were crammed to bursting all day from sunrise until evening."[175] "When the bather is quite undressed," writes Dr. Lortet, "he puts on some

Mount Qasyun
N. Yazid
N. Tawra
Barada
to Aleppo and Istanbul
to Palestine and Egypt
to the Hawran and Mecca

Christian cemetery
Muslim cemetery

N 0 500 m

Above. Damascus in the mid-19th century. **1** Al-Salihiyya. **2** Suq Saruja. **3** Al-Qasab. **4** Takiyya and al-Sulaymaniyya madrasa. **5** The Merjeh. **6** Qanawat. **7** Al-Suwayqa. **8** Midan Tahtani. **9** Midan Fuqani. **10** Camel market. **11** Bab al-Musalla. **12** Shaghur Juwwani. **13** Shaghur Barrani. **14** Jewish quarter. **15** Christian quarter.

double-heeled sandals (*kabkab*), and, conducted by two scantily clad boys, is brought to the hot-room, where he stays only a few moments, then to a second even hotter, and finally into a third, where the temperature is so high one can hardly breathe. . . . Then the entire body is soaped and lathered using a little packet of fiber from the loofah marrow. . . . Then, after being turned over repeatedly and rubbed every which way by pitiless masseurs, the patient, rinsed in lashings of water, toweled down, swaddled in soft, yielding wraps, a dressing gown rolled around his head, looking like one of Molière's *mamamouchi*, is lead back to the foyer, where, lounging on a couch, he is passed coffee and cigarettes."[176]

The closeness and promiscuity that reigned in these locales, as well as their layout, were naturally conducive to oft-condemned practices that flouted every prohibition. Flaubert describes a Cairo *hammam* where he was subjected to some highly unorthodox massage:

> I was alone at the back of the sweat-room, gazing as the day drew to an end through the great glass lenses fixed in the dome; hot water ran everywhere; stretched out like a calf, I was thinking of a mass of things and my pores set to quietly

dilating. . . . That day, my *kellak* rubbed me over gently and on arriving at my noble parts, rolled up my balls of love to clean them for me, then, all the while rubbing my chest with his left hand, placed the right on my cock, and, polluting me with a pulling movement, leant over my shoulder and kept on saying: *batchis, batchis* (that is, "tip, tip").[177]

As for the interiors of Damascene houses, in spite of the infiltration of European taste, they remained an object of amazement—"the only aspect of the city which can confidently defy the caprices of imagination . . . where all is coolness, silence, and a delight to the eyes," as Eugène Melchior de Vogüé put it.[178] If travelers all concur in stressing their cleanliness, elegance, and richness, as well as the refinement they reflect, they are struck above all by the ornamentation—all the more since furniture proper is practically nonexistent: "It is impossible to describe in detail the designs, decoration, and ornamentation of the houses of Damascus which are without doubt the most beautiful in any Arab city," was the Austrian Orientalist Alfred von Kremer's opinion. He goes on:

> An English traveler who had also visited the Alhambra told me that only there had he seen comparable decorative opulence and taste, and

Above. Maktab 'Anbar. The main courtyard arranged around the pool in the middle.
Maktab 'Anbar today contains the office of the Commission for the Old Town.

Below. Maktab ʿAnbar. Detail of ornamental banding running
above the doors and windows in the main courtyard.

The end of the "pink city"

that Damascus interiors reminded him of halls in
the Alhambra of the Moorish kings. For the most
part, decoration in Damascene rooms consists in
paintings on wood of a brilliance equaled only by
that on watercolors in German medieval
manuscripts. . . . Furniture in Arab houses is
generally very sparse. Couches against the walls
serve as armchairs. Tables and beds are unknown:
at night, mattresses are taken out of the *khazna*
[closets] and are laid either on carpets or on the
terrace. The only furnishings to be found . . .
consist in pipes and nargilehs. . . . The windows
are covered with tastefully worked grilles of
mauve wood; panes of glass, a novel feature in
Damascus, are still not very widespread.[179]

The ceilings were especially admired: "They are
of peerless grace and brilliance," wrote de Vogüé,
"sometimes possessing painted and gilded projecting
beams, and sometimes hollowed-out coffers in
whose cedar and sycamore the skilful carpenters of
old carved into luxuriant vegetation, with rosettes,
arabesques, and flowers, in sober and faded colors
picked out with touches of gold. . . . They are the
worthy rivals—in a lighter, brighter vein—of our
Renaissance choir stalls and woodcarvings."[180]

The majority of the more opulent residences that
can still be seen today date from the nineteenth
century. Those belonging to Jews were "much richer
and more splendid,"[181] because, as de Vogüé points
out, in addition to their high profile in the business
world, in contrast with the "uncaring Muslims," and
the "terrified Christians," they were the only builders.
Again according to de Vogüé, the most luxurious of
recently built residences was that of Ambhar ('Anbar),
a Jew who went to India as a servant, returning, as
rumor had it, with "his fez brimful of diamonds."[182]

Maktab 'Anbar. Carved stone medallion between the door arches in the principal courtyard.

Above. Detail of the *iwan* in Bayt Lisbuna.

Left. Maktab 'Anbar. Main courtyard,
decor over a niche.

Page 248. Courtyard in a house
in the Christian quarter.

Page 249. Courtyard in a house in Salihiyya.

247

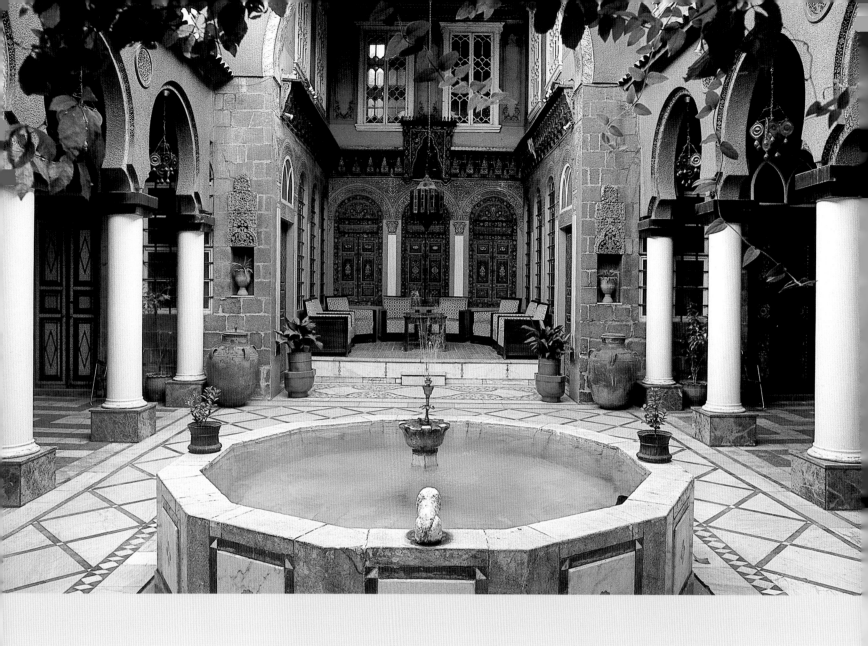

Top. The courtyard at Bayt Nassan. The only one of its kind in Damascus, the courtyard was reworked in the nineteenth century.

Bottom. Bayt Nassan. Detail of interlace on a door (timber incrusted with mother-of-pearl).

Bayt Nassan. The ceiling in the *iwan*.

Bayt Nassan. Door opening onto the courtyard (detail). Camel bone set in wood.

The end of the "pink city"

Left. Bayt Nassan. Two-leaf doorway opening onto
the courtyard (detail p. 250).
Below. Traditional wooden trunk showing the metal
and mother-of-pearl inlay.

Above. Bayt Barudi. Wall fresco showing the Mosque
at Medina. In the process of restoration
by the Faculty of Architecture, the residence
will soon house a study center for the Old City.
Left. Bayt Niyadu (formerly Stambuli house).
"Cupboard" door. The residence owed its original
name to a Jewish family from Istanbul that lived
there prior to the present occupant.
Facing page, top. Bayt Shamiyya. Ceiling detail. The
residence now houses a religious community.
Facing page, bottom. Bayt al-Yusuf Pasha,
emir of the hajj. Suq Saruja district.
Detail of the decoration.
Today in a sorry state, the house is occupied
by a number of families.

In step with the progressive Europeanization of its institutions, the evolution of nineteenth-century Damascus is marked primarily by the appearance of new public buildings and by the displacement of the center of urban gravity to the west of the ramparts. In the reign of Ibrahim Pasha (1832–40), a new seraglio—palace of the governor—and barracks were built near the citadel, while the Yalbugha mosque was transformed into a biscuit factory and the Tankiz mosque into a military academy. The quarter was not long in attaining the status of a new center; it was in any case the only one to elicit a positive response from Europeans. Baron Taylor regarded it as the "most beautiful of the city;" Comte de Pardieu, after stressing that the Turkish districts were "most beautiful," saw in their broad, paved, and "rather clean" streets, some of which were even planted with trees and provided with shops, nothing other than a reflection of Parisian boulevards; while for Lycklama a Nijeholt "the surroundings of the seraglio was Damascus's finest and wealthiest district."[183] It was a zone that offered a glaring

Top. View of the Jewish quarter. *Bottom.* Tinsmiths: A craft on the verge of extinction.

contrast to the intramural "maze," still little to the liking of Western travelers.[184] This area was all the more appreciated since, a short distance off to the west, lay the ancient Green Hippodrome (the Maydan al-Akhdar) and its immediate environs that served as a space for walking and recreation, as Blondel was to observe:

> On Fridays and Sundays, crowds of Damascenes leave the city to the promenade at the Maydan. Venerable walnut trees afford welcome shade in this joyous spot watered by the Barada. Amateurs of horse-riding exercise throw the *jerid* there to the vocal appreciation of an audience in the gallery who applaud the skill of the combatants. . . . Everywhere beneath the trees along the brook, are crowds of women enveloped in uniform white coats. As you walk by, and whenever they are not being too closely supervised by some importunate native, the youngest and prettiest of them obligingly draw aside their veil and address you.[185]

After the massacres and destruction of 1860, the Christian district was gradually rebuilt and, according to W. McC. Thomson, reconstruction had been essentially completed by the mid-1880s.[186] To forestall new outbreaks of disorder, in 1863 two barracks were stationed—one within the city walls along the southern side of Straight Street, and the other in the suburb of Midan Fuqani. In 1864–65, a decree put an end to encroachments onto the causeway, a practice that Muslim law had in general permitted and which had not escaped European observers: "It should be noted that, in this country," Blondel wrote, "nobody bothers about spilling over the public highway if he likes or feels the need; this

The courtyard in a Jewish house in Damascus. Nineteenth-century print of, what is undoubtedly, Bayt Lisbuna.

is tolerated and usually occurs without conse-quence."[187] In 1866, the banks of the Barada were developed. Between 1873 and 1884, a new suq—known by the name of al-Hamidiyya, after Sultan 'Abd al-Hamid (1876–1909)—was built at the entrance to the Umayyad mosque at the southwest corner of the citadel, whose parapets were used as a stone quarry. It is perfectly rectilinear and roofed with curved pieces of sheet metal; bordering its broad central alley are shops, with a floor above whose front, inspired by Baron Haussmann's style in Paris, is divided by fluted pilasters with Corinthian capitals.

During two years of sound governance in Damascus, between 1878 and 1881, the author of the 1876 Ottoman Constitution, Midhat Pasha, concerned to improve traffic congestion, built a new suq roofed with a barrel-vault in sheet-metal at the east end of Straight Street, between the spice suq and Bab al-Jabiya. As Charles Lallemand reported, passing through Damascus in July 1893, "this expeditious pasha, tired of seeing narrow, sordid lanes in the very heart of the city, simply set fire to the hovels to either side of them. And then, upon these expressly made and manageable ruins, had a superb bazaar built whose imposing central gallery bears his name."[188]

Greek Orthodox church. Detail of the bronze cladding on one of the leaves of the great central door. The Arabic inscription announces to the faithful as they enter the edifice: "This [church] is not only the House of God, it is [also] the Gate to Heaven." The other leaf bears the same inscription in Greek.

In the final decades of the century, a complex of public buildings betraying the manifest Europeanization of administrative life arose northwest of the citadel, around the Merjeh Square. In 1877–78, on the northern side, were erected law courts, a head office for the post and telegraph service, and a suq—the Suq 'Ali Pasha—connecting the concourse to the old Suq al-Khayl; in 1895, on the western side, a city hall; then, close by, a police headquarters, a new seraglio, and several hotels. In 1907, a column was raised in the center of the square to commemorate the Istanbul–Mecca telegraph line becoming operational. The new district was to centralize future development in the city to the northwest. The same year, a tram network entered service, with lines starting from the Merjeh serving the extramural districts. In 1908, the wells and old channels appearing inadequate and heavily polluted, new conduits were dug bringing in spring water from 'Ayn al-Fijeh. The Hijaz rail station, already under construction when Pierre Loti passed through the city in 1894, was completed in 1913. The following year, Maurice Barrès, arriving in Damascus by train, gave the following early description: "A rail station, telegraph wires, trams, all the trappings of a banal urban setting."[189] The earthly paradise so dear to the

Greek Orthodox church. Above the main door, a marble Gospel reproduces Matthew 16:18 in Greek and Arabic:
"And I say unto thee, That thou art Peter, and upon this rock I will build my church; and the gates of hell shall not prevail against it."

heart of Muslim authors—the marvelous pink city, Loti's beloved "Pearl and Queen of the East"— thus entered the annals of the past.[190]

In the nineteenth century more than ever "the suburb of Salehié [Salihiyya] at our feet, [which] burst suddenly upon our delighted fancy . . . a mile from the limits of the city but connected with it by gardens, orchards, and the villas of the rich,"[191] became increasingly residential, and prominent inhabitants and European consuls had summer abodes built there. In the little coffeehouses on the outskirts of Nahr Yazid, the "idlers of Damascus," as Blondel calls them, came to linger beneath the shade of the plane-trees, puffing on the nargileh, or sipping scented coffee.[192] Eastwards, Kurdish soldiers built spacious dwellings that soon formed a new district known as al-Akrad [the Kurds] that stretched up to the village of Berzeh. In 1870, according to Isabel Burton, it sheltered about fifteen thousand inhabitants and had a reputation of being the least tractable and roughest district in all Damascus—so much so that at night one could only venture down the road connecting it to the city being well armed and never alone.[193] At

the turn of the century, refugees from Rumelia and Crete settled on the slopes of Mount Qasiyun to the west of Salihiyya in a new district called al-Muhajirin. In marked contrast to the traditional principles observed in the city, its houses were built over three floors and its checkerboard plan signaled the appearance of "Western-style" town planning in Damascus. Attracted by the pleasant environs, by its "modern comforts," improved aeration, and the splendid panoramic view it afforded over the city, the luxurious residences built by notable Turks formed a prestigious residential development outside of the old Salihiyya. At the beginning of the twentieth century, the residential area of Qasiyun extended east–west over two miles (3.5 km).

Unlike Salihiyya, prolonging the city "in a long pink smudge in the middle of the green velvet of the trees,"[194] the suburb of Midan, inhabited by many Druzes, was regarded as the poorest and most "fanatical" quarter in Damascus—a breeding-ground for political and religious rioters, teeming with quaint ruins, mosques, and *hammams*.[195] On a visit to southern Syria, Flaubert entered the district on

Top. House at the end of a cul-de-sac.
Bottom. A tomb in the Christian cemetery of Bab Kaysan.

September 1, 1850, noting: "We go into an inter-minable suburb where our horses slip about on the paving stones. Wheat lies in heaps on the ground, cotton spinners, dyers, mosques, fountains, and trees hanging in clumps bear a tide of green that hovers over the countless colors waving in front of our eyes—some fine Turkish guardsmen [and] the road crosses a great cemetery with small branches of greenery stuck into the foot of each tomb. We enter the city . . . there are so many obstructions our mounts can make no progress."[196]

The "Arab," that is Bedouin, character of the district was much remarked upon: "As soon as one steps into this astonishing quarter," observed Charles Lallemandin in 1893, "one feels one's in an Arab country, as if a wind from Arabia blows in over it."[197] In 1914, Maurice Barrès bumped into "long lines of camels and Bedouins armed with spears or rifles in the midst of that odor so peculiar to Oriental towns, slightly sickening and heavy with beguiling images—here, images of animal power—of a transitory beauty, and proudly, filthily barbaric."[198]

Estimates of the population advanced by nineteenth-century travelers vary wildly, ranging from 35,000 inhabitants according to Taylor and Reybaud to 400,000 by Lamartine, who, employing a highly debatable method, reaches nearly a million when including the suburbs and the villages of the Ghuta.[199] According to the probably more reasonable figures of the Baedeker Guide, in 1906, Damascus was the most populated city in Syria, numbering some 200,000 inhabitants, made up of 144,200 Muslims; 16,500 Greek Orthodox; 15,000 Greek Catholics; 8,000 Jews; 1,420 Syrian Orthodox; 1,210 Armenians; 800 Syrian Catholics; 730 Protestants; 700 Roman Catholics; 450 Maronites; 380 Armenian Catholics; 320 Chaldean Catholics, and 150 Druzes.[200]

Facing page. The Hotel Victoria in a postcard from the beginning of the twentieth century. Built in 1898 and since demolished, it stood almost directly opposite the present Hotel Semiramis on the left bank of the Barada. It was there that T. E. Lawrence stayed following his entrance into Damascus on October 1, 1918.

261

Above, left. A street in the Suq Saruja district.
Above, right. A lane within the city walls to the north
of Straight Street. *Left*. Traditional wooden doorway.
Such examples are becoming increasingly rare.
Often these have been replaced by ghastly
metal doors (cf. figs. pp. 261, 264).
Facing page. A street in Damascus in a nineteenth-
century print. The original caption read: "The houses
on either side of the street almost touch
at the height of their upper balconies."

Façade of a house on Straight Street.

Top. The (intramural) Shaghur Juwwani district in 1989.

Bottom. District to the north of the Umayyad Mosque known as Bayn al-Surayn. Left, the Mameluk minaret of the Mosque al-Mu'allaq (photograph 1989).

Following pages. The Umayyad Mosque. In the foreground, the district known as Bayn al-Surayn.

The end of the Ottoman empire and the pangs of "Westernization"

"European colonization was a series of crimes perpetrated on weaker peoples. Its keystones were acquisitiveness, might is right, and usurpation. Words like "civilization" and "Christianization" were smokescreens that inadequately conceal the basest instincts of mankind."

Ferhat Abbas, *La nuit coloniale*, Paris, Julliard, 1962, p. 43.

Partition of Syria and the French occupation

World War I was to provide Western imperialism with a long-awaited opportunity to replace traditional policies of arm-twisting and interference with more direct action. If this was not a consequence of the "fall" of the Ottoman Empire that the Western halls of power had so dreaded, it proved to be the cause. French claims were based on the enduring tradition of her "protection" of local Christian communities, on far-reaching commercial interests, and—France already being mistress over the Maghreb—on a desire to consolidate her position as the "Muslim power in the Mediterranean." The minute minority of Syrians—primarily Christians—favorable to the independence of Syria under French aegis often quoted such far-from-negligible considerations. Thus, in 1916, the supremely conciliatory Nadra Moutran wrote: "France . . . cannot ignore Syria which is an essential complement to her African empire. For her, Damascus, the holy city, the gate to the Ka'ba, the city that preserves the traditions of the Arabs and of Islam, crowns an edifice whose pillars are Algiers, Tunis, and Fez. She does not have Cairo or Constantinople; she must have Damascus. . . . With the head in her grasp, the body will lie at her disposal."[1] In France, among profiteers, colonialists, and Catholics, the terms used were more extreme still. A certain Paul Pic, professor of international law at the University of Lyon, a city whose silk merchants possessed significant interests in the Orient, baldly regarded Syria as "a natural extension of France."[2]

The claims of Great Britain—already master over Egypt and southern Arabia—were of far greater scale and more vital to its interests: to protect the land and sea routes to its empire in the Indies and preserve intact the "Monroe zone"—i.e., a quadrilateral delimited by Egypt, Alexandretta [Iskenderun], Persia, and the Indian Ocean—to control the approaches to the Suez Canal, to extend its influence within Arabia, over the Persian Gulf and the greater part of the Syrian coast, and to keep France as far away as possible from these strategic zones. The poet Arthur Rimbaud showed his awareness of this disproportionate interest when writing from Aden on December 30, 1884: "I believe that no nation has as inept a colonial policy as France. If England makes mistakes and has to suffer the consequences, at least it has serious interests and real prospects."[3]

As the Ottoman Empire tottered, Great Britain saw the best means of achieving its objectives as being to constitute a vast Arab kingdom centered on Mecca and placed under its "protection." Before even the outbreak of hostilities, contacts established in Cairo between the British representative in Egypt, Lord Kitchener, and Abdallah, the son of Husayn, sharif of Mecca, made clear to the British the ambitions of the Hashemites and the feasibility of an Arab uprising against the Turks. At the same time, Britain kept channels open with the Hashemite rival, Ibn Sa'ud, the emir of Nadj, who was to prove

extremely useful when the moment came to dispose of the puppet of Mecca. In 1915, negotiations were opened between Husayn and Sir Henry McMahon, a British resident in Cairo, to whom the British government had given complete freedom to come to any agreement that might involve him in the affair.[4] Great Britain engaged to recognize "the 'independence of the Arabs' south of the latitude 37 deg., except in the provinces of Baghdad and Basra, where British interests [the exploitation of the oilfields] require special measures of administrative control, and except where Great Britain is 'free not to act without detriment to the interests of France.'"[5] A healthy delivery of weapons and a monthly pension of twenty thousand pounds dispelled any last misgivings on the part of sharif, who, on June 10, 1916, announced the revolt of the Arabs of the Hijaz against the government of Istanbul. This alliance with the Infidel, whose hypocrisy and imperialist aims were hardly shrouded in mystery, was far from achieving unanimity in the Muslim world, and ulemas in Damascus published a fatwa condemning the revolt of Husayn against the caliph.[6] Mecca was quickly occupied by the sharif's troops and the Hijaz liberated from the Turkish presence, except for Medina, which an armed force, linked to Damascus—the German-Turkish headquarters—by the Hijaz railroad, succeeded in keeping until January 1919. On October 30, 1916, Husayn suddenly had himself proclaimed "king of the Arabs"—a title that neither France nor Britain recognized since they had pictured him only as "king of the Hijaz."

Just as promises were being extended to the Arabs, Britain, France, Russia, and Italy were having secret negotiations aimed at determining exactly how to divide up the spoils of the Ottoman Empire. The Sykes-Picot agreement, concluded between France and Britain on May 16, 1916, sealed the fate of Syria by splitting the country in an arcane manner into the following five zones, with no regard for geographical and cultural circumstances:

1. A blue zone reserved for France; starting in Tyre, this formed a narrow strip along the coast that broadened northwards to include Cilicia, half of Kurdistan and Armenia with the towns of Diyarbakir, Sivas, Adana, and Urfa.

2. A red zone reserved for Britain, including the Lower Mesopotamian plain to upstream of Baghdad.

3. A Zone A, including the provinces of Aleppo, Damascus, Mosul, and the city of Kirkuk.

4. A Zone B, extending south of the preceding to the latitude of Aqaba.

5. A brown zone more or less covering Palestine that was to be placed under international aegis and within which Britain was to keep direct control over 'Akka and Haifa.

In Zones A and B, the two Powers committed themselves "to recognizing and protecting" an "independent" Arab state or a confederation of Arab states under the suzerainty of an Arab chief, with Zone A remaining under French and Zone B under British "influence." In the blue and red zones, the power concerned could set up any regime of its choice, but only "following agreement with the Arab state or confederation of states." Far more restrictive

than the agreements of 1915, and in contradiction with them on several points, the Sykes-Picot accord treated the commitments entered into with the sharif Husayn without compunction. Moreover, Husayn was only informed of this in November 1917, when Trotsky, denouncing the Tsarist alliance with the imperialist Powers, had it published in an edition of *Pravda* of February 21, 1918.[7]

In spite of the secret accords, British diplomacy continued to spin the lie: on June 11, 1917, a statement from Cairo confirmed the promises made in 1915, assuring "them that pre-war Arab states, and Arab areas freed by military action of their inhabitants during the war, shall remain entirely independent."[8] Meanwhile, as the Great Powers plotted their downfall, the Arabs, under the command of T. E. Lawrence and Faysal, one of Husayn's sons, took the fight to the Turks. On July 6, 1917, after an epic desert crossing, they entered Akaba, thus opening the road to Damascus. The waters were further muddied, when, on November 2, 1917, through the Balfour Declaration—a missive addressed by then British foreign secretary Arthur James Balfour to Lord Rothschild, leader of the Jewish community in Britain—in which His Majesty's Government, concerned to placate a Jewish community that was becoming more favorable to Germany and to satisfy American Jewish financiers likely to support the entrance of the United States into the war, announced its aims as regards Palestine. With a land it did not own at its disposal, the government made it known that it would deploy every effort to facilitate the establishment in Palestine of a "national homeland" for the Jewish people, "it being clearly understood," as the text adds, "that nothing shall be done which may prejudice the civil and religious rights of existing non-Jewish communities in Palestine."[9] In fact the declaration opened the door in the medium- to long-term of the transformation of this new legal entity—the "national homeland"—into a thoroughgoing

Map of the Sykes-Picot agreement.

state, "as Jewish as France is French and Great Britain, British," according to Dr. Weizmann's famous dictum.[10] The fate of the Arabs mattered little, apparently, since, as Balfour underlined, "Zionism [was] of far profounder import than the desires and prejudices of the 700,000 Arabs who now inhabit that ancient land."[11]

Balfour moreover extricated himself from the manifest incompatibility between the promises made to the Arabs and those made to the Jews with a cynicism true to type: "[S]o far as Palestine is concerned, the Powers have made no statement of fact which is not admittedly wrong and no declaration of policy which, at least in the letter, they have not intended to violate."[12] On December 27, 1917, reacting to the disclosure of the Sykes-Picot agreements by the Bolsheviks, the French Foreign Minister blithely declared to the Chamber of Deputies: "It was out of the question for France to annex or incorporate in any form whatsoever under the terms of right of conquest populations whose fate should rest with them and them alone."[13]

On the Arab side, engagements with the Turks intensified, as T. E. Lawrence recalled: "Feisal's courage and statesmanship made the Mecca revolt spread beyond the Holy cities, until it became a very active help to the Allies in Palestine. The Arab army, created in the field, grew from a mob of Bedouins into an organised and well-equipped body of troops. . . . This was a great service in our extreme need and we felt we owed the Arabs a reward; and to Feisal, their leader, we owed double, for the loyal way in which he had arranged the main Arab activity when and where Allenby directed."[14]

On September 27, 1918, while German-Turkish troops were falling back on Baalbek by way of the valley of the Barada,[15] British cavalry with its armored personnel carriers approached from Muzayrib. In Damascus, through which gangs of armed Bedouin roamed, where the population, agitated by Faysal's agents and bombarded with English leaflets, was in

uproar, the emir Sa'id, grandson of 'Abd al-Qadir, favorable to France and who hitherto had sided with the Ottoman through religious solidarity, took over the reins. With the assistance of his younger brother 'Abd al-Qadir, he proclaimed the independence of Syria. On September 30, while the last Turkish convoys entered the valley of the Barada under fire from the city's inhabitants, shooting "from roofs, doorways, balconies, and windows," the retreating forces blew up oil and gas stores, as well as arms and ammunition dumps, leaving the station of Kadem, the terminus for the Hijaz railway, burning fiercely.[16] On October 1, news arrived that the British had occupied Beirut and that the city had proclaimed its adherence to the Arab government. On the same day, Lawrence and Nuri Sa'id's Bedouin quotas penetrated into the ancient city of the Umayyad.[17] Lawrence wrote:

> When dawn came, we drove to the head of the ridge, which stood over the oasis of the city, afraid to look north for ruins we expected: but, instead of ruins, the silent gardens stood blurred green with

Street running along the Bab al-Saghir cemetery. Right, the dome and minaret of the al-Sabuniyya madrasa with, behind, the *turba* of Sheikh Hasan. Early twentieth-century watercolor by W. S. S. Tyrwhitt. *Facing page.* The same street, photographed in 2003.

river mist, in whose setting shimmered the city, beautiful as ever, like a pearl in the morning sun. . . . Quite quietly we drove up the long street to the Government buildings on the bank of the Barada. The way was packed, lined solidly on the sidewalks, in the road, at the windows, and on the balconies or house-tops. . . . Every man, woman and child in this city of a quarter of a million seemed in the streets, waiting only the spark of our appearance to ignite their spirits. Damascus went insane with joy. The men tossed up their tarbushes to cheer, the women tore off their veils. Householders threw flowers, hangings, carpets into the road before us; their wives leaned screaming with laughter through the lattices and splashed us with bath-dippers of scent. Poor dervishes made themselves our running footmen in front and behind, howling and cutting themselves with frenzy.[18]

Before the day ended, the provisional government of Emir Sa'id was abolished and Shukri Pasha, a former colonel in the Ottoman army, was named military governor as he awaited the arrival of Faysal,

officially proclaimed head of an independent Syria. On the following day, October 2, the British army made its entry into the city.

A provisional administration took the emergency measures needed in the circumstances: supplying water and electricity, maintaining law and order, preventing plunder, putting out fires in ammunition dumps, giving aid to the population, replenishing provisions, restarting the railroad, and organizing medical services, since the streets were strewn with the remnants of the German-Turkish army (abandoned carts and cars, baggage, and equipment) and corpses. A general civil, political and military amnesty was declared. A few days later, after an abortive uprising, Emir Sa'id was arrested and led under escort to Haifa, while his brother 'Abd al-Qadir escaped. On October 7, a French naval division disembarked in Beirut whence Faysal's representative was directed to withdraw, while Lieutenant-Colonel Piépape, appointed governor, took possession of the government headquarters and received official submission from notable citizens and from representatives of both the Christian and Muslim communities.

On October 31, Turkey laid down her arms and signed the armistice of Moudros. Four days later British troops took possession of the oil-rich Mosul region. Syria was immediately divided into four zones coinciding with the divisions in the Sykes-Picot agreement—all placed under the authority of the commander in chief of the British Army, General Allenby. The blue zone was handed over to French military administrators delegated by the British authorities. On November 17, in order to reassure Arabs the French and British issued a soothing but misleading declaration alleging that "their goal was the final and total liberation of a people so long oppressed by the Turks and the establishment of governments and national administrations deriving their authority from the initiative and unhindered choice of the indigenous populations."[19]

Invited by the British and accompanied by Lawrence, Emir Faysal embarked for France on November 22, 1918, to defend Arab interests—that is to say, the constitution of a unified state as vouchsafed by Sir Henry McMahon in 1915—at the Peace Conference charged with determining the fate of those territories no longer under Ottoman sway. On December 2, Georges Clemenceau, preoccupied exclusively with the left bank of the Rhine, made an initial concession to the British, and, in the teeth of opposition from the Quai d'Orsay, abandoned the rich oil-producing zone of Mosul, as well as Palestine, in exchange for a share of incomes from the exploitation of crude from Mesopotamia and Kurdistan, and the recognition "of the exclusive French influence over the rest of Syria."[20] Except for a few Maronites and a handful of intellectuals, who, in June 1917, had formed a Syrian Central Committee backed and funded by the French colonial party, Syrians as a whole rejected such influence over their affairs. "The Arabs would rather die than accept the French mandate,"[21] Faysal is supposed to have declared. This should have afforded no surprise to anyone given the consequences of the French occupation of Algeria (of which all Syria was cognizant), and considering the frequently denounced incompetence and amateurism of her political, governmental, and diplomatic personnel. Concerning Algeria, the testimony of Alexis de Tocqueville—a fervent partisan of the most savage colonialism, that of "total domination" and "territorial devastation"—is edifying: "Around us the lights have gone out, recruitment among men of religion and men of law has ceased; that is to say, we have rendered Muslim society much more wretched, disorderly, ignorant, and barbaric than what it was before we encountered it."[22]

As for the type of personnel sent "overseas," they hardly inspired confidence. In a letter of October 9, 1918, Paul Cambon, a onetime senior member of the government under Jules Ferry and ambassador to London, wrote: "for years now, we have done no good whatsoever in Syria. . . . There was no blunder we did not commit, and yet still our newspapers speak of annexation and protectorate when these words rile the Arabs, it being necessary to show an adroitness in dealings with them of which our political staff seem incapable."[23]

In an article in the *Revue des Deux Mondes* dated April 15, 1921, Raymond Poincaré drove the point home: "It seems as if certain ministries have taken pleasure in offloading in Syria their civil service rejects, and that the East has become a paradise for agents who have had the misfortune to come unstuck in the metropolis." General Catroux confirmed this: "Yet, just when special men of patent superiority were required . . . all too often he [Gouraud] was sent unsatisfactory personnel. . . . Consequently, what was an extremely disparate functionary body included, besides a handful of undeniable talent, a high proportion of staff insufficiently qualified for the job. Furthermore, only very few knew the Arabic language."[24] In less "diplomatic" terms, Alice Poulleau says the same thing: "Syria was thrown as a sop to parvenu *fils de 'bistro'*—'taproom bores' . . . It seems it served as somewhere in which to pour the detritus of our own country. . . . The majority were moreover blindingly ignorant: what they know of the East is summed up in newspaper commonplaces, worn-out stereotypes, outmoded ideas. . . . For them, any woman in a veil is a *moukère*—a 'bint,' any man in a tarbush is a carpet-trafficking *bicot*—a 'wog.'"[25]

These observations offer corroboration by experience of the presentiment Volney had had—even before Bonaparte's expedition—of the inaptitude of the French for the colonial adventure: "What need do we have of foreign land," he wrote, "when a sixth of our own is still uncultivated. . . . We will surely not act with a wisdom in foreign climes which we fail to employ at home. . . . Our agents will take with them the casual, aloof, scornful tone that makes us so insufferable to foreigners, and they will alienate every heart. There will be recurrent quarrels and seditions: punishments will be meted out . . . and what happened to the Spanish in America and the English in Bengal will happen to us . . . we will exterminate the nation: in vain we extol our gentleness, our humanity; it is circumstances that make men, and in our neighbors' place we too would have been cruel like them."[26] And from Algeria to Indochina and Madagascar, Volney's foresight has been borne out.

Nevertheless a broad swathe of public opinion stubbornly believed that France was the colonial power par excellence, as the groaningly complacent Henri Bordeaux opined: "Of all the European Powers, contrary to a misguided if widespread prejudice, we are the nation that understands best how to colonize, since we strive to understand the indigenous races, to distribute property equitably among them, and to bring them economic development, and not unwontedly to stand in the way of their following their customs and practices."[27]

At the meeting of the Peace Conference on January 29, 1919, this plot was made still thicker by the intervention of the United States. The president, Woodrow Wilson who had made a name for himself "invading Mexico and Haiti and by launching a counterinsurgency war in the Dominican Republic . . . with ample destruction and torture,"[28] announced "the right of the people to determine their own destiny," refusing to recognize the Sykes-Picot agreements negotiated before the United States entered the war, and proposed placing these "colonies" [sic] under the control of the Society of Nations and the tutelage of a power delegated to administer them.

This new theory of mandate acquired its final form in Article 22 of the Treaty of Versailles of June 28, 1919: the mandated state, designated by the Society in the interests of the population placed under it, was neither a sovereign, nor even a protector, but a guardian, whose authority, delegated by the Society of Nations and exercised under its control by the intermediary of a standing committee, was limited and, theoretically speaking, revocable. The mandate was therefore not a protectorate—and still less a colony—but, in principle at least, a consultative and aid mission designed to pave the way to independence. The only concession obtained by Faysal at the Conference was that an inter-Allied board of inquiry be sent to Syria (this was exclusively American after France and Britain both reneged)—the King-Crane Commission, instructed to test popular feeling.[29] Its report, submitted on August 28, recommended the reduction of the Zionist program, the creation of a unified Syrian state—including Palestine—under Faysal's authority, with the United States or Great Britain as mandatory Powers (but in no way France, as this would likely provoke serious disorder, as the report pointed out), and the limitation of the French mandate to the tiny Mount Lebanon, populated chiefly by Maronites.[30]

Rather than satisfying Arab public opinion, which favored instead the immediate halt of Zionism, the independence of Syria within the territorial integrity of its natural borders from the Taurus to Aqaba and from the Mediterranean to the Euphrates, the Commission's recommendations, which might have served as a provisional compromise, were shelved. In France, nevertheless, a tidal wave of public opinion, aided and abetted by the Catholic Church, extreme-right colonialist groups like the Comité Dupleix, by industrial special interest groups, in particular the Lyon silk-traders, and by the Chambers of Commerce of Lyon and Marseille, urged the government to broaden and strengthen its influence in Syria.[31] "Syria is a daughter of France—a mother does not abandon her children," exclaimed, with customary eloquence, the senator for Lyon, Édouard Herriot.[32] For their part, the usual Syrian suspects—members of the Central Committee—endeavored to give credit to the notion that the people rejected Faysal and Britain, and hankered solely after French supervision.[33]

In 1916, in his book *La Syrie de demain*, Nadra Moutran became an obsequious mouthpiece for the "rights and vital interests of France in the Orient." "We do not demand, before the final victory, that troops be transferred to free us from the hateful yoke." he remarked. "On the contrary, it is gladdening for us to suffer as long as the French suffer . . . We will not allow the French to be hoodwinked into thinking that ungrateful and forgetful Syrians might oppose their intervention in Syria."[34] And our spokesman—who had plainly not read Tocqueville—adds: "Syrians know very well that, in spite of the slanderous tittle-tattle, France does respect Islamic worship in its Muslim colonies."[35] He goes on cravenly to enumerate in minute and sometimes absurd detail all the various and varied interests that France—motivated by purely disinterested sentiments—would discover in Syria: a means of ensuring peace in her Muslim possessions in Africa, elements she might need to develop her industry, and many sources of natural, agricultural, mining, archeological, and tourist wealth.[36] Having just proven that Syrians were all dewy-eyed for the love for France, he concludes, clearly not above a contradiction or two: "Once the coast and the Lebanon are conquered, the rest of Syria would be condemned to fall, if not by arms, then by famine."[37]

In parallel, an ethno-racial litany—very much in vogue—strove to put the seal on the long-awaited Franco-Syrian rapprochement. "From the ethnographical point of view," wrote a certain Dr. J. Khalil unblushingly, "the French race is differentiated from the Syrian race only by nuances."[38] We were told some time ago that the Druzes descended from the Druids, or even the Comte de Dreux,[39] and we now learn that the Syrians are in fact Gauls! At a meeting organized at the Geographical Society on June 15, 1920, by the Comité Dupleix, a certain M. Saint-Yves gave a lecture that the right-wing paper *Action française*, reporting the event, characterized as "well documented from the ethnological point of view." An unnamed *Action française* journalist wrote:

He [the lecturer] has also shown that Syria is Syrian and not Arab, that furthermore one should regard Arab "nationality" and the Arab state, of which so much has been made, as a figment of the imagination. Strictly speaking there never has been an Arab civilization. Damascus was a center of Syrian civilization. Baghdad a center of Persian civilization. . . . Real Arabia is the Arabian Peninsula. The true Arab has never created anything, he is a Bedouin, a nomad. We demand that the Christian, Muslim, and other populations of various confessions in Syria over which France has had centuries-long rights not be delivered over to the Bedouins of King Husayn or Emir Faysal.[40]

Returning to Damascus from the Peace Conference at the end of April 1919, Faysal was given a triumphant welcome. On May 7, he reaffirmed his commitment to unconditional independence. In July, an elected Syrian General Congress published a series of far-reaching demands: "total and immediate independence for Syria, without protection or supervision, as a constitutional monarchy . . . opposition to Zionist claims in view of creating a Jewish 'commonwealth' in that southern part Syria known as Palestine . . . a formal demand that the southern part of the country should not be separated from the country of Syria . . . the rejection of any treaty proposing the partition of the Syrian nation."[41] In Damascus, anti-French demonstrations became more frequent and collaboration between the Arab administration and French "advisers" more difficult each day, while there was further friction between the army of occupation and Syrian troops in coastal zones. Faysal embarked for London, arriving on September 18, the day of the publication of the Franco-British agreement of September 15, which envisaged replacing British troops with the French Army "west of the Sykes-Picot line" from November 1. Although confined to the provisional regulation of "the military occupation, without prejudice to any final solution of the mandate and border questions," the switch nonetheless enshrined French power over the littoral, so the British government, playing Pontius Pilate, now urged Faysal to address negotiations to France. On November 27, Faysal signed an agreement with Clemenceau, which recognized him as king of Syria—where he was responsible for maintaining law and order and over which he was to impose his authority—but which also constrained him to accept French occupation on the coast and an exclusively French dimension in the areas of the economy and government.

In January 1920, Faysal ran up against a nationalist movement hostile to Syrian dismemberment and to foreign supervision. A second General Congress, convened on March 8, drafted a historic resolution: the independence of Syria "within its natural limits," the rejection of Zionist claims, a regime of decentralization for the Lebanese mountains, and the election of King Faysal, ruling in a unified and autonomous Syria. A Syrian national government was constituted under the presidency of

'Ali Ridha al-Rikabi, a retired Ottoman general. The Allies rejected the decisions of the Congress and President Millerand charged General Gouraud, French High Commissioner and the commander in chief of the army in the Levant since October 9, 1919, with informing Faysal that France viewed the decisions of the Congress as null and void.

Events quickly came to a head. Meeting in San Remo, the Supreme Council of the Allies, after much procrastination and horse-trading, ratified the partition of Syria on April 25, 1920, thus reneging on the promise of self-determination made to the Arabs in 1915. The northern part of the country—the only one to bear the name of "Syria"—was placed under French mandate, with Palestine, the Transjordan and Mesopotamia under British. These accords were confirmed at the Treaty of Sèvres and the Tripartite Convention signed by France, England, and Italy on August 10, 1920, which enshrined the dismemberment of the Ottoman Empire, with further territorial amputation for Syria: as a concession made to Kemalist Turkey, with which an armistice had been just signed on May 30, the northern border shifted south.[42]

There was an explosion of anger and indignation in the Arab world. In Palestine, whose population refused any separation from the rump of Syria, violent clashes opposed Arab tribes and British troops. In Damascus, the National Congress once again demanded total independence and rejected foreign control out of hand. In the occupied coastal zone, attacks against French forces and concerns multiplied. Impatient to impose the French mandate, General Gouraud, who had just taken delivery of reinforcements in the shape of an elite colonial corps in Beirut, issued an ultimatum to the Syrian government on July 14 that urged the acceptation of the mandate, the disarming of the Arab army, the occupation of Rayaq, Aleppo, Homs, and Hama by French forces, as well as the punishment of troublemakers. In Damascus, indignation reached

13. BEYROUTH — L Arrivée du Général Gouraud

Postcard showing the arrival of General Gouraud in Beirut.

fever pitch. Concerned above all to keep his throne, Faysal pitifully issued the order to disarm, while the Congress, accusing him of spinelessness, adopted a more intransigent stance. On July 20, on the pretext of having waited too long for an answer, Gouraud dispatched a second ultimatum to Faysal requiring that a French mission be received in Damascus so as to prepare the way for the application of the mandate. The same day, police opened fire with machine-guns on demonstrators, leaving around two hundred casualties. Three days later, the French Army began its progress towards Damascus, while Faysal ordered his troops to make no resistance. Nevertheless, on the morning of July 24, in Khan Maysalun, six hundred regulars, commanded by Ysuf al-'Azma, Minister for War, hastily joined by a few hundred volunteers from Damascus, were decimated by French forces equipped with tanks and 155-caliber artillery.[43] The following day, with a regiment of Moroccan spahis in front of line, a French army under the command of General Goybet made its entry into the city through deserted streets.[44] Faysal, who, up to the last minute, had hoped to "collaborate" with France, was ordered to leave Syria. Accompanied by his Foreign Minister and an entourage, he traveled to Haifa and embarked for Europe, where the British handed him the throne of Iraq in compensation.

Arriving at the Hijaz station before which the Moroccan spahi regiment presented a guard of honor, Gouraud made his official entrance in Damascus on August 7. He made a lengthy visit to the Umayyad mosque before going to the tomb of Saladin, where he made the famous sally: "Here we are, Saladin!"[45] A court martial was convened that sentenced in absentia several Syrians among the most active in the resistance to French aggression. Less than two years after its creation, the Arab kingdom of Damascus was thus extinguished. The Syrian Central Committee voiced its glee and, hailing it as a "glorious victory . . . that has liberated

Syria from the oppression of the Hijaz," published an address thanking "General Gouraud and his troops for their heroic action in the cause of justice and civilization."[46] In France, colonialists, racketeers, and Crusade revivalists were overjoyed. In a 1925 book dedicated to General Gouraud with the eloquent title *Le Chemin de Damas* (The Road to Damascus), the Tharaud brothers welcomed the event thus: "After so many centuries, we now reappear on Syrian coasts. . . . The Frankish kingdom of Syria is being rebuilt before our very eyes. Here begins our new Crusade."[47]

Nationalist revolt and the bombardment of Damascus

After the capture of Damascus, French forces set about "pacifying" (as officialese has it) the rest of the country. Aleppo, Homs, Hama, Dera'a and Dayr al-Zor were quickly occupied and, one after the other, the Bedouin tribes submitted. On June 22, 1921, in the outskirts of Qunaytra, General Gouraud escaped an attempt on his life during which his officer interpreter was killed.[48] After crushing an insurrection by Ibrahim Bey Hananu in the Aleppo region in July 1921, and in October another by Salih al-'Ali in the Ansariyeh mountains, the "pacification" of Syria was complete—all the more thoroughly, as the then head of the intelligence service, Lieutenant-Colonel Catroux, put it, because "the most active representatives of the idea of national unity had been rooted out of the territory."[49] In 1925, on the eve of the great Syrian uprising, France was to have no more than twenty thousand men left in the Levant.

Anxious to neutralize the aspirations to national unity threatening her authority, and with the fig-leaf of defending the minorities, France proceeded—contradicting the spirit of the mandate, but in accord with the maxim *divide et impera*—to dismember the nation.[50] On September 1, 1920, against the will of an

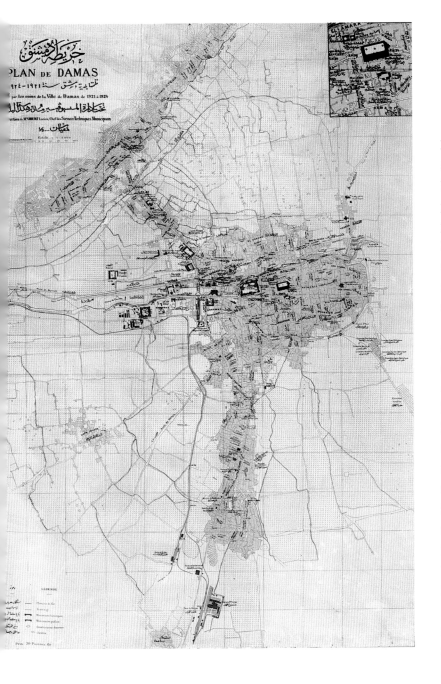

However, restored to the rank of chief town of its *wilaya*, Damascus lost its status as a capital to the benefit of Beirut. Concluding the exposition of partition, Catroux wrote: "Such is the regression, so painful to Syrian national self-esteem and especially humiliating for the proud Umayyad capital, that the deposition of Faysal on the occasion of the establishment of the mandate has accompanied all to do with aspirations to unity."[52]

In spite of installing indigenous governments in each of these states—that had been previously, as a decorous expression put it, "softened up"[53]—and in contradiction with the spirit of a mandate intended to bar direct intervention by the mandate nation, power in reality lay in the hands of the High Commissioner, the representative of the Republic, and the commander in chief of the army, assisted by a secretary-general and by delegates "supervising" indigenous administrations. In France, voices rose to condemn what was blatantly underhand colonization. During the sitting of December 30, 1920, senator Victor Bérard, recalling that the intervention of France in Syria had been promoted by the Chamber of Commerce of Lyon and Marseille, declared: "the intended aim is permanent occupation, administrated directly, a policy contrary to every engagement undertaken, to our future in that place, as well as to the desires and needs of the indigenous populations."[54]

Violent demonstrations erupted in Damascus, Homs, and Hama. With the declared purpose of "appeasing the idea of unity without, however, annihilating the autonomous states it constituted,"[55] the mandatory power proceeded to redraw the map: on June 30, 1922, the States of Damascus, Aleppo, and the Territory of the Alaouites were joined in a confederation. Demands for unity were not assuaged, however, and, in 1924, General Weygand, the new High Commissioner, amalgamated the states of Aleppo and Syria into a single Syrian state, with the State of the Alaouites remaining independent. Virulent

immense majority of the population, the State of Greater Lebanon was solemnly proclaimed, amalgamating with the tiny Lebanese mountain, with its Maronite majority, a series of mainly Sunni territories that were constantly to demand their reattachment to Syria, including the plain of the Beka'a, traditionally part of Damascus, and the entire coast from the 'Amil *jabal* to Tripoli.[51] The rest of the land was divided into three further states: the State of Aleppo, including the *sandjak* of Alexandretta given relative autonomy; the Territory of the Alaouites; and the State of Damascus from which the Druze *jabal* was detached shortly afterwards, in March 1921.

Plan of Damascus drawn up by the city authorities from 1921 to 1924 under the direction of Lucien Vibert, Head of Municipal Services.

opposition to the mandate power persisted. At the beginning of 1925, shortly after the nomination of the Radical and Freemason General Sarrail as High Commissioner, nationalist opposition gathered around Dr. Shahbandar in a People's Party; dissatisfaction was further exacerbated by the separation of southern Syria and by Western support for Zionism.

On April 8, 1925, ferocious demonstrations broke out during a visit to Damascus by Lord Balfour— he of the ill-fated Declaration—to inaugurate a Hebrew university in Palestine: the suqs were closed, the crowd invaded the Suq Hamidiyya and confrontations with the police left dead and injured. In the Druze *jabal* throughout July, troops had constant skirmishes with groups of armed patriots which French propaganda now dubbed "gangs of fanatics."[56] The Druze massacred a detachment of Tunisian spahis and Syrian legionnaires,[57] while the French garrison in Suwayda was holed up in the citadel. On August 3, a column three thousand strong going to its aid was routed. The rebellion soon extended to all the Druze areas. On October 18, rifle fire directed at the High Commissioner's train coach in the suburb of Midan triggered a riot that quickly spread to the city center. "Isolated soldiers . . . have their throats cut by a fanatical mob," wrote General Andréa: "An NCO post-orderly at the military hospital and an orderly accompanying him are killed in the street and impaled on stakes . . . elsewhere, seven Algerian riflemen surprised in the riot take refuge in a house which the insurrectionists torched, burning the poor wretches alive."[58] Joined by part of the local gendarmerie, the insurrectionists marched as a body on the 'Azm palace, the residence of General Sarrail. Set ablaze and pillaged, its furniture, precious rugs, and objets d'art were carried off; electric wires were ripped out, the library ransacked, and the museum stripped of its finest pieces, its cameras, and its priceless collection of photographic plates containing more than two thousand pictures of the monuments of Damascus,

Aleppo, Hama, and Upper Mesopotamia. As barricades sprang up everywhere and Europeans hastened to take refuge in their consulates, the citadel's guns, the air force and tanks rolled in action. The population of the lower city fled towards the districts of Muhajirin and Salihiyya, while a continuous line of cars wended its way to Beirut.

It was "a throwback to the era of gloom and barbarism,"[59] wrote Frenchwoman Alice Poulleau, an eyewitness to the events. After three days of fighting and bombing, Damascus looked like a war zone: "All along Straight Street up to Bab Sharqi, walls, doors, and house fronts [were] pockmarked with tank shells."[60] The Quwatli house, one of the most beautiful in all Damascus, full of treasures and incomparable antiquities, had been peppered with shells and all the houses around it burned.[61] The whole neighborhood around the Darwishiyya mosque had been laid waste. At the entry of the suburb of Midan, a hole gaped in the cupola of the Sinaniyya mosque, in which, by sheer chance, the shell had failed to explode. "Close to the Bank of

The *qa'a* of the 'Azm Palace following the pillage and conflagration of October 1925. The whole edifice was restored by architect Michel Écochard using photographs taken by Bonfils around 1885 (for the present state of the *qa'a*, see p. 211).

Syria, between the Suq Hamidiyeh and Suq Tawileh," Alice Poulleau observed, "there is another district of Dantesque horror where nothing remains standing, and where, in certain areas, as people have been buried under their own houses, there rises the stench of a mass grave. . . . Everywhere, in the inner courtyards, pathetic, dainty trees stand broken and singed; debris lies in piles near waterless pools. Bedouin women forage over the smoking ruins . . . electric cables trail everywhere and water from burst conduits floods into the lifeless alleyways . . . the most horrific zone, bordering the Suq Tawileh, brings to mind the entrance to a volcano with lava belching out smoke."[62] By the evening of the third day, some 250 houses and many historic buildings had been destroyed and 135 people crushed beneath the debris. The toll among the insurrectionists and the civil population reached several thousand. Less than three years later, wandering among the ruins of the bombarded districts, Roland Dorgelès found that they closely resembled villages he had seen at the Front, while the "broad avenues of rubble around the citadel churned up by shells" were to remind him of the horrors of the Great War.[63] Gradually rebuilt, the western districts within the city walls would earn the name Hariqa ("conflagration") in remembrance of France's civilizing mission. The bombing of Damascus was welcomed, however, by partisans of "modern" town-planning like Louis Jalabert, who defined it as the "development of civilized life." "In Damascus," he writes, "Sarrail's bombardment presented the advantage of allowing certain clearances to be effected."[64]

The brutal repression brought sharp protests from foreign consuls. In Arab countries as a whole, anger against France reached new heights. Domestically, an

DAMAS (Syrie). - Panorama général après l'incendie du 18 Octobre 1925

Districts west of the intramural city after French bombing in October 1925 (the future Lariqa quarter). Postcard.

indignant press campaign temporarily stirred the public from its accustomed slumbers: "General Sarrail has passed through Syria like a plague of locusts. . . . In Syria, he found a splendid heritage which he scandalously laid waste. Sanction must be sought. There must be a change of regime," fumed A. Gauvin in the *Journal des débats* dated October 30. On November 11, 1925, Sarrail stepped down to make way for Henri de Jouvenel, a liberal senator appointed to find a political exit strategy from the conflict. The "pacification" policy was not shelved, however—not least as the insurrectionists holed up in the Ghuta, seeing no change with the arrival of Jouvenel, carried on the struggle until July 1926. "A large city like Damascus," wrote General Gamelin, "meandering and tortuous in form, linked by a thousand lanes to the green spaces surrounding it, constituted an ideal field of operations for the rebels. In the guise of law-

abiding inhabitants, they could enter and leave it freely."[65] Thus, root-and-branch measures were called for: "To ensure stability," Gamelin continues, "headquarters has decided to ring the town with a mesh of barbed wire commanded by pillboxes armed with machineguns and with a limited number of entry points. This system has allowed movements to be monitored in earnest and quickly made it possible to return order to the interior of the great Muslim city, forcing unruly elements out of the area."[66]

It thus became crucial for the French authorities to cut the city off from the Ghuta with which it had lived in close symbiosis since the dawn of time. In a burst of zeal of which Paris's Baron Haussmann would have been proud, it bored thoroughfares for its troops and armored cars, thus allowing them to speed to any area in an old city seen as a prime hideout for the "gangs of fanatics." On December 10, the governor

Pacification *à la française*. Syrian resistance members hanged at Merjeh Square, February 1, 1926.

presented to the mayor and councilmen a plan for "beautifying" the city. The following day, without legal act of expropriation, "indigenous" workmen set to the task, under the protection of two Algerian rifle battalions "commanded to disperse the crowd if it takes it into its head to hinder matters."[67] On January 1, 1926, the northern sector was completed, and, at the beginning of February, over seven miles (12 km) of boulevard together with as many of barbed wire surrounded the city. Supine politicians, architects, and town-planners tried to justify these improvements, citing demands of vehicle traffic or a campaign against unsanitary conditions.[68]

The military authorities did not deal in tender-hearted circumlocutions: in a confidential report on the situation in Syria on January 1, 1926, Pierre Alype, the High Commissioner's envoy extraordinary wrote: "The gangs were severely harassed and punished, but the species has not for all that been entirely eradicated. The city of Damascus is now being organized as a kind of retrenched camp: in spite of the difficulties of the season and under the energetic and expert supervision of General Andréa—whose name will forever remain attached to this remarkable enterprise—immense engineering works are being fully and rapidly implemented: a circular boulevard is being constructed with broad thoroughfares more favorable to modern means of combat and a net of barbed-wire is steadily being woven round the city."[69]

The inhabitants inevitably took a dim view of these "improvements"—all the more so since they were funded by a charge of one hundred thousand *livres* levied on the population. "Actually, this is vandalism, and Damascus has no need whatsoever of an orbital for the cars of a few functionaries or pashas, forming a ring-road that has chopped up its districts, obliterated picturesque little corners, cut it off from its gardens, and where we will be forced to breathe dust perfumed with benzol,"[70] observed Alice Poulleau, before issuing this premonitory warning: "In ten years, Damascenes,

if you let things take their course, your ancient Sham will look more like Levallois-Perret [a rundown Paris suburb]."[71] In April, in spite of the blockhouses, bypasses, barbed wire, tanks, the "belts of iron and fire," the arrests, the torture, and in spite of hanging some nationalist leaders, combat raged once more in the Midan district. "I wonder what remains of the Midan," wrote Alice Poulleau on April 15: "Today a mosque from where shots were being fired on airplanes was burned together with a great number of houses round about. Almost all the houses still standing were pillaged and the inhabitants have fled the district. Two bombs dropped by plane that I saw explode in the distance killed some people at prayer. Often, rowdy children playing in the street are attacked by jumpy soldiers."[72]

On May 7, when it seemed the storm was abating, the Midan, unable to collect the required funds, was subjected to blanket bombardment. The quarter burned on until evening, two to three hundred houses were leveled, several historic buildings damaged, while occupants attempting to flee were mown down by soldiers encircling the quarter. At same time, a force of 8,500 men, bolstered by tanks and artillery, and under the orders of Colonel Andréa, regional commander for Damascus, set about "flushing out" the Ghuta. By July 10, "order" had been restored. Immediately, the Damascus worthies—the vast majority of whom, the mandatory power mischievously observed, were behind the insurrection—"hastened to ensure the envoy extraordinary that the city totally disassociated itself from the rebels."[73] By the end of 1926, with the "pacification" of the Druze *jabal*, the Hermon and southeast Lebanon complete, the last surviving "gangs" had been annihilated.

A last gasp for independence—
a disastrous assessment

While the nationalist revolt had petered out, if

anything Syrian opposition to the mandate increased. As for French policy, it was a sorry saga of blunders, inconsistencies, and gaffs that managed to earn the disapprobation even of her most faithful allies: "If the intention had been to give Syrians an impression of instability and uncertainty, to proclaim to the world just how incapable we are of carrying through a plan, to create a sense of revulsion among the populations under our mandate, in short," wrote Joseph Kessel in 1926, "if we had wanted to lose Syria, we could have acted no differently."[74] In 1939, faced with German threats, and keen to ensure Turkish neutrality, France yielded the *sandjak* of Alexandretta to Mustafa Kemal. After Palestine, the Lebanon, Transjordan, the community states, the loss of the Mosul region and the northern territories, this shameless violation of earlier promises and obligations that its mandatory status had imposed on France proved to be the final act in the piecemeal division of Syria.[75]

The debacle at the hands of Nazi Germany had profound repercussions in Syria, where nationalists were quick to point out that, as Vichy France had withdrawn from the Society of Nations in April 1941, the mandate had lost all validity in international law. When German planes on the way to Iraq to aid nationalist forces in an uprising against British Occupation availed themselves of airports at Aleppo and Damascus, the British army, supported by Free French forces, crossed the Syrian border. On June 24, de Gaulle made his entry into Damascus liberated from the Vichy party and declared before members of the Syrian government: "Free France has proclaimed the independence of Syria. It is imperative that this independence become a reality as soon as possible. General Catroux, *délégué général* of the Levant, will proceed with initial measures and all necessary steps as soon as the current crisis is over—that is to say, as I see it, in the very near future."[76] No better respected than the preceding ones, these new promises did not prevent five more years of grinding negotiations and a fresh

bombardment of Damascus, before—with an outcome at once deplorable and pathetic—the Syrian escapade came to end.

On December 1, 1943, in spite of noises from a France desirous of extorting a "treaty of alliance" and so protecting the interests she still hoped to preserve in the country, the Syrian Prime Minister declared the mandate to be at an end. The new Syrian state was recognized by the Soviet Union in July 1944 and by the United States in September. As France committed one last faux pas—unloading troop reinforcements at the Lebanese ports—fierce demonstrations erupted, particularly in Damascus, where the "Fidahi" group delivered to public vilification individuals guilty of "collaborating in any way with the French enemy or of maintaining any kind of connection with it."[77] The Syrian gendarmerie joined the rioters and its own police attacked the headquarters of the French commander in chief. In the Druze *jabal*, Syrian troops commanded by French officers passed with arms and materiel over to the irregulars. In Dmeir, native Meharists (camel corps) revolted and massacred their officers.

On May 28, 1945, French posts were encircled at Dayr al-Zor, in the Druze *jabal*, and in Dera'a. In Hama, in response to an attack on a convoy, French planes took to the air, killing about a hundred and injuring as many again. In Damascus, shots having been fired from the windows of the Parliament at the residence of General Oliva-Roget, the deputy in Syria, the French counterattacked with cannon and occupied the building. The citadel—the rioters' headquarters—was pummeled from the air. For two days, on May 29 and 30, Oliva-Roget, in an effort to restore order, had the city bombed, leaving several hundred casualties. The shooting ceased only on the third day at the injunction of the British, and after their 9th Army had been called into action. The Syrian and Lebanese governments then demanded the unconditional withdrawal of French

7. Damas — Pont de Bab-Touma

so disinterested—were not spared: "We left, insulted by our own wretched patients," confided one sister of Charity.[81]

Five centuries of and policy sank without trace in an ignominious failure that left untold psychological and material damage. After a final bout of double-dealing, the last French troops left Syria on April 7, 1946. Having miscarried in her ostensible mission to pave the way to independence, France left behind her a debilitated and traumatized country, poorly prepared for a stable political existence. For the entire Middle East and for ancient historical Syria in particular, the interference of the French, Americans, and British had proved catastrophic. Instead of promoting unity, as signed up to in 1915—a unity dictated by history and culture, with which the entire population concurred—the policy followed was politically divisive and simply placed the oil fields in the hands either of Western oil companies or in those of puppet emirs or monarchs compliant to imperialist interests—British and American for the most part.[82] Four states were created from the limbs of ancient Syria: Lebanon, to placate a Francophile Maronite minority;[83] the emirate of Transjordan where, at the end of 1920, the British placed on the throne Faysal's brother, the emir Abdallah; Palestine, now open to Jewish emigration and whose partition the UN, by rubber-stamping the transmutation of "national homeland" into "state," was on the point of enshrining; and finally, a nation that was ancient "Syria" in name only.[84] Damascus thus saw itself severed from its thousand-year-old links with the Holy Cities of Arabia and its natural "Lebanese" and "Palestinian" ports, and cut off from the Galilee and from the bread-basket of the Beka'a. Moreover, the proclamation on May 14, 1948, at 4 p.m., of the Jewish State of Palestine—under the Biblical name of Israel—set up on its doorstep, on a portion of southern Syria which hitherto had been solely under

troops. At midday on June 1, the evacuation of Damascus began, and British troops entered at 4 p.m.[78] Homs, Hama, the Druze *jabal* and the Hawran were evacuated in their turn. Elsewhere, awaiting the order to fall back and surrounded by a furious crowd who hurled taunts and insults, French troops were closeted in their barracks, protected only by British patrols.[79] As for the unfortunate French civilians, they poured out of homes that the mob was on the brink of ransacking—"with nothing more that the clothes they stood up in"—and fled in droves towards the Lebanon via the airport at Mezzeh that served as a transit camp.[80] Even the missions—so humane, and

its dependence, a Zionist and expansionist enemy, which was going to drag the region into a saga of crises and conflict.[85]

In such dire circumstances, there as elsewhere, the tattered mask of the "civilizing mission" was laid down, leaving little else for the mandatory Powers to do than trumpet their achievements in the material field.[86] These were strenuously puffed up in official reports—living monuments to ethnocentrism—in self-congratulatory propagandist tracts, such as *L'Œuvre de la France au Levant*,[87] in the star-struck accounts of many travelers, and in the speeches of ignorant politicians with their own agendas. In 1922, Henri Bordeaux had already written: "Lebanon and Syria . . . are being reborn under French protection and the vigilant eye of General Gouraud."[88] It is indeed beyond question that the French mandate promoted the development of an infrastructure essential to a modern economy. Road mileage was increased from 430 to 1,800 miles (700 to 2,900 km);[89] railways, bridges, and aqueducts destroyed by the Germans were rebuilt; the port of Beirut was cleared, and those of Alexandretta, Latakia, and Tripoli enlarged. Reforestation, irrigation, and drainage work were undertaken, and arable land significantly increased, especially in Jezira. Many hospitals and schools opened. Although progress in education benefited primarily the Christians, thus reinforcing denominational divisions, the number of schools in Syria and the Lebanon rose from 670 in about 1919 to 2,800 in 1939 and the numbers of pupils from 50,000 to 271,000.[90]

The historical and archaeological heritage was the object of special care on the part of the agent. In 1920, a Service of Antiquities was set up under the scientific direction of the Academy. Two years later, the Beirut Museum opened its doors, while an Institute of Art and Archaeology, a School of Fine Arts and a French Institute of Archaeology and Islamic Art started up in Damascus: many historic buildings were to be the subject of thorough study. Syria's immense heritage, which previously had received scant attention, was to emerge from the shadows. In 1924, the first methodical excavations were undertaken in Palmyra under Danish scholar Herald Ingholt. In 1926, in order to increase fiscal revenues and improve repartition of the rate, the first land survey of Damascus was drawn up. Since 1933, many monuments have been restored, in particular the parts of the 'Azm palace destroyed during the riots of 1925, using fragments dug out from among the debris and featuring in historic photographs. In 1939, Bab Kaysan was restored and the interior of the chapel of St. Paul rebuilt.

Damascus on the road to Westernization—monuments and districts in danger

By promoting the wholesale import of "modernity" into Damascus, the mandate triggered a complete rupture with the past. Thanks to these intrusions, unprepared and poorly monitored, all the checks and balances—social, ecological, economic, etc.—on the basis of which the city had previously flourished were upset. Initially, there was a considerable rise in population, swelled after 1930 by a massive influx from the countryside: from 173,000 inhabitants in 1922, it was to reach more than 300,000 by the end of the mandate.

The arrival of French functionaries and soldiers with their families accelerated the hitherto embryonic development of the districts of Shuada, 'Arnus, and Jisr, located along the road connecting Salihiyya to the intramural city. Numerically low but influential, and bathed in the glow of social and cultural prestige, this community attracted Europeans of all nationalities; soon the consulates of Britain, Italy, and Belgium, and certain echelons of Damascus's middle class—Muslim as well as Christian, who abandoned the old city all the more

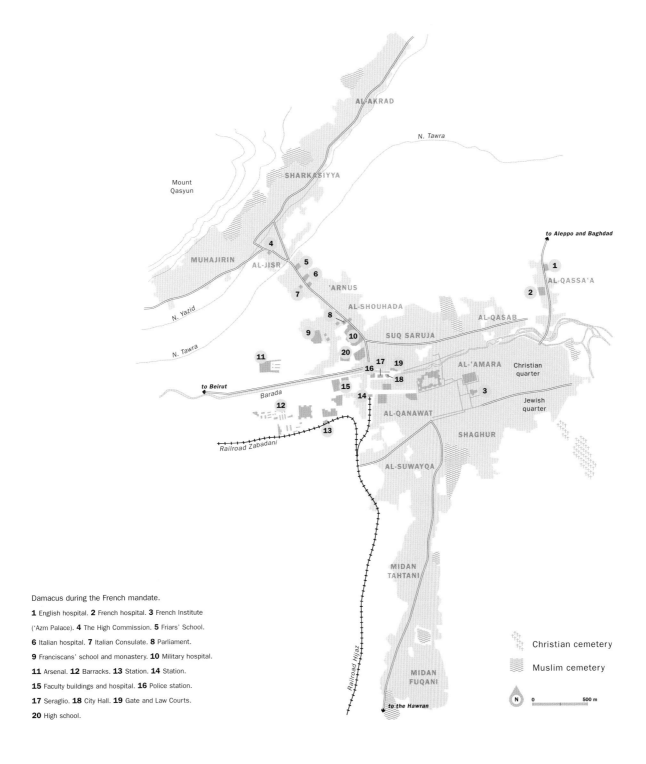

Damacus during the French mandate.

1 English hospital. **2** French hospital. **3** French Institute
('Azm Palace). **4** The High Commission. **5** Friars' School.
6 Italian hospital. **7** Italian Consulate. **8** Parliament.
9 Franciscans' school and monastery. **10** Military hospital.
11 Arsenal. **12** Barracks. **13** Station. **14** Station.
15 Faculty buildings and hospital. **16** Police station.
17 Seraglio. **18** City Hall. **19** Gate and Law Courts.
20 High school.

readily as rural populations settled there in large numbers—moved to live near European neighbors and in buildings thought of as more comfortable, better equipped, and more "modern." This population shift catalyzed a slow deterioration in the ancient fabric of the city. Thus, just as in Hellenistic times, a new city arose adjacent to the old, organized according to principles opposed to those of ancestral tradition: broad straight streets, with tree-lined avenues; "residential" blocks from four to five floors high with little balconies—of a distressing uniformity for the most part—and surrounded by small private gardens. Replacing the Merjeh square, this new urban center incorporated government services, banks, the treasury, post offices, regional general staffs, the war office, gendarmerie, military hospital, hotels, schools, and churches (such as the Church of St. Anthony of Padua erected in 1926) and soon the Parliament of Syria, on which construction began in 1932. Other districts experienced rapid development, including al-Muhajirin, linked to the city center by a tramline down Salihiyya Street, but more especially that of al-Kassa'a, northeast within the walls, whose growth accelerated following the building of the avenue of Baghdad in 1926, and in which successive waves of immigrants sought refuge: Christians from the Midan district fleeing bombardment in 1926 and 1927; Armenians and Greeks from Turkey—the former to escape massacre, and the latter fleeing a war that opposed them to Kemalist forces. To take account of this increase in population, in 1932, a new system supplying water from the 'Ayn al-Fijeh spring by a channel eleven miles (18 km) long was brought into service.

From the very start of the 1930s, anxious to exert control over urban growth and to safeguard the Ghuta, whose 62,000 acres (25,000 ha) of orchards and arable farming were threatened both by urbanization and by water pollution, the mandatory authorities commissioned city planner R. Danger and architect M. Écochard to draw up a regulatory plan. With regard to the Ghuta—the very lungs of Damascus—its recommendations were clear and unambiguous: to preserve and even to expand agriculture and the plantations, to limit the growth of the built-up zone and preferably to channel it towards the foothills of Mount Qasiyun and away from farmland, and to put a halt to unauthorized settlement that endangered particularly the orchards to the north of the avenue of Baghdad: "If one permits the clandestine mode of occupancy to continue," R. Danger warned, "the gardens will disappear and with them the green belt surrounding the city, and, in relatively few years, one will be amazed to see in their place a filthy and unsanitary shanty town forming a dangerous breeding-ground for epidemics."[91]

In spite of these dire warnings, unregulated and unauthorized urbanization currently remains one of the major stumbling blocks to proper development in Damascus. In addition to safeguarding the Ghuta and to planning for urban growth, the Danger-Écochard plan also dealt in depth with interregional and urban traffic. The Palestine road, the busiest at that time, and those to Beirut, the Hawran, Homs, and Baghdad, interlinked by a series of circular routes bypassing the city, were widened into divided highways. As regards sanitation, the suggestion was to overhaul the main bed of the Barada so as to forestall flooding in the city center, in particular in the vicinity of the Merjeh Square. Lastly, with a view to a "balance between archaeology and aesthetics,"[92] it was suggested that the area around certain historic buildings be cleared—starting with the citadel and the tomb of Saladin. Work started as early as 1936, a full year before the plan was finally approved: new thoroughfares and public gardens were laid down, monuments spruced up, and a new national museum constructed next to the Sulaymaniyya *takiyya* to plans by Messrs. Écochard and Pearson.

Despite the onslaughts of modernity, the arrival of "hordes of tourists"[93] and of movie houses that "displaced the old music-halls,"[94] in spite of the trams, rail stations, avenues, and the trundle of automobiles, the "exoticism" of the old city could still cast its spell. "For weeks I had been looking for the Orient of legend," wrote R. Dorgelès in 1928. "Finally I had reached it. I had only to enter the suqs, without asking, at random. All was there: pilgrims in their green turbans, dervishes with felt bonnets, the blind soothsayers, prostitutes with red waistbands, and the Bedouin with cropped beards, wearing their *abayas* with the air of a ruined lord. . . . Filled with wonder, I dived under arches and descended stairways . . . and, in the gloom of a Moorish coffeehouse, I sought out impassive smokers sliding chess pieces."[95] Other travelers, on the contrary, more sensitive to the gnawing of time, voiced their disillusion: "What remains of old Damascus today?" asked the Tharaud brothers in 1923. "Almost nothing if the truth be told. . . . One seeks vestiges of its former grandeur in vain. A few mosques, tombs, two or three palaces drowned in modern banality, a pleasant enough *turquerie* without much of interest, all rather pitiful compared to the stirrings the glorious name of 'Damascus' summons up from the depths of memory. . . . Is it the delights of their gardens, their heavenly abundance that conceals from Damascenes the decrepitude of their city? They don't notice its decadence, its faded beauty."[96]

After independence, developments in Damascus accentuated trends born during the mandate: deterioration of the ecological equilibrium, dilapidation of the ancient fabric of the city, increased illicit occupation—phenomena all stemming from a poorly controlled and exponential increase in population. To already accelerating demographic growth was added an influx of rural populations driven from their land by falling agricultural incomes—in 1975 only 14 percent of arable land was under irrigation—and attracted to the capital with its concentration of administrative, industrial, and commercial activities offering prospects of a more decent existence. In 1948, this was compounded by a large-scale influx of Palestinian refugees fleeing persecution by the Jews once the UN, under American pressure, had voted the partition of mandated Palestine on November 29, 1947.[97] Initially crammed into mosques, khans, *hammam*s and old houses, from 1955, they settled in the "camp" of Yarmuk that extends southwards from the suburb of Midan. From 300,000 in 1945, the population swelled to 1,700,000 inhabitants in 1988, while, at same time, the urban area grew from 4,700 acres (1,900 ha)—as against 333 (135) for the intramural city—to nearly 21,000 (8,500). In spite of

the recommendations of the Danger-Écochard plan, this extension occurred essentially at the expense of the Ghuta, which dropped from 57,000 acres (23,000 ha) to less than 25,000 (10,000), entailing the destruction of the orchards and the best agricultural terrain.

From the very early 1950s, the housing crisis became acute, caused by governmental policies and unsuitable and inadequate manufacturing infrastructures. The shortage affected primarily social categories on low incomes, which had recourse to large-scale unregulated settlement. Already thrown into relief by Écochard and Danger, this phenomenon—one of the most visible scourges of the urban crisis—has even accelerated since the late 1960s. Acting outside the law, under the obliging if not complicit eye of the authorities, speculative builders and unregulated developers, concerned solely with turning a quick profit, have overloaded building land. The result is unsurprising: high-rise blocks, unusable narrow roadways, nonexistent utilities, squalor, lack of maintenance, and water supply, drainage, sewerage, and electricity all reduced—when they exist at all—to the barest minimum. Approximately 70 percent of housing built in the 1980s belongs to this category: today, more than half the population subsists in an unregulated habitat scattered about a score or so zones throughout the city.

While this belt of concrete and perpend was severing the ancestral links Damascus had maintained with the Ghuta, the historical city too entered an accelerated process of decline, the consequence of an exodus on the part of the traditional middle class and the arrival of countrymen short of money and ready to put up with substandard housing conditions. A system of renting in small units—or even by the room—made its appearance, dividing the old residences into two or more parts, either partitioning the courtyards or by intercalating floors. Housing densities soared, with people living in close proximity in a manner at odds with traditional life: today, nearly 80 percent of houses in the old city have been converted and rented out in this manner, the average rate of occupation to a room being about 3.8. As low rental incomes mean that owners are unable to carry out the necessary refurbishment and maintenance works, the whole urban fabric is condemned to degrade rapidly, a process accentuated by the irruption—into streets far too narrow for them—of motor vehicles and their attendant congestion, noise, and pollution. Moreover, many houses—together with a number of khans and *hammams* that have been severely affected—have been converted into warehouses, craft workshops, or even into small-scale industrial plants. A way of life ousted by new hygiene practices, one by one the *hammams* have closed their doors. By 1960, only thirty remained active. The others had been abandoned, destroyed during rehabilitation, absorbed into new constructions, or converted into premises for such activities as welding, weaving, soapmaking, dyeing, cabinetmaking, or storing grain.

The historic center, plagued by unsanitary conditions, its fabric deteriorating, its traditional economic activities progressively disappearing, robbed of its symbolic cachet, accused of every evil—including being a hotbed for Islamist insurrection—was an easy target; calls for its partial or complete destruction came from those afflicted with the town-planning bug, from politicians with a mania for "Westernization" to developers with an eye to the vast profits to be made. Very early on, however, in the 1950s, concerned to curb urban expansion and conscious that the 1936 scheme was outdated, the authorities asked foreign experts to draw up a new master plan. A project drafted in 1957 by the Bulgarian Morozov being rejected as it would have condemned the old city, the municipality called upon architects Écochard and Benshoya, who presented

their new plan in 1968. Based on the principles of "functional urbanism" originating in the Athens Charter devised by architects unacquainted with the sociocultural realities of the Orient, it envisaged the control of urban growth up to 1984. Like its predecessor of 1936, and in accordance with the accepted ideas of the time, it accorded priority to the transport infrastructure. Keen to safeguard the Ghuta, it recommended urban expansion over the foothills of Mount Qasiyun towards the Berzeh sector in the east and the Mezzeh in the southwest. In order to meet the enormous demand for water, it envisaged the creation of dams and reservoirs to regulate the flow of the Barada, of the al-Awaj river, and the spring of 'Ayn al-Fijeh. A bypass was to deviate traffic away from the ramparts, rehabilitate the city gates, and reduce through-traffic. Lastly, after fine words concerning the intramural city in the declaration of intent ("We must drive home the exceptional, unique importance for the history of the world of this quadrilateral of only a few hectares"[98]), the old quarters were dispatched in a

Above: Storefront of a seller of *halawiyats*, sweets much loved by the inhabitants of Damascus (photograph 1983).

290   *Facing page.* In an antique dealer's shop: Damask silks, mother-of-pearl inlaid furniture, *'uds*, dolls, etc. (photograph 1994).

few short pages that, at the outset, dissociated historic buildings worth preserving and even restoring where necessary, from the traditional environment whose value it strongly contested. Heritage buildings, according to a thoroughly European approach antithetical to the spirit of the Arabo-Islamic city, were to be, as the saying went, "enhanced," whereas the rest—except for the most beautiful listed residences—would gradually be given over to demolition contractors and their bulldozers.

Paying scant regard to the integrity of the urban fabric, and neglecting the deep-rooted values of a living historic city, the Écochard plan administered a coup de grace to its unity and architectural coherence. Declaring that "everywhere significant areas need to be cleared, for various reasons—aesthetic, or to improve traffic circulation, safety, or links with the rest of the city,"[99] it divided the intramural city into three sectors of differing size. The northwestern sector—the most valuable, a reserve of historic buildings gathered around the

Umayyad mosque—was to be subjected to developments by means of which "the monuments might be easily reached by car, the warehouses readily supplied by truck, but also so that pedestrians might walk freely through the suqs and around the monuments, and that all the means of circulation created, car parks and empty spaces alike, are distributed to allow the plan of a given monument to be extricated from the surroundings and comprehended."[100] The development of the monuments in that sector occasioned the obliteration of many small plots, countering those who would have preferred "the 'oriental' character of the old town to be preserved in its entirety . . . without realizing that every day houses crumble and melt away in the rain, and that, even to keep up their external appearance would be infinitely more costly than to build a whole new house in modern materials."[101]

The other sectors of the intramural city were to be delimited by major thoroughfares; if the plan credited them with a "medieval character" worthy of preservation "in places," at other points they were to be sectioned off to create little squares or parking spaces, with various smaller plots being pared down to make way for the road infrastructure. In the event of total destruction for reasons of sanitation, the plan, however, stipulated that any new construction should employ solely traditional materials and could not be higher than a single story. As for the suburbs of Midan, Qanawat, Saruja, Salihiyyeh, etc.—apparently deprived of extenuating circumstances—they would be progressively demolished and replaced by modern constructions.

Though work did begin—several small plots were demolished, a street running from the Suq Midhat Pasha to Bab al-Saghir was widened, and a few buildings erected—the resulting outcry put a stop, within the city walls at least, to the execution of a plan whose ethnocentric, insensitive, and simplistic character was vilified on many occasions. It had been a shot across the bows, however, and subsequently

the defense of old Damascus was to be enshrined by administrative and legislative provisions. In 1972, a decree prohibited intramural demolition or rebuilding. In 1975, at the request of the Antiquities division, the city within the walls was placed on the UNESCO list of world heritage sites—all symbolic measures, without legal effect, but which nonetheless ensured international recognition of the value of the traditional urban fabric.

That same year, a department devoted exclusively to the old city was set up under the aegis of the Service of Antiquities, while a *Société des Amis de Damas* was constituted in order to increase awareness of the problems of urban regeneration and heritage protection among the public and responsible agencies. In 1977, an international

Aerial view of the southwestern districts. Shaghur, Qanawat, Suwayqa, and the Bab al-Saghir cemetery.
In the foreground, the al-Sinaniyya Mosque.

committee for the preservation of the city was established, including among its members the directors of the French and German institutes, which launched a program of systematic study of the historic quarters. The following year, a government committee, embracing representatives from the Antiquities department, City Hall, the Ministry of Tourism, various waqfs, and the Faculty of

Architecture, was convened to coordinate these studies and see them incorporated into the city's economic plan. Though wielding no great power, the committee nevertheless succeeded in having a number of measures adopted, none of which seem to have been honored to the letter: joint approval by the municipality and the Antiquities department is required for any alteration; the exclusive use of

Western districts without the city walls on either bank of the Barada. Merjeh Square, the main post office, the station of the Hijaz. In the background, the Citadel.

traditional materials: wood, sun-dried brick, stucco, etc.; a single-story height limit; a prohibition on raising roofs; the obligation to adhere to the cadastral survey of 1930; and a halt to the demolition—unfortunately already at an advanced and probably irreversible stage—of the Suq Saruja suburb.

In spite of the best intentions of UNESCO and various committees, the degradation of the old town and its monuments was to continue. In the 1960s, several new buildings were erected within the city walls; in 1962, in an effort to ease traffic congestion, the Barada—now little more than an open-air sewer—was covered for about a third of a mile (600 m) between the Sulaymaniyya *takiyya* and the western ramparts; in 1983, a thoroughfare was laid out from the al-Sandjaqdar mosque to Bab al-Barid:

houses were bulldozed without regard to the cadastral plan, and, in the process of clearing a small precinct before the western entrance to the Umayyad mosque, several houses, as well as the booksellers' and perfumers' suqs were obliterated. Yet it was in the suburbs, more exposed to "pressure" from transport infrastructures, that the damage was most severe.

The destruction of the Suq Saruja quarter, already eviscerated by the north–south divided highway, may start up again at a moment's notice. The Midan district, bisected by the Beirut–Aleppo motorway, has already been deprived of a number of historic residences. The Tawrizi district, which even twenty years ago possessed exemplary architectural coherence, is now disfigured by jerry-built concrete

Hammam Qarmani. *Left.* in 2003, after restoration. *Right.* in 1989, before restoration.
Facing page. View of Damascus taken from the top of the Minaret of Jesus: A series of high-rise blocks ruining the western faubourgs in the wake of speculative building development that now threatens the intramural city.

estates out of all proportion to the surroundings. At Salihiyya, several historic buildings, such as the Rukniyya, Hafiziyya, and Badriyya madrasas, have already been completely shorn of their traditional urban context, and a new development plan drawn up in 1980 that allots priority to relieving traffic congestion recommends the demolition of thirty-three monuments. Moreover, the majority of these districts have been afflicted by an evil from which, with some exceptions, the intramural city has been shielded: the presence on their periphery of high-rise buildings, which, as well as upsetting the microclimate by reducing sunlight in the winter and blocking off wind from the west, also have a sociological impact, since they violate the privacy of terraces and courtyards, the traditional refuge of women and their families. Historic buildings have fared little better. Incompetence and a dearth of financial resources have meant that restoration work has not measured up to the task: inadequate stone-dressing, coursing, and pointing; the abuse of coatings and seals; forms softened and muted; garish, slapdash paintwork; substandard calligraphy; unsuitable materials, etc. Since the beginning of the 1990s, few monuments have escaped this kind of treatment.[102] Even in the least inadequately restored, like the Khan As'ad Pasha, tourist amenities—museum, hotel, and restaurant—have ousted traditional activities, thus hastening the vitiation of the old city.

A survey of the city's deterioration would not be complete were we to omit the Ghuta, more than half

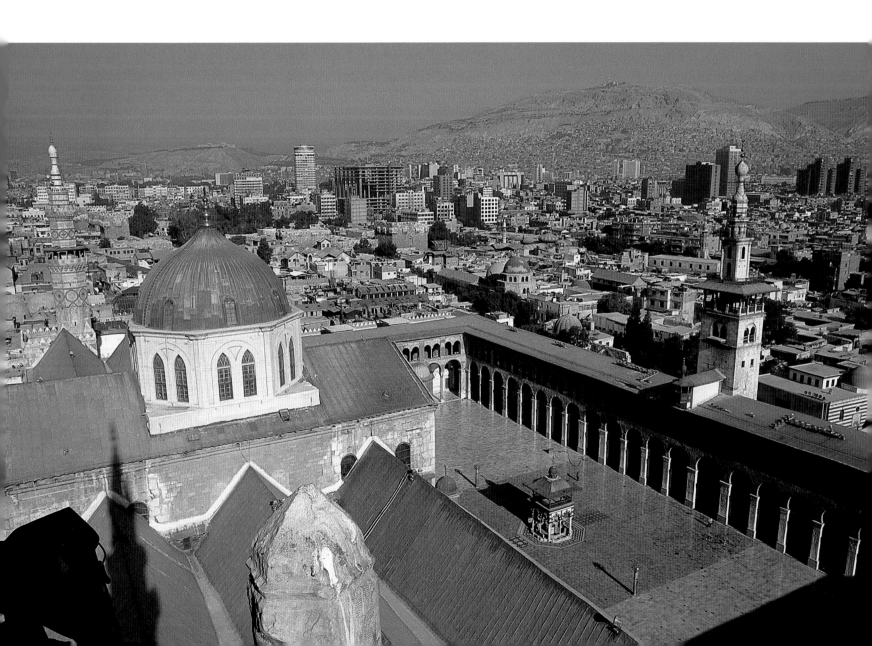

of which has already been swallowed up at a rate estimated at approximately 500 acres (200 ha) per annum. The first inroads date back to the mandate, when, after the revolt of 1926, the authorities leveled the earthen walls between the gardens, on the pretext that they supposedly helped the guerrillas. Gradually, and in spite of the prescriptions of the Danger-Écochard plan, the best irrigated and most fertile zone—next to the northern suburbs—has fallen prey to urbanization, and the villages of Mezzeh, Qadam, and Berzeh engulfed by the conurbation. Other villages of the oasis were not spared: swollen by an upsurge in immigration, illicit construction multiplied and absorbed hundreds of acres of arable land. Moreover, over a period of a few years, thousands of trees were cut down to feed new craft and industrial activities—glassmaking, small-scale engineering, furniture manufacturers, producers of perpend

(breeze-blocks), and tile manufactories, etc.—that have sprung up in the area. Beginning in 1954, Lakes 'Utayba and Hijaneh gradually dried up because of excessive pumping, over-extraction of water from the Barada and the Awaj, and an increasingly arid climate. To this must be added the pollution of the groundwater, whose level started to drop in 1930s following the introduction of motor-driven pumps, and that of surface water, relentlessly siphoned off for agriculture and arboriculture. In March 1990, the Minister for the Environment acknowledged that Damascus's liquid waste "was discharged untreated into the River Barada," whence thousands of offshoots flow through the gardens of the oasis.[103]

As Alice Poulleau had warned: "In ten years, Damascenes, if you let things take their course, your ancient Sham will look more like Levallois-Perret."[105]

In the foreground, the decaying district of the Suq Saruja; left, the summit of the minaret of the al-Shamiyya madrasa; in the background, "Levallois-Perret-style" new-town Damascus raises its ugly head (photograph 1989).

The principal monuments of Damascus

Inner Damascus

Umayyad

1 Umayyad Mosque – 705

Burid

2 Al-Aminiyya madrasa – 1120

Zengid

3 *Bimaristan* of Nur al-Din – 1154
4 *Hammam* of Nur al-Din – 1154–71
5 Bab al-Sharqi – 1164
6 Al-Nuriyya madrasa – 1167–71
7 Dar al-Hadith al-Nuriyya – 1171

Ayyubid

8 *Turba* of Saladin – 1195
9 Al-Silsila *hammam* – 12th/13th cent.
10 Usama *hammam* – 1204
11 Al-'Adiliyya madrasa – 1222–23
12 Bab al-Salam – 1243
13 Tower of al-Salih Ayyub – 1248
14 Al-Qilijiyya madrasa – 1253
15 Al-Badira'iyya madrasa – 1258
16 Al-Zahir *hammam* – founded in 978
    and overhauled in the Ayyubid epoch.

Mamluk

17 Al-Qaymariyya madrasa – 1266
18 Al-Najibiyya *turba* – 1268–69
19 Al-Zahiriyya madrasa – 1277–78
20 Dar al-Hadith al-Tankiziyya – 1327–28
21 Sitt Tankiz *turba* – 1330–31
22 Al-Qaymariyya *hammam* – 14th cent.
23 Al-Nasiri *hammam* – 14th cent.
24 Al-Ikhna'iyya madrasa – 1415–14
25 Al-Jaqmaqiyya madrasa – 1419–20
26 Mosque and minaret Hisham – 1427
27 Mosque and minaret al-Qal'i – 1470

Ottoman

28 Al-Yaghushiyya Mosque – 1597
29 Al-Bakri *hammam* – 1617
30 Al-Naufara *hammam* – end of the 17th cent.
31 Madrasa of Sulayman Pasha al 'Azm
    1757
32 Fathi Mosque – 1743
33 'Azm Palace – 1749
34 Bayt al-Siba'i – 1769
35 Bayt al-Nabulusi – 1780
36 Bayt al-Quwatli – 1797
37 Bayt Farhi/Dahdah – 18th cent.
38 Bayt Farhi al-Mu'allim – 18th cent.
39 Bayt al-Quwatli – 18th cent?
40 Bayt Lisbuna – 18th/19th cent.
41 Bayt al-Safarjalani – 18th/19th cent.
42 Bayt 'Abd al-Qadir – 18th/19th cent.
43 Bayt al-Mujallid – 18th/19th cent.
44 Bayt Nizam – 18th/19th cent.
45 Maktab 'Anbar – 19th cent.
46 Bayt Shamiyya – 19th cent.
47 Bayt al-Jabri – 19th cent.
48 Bayt Shatti – 19th cent.
49 Bayt al-Qudsi – 19th cent.
50 Bayt Shuta – 19th cent.
51 Bayt al-Baydawi – 19th cent.
52 Bayt 'Arida – 19th cent.
53 Bayt al-Hulwani – 1807
54 Bayt Yusuf Baddun – 19th cent.
55 Bayt Niyadu – 19th cent.
56 Synagogue – 19th cent.
57 Synagogue – 19th cent.
58 Synagogue – 19th cent.
59 Armenian Orthodox church – 19th/20th cent.
60 Greek Catholic church, patriarcate, school
    and monastery – 19th/20th cent.
61 Armenian Catholic church – 19th/20th cent.
62 Syriac Catholic church – 19th/20th cent.
63 Franciscan church and monastery
    19th/20th cent.
64 Protestant church – 19th/20th cent.
65 Jesuit church – 19th/20th cent.
66 St. Mary's Greek Catholic church
    19th/20th cent.
67 Syriac church – 20th cent.
68 Maronite church and patriarcate – 20th cent.
69 Synagogue – 1930

Salihiyyeh

Zengid

1 Al-'Imadiyya *turba* – 1169

Ayyubid

2 'Umariya madrasa – end 12th cent.
3 Al-Khatuniyya *turba* – 1182
4 Al-Sitt Yasmin *turba* – 1203
5 Hanabila Mosque – 1203
6 Jaharkasiyya madrasa – 1211
7 Ibn Salama *turba* – 1213
8 *Turba* of Mithqal – 1224
9 Al-Farnathi *turba* – 1224
10 Al-Rukniyya madrasa – 1224
11 Dar al-Hadith al-Ashrafiyya – 1236
12 Al-Atabikiyya madrasa – 1242
13 Qubba Rayhan – 1243
14 Sahibiyya madrasa – 1245
15 Al-Latif *turba* – 1247
16 Al-Qaymari *bimaristan* – 1248
17 Al-Murshidiyya madrasa – 1253
18 Qaymariyya *turba* – 1256

Mamluk

19 Al-Takritiyya madrasa – 1298
20 Ghorlo *turba* – 1319
21 Al-Kajkariyya *turba* – 1322
22 Al-Jadid Mosque – 1388
23 Al-Muqaddam *hammam* – 14th cent.
24 Al-Dulamiyya madrasa – 1443
25 Al-Hajib *hammam* – 1451

Ottoman

26 Shaykh Muhyi al-Din ibn 'Arabi Mosque
    1517
27 Al-Salimiyya takiyya – 1518
28 Abd al-Ghani al-Nabulusi Mosque – 1731

Western and southern outskirts (Midan)

Fatimid

1 Fatima's Tomb – 1048
2 Abu Fulus Mosque – 11th cent.

Seljuk

3 Tomb of Sukayna – beginning 12th cent.

Zengid

4 Bah al-Saghir – 1156 and 1168
5 Bab al-Jabiya – 1164
6 Tower of Nur al-Din – 1173

Ayyubid

7 Al-Jarrah Mosque – 1183
8 Mosque of al-Musalla – 1209
9 Al-Jadid *hammam* – mid-13th cent.
10 Suhayb al-Rumi Mosque – 13th cent.

Mamluk

11 Tankiz's mosque and *turba* – 1317
12 Al-Karimi/al-Duqaq Mosque – 1318
13 Ba'adur 'As *turba* – 1329
14 Afriduniyya madrasa – 1348
15 Sandjaqdar Mosque – 1348
16 *Turba* of Arak – 1349
17 Shaykh Hasan *turba* – 1350
18 Sayf al-din Ji'an/Wali al-Shaybani *turba*
    1353
19 Baba Kaysan – 1363
    (chapel of St. Paul – 1939)

20 Zawiya Rifa'iyya – before 1372
21 Rashidiyya madrasa – after 1389
22 Sunqur *hammam* – 13th/14th cent.
23 Manjak Mosque – 1391
24 Al-Zayn *hammam* – 14th cent.
25 Zawiya Abu Bakr al-Mawsili – before 1394
26 Al-Taynabiyya Mosque – 1399
27 Al-Mawsili *hammam* – end 14th cent.
28 Al-Darb *hammam* – end 14th cent.
29 Al-Tawrizi Mosque – 1420
30 Al-Tawrizi *hammam* – 1441
31 Al-Shadbakliyya madrasa – 1453
32 Al-Sabuniyya madrasa – 1459
33 Zawiya 'Abd al-Karim al-Mawsili
    before 1513
34 Al-Siba'iyya madrasa – 1515

Ottoman

35 Takiyya al-Sulaymaniyya – 1554
36 Al-Sulaymaniyya madrasa – 1566
37 Al-Darwishiyya Mosque – 1574
38 Murad Pasha Mosque – 1575
39 Rifai *hammam* – 16th cent.
40 Darwish Pasha *turba* – 1579
41 Al-Sinaniyya Mosque – 1591
42 Maktab al-Sinaniyya – end 16th cent.
43 Fathi *hammam* – 1745
44 Bayt Abu Shamad – 18th/19th cent.
45 Sa'id al-Din Mosque – 18th/19th cent.
46 Bayt Barudi – 19th cent.
47 Station for the Hijaz – 1913

Northern outskirts
(between the Tawra and the Barada)

Seljuk

1 Site of the tomb of Safwa al-Mulk – 1111
    (destroyed in 1939)

Zengid

2 Bab al-Faraj – 1154

Mamluk

3 Al-Shamiyya madrasa – end 12th cent.
4 Al-Badriyya madrasa – end 12th cent.
5 Al-Ammuneh *hammam* – end 12th cent?
6 'Ala al-Din *turba* – 1173
7 Al-Mansur Hasan *turba* – 1179
8 Farrukhshah *turba* – 1183
9 Al-'Izziyya madrasa – 1224
10 Al-Shibliyya madrasa – 1226
11 Bab Tuma – 1228
12 Maridaniyya madrasa – 1228
13 *Turba* of Bahramshah – 1229
14 Bab al-Faradis/Bab al-'Amara – 1232
15 Al-Tawba Mosque – 1234
16 Hafiziyya madrasa – 1250
17 Al-'Umari *hammam* – 13th cent.
18 Al-Jawza *hammam* – 13th cent.
19 Al-Ashraf *hammam* – 1295
20 Al-Shaybani *turba* – 1333
21 Al-Yunusiyya khanqah – 1382
22 Al-Ward *hammam* – 14th cent.
23 Al-Mu'ayyad Mosque – 1399
24 Al-Jawza Mosque – 1402
25 Al-Aqsab Mosque – 1408
26 Al-Saqifa Mosque – 1411
27 Al-Ward Mosque – 1427
28 Al-Nahhasiyya khanqah – 1458
29 Mosque and *turba* of Shaykh Raslan – 1504
30 Al-Mu'allaq Mosque – beginning 16th cent.

Ottoman

31 Mosque of Sinan Agha – 1564
32 Bayt Khalid al-'Azm
33 Bayt al-Yusuf

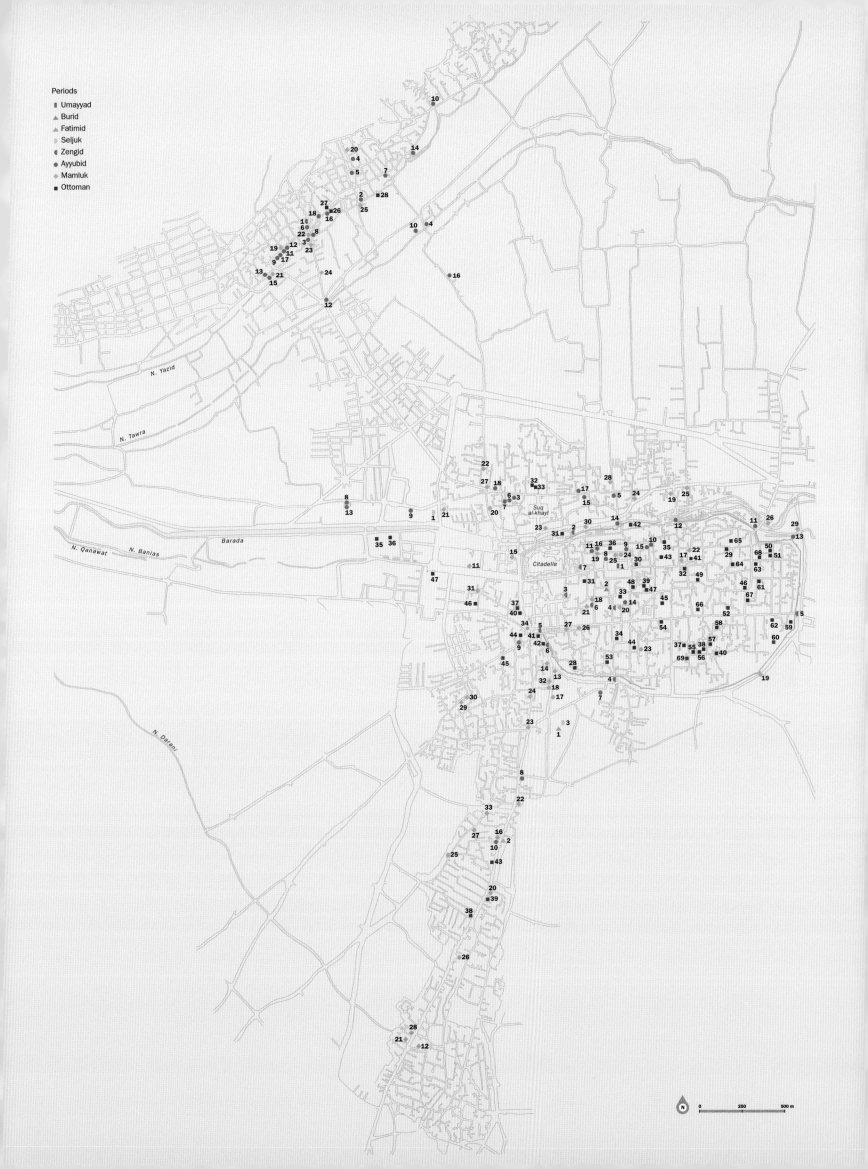

Periods

	Umayyad
	Burid
	Fatimid
	Seljuk
	Zengid
	Ayyubid
	Mamluk
	Ottoman

N. Yazid

N. Tawra

N. Qanawat   N. Banias   Barada

N. Darani

Suq al-khayl

Citadelle

N

0   250   500 m

Notes

Introduction

1. Immanuel Kant, *Anthropology from a Pragmatic Point of View* (tr. M. J. Gregor), The Hague, 1974, p. 40 [1:25a].
2. C. 1500, Dimashqi writes in his *Manual of Cosmography*: "Syria stretches from Malatia [Malatya] to al-Arich over a length of twenty-seven days, its broadest point lying between Manbij and Tarsus." *Manuel de la cosmographie du Moyen-Âge*, Copenhagen, 1874, p. 257. It should be noted that Malatya, situated in what is today Turkey, lies far to the north of the present-day northern frontier of the country. For his part, Herodotus locates Cappadocia in Syria (*Histories*, V, 49). On the division in 1920 of this geographical entity from which arose contemporary Syria, cf. infra p. 270–71.
3. The Lebanon and Anti-Lebanon form part of a double mountain range running parallel to the shores of the Mediterranean whose altitude, roughly speaking, decreases from north to south, from the Lebanon to the hills of Judaea. The Lebanon culminates at 10,138 feet (3,090 m), the Anti-Lebanon at 9,186 feet (2,800 m), while Mount Hermon, which prolongs the latter southwards, peaks at 9,232 feet (2,814 m). Syria's water reservoir, these two solid masses are separated by the Beka'a Valley, also known as Coele-Syria, where the Litani (Leontes), Orontes, and Jordan have their source.
4. A *ghuta* is a well-watered verdant valley. With an uppercase "G" the term invariably designates the *ghuta* of Damascus.
5. Ibn Hawqal, *Configuration de la Terre*, Paris/Beirut, 1964, vol. 1, p. 171. He adds (vol. 2, p. 455): "It is common knowledge that the most beautiful sites in the world are the Samarkand Sughd, the estuary of Obolla, the Ghuta at Damascus." Obolla was a port on the Tigris estuary at the mouth of a channel running from Basra.
6. P. Belon du Mans, *Les Observations de plusieurs singularitez et choses mémorables trouvées en Grèce, Asie, Judée, Égypte, Arabie et autres pays estranges*, Paris, 1555, p. 149.
7. The waters of the 'Awaj disgorge to the east into Lake Hijaneh, which, at one time, merged with those of the 'Utayba. At the beginning of the fourteenth century, Dimashqi recorded a single lake fed by the 'Awaj and the Barada. Since 1954 an increasingly dry climate, a swelling population, and intensive use of water have gradually drained both lakes. (Total consumption for Damascus has rocketed from 5,500,000 gallons (20,000 m³) per day in 1932 to 110,000,000 gallons (400,000 m³) in 1980). Nevertheless, Muslim tradition preserves the memory of an era long ago when rainfall and moisture were much greater than today. Tabari has it that the Syria of Abraham's time was "completely covered over with trees, greenery, flowing water, and cultivated fields." *Chronique*, Paris: Sindbad, 1980, vol., 1, p. 167. Other texts refer to a cedar forest in the valley of the Barada, cf. M. Gaudefroy-Demombynes, *La Syrie à l'époque des Mamelouks d'après les auteurs arabes*, Paris, 1923, p. 42.
8. Altitude 3,770 feet (1,149 m).
9. Prior, of course, to the meteoric growth of the city, which, beginning at the end of the nineteenth century, has driven the population from around 100,000 up to more than three million today—greatly to the detriment of the Ghuta.
10. Located in the center of a bustling city, these tells cannot be systematically explored today. The only in-depth excavations to reveal information concerning Damascus before the Iron Age were undertaken very recently on the stretch of ground within the citadel. Eight surveys carried out between mid-January and mid-March 2002 exposed for the first time vestiges dating from the middle of the third millennium. Cf. the forthcoming article by P. Leriche, Gelin M. al-Maqdissi, and E. Al-Ejji, *La fouille des états antiques de la citadelle de Damas*.
11. Tabari, *Chronique*, op. cit., p. 102.
12. Al-Muqaddasi, *La Meilleure Répartition pour la connaissance des provinces*, Damascus, 1963, p. 80 and pp. 152–53.

13. Ibn Khurdadhbeh, *Le Livre des routes et des provinces*, Paris, 1865, p. 273.
14. Dimashqi, *Manuel*, op. cit., pp. 259 and 261.
15. *The Travels of Ibn Battuta, A. D. 1325–1354* (tr. H. A. R. Gibb), Cambridge, 1958, vol. 1, p. 118
16. Quoted by Ibn Battuta, ibid., p. 120
17. J. Palerne, *D'Alexandrie à Istanbul. Pérégrinations dans l'Empire ottoman, 1581–1583*, Paris: L'Harmattan, 1991, p. 208.
18. Al-Muqaddasi, *Meilleure Répartition*, op. cit., p. 174. Genesis 15:2 states boldly that Damascus was the hometown of Abraham's servant Eliezer: "And Abram said, Lord God, what wilt thou give me, seeing I go childless, and the steward of my house is this Eliezer of Damascus?"
19. Ibn Rusteh, *Les Atours précieux*, Cairo, 1955, p. 228.
20. Mas'udi, *Les Prairies d'or*, Paris: Société asiatique, 1965, vol. 2, p. 451.
21. Ibn Battuta, *Travels*, op. cit., vol. 1, p. 143; Ibn Jubayr, *Voyages*, Paris, 1949–56, vol. 6, p. 317.
22. Ibn Jubayr, ibid.; Ibn 'Asakir, *La Description de Damas*, Damascus, 1959, pp. 184 and 187; Mas'udi, *Prairies d'or*, op. cit., vol. 1, p. 27.
23. Ibn Jubayr, ibid.
24. Ibn 'Asakir, *Description de Damas*, op. cit., p. 185.
25. This tradition derives from a somewhat forced interpolation in the Koran, 23, 52. Cf. Tabari, *Chronique*, op. cit., vol. 2, p. 102; Ibn 'Asakir, *Description de Damas*, op. cit., p. 184; Ibn Jubayr, *Voyages*, op. cit., vol. 6, p. 318.
26. Ibn 'Asakir, *Description de Damas*, op. cit., p. 195.
27. Ibid., p. 203.
28. Ibn Jubayr, *Voyages*, op. cit., vol. 6, p. 320. See also, Koran 6, 74.
29. Cited by Ibn Jubayr, *Voyages*, op. cit., vol. 6, p. 516. Ibn 'Asakir, *Description de Damas*, op. cit., p. 305, relates that the tombs of both Moses and Mary, Mother of Jesus, are supposed to be in Damascus.
30. Ibn 'Asakir, *Description de Damas*, op. cit., p. 305.
31. Ibn Jubayr, *Voyages*, op. cit., vol. 6, p. 328. Another tradition says that Christ will descend from the east minaret of the 'Umayyad mosque—which moreover bears his name.

Chapter I

1. R. Thoumin, *La Maison syrienne*, Damascus: PIFD, 1932, p. 9.
2. Recent excavations in Anatolia may put this widely held idea to the test: the "sanctuaries" discovered at Çayönü and Nevali Çori would be older by a millennium than those at Obeid (Ubaid). Cf. J. Cauvin, *Naissance des divinités, naissance de l'agriculture*, Paris, 1998, p. 161.
3. As Ernest Renan had already observed (*Histoire générale et système comparé des langues sémitiques*, Paris, 1868, pp. 40–43), the choice of the term "Semite" to designate a family of languages comprising Akkadian, Hebrew, Arabic, Aramaean, etc., owed to the philologist Eichhorn, is an awkward one. Only one of the sons of Sem (as mentioned in Gen. 10), Aram, can be called a Semite; Elam, Arphaxad, Asshur being Aryan in the strict sense in which such terms should be employed in philology. By analogy with the appellation "Indo-European," the family of Semitic languages should be termed "Syro-Arabic."
4. W. T. Pitard, *Ancient Damascus*, Winona Lake, 1987, p. 49.
5. Six of these missives are written by a certain Abdi-Heba, "king" of Urushalim (modern Jerusalem), which, at the time, was just a modest hamlet in southern Syria that controlled at most a handful of agricultural villages and the pastoral population in the surrounding area. "We can say nothing precise regarding David as an historical figure. It is hard though not to note the strange resemblance between these miscreant Habirus, whose hordes plagued Abdi-Heba, and Biblical tales of an outlaw named David who with his men ranged over the mountains of Hebron and the

desert of Judea," observe I. Finkelstein and N. A. Silberman, in *La Bible dévoilée*, Paris, 2002, p. 274.
6. W.T. Pitard, *Ancient Damascus*, op. cit., pp. 82–84. See also J. Starcky, *Palmyre*, Paris, 1985, p. 34; J. Briend and M.-J. Seux, *Textes du Proche-Orient ancien et histoire d'Israël*, Paris, 1977, p. 72; G. Degeorge, *Damas des origines aux Mamluks*, Paris, 1997, p. 43.
7. Cf. I. Finkelstein and N. A. Silberman, *Bible dévoilée*, op. cit. These fables and, in particular, the authenticity of the Pentateuch, have long been undermined by philological investigations and historical criticism. See also Voltaire, *The Philosophical Dictionary*, art. "Moses."
8. "The picture entertained in Jerusalem of the era of David and more so of his son, Solomon, has for centuries been based on myth and a romanticized image." I. Finkelstein and N. A. Silberman, op. cit., *Bible dévoilée*, p. 159.
9. II Sam. 8:1–14; 10:1–19, and Chr. 18:1–16; 19:1–19.
10. Recent authors place these events more than a century later, under Jehoash (Joash) (800–784) and Amasias (798–769). Cf. H. Sader, *Les États araméens de Syrie depuis leur fondation jusqu'à leur transformation en provinces assyriennes*, Beirut/Wiesbaden, 1987, p. 253.
11. Cf. J. Briend and M.-J. Seux, *Textes du Proche-Orient*, op. cit., p. 87. Among the coalition forces the text mentions one thousand camels from "Gindubu in the land of 'Araba," that is to say, the Arabs who are cited here for the first time in literature. It should be stressed, however, that the term "'Araba" refers more likely to the nomadic lifestyle than to an ethnic group. This is also the first occurrence of a king of Israel in a non-biblical text.
12. The text is carved on a stone slab discovered at Nimrud (Iraq), twenty-five miles (40 km) to the southeast of Mossul: "At Dimashqa, his native city, in his palace, I received 2,300 silver talents, 20 gold talents, 3,000 bronze talents, 5,000 iron talents, garments with multicolored trimmings, linen, a bed and a couch with bedding, and inlayed with ivory, and countless other goods and property from him." J. Briend and M.-J. Seux, ibid., p. 95.
13. Isaiah 17:1. See also Amos 1:3–5. "Thus saith the Lord; For three transgressions of Damascus [...], I will send a fire into the house of Hazael [...], I will break also the bar of Damascus [...]. And the people of Syria shall go into captivity unto Kir."
14. On the deportations of Sargon II, see I. Finkelstein and N.A. Silberman, *Bible dévoilée*, op. cit., pp. 255–57, and A. Causse, *Les Dispersés d'Israël*, Paris, 1929, p. 12 sq.
15. The Muslim historian Mas'udi refers to "a remarkable construction named al-Baris, still standing in the center of the city" in the first half of the tenth century. Cf. *Les Prairies d'or*, Paris: Société asiatique, 1965, vol. II, p. 545.
16. *Au Pays de Baal et d'Astarté* (exh. cat.), Paris, 1985, pp. 214–17.
17. Strabo, *Geography*, XVI, 20.
18. Aristotle, *Politics*, II, 7; G. Degeorge, *Damas des origines aux Mamluks*, op. cit., p. 56. It should be said that the "grid" town plan, as seen at Miletus, Priene, and Cnidus, if it was indeed systematized by Hippodamos, is already to be found in the Orient at a far earlier era date, in Amorite Babylon in the eighteenth century B.C.E., for example, and that, contrariwise, so-called "Oriental" or occasionally "Arab" or "Islamic" urbanism, is by no means specific to the East nor to the Arabs, and still less to Islam, and may be encountered in many other countries and regions.
19. J. Sauvaget, "Le plan antique de Damas," *Syria*, XXVI, 1949, p. 332.
20. Emperor Julian had sent from Damascus to his friend Serapion "a sweet assortment of dried long-stalked figs." *Œuvres complètes*, Paris: Plon, p. 376. In the first century C.E., the Latin poet Martial sang the praises of Damascus prunes (*Epigrams*, V, 18), and Pliny the Elder lauded the whiteness of its alabaster (*Naturalis Historia*, XXXVI, 61).
21. Julian, ibid., p. 378.
22. Flavius Josephus, *The Jewish Wars*, I, 21.

23. J. Sauvaget, "Le plan antique de Damas," art. cit., p. 350.
24. It was probably during the dispersion of the Christians from Jerusalem following the persecution of Stephen that the Gospel was taken to Damascus. Cf. Loisy, A., *Les Mystères païens et les mystères chrétiens*, Paris, 1930, p. 307, n. 1, and p. 316.
25. The pilgrim from Piacenza who visited Damascus around 570 signaled the presence of a monastery on the site of the conversion. He mentions in addition the street "they call Straight," where, he says, "many miracles were accomplished." Cf. Maraval, P., *Récits des premiers pèlerins chrétiens au Proche-Orient*, Paris: Le Cerf, 1996, p. 235.
26. Acts 9:8–9.
27. Acts 9:23.
28. I Cor. 7:18–19.
29. It is obvious, no matter what the more devout think, that, as Nietzsche remarks [1881] in *Daybreak* (tr. R J Hollingdale), Cambridge, 1982, p. 39: "[...] without the storms and confusions of such a mind, of such a soul, there would be no Christianity; we would have hardly heard of a little Jewish sect whose master died on the cross." In fact, Jesus constantly maintained that his mission lay within Judaism: "I am not sent but unto the lost sheep of the house of Israel" (Matt., 15:24); "Go not into the way of the Gentiles, and into any city of the Samaritans, but go rather to the lost sheep of the house of Israel" (Matt., 10:5–6); "Think not that I come to destroy the law, or the prophets: I am not come to destroy but to fulfill" (Matt., 5:17); "The scribes and the Pharisees sit in Moses' seat: All therefore whatsoever they bid you observe, that observe and do" (Matt., 23:2–3). It is difficult to see universal meaning in such teaching and, moreover, Paul, who turned Jesus into a "minister of the circumcision [...] to confirm the promises made to the fathers" (Rom., 15:8), was perfectly cognizant of the divergence. See on this subject J. Isaac, *Jésus et Israël*, Paris, 1948, pp. 285–89, and Voltaire, *Philosophical Dictionary*, art. "Christianity." The break between Christianity and Judaism does not seem to date from before the mid-second century. Around that time, a disciple of Paul, Marcion, founded a new religion that severed all links with Judaism.
30. I Cor. 6:13; 6:15; 6:19; I Cor. 7:1: "It is good for a man not to touch a woman"; and I Cor. 7:8: "I say therefore to the unmarried and widows, It is good for them if they abide even as I. But if they cannot contain, let them marry; for it is better to marry than to burn." This was chanted throughout Early Christian literature. John Chrysostom devoted an entire book in praise of virginity that "alone permits creatures of the flesh, to accede and enjoy closeness to God." St. Augustine affirms: "But if equal in other things, who would hesitate to prefer the continent man to the married?" *The City of God*, XVI, 36; tr. M. Dods, Glasgow, 1871. See also the letters of St. Maximus Confessor, *Lettres*, Paris: Le Cerf, 1998, pp. 71 and 78: "[One must] put out the fires of the flesh by fasting, vigil, [and] meditation on the Holy Scriptures [...] and utterly despise the pleasures of the flesh, that corrosive illusory abomination." Methodus utters the following delicious observation: "It is absolutely necessary, if one wishes to be without sin in the exercise of purity, to keep all one's organs intact and one's senses locked up so as to stop up every part through which sin might seep in from the outside." *Banquet*, XI, 1.
31. John Chrysostom, *On Virginity*, lxxviii, 1.
32. Matt. 19:12. The cost to Origen is well known.
33. I Cor. 8:1–2.
34. Mas'udi, *Prairies d'or*, op. cit., vol. II, p. 278. See also E. Renan: "This [Paul] was no scholar; one can even state that he did much damage to science by his paradoxical scorn for reason, by his vaunting apparent madness, by his apotheosis of transcendental absurdity." *Saint Paul*, op. cit., pp. 567–68. The condemnation of science, even of mere curiosity, is profound among Fathers of the Church. Tertullian, lambasting philosophy and decrying "the pitiable Aristotle," writes in *De praescriptione haereticorum*, VII, 9: "What indeed has Athens to do with Jerusalem? What concord is there between the Academy and the Church? [...] We want no curious disputation after possessing Christ Jesus, no inquisition after enjoying the gospel." *The Prescription Against Heretics*, tr. P. Holmes. And in effect, what could Aristotle or Athens have to do with a man who uttered such emblematic formulae as: "It should be believed because it is inane." Cf. *Apologétique*, Paris, Les Belles Lettres, 1998, p. xv; a saying paraphrased by St. Thomas Aquinus into "I believe because it is absurd" (ibid., p. xv). The same idea occurs in Augustine: "There is no point in plundering Nature in the way of those the Greeks called physicists." And, once more, the monk Evagrius [Vita Pachomii, 5] declares: "Blessed is he that has attained infinite ignorance." R. MacMullen, Princeton, *Changes in the Roman Empire*, 1990, p. 125. Rutilius Namatianus in the fourth century saw Christianity as "the sect that renders souls stupid." Cited by L. Rougier, *Celse*, Paris: A. Delpeuch, 1925, p. 112. Contrary to what is occasionally stated, things were no better with the Reformation, and Luther had no hesitation in writing: "One should leave reason alone as it is the sworn enemy of faith," *Table Talk*, II, 135. This is more or less the rabbinical attitude too: "It would better that he who reflects on these four things, whatever is on high, whatever is below, whatever is before, whatever is after, says the Talmud, had never been born." *Khagiga*, 2:1. Ancient Greek philosophy is also once more condemned: "Cursed be he who has taught his son Greek philosophy." *Baba Kamma*, 82.b. Nothing, in effect, demonstrates better than the Talmud the rabbis lack of knowledge in matters of Greek philosophy. In this respect, Islam's attitude will be totally different and the fortune of Greek philosophy in Islamic lands is well known. Numerous Koranic texts and many *hadith* celebrate *'ilm*, or science. "The first duty of every sane man is to try to reason so as to convince himself of knowledge of the world," wrote the theologian Juwayni in the eleventh century, quoted by L. Gardet and M.-M. Anawati, *Introduction à la théologie musulmane*, Paris: Vrin, 1981, p. 66. It was not until the eighteenth century that Western voices, braving the ecclesiastical authorities, would be raised against this institutional and universal obscurantism: "People who lay no claims to reason for themselves, are not able to prove by reason their assertion; and if they hawk about something superior to reason, it is a mere figment," Spinoza writes in Book IV of *The Theologico-political Treatise* (tr. R. Elwes), New York: Dover, 1951, p. 93.
35. Rom, 13:1–2, and Tertullian, *Apologetic*, XXXII, 2: "We look up to the judgment of God in the emperors, for He set them over the races of the world" (tr. Alexander Souter). Much the same in the Talmud: "Whosoever he be that shall rebel against thy [the King's] commandments and shall not hearken unto thy words in all that thou commandest him, he shall be put to death." *Sanhedrin*, 49*a* (tr. J. Shachter and H. Freedman).
36. Tertullian, *Apologetic*, XXIV, 5, 6.
37. Considered as the supreme act, the apotheosis of asceticism to which all veritable athletes of Christ ought to aspire, martyrdom formed part of the divine plan—as did the crucifixion of Jesus—and fostered the expansion of Christianity. "The blood of the Christians is the seed of a new life," writes Tertullian, *Apologetic*, L, 13 (tr. Alexander Souter). The endurance of those martyred, which a specialist literature relates in gory detail, had its effect, since it was this that caused the conversion of the Stoic St. Justin, himself a martyr at his own behest in 167 during the reign of Marcus Aurelius, that emperor who admittedly displayed little sympathy for Christianity.
38. "Christianity, which had traversed three hundred years of persecution, having become dominant in its turn, persecuted more fiercely than any other previous religion," Renan rightly observed. *Les Apôtres*, Paris, 1866, p. 146. But it should be recalled that that intolerance stems not from Jesus' teaching, but from that of Paul and Judaism. Paul's formulae often seem to anticipate those of the Inquisition: "In the name of our Lord Jesus Christ, when ye are gathered together, and my spirit with the power of our Lord Jesus Christ, To deliver such a one [i.e. a fornicator] unto Satan for the destruction of the flesh, that the spirit may be saved in the day of the Lord Jesus" (I Cor. 5:4–5). "Heresy is a sin by which one deserves to be excluded from the world through death," Thomas Aquinus railed (L. Rougier, *Celse*, op. cit., p. 183). As for Jewish history, it offers numerous examples of forcible conversions and circumcisions (Flavius Josephus, *Antiquitates Iudaicae*, 11, 3; 13, 9; 15, 7–9, and the *Bellum Iudaicum* [The Jewish Wars], II, 17, 10, etc.). Even Maimonides calls for the extermination of infidel Jews in his *Book of Knowledge*, and, anticipating in this Gobineau, he puts the Mongols, nomads, and Blacks among the lower entities, "who do not attain the rank of human beings" and whose nature "is similar to that of a dumb animal." Cf. Israël Shahak, *Histoire juive. Religion juive. Le poids de trois millénaires*, Paris, 1996, p. 62. This is summed up by Renan: "Christianity was intolerant, but intolerance is not an essentially Christian fact. It is a Jewish one, in the sense that Judaism erects for the first time a theory of the absolute in matters of faith and poses the principle that every individual turning away the people from its true religion [...] should be greeted with stones, lapidated by all, without trial. [...]. The Pentateuch was thus the first code of religious terror." *Vie de Jésus*, Paris: Gallimard/Folio, 1974, p. 394. It was again in the Scriptures that the most brutal *conquistadores* and colonizers unearthed justification for their atrocities. During the conquest of Algeria, General Changarnier thus advocated the *razzia* system of collective punishment, of the massacres and the scorched earth: "Holy Scripture teaches us that Joshua and other leaders blessed by God [*sic*] performed truly terrible *razzias*." *Mémoires du général Changarnier*, Paris, 1930, p. 215
16. Similarly, the curse of Sham was a favorite argument among slave-owners. Cf. L. Sala-Molins, *Le Code noir ou le Calvaire de Canaan*, Paris: PUF, 2002, pp. 21–25. Every monotheism, as Freud [1939] observed, can be little else other than intolerant: "[It] was a strict monotheism [...] and along with the belief in a single god religious intolerance was inevitably born, which had previously been so alien to the ancient world [...]." *Moses and Monotheism* [...] (ed. J. Strachey), *The Standard Edition* [...], London, 1964-, vol. 23, p. 20. Renan was of a similar opinion: "The intolerance of the Semitic peoples is a consequence of their monotheism." *Histoire générale*, op. cit., p. 7. Nonetheless, the tolerance of Islam—the least intolerant of the three monotheisms—has been emphasized on many occasions: "Everywhere the Moslem sees the idea of God in the thoughts of his brothers, he bows and respects. [...]. It is the only tolerant people," Lamartine was to observe, cited by R. Edwards, *La Syrie 1840-1862*, Paris, 1862, p. 34. See also note 88, chap. IV.
39. A Platonic school survived at Harran in northern Syria until the arrival of the Seljukid Turks in the eleventh century.
40. See the text of the dogmatic decree in G. Degeorge, *Damas des origines aux Mamluks*, op. cit., p. 72.
41. John of Asia, cited by E. Rabbath, *L'Orient chrétien à la veille de l'islam*, Beirut, 1980, p. 24.
42. Michael the Syrian, *Chronique syriaque*, Paris, 1899–1914, vol. 2, p. 195. Michael the Syrian was the Jacobite patriarch of Antioch from 1166 until his death in 1199.
43. John of Asia, *The Third Part of the Ecclesiastical History of John...*, Oxford, 1860, p. 8.
44. John of Asia, "Histoire ecclésiastique," *Revue de l'Orient chrétien*, 1897, p. 467.
45. *Code*, I, 11, 10, 5.
46. John of Asia, "Histoire ecclésiastique," art. cit., p. 481. Concerning the persecutions, see also J. Maspéro, *Histoire des patriarches d'Alexandrie*, Paris, 1923, p. 122. At the end of the fourth century, Emperor Julian, who considered the "the impious Galileans [the Christians] as a cancer of human society," castigated their methods in the following terms: "You destroy the temples and altars; you cut the throats not only of those who keep faith with the rites of their fathers [the 'pagans'], but those among you whom you call infected with heresy and who do not adore the dead one [Jesus] in the same manner as you do." *Œuvres complètes*, op. cit., pp. 439 and 430.
47. Michael the Syrian, *Chronique*, op. cit., vol. 2, p. 412.
48. Ibid.
49. Procopius, *De bello persico*, II, 8.
50. According to a Greek inscription known only through a translation into Arabic, the transformation was to have occurred during the reign of Arcadius (395–408).
51. Ps., 145:13. In reality the Psalm sung by David is addressed to Yaweh.
52. Quoted from Mgr Nasrallah, "Damas et la Damascène: leurs églises à l'époque byzantine," *Proche-Orient chrétien*, XXXV, 1–2, 1985, p. 42.

53. Cf. Abd al-Qadir al-Rihawi, *Damascus: Its History, Development and Artistic Heritage*, Damascus, 1977, p. 47; See also Mas'udi, *Prairies d'or*, op. cit., vol. 2, p. 545.
54. On this unsatisfactory term, see n. 18.
55. John of Asia, "Histoire ecclésiastique," art. cit., p. 485
56. Cited by M.-J. de Goeje, *Mémoire sur la conquête de la Syrie*, Leiden, 1900, p. 106. The *Tayy* denotes the Arabs: in Syriac literature, the latter are often so called from the name of one of their largest tribes.
57. T. Wright, *Early Travels in Palestine*, London, 1848, p. 10. The four rivers are the Barada itself and the three chief channels, the Banias, the Tawra, and the Qanawat, which existed at the time. See also P. Maraval, *Récits*, op. cit., p. 275.
58. Ibn 'Asakir, *La Description de Damas*, Damascus, 1959, p. 30.
59. Ibn Jubayr, *Voyages*, Paris, 1949–1956, vol. 6, p. 340–41.
60. Ibn 'Asakir, *Description de Damas*, op. cit., p. 58.
61. Ibn Battuta, *Travels*, op. cit., vol. 1, p. 124.
62. Cf. E.-M. Quatremère, *Histoire des sultans mamelouks de l'Égypte*, Paris, 1837–1845, vol. 2, 1, p. 280.
63. Ibn Jubayr, *Voyages*, op. cit., vol. 5, p. 309.
64. Cf. E.-M. Quatremère, *Histoire des sultans*, op. cit., vol. 2, 1, p. 273, and Lamartine, *Voyage en Orient*, Paris, 1846, vol. 2, p. 72: "The great doors of the mosque were shut with heavy curtains; I was unable to see inside." The curtains are depicted drawn open in two mosaic panels opposite one another in the west vestibule, on one side fixed to the center, on the other, opening to the sides.
65. As the cycle of destruction and rebuilding unfolded, on the north portico and the front of the prayer-hall, the columns were replaced by pillars, easier to produce and, especially, less costly. The magnificent eurhythmy of the original has thus been broken, resulting in a building of a very different nature. On this subject, and for a complete description of the mosque: cf. G. Degeorge, *Damas des origines aux Mamluks*, op. cit., p. 107–128. For a recent study, cf. F.B. Flood, *The Great Mosque of Damascus*, Leiden: Brill, 2001.
66. Ibn Hawqal, *Configuration de la Terre*, Paris/Beirut, 1964, p. 171.
67. Ibn Jubayr, *Voyages*, op. cit., vol. 6, p. 302.
68. Literally "house of Islam," that is to say the sum of the territories under Muslim authority.
69. It is strange to note that, in spite of the claims by the best-informed Muslim authors, al-Muqaddasi (originally from al-Qods, and hence perfectly familiar with Damascus) wrote in the tenth century: "There are few trees or known lands that are not in this way represented on the walls." *Meilleure Répartition*, op. cit., p. 169. In spite of the huge disparity between this pictorial program and the descriptions of the Islamic paradise, in spite of the presence of the *Ka'ba*, many authors of all origins, ancient and contemporary, have been unafraid to affirm that these mosaics present an image of paradise as promised to believers. Cf. D. Clévenot, and G. Degeorge, *Splendors of Islam*, New York: Vendome, 2002, p. 79; F. B. Flood, *The Great Mosque*,op. cit., p. 25 and passim; see J. D. Hoag, *Islamic Architecture*, London, 1975, p. 17: "The Koranic Paradise is probably the subject but it is one without human inhabitants." It is true that Damascus is surrounded by a paradisiacal halo; even the *Talmud* considers it one of the gates to paradise, along with Jerusalem, but even so! Fiction did not lag far behind, and Damascus as paradise has become a stock image: "Adam and Eve were then created by God and placed in Eden, in the plain of Damascus, that lovely garden resplendent with sunlight and colour, teeming with luxuriant vegetation. The fruitful earth gave them her bounty: beasts and birds were their willing servants: they knew not the ills our flesh is heir to, disease and poverty and death: for all that a great and generous God could do for them was done." J. Joyce, *The Portrait of the Artist as a Young Man*, Harmondsworth, p. 53.
70. A *hadith* recorded by Ibn 'Asakir affirms: "For any who builds a sanctuary, be it the size of a sandgrouse nest on bare ground, God will build him a house in paradise." *Description de Damas*, op. cit., p. 83.
71. Cf. E.-M. Quatremère, *Histoire des sultans*, op. cit., II, 1, p. 283. See also Ibn Battuta, *Travels*, op. cit., vol. 1, p. 133.
72. J. Sauvaget, *Revue des études islamiques*, 8, 1934, p. 448.
73. Cf. E.-M. Quatremère, *Histoire des sultans*, op. cit., 2, 1, p. 269, and al-Muqaddasi, *Meilleure Répartition*, op. cit., p. 166: "These are the finest baths to be seen anywhere."
74. Mas'udi, *Prairies d'or*, op. cit., vol. 4, p. 931.
75. Ibid.
76. J. Sauvaget, *Historiens arabes*, Paris, 1988, p.59. Only 'Abd al-Rahman b. Mu'awiya, grandson of Hisham, escaped the massacre and managed to reach Andalusia, where in 756 he founded the emirate of Cordoba to which thronged clients and partisans from Syria.
77. Ya'qubi, *Les Pays*, Cairo, 1937, p. 74; al-Muqaddasi, *Meilleure Répartition*, op. cit., p. 173.
78. The Jacobites had translated Aristotle and Porphyry into Syriac as early as the fourth century.

Chapter II

1. "Our lord is Allah and we adore only Allah. The construction of this mosque and the destruction of the church which once stood there were ordered by the servant of God, al-Walid, Emir of the Believers, in the month of *dhul-hijja*, in the year 87 [Nov–Dec 706]." Nevertheless Mas'udi states that the inscription was still visible in 943–44, *Prairies d'or*, op. cit., vol. 3, p. 844.
2. Mas'udi, ibid., vol. 7, p. 257.
3. Ibn 'Asakir, *Description de Damas*, op. cit., p. 288.
4. Ibid., p. 289.
5. Ibid.
6. Ibid.
7. Ibid., p. 290.
8. On the Aleppo Hamdanids, cf. J.-C. David and G. Degeorge, *Alep*, Paris: Flammarion, 2002, pp. 74–81.
9. J. Sauvaget, *Historiens arabes*, op. cit., p. 83.
10. Ibid., p. 85.
11. H. Sauvaire, "La description de Damas," *Journal asiatique*, 9th series, vol. 8, ii, 1896, p. 209.
12. J. Sauvaget, "La citadelle de Damas," *Syria*, XI, 1930, p. 63. Recent excavations have revealed the "Seljukid" compound, a vast irregular quadrilateral of approximately 689 x 426 feet (210 x 130 m), built between the end of the eleventh and the middle of the twelfth centuries; cf. S. Berthier, Introduction to the Supplement to *Citadelle de Damas*, *Bulletin d'études orientales*, Damascus, 2002, p. 39. A foundation inscription dated 1085–86 unearthed on the façade of a tower (T. 25) of the west front, has been published by M. Hanisch, "Die seldschukidischen Anlagen der Zitadelle von Damascus," *Damaszener Mitteilungen*, 6, pp. 488–489. The enormous edifice visible today, and which doubled the earlier enclosure, dates for the most part from a major rebuilding program at the beginning of the thirteenth century.
13. See chap. I, n. 18.
14. al-Muqaddasi, *Meilleure répartition*, op. cit., p. 167.
15. The majority of European observers, including celebrated Orientalists, admirers of the Greco-Roman "model," have been unable to perceive the coherence of this type of urban fabric. An instance of this is Renan, *Saint Paul*, op. cit., p. 333: "What strikes the traveler as he weaves his way though a maze of sickening bazaars, narrow and filthy yards, with teetering, rickety structures, is the utter dearth of nobility, and of political, even municipal spirit." See also *Mémorial Jean Sauvaget*, Damascus, 1954, p. 90; and, on Aleppo: "We should acknowledge that the Moslem era made no positive contribution here. Its most visible effect has been to accelerate and aggravate the degradation of a city that it had annexed in good order, with all its organs in place and operational." *Essai sur le développement d'une grande ville syrienne, des origines au milieu du XIXe siècle: Alep*, Paris: Geuthner, 1941, quoted in R. Avez, *L'Institut français de Damas au palais Azm (1922-1946) à travers les archives*, Damascus: PIDF, 1993, p. 261.
16. al-Muqaddasi, *Meilleure répartition*, op. cit., p. 165.
17. Ibid., p. 165.
18. From the Greek *pandokéion*. *Khan* is an Iranian term; *qaysariyya* derives from Caesar.
19. al-Muqaddasi, *Meilleure répartition*, op. cit., p. 171.
20. Ibid., p. 166.
21. Ibn Hawqal, *Configuration de la Terre*, op. cit., vol. 1, p. 171, and vol. 2, p. 455.
22. Ibn al-Qalanisi, *Damas de 1075 à 1154* (French tr. R. Le Tourneau), Damascus, 1952, p. 57.
23. Ibid., p. 38.
24. Voltaire, *Essai sur les mœurs* [1756], Paris: Garnier, 1963, vol. 1, p. 573.
25. *Histoire anonyme de la première croisade*, Paris: Les Belles Lettres, 1964, p. 111.
26. Ibid., pp. 177–79.
27. Ibid., p. 203 sq.
28. Ibn al-Qalanisi, *Damas*, op. cit., p. 43. The anonymous Crusader, who would have surely categorized them like the Muslims among the "pagan" race, has not a word to say of the Jews. "In the Temple [the Dome of the Rock] and in the porch of Solomon, the horses walked through blood up to their knees and bridle," wrote Raimond d'Aguilers, CIII, 300, quoted by P. Alphandéry, *La Chrétienté et l'idée de croisade*, Paris: Albin Michel, 1954, vol. 1, p. 123.
29. On Palestinian refugees in Damascus, cf. J.-M. Mouton, *Damas et sa principauté sous les Saljoukides et les Bourides*, Cairo, 1994, pp. 302–10.
30. Historian Kamal al-Din reaffirms this in these terms: "The princes of the time wanted to prolong the occupation of the Franks to conserve their grip on power." *RHOC* (*Recueil des historiens orientaux des croisades*), vol. 3, p. 607. Such a situation indeed meets with many parallels in the contemporary Middle East.
31. Ibn al-Qalanisi, *Damas*, op. cit., pp. 103–04.
32. J. Sauvaget provides a detailed description in *Les Monuments ayyubides de Damas*, Paris, 1938, pp. 1–13.
33. Koran, 2, 256.
34. *R.C.E.A.* (*Répertoire chronologique d'épigraphie arabe*), vol. 8, no. 2918.
35. Ibid., no. 2933.
36. Ibid., no. 2980.
37. Ibn Khallikan, *Biographical Dictionary*, Paris, 1842–1871, vol. 1, p. 339.
38. Cf. F. Gabrieli, *Chroniques arabes des croisades*, Paris, 1977, p. 67.
39. Ibn al-Qalanisi, *Damas*, op. cit., p. 193.
40. Ibid., p. 208.
41. Cf. F. Gabrieli, *Chroniques*, op. cit., p. 85.
42. Idrisi, *Géographie*, Paris, 1836–1840, vol. I, pp. 349–50.
43. Ibid., vol. 1, p. 352. The produce of Tinnis on the Nile Delta was much vaunted.
44. Ibid. In the first century C.E., the Latin poet Martial had already praised the prunes of Damascus (*Epigrams*, V, 18).
45. Ibn al-Qalanisi, *Damas*, op. cit., p. 313.
46. On *madrasas* predating Nur al-Din, cf. G. Degeorge, *Damas des origines aux Mamluks*, op. cit., p. 177. The earliest *madrasa*, the Sadiriyya, was constructed in 1098 by an emir of Duqaq near Bab al-Barid, the west door of the Umayyad mosque.
47. The *bimaristan* of al-Walid had probably disappeared by the period of Nur al-Din, as the Andalusian traveler Ibn Jubayr, in 1184, only mentions two *bimaristans*, one of which is that of Nur al-Din and the other surely that of Duqaq.
48. Ibn Jubayr, *Voyages*, op. cit., vol. 6, pp. 329–30.
49. Ibn al-Jawzi, *La Pensée vigile*, Paris, 1986, p. 56.
50. Ibid., p. 81.
51. Abu Bakr al-Razi, *Guide du médecin nomade*, Paris: Sindbad, 1980, p. 92. See also Pierre Bayle, quoted by Abbé du Laurens, *L'Arétin moderne*, Paris, 1920, p. 162: "Victories over chastity are a daily occurrence. One emerges triumphant from such battles covered with wounds." In Islam, as elsewhere, "Puritanical" currents did exist, however. Ibn Batta, for instance, forbade members of a couple to look at each other's genitals, *Profession de foi*, Damascus, 1958, p. 152. Others basing their ideas on *hadith* denounced the *hammam* as a place of abomination "because one removes one's clothes and also because there are pictures and statues." Cf. W. Marçais, *Articles et conférences*, Paris, 1961, p. 67.
52. Ibn al-Jawzi, *La Pensée vigile*, op. cit., p. 81. Contrary to a prevalent idea, women were not forgotten: "Then, when the husband achieves his goal, he should await his partner so that she too can satisfy her needs. In effect, the ejaculation of the woman is often rather delayed [...]." Ghazali [d. 1111 CE], *Le Livre des bons usages en matière de mariage*, Paris, 1989, p. 86. Such advice is unlikely to be found in the works of Augustine or Thomas Aquinus.
53. Ibid., p. 157
54. Rom., 7:24

55. Ibn Jubayr, *Voyages*, op. cit., vol. 6, pp. 311–12; cf. also F.B. Flood, *The Great Mosque*, op. cit., pp. 114–138.
56. Koran, 39, 73.
57. Sufism, according to Junayd, the great *sufi* of Baghdad († 911), is "to die unto oneself and to live in God." A further etymology derives the word *sufi* from the verb form *sufiya*, "he has been purified." Cf. E. Geoffroy, *Initiation au soufisme*, Paris: Fayard, 2003, p. 13.
58. Ibn Jubayr, *Voyages*, op. cit., vol. 6, pp. 330–31.
59. These are the terms used by Ibn Batta, *Profession de foi*, op. cit., p. 158.
60. Ibn al-Jawzi, *La Pensée vigile*, op. cit., p. 166.
61. Ibid., p. 122.
62. Ibid., p. 123.
63. Cf. J. Sauvaget, *Relation de la Chine et de l'Inde*, Paris, 1948, p. 11. This type of observation is often to be encountered among Muslim authors. Ibn al-Faqih says the following on the Chinese: "They do not wash after going to the stool," and of the Indians: "They do not purify themselves after carnal congress." *Abrégé du livre des pays*, Damascus, 1973, p. 17. Ibn Fadlan, in the tenth century, lambastes the Turks: "They do not wash after soiling with excrement or urine. They do not wash after major foulness or other foulness." *Voyage chez les Bulgares de la Volga*, Paris: Sindbad, 1988, p. 38. Likewise for the Russians, whom Ibn Fadlan considered "the most unclean of God's creatures." Ibid., p. 73.
64. Al-Qayrawani, *La Risala*, Algiers, 1952, pp. 36–37. The same goes inevitably for micturition. The Benedictine Diego de Haëdo observed in sixteenth-century Algiers: "As soon as they have urinated, they wash the male member with water or earth, rub it on some stone or against a wall." *Topographie et histoire générale d'Alger*, Paris, 1998, p. 163. The fastidious hygiene in the East obviated the annoyance met with in Europe, specifically in France, that an author from the end of the nineteenth century described as follows: "Travel through the middle of Istanbul, Pera, and Galata, in modern trams, often crammed with soldiers, men of the people, and poor women, and you will never notice those peculiar odors, a dreadful mix of wine, beer, liquor, garlic, onions, rank sweat, and nauseating filth, which you all too often encounter in similar vehicles running through popular districts in our great European cities." Paul de Régla, *El ktab des lois secrètes de l'amour*, Paris, n.d., p. 187. Countless European travelers, moreover, confessed to the superiority of Islam in matters of hygiene: "Muslims observe with regard to their person much greater cleanliness than do Europeans. Not only do they wash and bathe very often, and keep their nails very short; but they also cut the hairs from their ears and nose, [...], shave under the armpits and depilate other parts with a paste so that no impurities remain on the body." C. Niebuhr, *Description de l'Arabie*, Copenhagen, 1773, p. 55.
65. Ibn al-Jawzi, *La Pensée vigile*, op. cit., p. 123.
66. Cf. Flaubert, G., *Correspondance*, Paris: Gallimard/Pléiade, p. 198 (see *infra*, p. 244). Cf. Byron's mellifluous aside in a letter of August 2, 1819: "A Turkish bath—that marble paradise of sherbet and sodomy." *Letters and Journals 1818-1819* (ed. L. A. Marchand), vol. 6, London, 1976, p. 207; or this delicious poem by Abu Nuwas—one of the greatest Arab poets who died in Baghdad in 815—celebrating youthful beauty in accents worthy of Martial or Strato of Sardis: "What the trousers concealed is revealed/All is made visible. Feast your eyes with leisure/One whispers pious phrases.../Lord, the bath is truly delicious!/Even when, coming in with their towels, the bath boys disturb the fun." *Le Vin, le vent, la vie*, Paris: Sindbad, 1979, p. 102. The baths inevitably sat ill with Christian ideas. By an order of January 1, 1567, Philip II of Spain forced the Moriscos to demolish their *hammams*, and the Grenadian historian Bermudez de Pedraza spoke of them as something impious: "They washed—even though we were in December!" Cf. L. Poliakov, *De Mahomet aux Marranes*, Paris, 1961, p. 528.
67. The network remained largely unchanged until the development in 1928 of a system bringing drinking water from the spring of al-Fijeh. In Islamic lands to provide water for passersby was considered an act of piety. Cf. P. Belon, *Voyage en Égypte*, Cairo, 1970, p. 134: "There is scarce a crossroads in Cairo, nor in the other towns of Egypt or Syria, and in Turkey too, where there is not a great pot that is filled everyday with water to quench the thirst of passersby."
68. Ibn 'Asakir, *Description de Damas*, op. cit., p. 255.
69. Ibn Jubayr, *Voyages*, op. cit., vol. 6, pp. 301 and 315.
70. Benjamin of Tudela, *Voyage*, The Hague, 1735, p. 27.
71. Ibn Jubayr, *Voyages*, op. cit., vol. 6, p 335.
72. Ibid., p. 336.
73. Nizam al-Mulk, *Traité de gouvernement*, Paris, 1984, p. 92.
74. Plural of *sharif*.
75. Benjamin of Tudela, *Voyage*, op. cit., p. 28.
76. John of Würzburg, *Description of the Holy Land*, PPTS, vol. 5, p. 64.
77. Benjamin of Tudela, *Voyage*, op. cit., p. 27.
78. Ibn Jubayr, *Voyages*, op. cit., vol. 6, p 528.
79. *RHOC*, vol. 3, p. 91.
80. F. L. C. Marin, *Histoire de Saladin, sulthan d'Égypte et de Syrie*, Paris, 1758, vol. 2, p. 396.
81. Cf. F. Gabrieli, *Chroniques*, op. cit., pp. 299–300.
82. Maqrizi, *Histoire des sultans Mameluks de l'Égypte*, Paris, 1837–1845, I, 1, p. 85.
83. Ibid., p. 85.
84. Ibid., p. 98.
85. Ibid., p. 106.
86. Ibid., p. 107.
87. Ibid.
88. Yaqut, cited by Rihawi Abd al-Qader, *Damascus*, p. 61.
89. *RCEA*, vol. 10, no. 3650.
90. L. d'Arvieux, *Mémoires du chevalier d'Arvieux*, Paris, 1735, vol. 2, p. 450. On this columnated hall—a jewel of Ayyubid architecture, which anticipates that in the Khan As'ad Pasha—see the recent study by S. Berthier, Supplement to *Citadelle de Damas*, op. cit., p. 56, and *Bilan préliminaire sur la fouille de la salle à colonnes (2000–2001)*, no. 58 of *AAS*, 2004. It should be added that the large building on the southwest corner that Sauvaget, interpreting the stucco on the ground floor, called "the Ayyubid palace," is in fact part of the earlier fortification built before 1203 at the onset of the construction of the Ayyubid enclosure.
91. J. Sauvaget, "Le cénotaphe de Saladin," *Revue des arts asiatiques*, vol. 6, 1929–30, p. 168.
92. Ibid., p. 175.
93. Ibid., p. 168.
94. Quoted by Dussaud, Deschamps, Seyrig, *Syrie antique et médiévale illustrée*, Paris, 1931, p. 92.
95. *RCEA*, vol. 9, no. 3552.
96. *RCEA*, vol. 12, no. 4411.
97. Cf. H. Sauvaire, "La description de Damas," art. cit., vol. 6, 2, 1895, pp. 263–64.
98. Ibid.
99. Ibid.
100. Ibid.
101. Though the river is not overly large, flooding could cause serious devastation. Thus, in 1516–17, following a spate, 895 houses, 17 furnaces, 11 mills, 40 gardens, 21 mosques, and 5 *madrasas* were flattened. Cf. J. Sauvaget, "*Les Trésors d'or*" *de Sibt Ibn al-'Ajami*, Beirut, 1950, p. 9.
102. 'Abd al-Latif, *Relation de l'Égypte*, Paris, 1810, pp. 415–16.
103. Ibn 'Asakir, *Description de Damas*, op. cit., p. 208.
104. Koran, 23, 52. However, there is no mention in the Koran that this is al-Rabwa.
105. Ibn Jubayr, *Voyages*, op. cit., vol. 6, p 316.
106. Ibid., p. 319.
107. Kings, 1:19. On this cave that became a kind of underground synagogue and which "is also used as a refuge in times of danger," cf. Keith, Black, Bonar, and MacCheyne, *Les Juifs d'Europe et de Palestine*, Paris, 1844, p. 461: "They [the Jews of Damascus] maintain that a cave approximately three miles from the city was the one that the prophet Elijah lived in at the time he was sent to kill Hazael, king of Syria. This cave has become a kind of underground synagogue: it is visited on the last day of every month, a day of prayer and supplication. It is also used as a refuge in times of danger."
108. Ibn Jubayr, *Voyages*, op. cit., vol. 6, p. 316.
109. Flavius Josephus, *Antiquitates Iudaicae*, I, 7.
110. Ibn 'Asakir, *Description de Damas*, op. cit., pp. 173–74. In the fourteenth century, the traveler Ibn Battuta only recorded the tradition concerning Moses' foot.
111. Ibn Battuta, *Travels*, op. cit., vol. 1, p. 146.
112. Ibn Jubayr, *Voyages*, op. cit., vol. 6, p 532.
113. Ibid.
114. Ibid., p. 333.
115. Ibid., p. 345.
116. Ibid.

Chapter III

1. Al-Makin Ibn al-'Amid, *Chronique des Ayyubides*, Paris, 1994, p. 123.
2. Maqrizi, *Histoire des sultans*, op. cit., 1, i, p. 151.
3. Ibid., 1, ii, p. 78.
4. Cf. M. Gaudefroy-Demonbynes, *La Syrie à l'époque des Mameluks d'après les auteurs arabes*, Paris, 1923, p. 36.
5. Maqrizi, *Histoire des sultans*, op. cit., 1, ii, p. 90.
6. Barhebraeus (Abu al-Faraj), *Chronicon syriacum*, Leipzig, 1789, pp. 458–59.
7. Maqrizi, *Histoire des sultans*, op. cit., 1, ii, p. 33.
8. Ibid., p. 35.
9. Cf. F. Gabrieli, *Chroniques*, op. cit., p. 372.
10. J. Phocas, "The Pilgrimage of J. Phocas in the Holy Land," in *Palestine Pilgrim's Text Society*, vol. 9, London, 1889, p. 9.
11. Maqrizi, *Histoire des sultans*, op. cit., 2, p. 103.
12. Cf. F. Gabrieli, *Chroniques*, op. cit., p. 372.
13. G. Wiet, *L'Égypte arabe*, Paris, 1937, p. 456.
14. Cf. J. Sauvaget, *La Chronique de Damas d'al-Jazari*, Paris, 1949, p. 8.
15. Ibid., p. 6.
16. Abu'l Fida, quoted by F. Gabrieli, *Chroniques*, op. cit., p. 378.
17. J. Sauvaget, *La Chronique*, op. cit., p. 11.
18. Abu'l Fida, *Géographie*, Paris, 1835, p. 10.
19. Ibid., p. 17.
20. Ibid., p. 18.
21. Ibid., p. 20.
22. Ibid., p. 21.
23. Ibid., p. 22.
24. Ibid., p. 52.
25. Ibid., p. 53.
26. Ibid., p. 47.
27. Ibid., p. 54.
28. Ibid., p. 61.
29. Maqrizi, *Histoire des sultans*, op. cit., 2, p. 153.
30. Ibid., 2, ii, p. 150.
31. After Nuwayri, cf. Maqrizi, *Histoire des sultans*, op. cit., 2, ii, pp. 152–154.
32. Ibid.
33. Maqrizi, *Histoire des sultans*, op. cit., 2, ii, p. 161.
34. Ibid., p. 160.
35. Ibid.
36. Ibid., pp. 161–62.
37. Ibid., p. 168.
38. Ibid., p. 170.
39. Ibid., p. 175.
40. Ibid., p. 199.
41. Ibid., p. 200.
42. Ibid., p. 202.
43. Ibid., p. 211.
44. Cf. H. Sauvaire, "La description de Damas," art. cit., vol. 3, ii, 1894, p. 284.
45. Cf. H. Laoust, *Les Gouverneurs de Damas sous les Mamlouks et les premiers Ottomans*, Damascus, 1952, pp. 8–9.
46. Cf. H. Sauvaire, "La description de Damas," art. cit., vol. 3, ii, 1894, p. 285
47. Ibn Battuta, *Travels*, op. cit., vol. 1, p. 136.
48. Cf. H. Sauvaire, "La description de Damas," art. cit., vol. 3, ii, 1894, p. 315.
49. Ibn Sasra, *A Chronicle of Damascus*, Berkeley, 1963, pp. 241–42.
50. Cf. Héthoum, *L'Hystore merveilleuse [...] du grand empereur de Tartarie...*, Paris, 1529, f. 81.
51. James of Verona, "Le Pèlerinage du moine," *Revue de l'Orient latin*, vol. 3, no. 2, Paris, 1895, p. 291.
52. Ludolphe von Sudheim, "De itinere Terre Sancte," *Archives de l'Orient latin*, vol. 2, Paris, 1884, p. 560 (French tr. P. Sebag).
53. Ibid.
54. Cf. M. Gaudefroy-Demonbynes, *La Syrie à l'époque des Mameluks*, op. cit., p. 35.
55. Ibid., p. 45. The *qarath* is a tanning agent derived from a tree resembling walnut (p. 45, n. 2).
56. James of Verona, "Le Pèlerinage du moine," op. cit., p. 292.
57. M. Gaudefroy-Demonbynes, *La Syrie à l'époque des Mameluks*, op. cit., p. 37. The birds apart—this description is reminiscent of mosaics in the Great Mosque.
58. Ibid., p. 38.
59. Ibid.
60. Ibid., pp. 46–47.
61. Ibid., p. 45.
62. Ibid., p. 37.
63. Ibn Battuta, *Travels*, op. cit., vol. 1, p. 150.
64. Ibid., pp. 124–54.

65. The repression of the Bedouin was in general carried out most ruthlessly. Thus, Maqirzi reports that in 1302 in Upper Egypt tribal Arabs having prevented the collecting of taxes, lawyers and qadis declared the legality of armed force: "The inhabitants were put to the sword [...]. All had their throats cut without pity. Approximately sixteen thousand men were disemboweled [...]. The whole country choked in the stench of corpses." *Histoire des sultans*, op. cit., II, 2, pp. 187–89.
66. Cf. H. Laoust, *Les Gouverneurs de Damas*, op. cit., p. 14.
67. Ibn Sasra, *A Chronicle of Damascus*, op. cit., pp. 111–12.
68. Ibid., p. 115.
69. Ibid., p. 140.
70. Cf. D.S. Margolieuth, *Cairo, Jerusalem and Damascus*, London, 1907, p. 271.
71. Sharaf al-Din, *Histoire de Timur-Bec*, Paris, 1722, vol. 3, p. 338.
72. D S. Margoliouth, *Cairo*, op. cit., p. 273.
73. Ibid.
74. Sharaf al-Din, *Histoire de Timur-Bec*, op. cit., p. 344.
75. Cf. E.-M. Quatremère, *Histoire des sultans*, op. cit., II, 1, p. 286.
76. Sharaf al-Din, *Histoire de Timur-Bec*, op. cit., p. 346.
77. D. S. Margoliouth, *Cairo*, op. cit., p. 274.
78. Ghillebert de Lannoy, *Œuvres de Ghillebert de Lannoy, voyageur*, Louvain, 1878, p. 158.
79. Bertrandon de La Broquière, *Le Voyage d'outremer* [...], Paris, 1892, p. 33.
80. Cf. W. Heyd, *Histoire du commerce Levant au Moyen Âge*, Leipzig, 1885, vol. 1, p. 469.
81. Bertrandon de La Broquière, *Le Voyage d'outremer*, op. cit., p. 60.
82. L. Frescobaldi, G. Gucci, and S. Sigoli, *Visit to the Holy Places* [...], Jerusalem, 1948, p. 142.
83. Bertrandon de La Broquière, *Le Voyage d'outremer*, op. cit., p. 33. See also R. Bouvier, *Jacques Cœur*, Paris, 1928.
84. Ibn Khaldun, *Discours sur l'histoire universelle*, Paris, 1967–68, vol. 3, pp. 1238, and passim.
85. Ibid., p. 1049.
86. Mas'udi, *Les Prairies d'or*, op. cit., vol. 2, p. 278. Let us recall that if European science gathered pace in the thirteenth century, it was largely thanks to the scholars of Arab culture whose works translated into Latin became widely disseminated in Western universities. Similar observations on Christianity as obscurantist in Ibn Khaldun (ibid, p. 1046): "[...] Christianity that prohibits the intellectual sciences..." In point of fact, the intellectual emancipation of Europe took place despite Christianity. One should equally recognize that Ibn Khaldun, despite the admiration one may have for his work, also indulges in a certain amount of obscurantism peculiar to men of religion in all climes, as testified by, among other remarks, this prescription against logic: "No one should begin logic without having first become master of the Islamic religious sciences. Otherwise he is likely to become its victim." (p. 1184.)
87. Ibn Iyas, *Histoire des Mamlouks circassiens*, Cairo, 1945, vol. 1, p. 21.
88. H. Laoust, *Les Gouverneurs de Damas*, op. cit., p. 121.
89. Ibid., p. 122.
90. Ibn Iyas, *Histoire*, op. cit., vol. 1, p. 176. Harking back to the Crusades and their exploits, European expansionism, marked on all continents by renewed cruelty, began an era of atrocities. Vasco da Gama and Albuquerque, combining two virtues that have always proved capital bedfellows—greed and religious fanaticism—eloquently air such views. In the course of his second expedition in 1502–03, the former reports, glowing with self-satisfaction: "We encountered a large vessel from Mecca laden with precious cargo [and] manned with 286 pagans [*sic*], six women and twelve young children [...]. We took along the children and four of the women as well as nearly all the goods; we killed 186 Moors and burned them together with their ships." *Voyages de Vasco de Gama*, Paris: Chandeigne, 1995, p. 313. As for Afonso de Albuquerque, see G. Bouchon, *Albuquerque. Le lion des mers d'Asie*, Paris, 1992, p. 188: "I burned the city [of Goa] and all were put to the sword [...]. Everywhere we managed to gain entrance, we let no Moslem escape with his life; they were packed into mosques that were set ablaze. We counted six thousand dead Moslems of both sexes. It was [...] a very great deed, a feat of arms well executed and well completed [...]."
91. Ibn Iyas, *Histoire*, op. cit., vol. 1, p. 369.
92. H. Laoust, *Les Gouverneurs de Damas*, op. cit., p. 142.
93. Ibid.
94. Ibn Iyas, *Histoire*, op. cit., vol. 2, p. 166.
95. Ibid., p. 171.
96. Ibid., p. 218.
97. J. Thénaud, *Le Voyage d'Outremer*, Paris, 1884, p. 114.
98. Cf. J. Gaulmier, *La Zubda Kachf al-Mamalik*, Beirut, 1950, p. 99.
99. Cf. M. Gaudefroy-Demonbynes, *La Syrie à l'époque des Mameluks*, op. cit., p. 145.
100. Abu al-Baqa', in H. Sauvaire, "La description de Damas," art. cit., vol. 8, iii, 1896, p. 427.
101. L. von Sudheim, "De itinere Terre Sancte," op. cit., p. 360.
102. Bertrandon de La Broquière, *Le Voyage d'outremer*, op. cit., p. 38.
103. Maqrizi, *Histoire des sultans*, op. cit., 2, ii, p. 69 (in 1298, for example).
104. J. Gaulmier, *La Zubda*, op. cit., p. 198.
105. Fra N. da Poggibonsi, *A Voyage Beyond the Sea (1346–50)*, Jerusalem: Franciscan Press, 1945, p. 78. Such quotations allow recent climate changes to be gauged. Snow has become increasingly rare in Damascus.
106. L. Frescobaldi, G. Gucci, and S. Sigoli, *Visit*, op. cit., p. 183.
107. Al-Jazari, in J. Sauvaget, *La Chronique*, op. cit., p. 70.
108. Dismashqi, *Manuel de la cosmographie du Moyen Âge*, Copenhagen, 1874, p. 26.
109. Ibn Battuta, *Travels*, op. cit., vol. 1, p. 118.
110. Ludovico di Varthema, *The Itinerary of Ludovico Di Varthema of Bologna from 1502 to 1508*, in Poggio Bracciolini and Ludovico di Varthema, *Travelers in Disguise: Narratives of Eastern Travel* (tr. J.Winter Jones), Harvard, 1963, p. 57.
111. J. Thénaud, *Le Voyage d'Outremer*, op. cit., pp. 113–14.
112. Bertrandon de La Broquière, *Le Voyage d'outremer*, op. cit., p. 38. James of Verona cites a figure of "100,000 men able to bear arms" ("Le Pèlerinage du moine," op. cit., p. 291), and Poggibonsi (*A voyage*, op. cit., p. 77), in 1348, heard the French say that there were more people in Damascus than in Paris. Statistics established between 1520 and 1530 by the Ottomans estimated the population at about fifty-seven thousand.
113. L. Frescobaldi, G. Gucci, and S. Sigoli, *Visit*, op. cit., p. 143.
114. James of Verona, "Le Pèlerinage du moine," op. cit., p. 291.
115. Ibn Battuta, *Travels*, op. cit., vol. 1, p. 144.
116. Cf. H. Sauvaire, "La description de Damas," art. cit., vol. 7, ii, 1896, p. 427.
117. L. Frescobaldi, G. Gucci, and S. Sigoli, *Visit*, op. cit., pp. 181–82.
118. Al-Jazari, in J. Sauvaget, *La Chronique*, op. cit., p. 70.
119. L. von Sudheim, "De itinere Terre Sancte," op. cit., p. 361. (The figure seems a gross exaggeration.)
120. Fra N. da Poggibonsi, *A voyage*, op. cit., p. 79.
121. E. N. Adler, *Jewish Travellers*, London, 1930, p. 199.
122. J. Sauvaget, *"Les Perles choisies" d'Ibn ach-Chihna*, Beirut, 1933, p. 49.
123. Bertrandon de La Broquière, *Le Voyage d'outremer*, op. cit., p. 291.
124. Ibid., p. 38.
125. E. N. Adler, *Jewish Travellers*, op. cit., p. 198.
126. R. P. J. Masson, *Voyage en Égypte de Félix Fabri 1483*, Paris, 1975, p. 697.
127. F. C. Lane, *Andréa Barbarigo, Merchant of Venice*, Baltimore, 1944, p. 107.
128. Quoted by R. Bouvier, *Jacques Cœur*, op. cit., p. 60.
129. Fra N. da Poggibonsi, *A voyage*, op. cit., p. 77.
130. L. Frescobaldi, G. Gucci, and S. Sigoli, *Visit*, op. cit., pp. 182–83.
131. Ibn Jubayr, *Voyages*, op. cit., vol. V, p. 140. Further on he alleges that in spite of interdiction of the law (Koran, 12:21) the sacred mosque itself became one huge marketplace (p. 210).
132. G. Wiet, *Journal*, vol. 1, p. 32.
133. J. Jomier, "Le Mahmal et la caravane égyptienne des pèlerins de La Mecque (XIIIe-XXe siècles)," *Rech. arch. phil. hist.*, XX, Cairo, 1953, p. 21.
134. Ludovico di Varthema, *Itinerary*, op. cit., pp. 57, 64.
135. Bertrandon de La Broquière, *Le Voyage d'outremer*, op. cit., p. 55–56. Ibn Jubayr pointed out that in the twelfth century the caravan traveled by night (this was only in April, however) by the light of torches carried by people on foot (*Voyages*, op. cit., vol. 5, p. 215). Among the participants that year was a twenty-five-year-old princess who disposed of nearly one hundred horses for the transport of her personal effects and provisions alone (p. 212). On the supposed presence of the Koran in the Mahmal, see J. Jomier, "Le Mahmal et la caravane...," art. cit.
136. Ibn Battuta, *Travels*, op. cit., vol. 1, p. 159; James of Verona, "Le Pèlerinage du moine," op. cit., p. 291.
137. L. Frescobaldi, G. Gucci, and S. Sigoli, *Visit*, op. cit., p. 183.
138. Fra N. da Poggibonsi, *A voyage*, op. cit., p. 77.
139. L. Frescobaldi, G. Gucci, and S. Sigoli, *Visit*, op. cit., p. 145.
140. Ludovico di Varthema, *Itinerary*, op. cit., p. 60.
141. Ibid.
142. G. Degeorge, "Sous la Grande Mosquée de Damas," *Notre histoire*, 108, Feb. 1994, pp. 20–24.
143. James of Verona, "Le Pèlerinage du moine," op. cit., p. 291.
144. Ibid., p. 292.
145. Fra N. da Poggibonsi, *A voyage*, op. cit., p. 79.
146. Maqrizi, *Histoire des sultans*, op. cit., 2, ii, p. 158.
147. Cf. G. Degeorge and Y. Porter, *The Art of the Islamic Tile*, Paris: Flammarion, 2001, p. 192. Recent Franco-Syrian excavations carried out in the citadel have brought to light a significant collection of 150,000 shards ranging in date, for the most part, from the ninth to the nineteenth centuries. Once their study has been concluded, knowledge of ceramics and pottery in Damascus will be much improved. See contributions by S. McPhillips and V. François to the Supplement, *Citadelle de Damas*, *Bulletin d'études orientales*, LIII–LIV, IFEAD, 2001–2002, pp. 139–170.
148. Cf. E. Atil, *Renaissance of Islam, Art of the Mamluks* (exh. cat.), Washington, 1981, pp. 176–82.
149. Cf. H. Sauvaire, "La description de Damas," art. cit., vol. 4, ii, 1894, p. 263.
150. "His body was left abandoned in a field to be scavenged by wolves and wild animals [...]. His power vanished from view as if he had never existed." Ibn Iyas, *Histoire*, op. cit., vol. 2, pp. 84 and 67.

Chapter IV

1. Cf. H. Laoust, *Les Gouverneurs de Damas*, op. cit., p. 158.
2. Ibid., p. 173.
3. Ibid.
4. Jacques de Villamont, *Les Voyages du seigneur de Villamont*, Arras, 1606, p. 449.
5. B. Lewis, *A Jewish Source on Damascus Just after the Ottoman Conquest*, BSOAS, X, 1/ 1939/, p. 179.
6. P. Belon, *Les Observations de plusieurs sigularitez et choses mémorables*, Paris, 1555, pp. 149–152.
7. In less than a half a century, from 1500 to 1550, it is estimated that the Amerindian population plummeted from eighty to ten million, a hecatomb that cannot be compared in size and cruelty even with the genocides of the twentieth century. On the brutality of the Spanish in the New World, cf. Bartolome de Las Casas, *The Devastation of the Indies* [1542], Harmondsworth, 1992
8. T. Todorov, *The Conquest of America*, New York/London, 1999, pp. 18–20.
9. *Le Régime des Capitulations, par un ancien diplomate*, Paris, 1898, p. 57.
10. J. Besson, *La Syrie et la Terre sainte au XVIIe siècle*, Paris, 1862, pp. 196 and 199.
11. Cf. R. Ristelhuber, *Les Traditions françaises au Liban*, Paris, 1925, pp. 88, 129, and 208, and M. Barrès, *Une enquête aux pays du Levant*, Paris, 1923, vol. 2, p. 217, n. 5.
12. P. Dib, *Histoire de l'Église maronite*, Beirut, 1962, p. 136.
13. England was only authorized to begin trading under its own flag in 1583, the Dutch in 1613, and the Austrians in 1615.
14. Pierre Loti visited the tomb in 1894: "Come evening, in the reddening sun, we arrived in the remote outskirts at the tomb of Mouhied-din Ibn-el-Arabi, who was the great mystical thinker of ancient Damascus. [...] In this calm place, surrounded by so many prohibitions and so much

mystery, dwells the quintessential charm of Muslim sacred art, that immaterial something in the design, in the shape of things, which arouses an impression of especial peace alien to our Western souls [...]." *La Galilée*, Paris, 1896, pp. 167–68.
15. Jacques de Villamont, *Les Voyages*, op. cit., p. 435. Muhammad's tomb is not of course in Mecca at all, but in Medina.
16. H. Laoust, *Les Gouverneurs de Damas*, op. cit., p. 186.
17. I. Burton, *The Inner Life of Syria, Palestine and the Holy Land*, 1875, vol. 1, p. 51.
18. Cf. B. Lewis, *Istanbul and the Civilization of the Ottoman* Empire, Norma, 1963, pp. 132–135.
19. B. de Monconys, *Journal des voyages de Monsieur de Monconys*, Lyon, 1665, vol. 1, p. 345. In the seventeenth century, Father Besson speaks of coffee in the following terms: "[...] black and boiling water, healthy rather than pleasant, unknown in France where it would be thought a drink fit for a hobgoblin." *La Syrie*, op. cit., p. 436.
20. Not to be confused with the preceding.
21. On the position of the khan, cf. J.-P. Pascual, *Damas à la fin du XVIe siècle*, Damascus, 1983, pp. 106–115, and F. Yahya, *Inventaire archéologique des caravansérails de Damas*, 1979, p. 389.
22. P. Belon, *Les Observations*, op. cit., p. 150.
23. Ibid., p. 152. Trade seems to have played a mounting role in the pilgrimage, as Baron Taylor observed in 1838: "For several centuries now, the goal of this caravan, religious solely in terms of the institution's origins, has been of a mercantile and speculative character. The caravan is less of a pilgrimage than a safe and ready means of exploiting every branch of Asian and African commerce. It is a real perpetual bazaar, to which each traveler brings wares from his own country that he exchanges, either on the way or in Mecca itself, sometimes for muslin or veils from the Indies, shawls from Cashmere or amber from the Deccan, or sometimes for pearls of Ceylon, pepper from Sumatra, or coffee from the Yemen. Several of these *hajjs*—venerable brokers of the caravans—have covered the route to Mecca ten times and so turned huge profits." *La Syrie, la Palestine et la Judée*, Paris, 1855, p. 120.
24. Jacques de Villamont, *Les Voyages*, op. cit., pp. 431–36. The Villamont quotation is significant because it appears to show that houses in unfired earthen brick—like those one still sees today—began to replace earlier dwellings that were higher and probably stone-built in the sixteenth century.
25. E. Roger, *La Terre sainte, ou Description topographique*, Paris, 1646, p. 297.
26. Ibid., p. 313.
27. Laurent d'Arvieux, *Mémoires*, op. cit., vol. 2, p. 464.
28. Cf. A. Vandal, *Les Voyages du marquis de Nointel*, 1900, p. 154.
29. Pietro Della Valle, *Voyages de Pietro Della Valle dans la Turquie*, Rouen, 1745, vol. 2, p. 133.
30. R.P. Coppin, *Relation des voyages faits dans la Turquie*, Lyon, 1720, p. 232.
31. L. d'Arvieux, *Mémoires*, op. cit., vol. 2, p. 291.
32. J. Goujon, *Histoire et voyage de la Terre sainte*, Lyon, 1672, p. 303.
33. E. Roger, *La Terre sainte*, op. cit., p. 208.
34. J. Besson, *La Syrie*, op. cit., p. 7, p. 176., p. 364.
35. *Lettres édifiantes et curieuses*, vol. 4, p. 87.
36. E. Roger, *La Terre sainte*, op. cit., p. 391.
37. Cf. A. Vandal, *Les Voyages*, op. cit., p. 248.
38. J. Goujon, *Histoire et voyage*, op. cit., pp. 52–53.
39. L. d'Arvieux, *Mémoires*, op. cit., vol. 2, pp. 291–92.
40. J. Mocquet, *Voyages en Afrique, Asie, Indes*, Paris, 1617, p. 378.
41. G. Fermanel, *Le Voyage d'Italie et du Levant de MM. Fermanel*, Rouen, 1664, p. 314.
42. B. de Monconys, *Journal*, op. cit., vol. 2, p. 342. The houses were still visible at the beginning of the 1930s, cf. *Mémorial Jean Sauvaget*, Damascus, 1954, vol. 2, p. 99.
43. L. d'Arvieux, *Mémoires*, op. cit., vol. 2, p. 458; and also B. de Monconys, ibid., vol. 1, p. 343, and H. Maundrell, *Voyage d'Alep à Jérusalem*, Utrecht, 1705, p. 206.
44. L. d'Arvieux, ibid., vol. 2, p. 477. The walls were surely double, since, in the early 1880s, Victor Guérin, a reliable observer, refers on several occasions to a second rampart, cf. *La Terre sainte, son histoire, ses souvenirs, ses sites, ses monuments*, Paris, 1884, vol. 1, p. 411 and passim. Similar observations in J. Besson, *La Syrie*, op. cit., p. 63, and from 1583 in J. Palerne, *D'Alexandrie à Istanbul. Pérégrinations dans l'Empire ottoman 1581-1583*, Paris: L'Harmattan, 1991, p. 208.
45. B. de Monconys, *Journal*, op. cit., vol. 2, p. 465.
46. L. d'Arvieux, *Mémoires*, op. cit., vol. 2, p. 448
47. H. Maundrell, *Voyage d'Alep*, op. cit., p. 210.
48. R.P. Coppin, *Relation*, op. cit., p. 465.
49. J. Besson, *La Syrie*, op. cit., p. 79.
50. II, Kings, 5.
51. G. Fermanel, *Le Voyage d'Italie*, op. cit., p. 317.
52. C. Niebuhr, *Voyage de M. Niebuhr en Arabie*, 1780, vol. 2, p. 274 and pp. 177–78; see also C. Niebuhr, *Travels through Arabia* (tr. R. Heron), Edinburgh, 1792.
53. T. Shaw *Travels, or Observations Relating to Several Parts of Barbary and the Levant*. Edinburgh, 1808, p. xvii
54. Quoted by S. Shamir, *The Azm Walis of Syria, 1724-1785*, Ph. D, 1961, p. 7.
55. H. Laoust, *Les Gouverneurs de Damas*, op. cit., p. 248.
56. Quoted by S. Shamir, *The Azm Walis*, op. cit., p. 137.
57. Ibid., p. 136.
58. C.-F. de Volney, *Voyage en Syrie et en Égypte*, Paris, 1823, vol. 2, p. 383.
59. Ibid.
60. Ibid., p. 236.
61. Ibid., vol. 3, p. 103.
62. Quoted by F.-C. Roux, *Les Échelles de Syrie et de Palestine au XVIIIe siècle*, Paris, 1928, p. 139.
63. Lev. 24:16; Deut., 13:2 and 18:2.
64. Cited by H. Laurens, *Le Royaume impossible*, Paris, 1990, p. 16. Let us also quote Bonaparte's declaration to his men at Toulon on March 10, 1798, which established France as an arbiter of world affairs: "The Spirit of Liberty that made the Republic at its birth arbiter in Europe [now] desires she do likewise over the high seas and in the remotest regions." Cf. J. de Metz and G. Legrain, *Aux pays de Napoléon, l'Égypte*, Grenoble, 1913, p. 15. Less than receptive to the "sophisticated civilization" others wished to impose upon them, the inhabitants of Cairo revolted and Bonaparte was obliged to resort to more traditional processes of European colonialism: slaughter and terror. "One has," he wrote to General Zayonchek, "to treat the Turks [Muslims] with the utmost severity; every day, here, I have three heads cut off and paraded through Cairo: this is the only way of getting anywhere with these people." Cf. F. Charles-Roux, *Bonaparte gouverneur d'Égypte*, Paris, 1935, p. 53.
65. C.-F. de Volney, *Voyage en Syrie*, op. cit., vol. 2, pp. 50, 53, 52, 54, and 61.
66. W. G. Browne, *Travels in Africa, Egypt and Syria from the Year 1768 to 1798*, London, 1806, p. 458.
67. Venture de Paradis, *Notes diverses sur la Grèce, l'Archipel, l'Égypte et la Syrie*, Paris, Bibliothèque Nationale, Mss. fr. nouv. acq. 9135, f. 81.
68. Ibid., f. 84.
69. C.-F. de Volney, *Voyage en Syrie*, op. cit., vol. 3, p. 375.
70. Ch. de Saint-Maure, *Nouveau Voyage de Grèce, d'Égypte, de Palestine*, Paris, 1724, p. 71.
71. R. Pococke, *Description of the East and of Some Other Countries*, London, 1743–45, vol. 2, i, p. 121.
72. C.-F. de Volney, *Voyage en Syrie*, op. cit., vol. 2, p. 397.
73. Guide Baedeker, 1906, p. 300.
74. A. de Lamartine, *Voyage en Orient*, op. cit., vol. 2, p. 72.
75. Ibid.
76. L. d'Arvieux, *Mémoires*, op. cit., vol. 2, p. 447.
77. M. Busch, *L'Orient pittoresque*, Trieste, 1863, p. 88.
78. A. de Lamartine, *Voyage en Orient*, op. cit., vol. 2, p. 57.
79. H. Maundrell, *Voyage d'Alep*, op. cit., pp. 209–10.
80. It should be noted that in 1348, Poggibonsi observed that Damascus houses were very tall (*A Voyage Beyond the Sea*, op. cit., p. 77) and that Pierre Belon in 1555 was still of the opinion they closely resembled those in Cairo (*Les Observations*, op. cit., p. 152).
81. In a Muslim house with only one courtyard, the lower level serves as the *selamlik* and the upper as the haremlik.
82. D. Badia y Leyblich, *Travels of 'Ali Bey*, op. cit., vol. 2, p. 272.
83. E. de Lorey and J. Sauvaget, "Le palais 'Azm à Damas," *La Revue de Paris*, March-April, 1926, p. 444.
84. A. de Lamartine, *Voyage en Orient*, op. cit., pp. 187–88.
85. J. Michaud and B. Pouloujat, *Correspondance d'Orient*, Paris, 1833–35, vol. 6, p. 158. Undertaken as late as 1830, the conquest of Algeria was nonetheless an idea long cherished by French colonialism. Plans were already being laid under Louis XIII. At the end of his life, St. Vincent de Paul, lambasting the indifference of the European powers before the misery of their nationals held captive by the Barbaresques, tried to mount an expedition against Algiers. The great idea designed to advance the enterprise was that the Moors would rise up against the Turks. On July 22, 1664, a French task force disembarked between Bougie [Bejela] and Bone and succeeded in maintaining a bridgehead for more than two months before being pushed back. In 1682, a squadron commanded by Duquesne bombarded Algiers. In July 1688, more than 10,000 bombs launched by the squadron of the Maréchal d'Estrées landed in the city. In July 1728, more than 1,800 shells were fired on Tripoli by the squadron of M. de Granpré. In 1808, planning for a future disembarkation, Napoleon sent the commander of the Engineers, Yves Boutin, to reconnoiter. In 1816, Algiers was once again bombarded during an Anglo-Dutch expedition. Cf. F. Charles-Roux, *France et Afrique du Nord avant 1830*, Paris, 1832. The United States too had their work cut out with the Regency: in 1793, eleven of their ships were captured and their crews enslaved. In 1795, a peace treaty was signed in which the United States was engaged to pay $721,000 together with an annual tribute of $22,000. In 1812, hostilities flared up again and the American consul, declared persona non grata, had to quit the Regency. In May 1815, a squadron left New York, and, in June 30, a new peace treaty was ratified. The new American consul, William Shaler, wrote: "Within half a century, the United States has solved several political problems of the deepest interest to mankind. They have, also, stripped the phantom of Barbary importance of its imaginary terrors and exposed to derision the frauds, by which it has been so long upheld." *Sketches of Algiers* [...], Boston, 1826, p. iii. After the conquest, Jean-Toussaint Merle, private secretary to General de Bourmont, wrote: "[The conquest of Algiers] brought back all the wonders of the Crusades, the [French] nationality of the Egyptian expedition, and the glories of victories of Fernand Cortez. [...] It served the cause of morality and humanity; it was to be of major assistance in the advance of agriculture, trade, industry, and civilization." *La Prise d'Alger racontée par un témoin*, Paris: H. Jonquières, 1930, p. 3.
86. A. de Lamartine, *Voyage en Orient*, op. cit., vol. 2, p. 67. As to this supposed fanaticism, two contemporary observers remarked: "And finally, when will people forego the erroneous opinion concerning the fanaticism of the Moslems, who are, in the ordinary circumstances of life, the most tolerant people on earth?" Maxime Du Camp, *Le Nil*, Paris, 1860, p. 204. Goupil Fresquet, traveling through the Orient with the painter Horace Vernet, noted that in Alexandria: "The Christians and Jews of the country [...] are treated with much tolerance by the Turks and the Arabs. Why then in France, where we have enshrined freedom of opinion and worship, do we not have a single mosque where a Muslim might observe his religion in a single one of our cities?" *Voyage d'Horace Vernet en Orient*, Paris, 1840, p. 47.
87. E. Blondel, *Deux Ans en Syrie et en Palestine (1838-1839)*, Paris, 1840, p. 164.
88. J.-J. Ampère, *Voyage en Égypte et en Nubie*, 1868, p. 236.
89. J. Michaud and B. Poujoulat, *Correspondance d'Orient*, op. cit., vol. 5, p. 247. J.-J. Ampère acknowledges "the wretched state of Egypt" (ibid., p. 254) and points out that: "Muhammad 'Ali abuses oppression and impoverishes a country he exploits to a singular degree" (p. 253). Maxime du Camp did not mince his words when speaking of "the flock of vultures that is Muhammad 'Ali's family" (*Le Nil*, op. cit., p. 7.), and "the inane, debased government that is a deadweight on Egypt" (p. 32). In general terms, business and religious sectors, and all the partisans of the imposition—be it by force—of the supposed "values" of Western civilization, were wont to give a favorable assessment of Muhammad 'Ali's policies.
90. Saint-Marc Girardin, *La Syrie en 1861*, Paris, 1862, p. 126.

91. P. Lortet, *Revue du Lyonnais*, Lyon, 25 December, 1840. For his part, B. Poujoulat writes: "This admirable country of Syria is surely not condemned to live forever under the barbaric dominion of the Muslim; the Cross, this great standard of the new age of the world will take the place of the Crescent in the lands of Asia [...]." *Voyage à Constantinople*, Brussels, 1841, vol. 2, p. 86.
92. Cited in B. Lewis, *The Jews of Islam*, London, 1984, p. 160. "Much has been said this last year about the English plan to found a new kingdom of Israel in Syria," wrote Poujoulat in 1841: "[...] An article by my brother published in *La Quotidienne* in August 1840 gave the true position of the Israelites in Palestine and the absurdity of the plan for a new Jewish kingdom in that country." *Voyage à Constantinople*, op. cit., vol. 2, pp. 294–95.
93. T. Herzl, *Journal 1895–1904*, Paris, 1990, pp. 87, 91, 302, and passim.
94. Cf. B. Poujoulat: "This *hatt-i humayun* [of 1856] [...] raised the irritation of the Muslims against Oriental Christians to fever pitch." *La Vérité sur la Syrie et l'expédition française*, Paris, 1861, p. 97. Contrary to what one might think, the Christians were no more pleased with it than the Muslims: "[The Christians] viewed the *hatt-i humayun* with feelings of mistrust and even fear," observed Poujalat. "Their condition as *rayas* seemed preferable in their eyes to the independence they were promised." Ibid., p. 316. The religious hierarchies, who saw themselves deprived of their privileges by the equality of all before the law, were the most opposed to the reforms. An instructive parallel may be drawn with the Crémieux decree, which was greeted without great enthusiasm by Algerian Jews as it stripped them of legal autonomy and subjected them to French civil law, particularly in matters of matrimony—one of the causes behind the insurrection of 1871; cf. T. Reinach, *Histoire des israélites*, Paris, 1901, p. 318.
95. A perceptive observer of the international political landscape called the 1856 treaty "a writ of sequestration delivered upon the Turkish Empire." Louis de Baudicourt, quoted by Saint-Marc Girardin, *La Syrie en 1861*, op. cit., pp. 390–91.
96. Ceaselessly, but vainly, the Porte protested against the scourge of the Capitulations; thus one reads in a report of July 7, 1869, addressed to the ambassadors: "It is known that in practice they are granted a latitude from which they do not forebear, and that, besides the already exceptional privileges granted by these acts, there exist manifest abuses which give rise to constant difficulties." *Le Régime des Capitulations*, op. cit., p. 278. The misuse of the Capitulations on a judicial level was thrown into relief by Sir Alfred Milner, *England in Egypt*, London, 1892, passim.
97. "The condition of the Christians has so improved that it has become dangerous to them: the Moslems are jealous of their commercial prosperity and irritated by the arrogance of those Christians afforded protection by European consuls." M. Skene, British Consul at Aleppo, quoted by R. Edwards, *La Syrie, 1840-1842*, Paris, 1862, pp. 82–83.
98. The rise of Beirut had been noticeable for a number of years, as the Comte de Pardieu observed in 1849: "Beirut has become Syria's main trading center. It is the port for Damascus. All the states of Europe have their consuls there. There is a host of Europeans [and] French and Italian is spoken everywhere." *Excursion en Orient. L'Égypte et le mont Sinaï, l'Arabie*, Paris, 1851, p. 327.
99. Arriving at Dayr al-Qamar with the French army, Édouard Lockroy wrote: "[...] when we came into the city later on [...], our horses waded up to their knees through putrefying flesh." *Ahmed le boucher*, 1888, p. 183.
100. B. Poujoulat, *La Vérité sur la Syrie*, op. cit., p. 390.
101. Ibid., p. 395. "It was not just in homes that throats were cut, but in the street as well. Their executioners had blocked off every exit. The victims were packed in like flocks of sheep for the butcher's, and the human butchery began, and again and again, incessantly, the blood flowing in torrents; the slaughtermen were covered in it, and those who had had their throats cut were trodden underfoot by the Muslims, all chopped into such tiny pieces that they were practically without form." Ibid., p. 393.
102. Cited by V. Guérin, *La Terre sainte*, op. cit., p. 402. Poujoulat proposes a figure of 3,800 houses, ibid., p. 45.
103. Quoted by Jobin, *La Syrie en 1860 et 1861. Lettres et documents*, Paris, 1880, pp. 150–51.
104. C. Lallemand, *D'Alger à Constantinople, Jérusalem, Damas*, Paris, n.d., p. 115.
105. L.-C. Lortet, *La Syrie d'aujourd'hui*, Paris, 1884, p. 608.
106. Speech pronounced on August 7, 1860, at the camp of Châlons. Quoted by Jobin, *La Syrie*, op. cit., p. 235. The conservative and colonialist Catholic right exulted, voicing the opinion that the longed-for revenge for the Crusades was nigh. Aboard *Le Borysthène* that brought him to Beirut with the Sixteenth Battalion of Chasseurs from Vincennes, Poujoulat wrote on August 15: "What were our old Crusaders doing in the Orient? Quite simply, what the expeditionary force of 1860 will do: combating Muslim savagery. [...] The thought that pushed the West towards the Orient in the Middle Ages is no different from the one propelling it there today: the expulsion of Islam to the deserts whence it should never have emerged." *La Vérité sur la Syrie*, op. cit., p. 12.
107. R. Edwards, *La Syrie, 1840–1842*, op. cit., p. 201.
108. E.-M. de Vogüé, "Affaires de Syrie," *Le Correspondant*, October, 1860, pp. 341–42.
109. Quoted by H. Laurens, *Le Royaume impossible*, op. cit., p. 142. For several centuries, it is true, Europeans had already rendered, as Jules Ferry put it, priceless and capital services "to the cause of civilization" via brutality. And the same gentleman declared: "Superior races have rights with respect to lower races [...] because there exists a duty towards them. [They] have the duty of civilizing inferior races." *Journal officiel*, July 29, 1885. The racial theories that had been bandied about for a few years since Gobineau's famous essay on their inequality appeared in 1855 gave unexpected succor to the colonial companies. Renan observed: "The Aryan and the Semitic races moreover are destined to conquer the world and to restore unity to mankind, so that, with respect to them, the rest exist only as experiments, obstacles, or auxiliaries [...]." *De l'origine du langage*, Paris, 1858, pp. 232–33. This was an observation that Zionist Jews, believing themselves to be the "chosen people," were to apply in Palestine. Many of them, however, failed to fully appreciate the noble ideals promulgated by Jules Ferry—like Anatole France who did not shirk from writing: "Colonial policy is the most recent form of barbarism, or, if one prefers the term, civilization." Cf. *La France colonisatrice*, Paris: Diana Levi, 1983, p. 224.
110. Against the backdrop of imperialist competition with France, the occupation of Egypt was a long-cherished idea of Great Britain's, anxious to protect the route from the Indies. The Suez Canal was inaugurated in 1869, but long before, Lord Palmerston had averred that, were a canal ever bored, sooner or later, Great Britain would feel obliged to occupy Egypt; see J. Tonnelé, *L'Angleterre en Méditerranée*, Paris, 1952, p. 153. Fixated by the Vosges Line, Clemenceau refused the partnership Great Britain offered him.
111. Quoted by N. Moutran, *La Syrie de demain*, Paris, 1916, p. 210. This policy was not even an innovation; it was the same as Danton's and that of the Comité de Salut Public when commanding the consuls "to proclaim loud and clear that France continued to ensure the safety of the Christians." Cf. R. Ristelhuber, *Les Traditions françaises au Liban*, op. cit., p. VII. See also G. Charmes, *Voyage en Syrie*, Paris, 1891, p. 32: "The Convention that was beheading French bishops busied itself at the same time having Catholicism respected in the Lebanon." Quoted by R. Ristelhuber, ibid., pp. 289–90.
112. M. Barrès, *Une enquête*, op. cit., vol. 1, p. 33. Albert Vandal says: "Wherever they gained access, the monks became useful sources of information for us. Through their efforts, the government gathered information concerning the resources of the country as well as on the openings for trafficking and for establishing concerns there. Everywhere missionaries opened up fresh trade opportunities, leading the way for our merchants and consuls, serving as France's advance guard." *Une ambassade française en Orient sous Louis XV*, Paris, 1887, p. 16. In the words of a foremost Ottoman statesman, the missionaries made "France sprout beneath their feet." Ibid., p. 449. Cf. the Baron de Courcel's declaration in a report dated March 13, 1902: "It has become almost trite to boast of the crucial contribution made by Brothers of the Christian schools in the East to the development of our political and commercial interests, and to the diffusion of our language and civilization [...]." *Congrès français de la Syrie*, fasc. III, "Section Enseignement," Paris, 1919, p. 64.
113. A. Hourani, *La Pensée arabe et l'Occident*, Paris, 1991, p. 143.
114. Baron I. J. S. Taylor, *La Syrie, la Palestine*, op. cit., pp. 49 and 421.
115. E. Blondel, *Deux Ans en Syrie*, op. cit., p. 169.
116. Comte C. de Pardieu, *Excursion en Orient*, op. cit., p. 345.
117. W. McC. Thomson, *The Land and the Book, Lebanon, Damascus*, London, 1881–86, p. 412.
118. Comte de Paris, *Damas et le Liban. Extraits du journal d'un voyage en Syrie au printemps 1860*, London, 1861, p. 52.
119. L.-C. Lortet, *La Syrie d'aujourd'hui*, op. cit., p. 580.
120. *La Syrie et le Liban en 1922*, p. 264.
121. E. Ben-Yehuda, *Le Rêve traversé*, Paris, 1998, p. 135–37. It should be noted that the oppression evoked by Ben-Yehuda was far from peculiar to Jews since he observes: "One can in general affirm that Jews, even Turkish citizens, were less downtrodden than Arab *fellahs*," p. 134. Moreover, Jewish historians are unanimous in hailing Muslim tolerance, in marked contrast to European anti-Semitism: "Under Muslim domination, the Jews of Spain, like those of Mesopotamia and Africa, could breathe at last," wrote T. Reinach, *Histoire des israélites*, op. cit., p. 67, while L. Poliakov adds: "Islam, religion of tolerance par excellence [has been] less inclined than Christianity to plunge humanity into blood." *Histoire de l'antisémitisme, de Mahomet aux Marranes*, op. cit., pp. 25–26. The effect of the *himaya* was such that Jews originating in a country which did not enjoy a bona fide treaty sought to obtain the "protection" of a great power: thus, in 1885, Romanian Jews pleaded for French protection and naturalization to counter Ottoman intimidation." Cf. I. Margalith, *Le Baron Edmond de Rothschild et la colonisation juive en Palestine, 1882–1899*, Paris, 1957, p. 186. In addition, even anti-Semite governments, like Russia for example, would defend their nationals in Syria (Jew and non-Jew alike)—"not out of love for them," as Ben-Yehuda makes clear, but for "the honor of Russian nationality." Ibid., p. 137.
122. Contrary to a commonly-held notion, nostalgia for Zion was seldom the reason for emigration. Certain clerics resolutely forbade departure from Mesopotamia, even for Palestine: "He who leaves Babylon for Palestine infringes explicit Biblical command," declared R. Judah ben Ezechiel, referring to Jeremiah 27:22: "They shall be carried to Babylon, and there shall they be until the day that I visit them, saith the Lord." Cf. L. Poliakov, ibid., p. 8.
123. E. Ben-Yehuda places "the greed of civil servants for bribes" on a par with the Capitulations among the factors that paved the way for "national resurrection." *Le Rêve traversé*, op. cit., p. 137. "Two factors explain why Zionist immigration nevertheless could continue from 1882 to 1941: the ceaseless intervention of the Western powers under cover of the Capitulations [...] and the tireless corruption of the Turkish administration," summarizes N. Weinstock, *Le Sionisme contre Israël*, Paris: Maspéro, 1969, p. 90. Bribery remained (and indeed remains) effective long after the fall of the Ottoman Empire. Weizmann was convinced that the majority of Arab leaders could be suborned, cf. Kayyali, *Histoire de la Palestine 1896–1940*, Paris, 1958, p. 181. In 1949, "Ben Gourion suggested offering pay-offs to Arab leaders to incite them to show more lenience towards Israel." Cf. T. Segev, *Les Premiers Israéliens*, Paris, 1998, p. 60. Nevertheless, the restrictions of the Porte must have been of some effect since, among a million Jews leaving Eastern Europe between 1881 and 1900—a tide of emigration of unprecedented size—the vast majority went to the United States and the New World, with only twenty to twenty-five thousand moving to Palestine.
124. Viennese writer N. Birnbaum coined the word "Zionism" in 1890 to designate national renaissance in Palestine. The idea was already present in the declaration (which came to nothing) addressed by Bonaparte in Gaza to the Jews of Syria in 1799, inviting "the legitimate heirs to Palestine" to rebel as one so as "to restore their rights." Traces also surface in Spinoza's correspondence; Oldenburg (December 8, 1665),

asks the philosopher's advice on "a rumour in everybody's mouth that the Jews who have been dispersed for more than two thousand years, are to return to their country. Few in this place would believe it, but many wish it. For my part I cannot put any confidence in this news . . . [it is] an important announcement which if it were true would seem to bring a crisis into the world." *Correspondence of Spinoza* (ed. and tr. A. Wolf), London, 1928, p. 217. (Spinoza's response does not appear to be known.) Voltaire wrote in his *Treatise on Tolerance*: "If the Jews reasoned thus today [wanting to recover property and land that the Muslims expropriated more than one thousand years ago], it is clear that the only possible response would be to clap them in the galleys." *Traité de la Tolérance*, Paris: Flammarion, 1989, p. 123.
125. J. Zineman, *Histoire du sionisme*, Paris, 1950, p. 101.
126. T. Herzl, *Journal*, op. cit., p. 302.
127. Ibid., p. 191. And, when the "advantages" are not convincing enough, Herzl, foreshadowing the "pressures" that would later be brought to bear on various states by a range of Jewish organizations, turns instead to threats. In 1901, he asked the Professor Vamberg, about to leave for Constantinople, to "suggest to the Sultan that things would be hard indeed for Turkey should world Judaism embark on a fight against her." J. Zineman, *Histoire du sionisme*, op. cit., p. 173. It should be recalled that the most virulent opponents of Zionism came from within Judaism itself, from partisans of integration and assimilation, and especially from traditionalists and the orthodox, for whom the gathering of the dispersed could only be the supernatural work of God and who considered the normalization of Jewish existence within a political framework as undermining the passive Messianic vision. The Agudat Israel party was created in 1912 as a war machine against Zionism; its first president, Jacob Rosenheim, stated that "Zionism has demoted the Jewish nation to the level of a political nation among the nations." Cf. A. Dieckhoff, *L'Invention d'une nation*, Paris, 1993, p. 175. The historian T. Reinach wrote in 1900: "For a quarter of a century Palestine has been one of the favorite goals of Jewish emigration from Western Europe. The miseries and tribulations of all kinds endured by the Jews of Russia and Romania have sown in several minds the fanciful idea of rebuilding a Jewish state [...]. One understands, one readily excuses these aspirations; they are the bitter and legitimate fruit of persecution; but the political and religious conditions of Syria oppose insurmountable obstacles to their realization. Furthermore they blatantly contradict the historical evolution of Judaism, which has demonstrated a gradual, very slow, hotly disputed, but seamless transformation from being a national to being a religious fact." *Histoire des israélites*, op. cit., pp. 363–64. On the other hand, anti-Semites were very often favorable to Zionism; this is the case, for example, of the Tharaud brothers and also of L.-F. Céline, whose anti-Semitic hysteria is notorious (cf. *Bagatelles pour un massacre*, Paris: Denoël, 1937, pp. 317–18). Little after the war of June 1967, once back in Paris, A. Francos observed: "I read articles published in the anti-Semitic press, in *Rivarol*, *Aspects de la France*, *Défense de l'Occident*, all notorious collaborators, who all 'shopped' Jews in the past, took up their pens as one to acclaim Israel." *Les Palestiniens*, Paris: Julliard, 1968, p. 214. In 1974, Paul Morand noted in his *Journal inutile* (Paris, 2001, vol. 2, p. 372): "All change at the Academy· the Right, once anti-Semite, has become Zionist [...]." See also vol. 1, p. 443.
128. T. Herzl, *Journal*, op. cit., p. 104.
129. A.-W. Kayyali, *Histoire de la Palestine 1896–1940*, Paris, 1985, p. 13.
130. It was obviously the political methods and aims, which were a secret for no one, and not Jewish emigration as such that caused rejection, disquiet, and condemnation: "We are by no means hostile to the return of a great number of Jews in Palestine," wrote George Samné in about 1919, "but we ask them to enter the Syrian Federation with all proper sincerity and without cherishing ulterior motives of domination." *La Syrie*, Paris, 1920, pp. 408–409.
131. Quoted by B. Lewis, *Semites and Antisemites*, London, 1986, p. 171.
132. A.-W. Kayyali, *Histoire de la Palestine*, op. cit., p. 39. The parallels between the history of the United States and that of Zionism, in terms of the historical circumstances, the ideologies in play, the political objectives, and the methods employed were naturally far from news to the Zionist leaders themselves: thus, the young Ben Gourion had no hesitation in citing the example of the United States. "We who want to build a new country in the desert [*sic*], we should observe how exiles persecuted in England built such a wealthy state of unparalleled power." *Mémoires*, Paris: Grasset, 1974, p. 71. "Desert" here designates Palestine and refers to Herzl's well-known formula, the basis of Zionist propaganda: "A land without people for a people without land."
133. Quoted by G. Samné, *La Syrie*, op. cit., p. 316.
134. Quoted by J. Thobie, *Intérêts et impérialisme français dans l'Empire ottoman 1895–1914*, Paris, 1977, p. 92. This was a time-worn saying in France—as much among the Catholic Right as in the colonialist Left: "Syria is a French land," B. Poujoulat had written in all seriousness in 1860 in *La Vérité sur la Syrie*, op. cit., p. 9. Every conceivable ploy was employed in an effort to establish its right of ownership (mythical ancestors, imaginary filiations, historical sleight of hand...). In 1911, M. Barrès did not flinch from writing: "Algeria is France [...] Europe completes itself with the Mediterranean. The shores of the Mediterranean, lands from Egypt to Morocco, belong to Europe. They did in Roman times. It is in fact the heritage of Rome." N. Priollaud, *La France colonisatrice*, Paris, 1983, p. 101.
135. Quoted by H. Lammens, *La Syrie, précis historique*, Beirut, 1921, vol. 2, p. 218.
136. Von Kressenstien, *Zwischen Kaukasus*, 34, 38, cited by H. Lammens, ibid., p. 230.
137. L. von Sanders, *Cinq Ans de Turquie*, Paris, 1923, p. 45.
138. M. Busch, *L'Orient pittoresque*, op. cit., p. 89. "The fact that so many pilgrims on their way to refresh their religious faith at the very cradle of Islam pass through the city does much to sustain the characteristic fanaticism of the Damascenes." V. Guérin, *La Terre sainte*, op. cit., p. 419 (written at the beginning of the 1880s).
139. F. Charles-Roux, *Bonaparte gouverneur d'Égypte*, op. cit., p. 302.
140. D. Badia y Leyblich, *Travels of 'Ali Bey*, op. cit., vol. 2, p. 273.
141. J. Michaud and B. Pouloujat, *Correspondance d'Orient*, op. cit., vol. 6, p. 157.
142. Baron I. J. S. Taylor, *La Syrie, la Palestine*, op. cit., p. 121.
143. A. de Lamartine, *Voyage en Orient*, op. cit., vol. 2, p. 50.
144. Comte C. de Pardieu, *Excursion en Orient*, op. cit., p. 339.
145. G. Flaubert, *Voyage en Orient*, Paris, 1949, p. 190.
146. Guide Baedeker 1906, Introduction, p. LIX.
147. In the sixteenth century, Diego de Haëdo had already said of the mosques of Algiers: "If any Christian enters therein, he would have had to turn Moslem, for if not they set him ablaze or throw him alive onto hooks." *Topographie et histoire générale d'Alger*, op. cit., p. 162. A little later, in 1631, V. Stochove pointed out that in Cairo entry to mosques was forbidden to Christians, though not in Istanbul. *Voyage en Égypte*, Cairo, 1975, p. 50.
148. A. de Lamartine, *Voyage en Orient*, op. cit., vol. 2, p. 72.
149. T. M. Lycklama a Nijeholt, *Voyage en Russie, au Caucase et en Perse, dans la Mésopotamie, le Kurdistan, la Syrie, exécuté pendant les années 1866, 1867 et 1868*, Paris, 1872–74, vol. 6, p. 331. In exceptional circumstances, before 1860, certain Europeans were able to visit the building: Badia y Leyblich in 1807 as a Muslim; the Englishman Buckingham, who in 1816 tricked his way in; the Duke and Duchess of the Brabant by exceptional authorization in 1846; the Comte de Paris, in May 1860, also by exceptional authorization, though at night. Cf. G. Degeorge, *Damas des Ottomans à nos jours*, Paris: L'Harmattan, 1994, p. 138.
150. J. Kelman, *From Damascus to Palmyra*, London, 1908, p. 123.
151. G. Robinson, *Travels in Palestine and Syria*, London, 1837, vol. 1, p. 218.
152. A. de Lamartine, *Voyage en Orient*, op. cit., vol. 2, p. 63.
153. C. Greenstreet Addison, *Damascus and the Palmyra: Journey to the East*, London, 1838, vol. 2, pp. 140–41 and 121. In 1840, European dress had already invaded Istanbul: "Everywhere," writes G. Fesquet, "the European frock-coat and children in caps present themselves to the eyes of the crestfallen artist." *Voyage d'Horace Vernet en Orient*, 1840, p. 221.
154. I. Burton, *The Inner Life*, op. cit., vol. 1, p. 23.
155. L.-C. Lortet, *La Syrie d'aujourd'hui*, op. cit., p. 586.
156. R. Dorgelès, *La Caravane sans chameaux*, Paris, 1928, p. 135.
157. G. Flaubert, *Voyage en Orient*, op. cit., pp. 194 and 187. Inhabitants of Damascus even today favor the Louis XV style.
158. Major Fridolin, "Damas, Jérusalem, le désert et la caravane de La Mecque," *Revue des Deux Mondes*, April 1854, p. 93.
159. E.-M. de Vogüé, "Affaires de Syrie," art. cit., p. 79.
160. A. Leroux, *Le Liban et la mer: Beyrouth, Baalbek, Damas*, Nantes, 1881, pp. 68 and 71.
161. P. Loti, *La Galilée*, op. cit., p. 137 and 145–46.
162. Guide Baedeker, 1906, p. 297.
163. M. Barrès, *Une enquête*, op. cit., vol. 1, p. 146.
164. P. Loti, *La Galilée*, op. cit., p. 145.
165. Fra N. da Poggibonsi, *A Voyage Beyond the Sea*, op. cit., p. 78.
166. M. Busch, *L'Orient pittoresque*, op. cit., p. 88.
167. E.-M. de Vogüé, "Affaires de Syrie," art. cit., pp. 72–73.
168. G. Robinson, *Travels*, op. cit., p. 223–24.
169. Cf. A. de Lamartine, *Voyage en Orient*, op. cit., vol. 2, p. 68; E. Blondel, *Deux Ans en Syrie*, op. cit., pp. 163 and 169; Comte C. de Pardieu, *Excursion en Orient*, op. cit., p. 345; T. M. Lycklama a Nijeholt, *Voyage en Russie*, op. cit., vol. 4, p. 347; J. Michaud and B. Poujoulat, *Correspondance d'Orient*, op. cit., vol. 6, pp. 168–69.
170. A. de Lamartine, *Voyage en Orient*, op. cit., vol. 2, p. 66. I. Burton, *The Inner Life*, op. cit., vol. 2, p. 42. G. Fesquet, *Voyage d'Horace Vernet*, op. cit., p. 213. C. Greenstreet Addison, *Damascus and the Palmyra*, op. cit., vol. 2, p. 144.
171. G. Flaubert, *Notes de voyage*, Paris: Conard, 1910, p. 341. Sexual activity in the open air was inevitably much more frequent than the generally restrained pen of our authors might imply. In sixteenth-century Algiers, Diego de Haëdo already alludes to the kind of scene described by Flaubert: "A few marabouts serve as stallions to these ladies, and the husbands see nothing wrong with this as they regard their wives entering into congress with these individuals with gladness and as a fortunate event." *Topographie et histoire générale d'Alger*, op. cit., p. 116. In the following century, V. Stochove speaks "of these women [in Cairo] who give themselves to everyone for the love of Mahomet, believing in this to perform works of mercy." *Voyage en Égypte*, op. cit., p. 52. The same applied in Morocco, as this extract from the report of Commodore Stewart's mission in 1721 testifies: "All actions of the saints are legal because it is supposed that divine inspiration animates all their doings [...]. A few years ago, one of them threw himself stark naked on a girl in the middle of the street: not understanding the sanctity of his intentions, the girl started by resisting, but some saints of the same tribe as the ravisher being nearby, seized her by the heels and covered the couple with their coats." Cf. Defontin-Maxange, *Le Grand Ismaïl, empereur du Maroc*, Paris, 1929, p. 310. According to Diego de Haëdo, even homosexuality was not a private matter: "To practice pederasty in broad daylight and before all eyes is an act that surprises no one here." Ibid., p. 190. Even the most shameful vice of sodomy—the "sin that has no name" as the tribunals of the Holy Office called it—was practiced in public, as Diego de Haëdo once again records: "They [the marabouts] even commit this bestial sin in the midst of the souk and in the main streets before the eyes of the whole city." Ibid., p. 121. Lastly, and again in Damascus, Flaubert observes "two pupils, around twelve years old, f...ing [*sic*] at the gateway to a monastery." Ibid., p. 330. In the fifteenth century, Maqrizi noted in relation to Cairo: "I have heard it said that there were people who followed young boys or women [...]. They performed their antics as they walked, without anyone realizing it due to the crowd, and because each individual was intent solely on his own pleasure." Quoted by G. Wiet and A. Raymond, *Les Marchés du Caire*, Cairo: IFAO, 1979, p. 221. Nothing, then, had changed since the days of John Chrysostom, who observed in fourth-century Antioch: "Thus, in the middle of town, males practice turpitudes on other males as

if one were in the depths of the desert." Cf. A. J. Festugière, *Antioche païenne et chrétienne*, Paris: E. de Boccard, 1959, p. 207.

172. J. Michaud and B. Poujoulat, *Correspondance d'Orient*, op. cit., vol. 6, p. 177. At the end of the seventeenth century, H. Maundrell already included coffeehouses among the "curiosities" of Damascus. *Voyage d'Alep*, op. cit., vol. 2, p. 51.

173. C. Greenstreet Addison, *Damascus and the Palmyra*, op. cit., vol. 2, p. 144.

174. J. Michaud and B. Poujoulat, *Correspondance d'Orient*, op. cit., vol. 6, p. 178.

175. Ibid., p. 177.

176. L.-C. Lortet, *La Syrie d'aujourd'hui*, op. cit., p. 585.

177. G. Flaubert, Letter to Louis Bouillet, January 15, 1850, in *Correspondance*, vol. 1, Paris: Gallimard/Pléiade, 1980 [1830–1851]. It should be understood that the *hammam* does not possess only hygienic and therapeutic virtues, as the feverish pen of Omar Haleby implies: "These baths, with their damp, hot vapor, are useful and even necessary in combating the great number of diseases and in properly cleaning the skin [...]; but what is harmful is the abuse you make of them, the long hours your women and you spend in them, the former for the most part in discussing amorous subjects [...]; and you [...] alas! all too often in indulging in pederasty with your young masseurs and other bathers [...]." Cf. P. de Régla, *El Ktab des lois secrètes de l'amour*, Paris, n.d., p. 179. Such scandalous practices were so widespread that the goodwives of Trebizond, for example, "addressed a petition to the *wali* pleading with him to close the baths down because their husbands forsook them entirely for the fine young men attached to the *hammams*." *Ananga Ranga*, Paris, 1910, p. 16. As for the ladies, it is unlikely they merely discussed "amorous subjects," as a seventh-century connoisseur of such matters, Brantôme, alleges: "Turkish women go to the baths," he writes, "more for this lewdness [lesbianism] that for anything else, being extremely partial to it." *Vie des dames galantes*, Paris: Bibliothèque des Curieux, 1913, p. 117. Moreover, if one is to believe Laugier de Tassy (*Histoire du royaume d'Alger. Un diplomate français à Alger en 1724*, Paris, 1992, p. 108), they also met up with their fancy men: "The women have their own special baths where men would not dare enter under any pretext whatsoever. They are inviolable and ideal sanctuaries for gallantry; for, as the women there are served by female slaves, they often introduce young male ones masquerading as girls."

178. E.-M. de Vogüé, "Affaires de Syrie," art. cit., pp. 77 and 79.

179. A. von Kremer, *Topographie von Damaskus*, Vienna, 1854; extract cited in *Cahiers de la recherche architecturale* 10/11, Paris, 1982, p. 114. The *khazna*, literally "treasury," here designates a large, double-door built-in closet in the walls of the room.

180. E.-M. de Vogüé, "Affaires de Syrie," art. cit., pp. 78–79.

181. G. de Salverte, *La Syrie avant 1860*, Paris, 1861, p. 52. See also P. Loti, *La Galilée*, op. cit., p. 146.

182. E.-M. de Vogüé, "Affaires de Syrie," art. cit., pp. 80–81. Vogüé was in Damascus in 1872, only twelve years after the massacres of 1860. The house that he refers to is 'Anbar's, converted into a school in 1890 and today known as the 'Anbar *maktab*.

183. Baron I. J. S. Taylor, *La Syrie, la Palestine*, op. cit., p. 115; Comte C. de Pardieu, *Excursion en Orient*, op. cit., pp. 344 and 346; T. M. Lycklama a Nijeholt, *Voyage en Russie*, op. cit., vol. 4, p. 345. It should be recalled that, at the beginning of the nineteenth century, the suburbs of Damascus, already very extensive, represented 58 percent of the total surface of the city.

184. "Wherever one looks, in effect," writes V. Guerin, "Muslim neglect cries out at every step; the streets are generally narrow, poorly laid and still worse maintained; they intertwine chaotically and constantly disconcert the foreigner venturing for the first time into what is an inextricable maze." *La Terre sainte*, op. cit., p. 413.

185. E. Blondel, *Deux Ans en Syrie*, op. cit., p. 178.

186. W. McC. Thomson, *The Land*, op. cit., vol. 3, p. 409.

187. E. Blondel, *Deux Ans en Syrie*, op. cit., p. 180.

188. C. Lallemand, *D'Alger à Constantinople, Jérusalem, Damas*, Paris, n.d., p. 101.

189. M. Barrès, *Une enquête*, op. cit., vol. 1, p. 141.

190. P. Loti, *La Galilée*, op. cit., p. 135: "But alas! behind the beautiful veils, little by little Damascus is opening up: an iron bridge, a station under construction, Cook hotels, and hackney-cabs. What, these things here! Can this truly be the threshold of the marvelous pink city that is still named Pearl and Queen of the Orient!..."

191. G. Robinson, *Travels*, op. cit., vol. 1, p. 218.

192. E. Blondel, *Deux Ans en Syrie*, op. cit., p. 177.

193. I. Burton, *The Inner Life*, op. cit., vol. 1, p. 29.

194. P. Loti, *La Galilée*, op. cit., p. 169. "Today [...], this suburb of Meydan is filled as usual with singular visitors: Druze farmers selling cereals; Kurds bringing in herds of sheep; Bedouins of a type unknown to us; and, leery, flustered, villainous, gazelle-hunters from the solitudes of the Levant, armed with very long spears, alf-naked on scrawny horses." Ibid., p. 165.

195. I. Burton, *The Inner Life*, op. cit., vol. 1, p. 39.

196. G. Flaubert, *Voyage en Orient*, op. cit., p. 186.

197. C. Lallemand, *D'Alger à Constantinople*, op. cit., p. 117.

198. M. Barrès, *Une enquête*, op. cit., vol. 1, p. 142.

199. Baron I. J. S. Taylor and L. Raybaud, *L'Égypte, la Palestine et la Judée 1835–1838*, vol. 1, p. 129; A. de Lamartine, *Voyage en Orient*, op. cit., vol. 2, p. 79.

200. Guide Baedeker, 1906, pp. 292–93.

Chapter V

1. N. Moutran, *La Syrie de demain*, Paris, 1916, p. 48.

2. P. Pic, *Syrie et Palestine*, Paris, 1924, p. VII.

3. Cf. *La France colonisatrice*, Paris, 1983, p. 113.

4. "Secret Report," in, *The Letters of T. E. Lawrence* (ed. D. Garnett), London, 1938, p. 266.

5. Letter from Sir H. McMahon, October 24, 1915, cited in a letter by Lawrence to *The Times* of September 1919, in *Letters*, op. cit., p. 281.

6. G. Samné, *La Syrie*, op. cit., p. 455. With his customary lucidity, T. E. Lawrence got to the root of the Arab revolt against the sultan when he saw it as "the final triumph, the most brilliant demonstration there could be in Western Asia of nationalism as a basis for political action, as opposed to the principle of world religion that is a supra-national belief." *Oriental Assembly* (ed. A. W. Lawrence), London, 1939, p. 124. Let us also recall Rashid Rida's damning indictment of the Hashemites: "This dynasty was thus one of the first to help a non-Moslem foreign power [Great Britain] to colonize Arab countries." Cf. H. Laoust, *Le Califat dans la doctrine de Rashid Rida*, Paris, 1986, p. 125. The Iraqis having disposed of their last Hashemite lackey in July 1958, the phenomenon endures today only in Jordan, where the United States—helped by Israeli mercenaries—have supplanted Britain.

7. The "diplomatic lie" was to become the rule in the affairs of the Middle East. In 1892, Sir Alfred Milner offered the following justification: "But the fulfillment of the professions made by a nation in the act of going to war is not common human practice—whatever ought to be the case in the ideal—apt to be rigidly exacted of the same nation at the moment of victory." *England in Egypt*, London, 1892, p. 8. Long before, French writer and statesman Chateaubriand had already written: "The English consider solely positive policy, that is to say their interests; keeping faith with treaties and moral scruples seems puerile in their eyes." *Mémoires d'outre-tombe*, XIX, xviii, Paris: Gallimard/Pléiade, 1951, vol. 1, p. 736.

8. T. E. Lawrence, *Letters*, op. cit., p. 282.

9. R. Neher-Bernheim, *La Déclaration Balfour*, Paris: Julliard, 1969, p. 4.

10. Quoted by R. Neher-Bernheim, ibid., p. 366. For his part, Vladimir Jabotinsky, head of the Fascist-tinged revisionist party, defining Zionism as a movement aiming "to establish a Jewish majority in Eretz-Israel on both sides of the Jordan," declared that the term *homeland* "has no precedent and had been chosen simply so as not to irritate the Turkish authorities." Cf. Ben Gourion, *Mémoires*, op. cit., p. 320. In early December, 1917, an Undersecretary of State to the Foreign Office was even more trenchant: "Our wishes are that the Arab countries be for the Arabs, Armenia for the Armenians, and Judaea for the Jews" (cited by J. Pichon, *Le Partage du Proche-Orient*, Paris, 1938, p. 133), a formula that echoes the slogan of Polish Jewry's brown-uniformed *jeunesse dorée*: "Germany to Hitler, Italy to Mussolini, Palestine to us." Quoted in M. Rodinson, "Israël, fait colonial?" *Les Temps modernes*, June 1967, p. 52, and I. Halevi, *Question juive*, Paris, 1981, p. 187.

11. "Memorandum on Syria, Palestine, Mesopotamia," August 11, 1919; cited in Leonard Stein, *The Balfour Declaration*, London, 1961, p. 650

12. Ibid., p. 649.

13. *Journal officiel*, December 28, 1917. See also: Syrian Central Committee, *L'Opinion syrienne à l'étranger pendant la guerre. Documents*, Paris, 1918.

14. T. E. Lawrence, *Letters*, op. cit., p. 312. French officers, however unfavorable to the action of Lawrence and his Arab auxiliaries, recognized the impact of their action: cf. J. Pichon, *Sur la route des Indes*, Paris, 1952, p. 151. P. Lyautey makes similar observations: "[...] from the solely military point of view, the Palestine campaign would have been inconceivable without Arab participation [...]. The English were quite right to secure Arab collaboration, which enabled them, two months before the Armistice, to put an end to our domination over the Levant." *Le Drame oriental et le rôle de la France*, Paris, 1924, p. 124.

15. On the retreat of the Germano-Turkish forces in the Barada valley, cf. J. Pichon, ibid., p. 122.

16. Liman von Sanders, *Cinq Ans de Turquie*, Paris, 1923, p. 350, and J. Pichon, ibid., p. 125.

17. The chaos customary in such circumstances did not save the city: "As events progressed," noted J. Pichon, "nomads and Druze peasants trickled into the city, lured by the attraction of plunder. It was then that unprecedented scenes began. Everyone fell upon the wretched unarmed Turks and massacred them, not even the patients and the injured hospitalized in the medical units run by the Red Crescent were spared. There were no police—the agents were in hiding, afraid for their lives. The pillage was systematically organized and the terrorized population of Damascus dared not react." Ibid., pp. 144–45.

18. T. E. Lawrence, *Seven Pillars of Wisdom—A Triumph*, London, 1935, pp. 644–47.

19. Quoted by Comte R. de Gontaut-Biron, *Comment la France s'est installée en Syrie*, Paris, 1922, p. 74.

20. Dubbing Syria "the sands" and Palestine "a spat among clerics," Clemenceau's ignorance in respect of the Near East was legendary: "He couldn't find Mossul on a map and scarcely Palestine, and would mix up Alexandretta and Alexandria." P. du Véou, *La Passion de la Cilicie 1919–1922*, Paris, 1954, pp. 80 and 78.

21. Cf. T. E. Lawrence, *Letters*, op. cit., p. 275, and also J. Pichon, *Sur la route des Indes*, op. cit., p. 258: "From numerous conversations with Moslem dignitaries I have gathered the impression that many no more want English dominion than our own. They aspire to total independence." (February 24, 1919.)

22. A. de Tocqueville, *De la colonisation en Algérie*, Paris, 1988, p. 170. See also C.-A. Nallino, *La Littérature arabe*, Paris, 1950, p. 33: "In Algeria, after the French occupation, the flame of Arab science flickered and literature completely died out, so that [...] the famous Arab schools of earlier centuries at Constantine, Bougie [Bejela], and Tlemçen simply ceased to exist and knowledge of Arab works practically disappeared." Almost all the artist-travelers denounced the destruction of the architectural heritage: "Alas, Algiers today, when one looks at it too closely, has perhaps more to sadden than to delight the eye. It has been much damaged, much disfigured, half destroyed; and the really sad thing is these acts of vandalism are to be laid at the door of Europeans alone." E. Feydeau, *Alger*, Paris, 1862, pp. 7–8. Similar observations were made by G. Guillaumet, *Tableaux algériens*, Paris, 1891, p. 269; by L. de Baudicour, *La Guerre et le gouvernement de l'Algérie*, Paris: Sagnier et Bray, 1853, p. 39; and by E. Delacroix, *Souvenirs d'un voyage dans le Maroc*, Paris; Gallimard, 1999, pp. 109–10. For the impressions of a "native" of the country, as texts would say, see H. Khodja, *Le Miroir*, Paris: Sindbad, 2003, pp. 12, 50, 231, and passim, which affords a blow by blow account of the conversion of mosques into hospitals, stores, or churches, of the evisceration of cemeteries, the destruction of *waqfs* and suqs, of the profanation of tombs of the marabouts, etc. Around 1884, the author Guy de Maupassant, a witness to the expulsion of the Arabs from their land to the profit of the colonists, gave his own judgment of the

occupation of Algeria: "Since our system of colonization consists in ruining the Arabs, in dilapidating them without stint, in harassing them mercilessly, and impoverishing them to death, more insurrections will be in store." *Au soleil*, Paris: Librairie de France, 1935, p. 26.
23. P. Cambon, *Correspondance 1870–1924*, Paris, 1940, vol. 2, p. 143.
24. General Catroux, *Deux Missions en Moyen-Orient, 1919–1922*, Paris, 1958, pp. 129–30.
25. A. Poulleau, *À Damas sous les bombes*, Yvetot, 1930, pp. 40–41. The words after the dashes are the translator's equivalents of the French insults. High-ranking Muslims in Damascus confided to R. de Gontaut-Biron that French representatives were all too often "unpolished, mediocre little personages." *Sur les routes de Syrie après neuf ans de mandat*, Paris, 1928, p. 63. See also Maupassant, "Le Gaulois," August 2, 1881, in *La France colonisatrice*, p. 79; and Victor Hugo, "Discours sur l'Afrique," May 18, 1879, in ibid., p. 111.
26. Volney, "Considérations sur la guerre des Turcs," *Voyage en Syrie et en Égypte*, vol. 3, pp. 360–368.
27. H. Bordeaux, *Voyageurs d'Orient*, Paris, 1926, vol. 1, p. 243.
28. N. Chomsky, "Intervention in Vietnam" in *The Chomsky Reader*, New York, 1987, p. 327. The intervention in the Dominican Republic led to the military dictatorship of Trujillo, one of most brutal and corrupt in all Latin America.
29. "It is necessary at all costs to avoid sending a board of inquiry to Syria," reads one confidential French memo. "Consultation with the Syrians concerning the consignment of the mandate to a foreign power will not prove favorable to us, especially at the present juncture [...]." Quoted by J. Hajjar, *L'Histoire politique de la Syrie contemporaine (1918-1990)*, 1, Damascus, 1993, p. 179.
30. Zionism aroused a flurry of concern among the Syrians: "Syria is one," wrote G. Samné. "[...] Israelite elements should not be allowed to block the aspirations of the people; it should not think that it will be able to institute a Jewish state on the ruins of the homeland of others." *La Syrie*, op. cit., p. 410. On their side, Zionists leaders tried to show a reassuring face: "Is it not imperative," questioned Dr. Weizmann, "is it not logical that in Palestine we, who have suffered so much from the abuse of physical force, should endeavor to rebuild a reign of justice and universal rights? It is strange in truth to hear how afraid people are of the Jew becoming the aggressor in Palestine—the Jew who has always been the victim, the Jew who has always fought on the side of freedom for others, should suddenly turn into an aggressor, just because he has stepped on the land of Palestine." Ibid., p. 422. It is worth noting that G. Samné was secretary to the Syrian Central Committee and editor of the periodical, *Correspondance d'Orient*—the organ of that French propaganda organization in the East.
31. Chekri Ganem, president of the Syrian Central Committee—on the occasion of a conference convened on December 21 at the headquarters of the Lyon mutual benefit insurance company under the patronage of the Lyon arm of a committee of French interests in Syria, of which E. Herriot, French senator and mayor of Lyon, was one of the honorary presidents—obligingly declared: "If Lyon is France's second city, it is Syria's first. It has been its economic capital, and for a few years, its intellectual capital." C. Ganem, *Écrits politiques*, Beirut, 1994, p. 162.
32. Quoted by M. Seurat, *L'État de barbarie*, Paris, 1989, p. 212.
33. "No difficulty, no dissent over the choice of mandatory power. It can only be France, which has inculcated her culture into the Syrians [...] and maintains with them enduring bonds of friendship." Extract from a report on Syrian claims made by Ganem at the Peace Conference, quoted by G. Samné, *La Syrie*, op. cit., p. 543. Evidently, the missions had done their work thoroughly.
34. N. Moutran, *La Syrie de demain*, op. cit., pp. V and VI.
35. Ibid., p. 35.
36. Ibid., p. 33.
37. Ibid., p. 36.
38. Quoted by M. Seurat, *L'État de barbarie*, op. cit., p. 212.
39. The legend of the European origin of the Druzes would date from the seventeenth century, the fruit of the overactive imagination of a missionary. Cf. G. Puaux, *Deux Années au Levant 1939–1940*, Paris, 1952, p. 151.
40. *Action française*, June 16, 1920.
41. Cf. A.-W. Kayyali, *Histoire de la Palestine*, op. cit., p. 76.
42. Neither the Treaty of Sèvres nor the Tripartite Convention came into force instantly. The United States, which was not a member of the Society of Nations, gave assent only on April 4, 1924, in an understanding signed at Paris and ratified on July 13. It was thus only from this date that France was officially able to exercise her mission, without diplomatic restriction, over the states placed under her mandate.
43. On the French side, there were forty-three killed and approximately two hundred wounded. On the Syrian, losses were "very high." Ysuf al 'Azma also died on the field. Cf. J. Pichon, *Sur la route des Indes*, op. cit., p. 330.
44. Gouraud nonetheless telegraphed Paris: "[...] the troops paraded in splendid order amid a sizable and respectful crowd. They have set up camp beneath the walls of the city, occupying stations and public buildings without incident." Quoted by J. Hajjar, *L'Histoire politique*, op. cit., p. 364. A craven press was to publish Gouraud's communiqué more or less in extenso, cf. *La Croix*, July 30, 1920. Cf. also, P. du Véou, *La Passion de la Cilicie*, op. cit., p. 242: "Goybet entered Damascus to the cheers of the men and the ululations of the womenfolk."
45. Cf. G. Puaux, *Deux Années au Levant*, op. cit., p. 29. This "Crusades complex" was a recurrent French ailment. Recalling that Damascus had never been taken by the Crusaders, G. Puaux, the French ambassador and member of the Institute, wrote with satisfaction on the seizure of the city on October 1, 1918: "The entry of the English [*sic*], in the company of a French quota, into the city of St. Paul [...] marked the first steps in the return of Christian dominion over the Umayyad capital." Ibid.
46. G. Samné, *La Syrie*, op. cit., p. 673.
47. J. and J. Tharaud, *Le Chemin de Damas*, Paris, 1923, pp. 53–54. Later however, as the painful fiasco of the mandate sunk in, the same Tharauds, along with many others, were forced to "face facts": "At the beginning of the mandate, at a time of widespread hope, everyone thought that France, with wisdom and authority, would return to undertake the great task begun by the Crusaders and continued with such resilience by our kings, missionaries, seafarers, and by all those Marseille tradesmen who forged bonds of commerce and friendship with the Ports of the Levant... Alas! We must now face facts! We have made so many mistakes [...] that I can feel none of the enthusiasm which then fired [...] those Frenchmen that good luck, happenstance, or a desire to make their fortune had brought there." *Alerte en Syrie*, Paris, 1937, p. 22. In a brief but widely distributed colonialist booklet, the bombast becomes earsplitting: "[...] the Franks have returned. With their new Crusade, they bring freedom for Syria, and the renewed miracle in this land of Roman peace; [...] and the *fellah* will soon say with pride: 'I am a spiritual son of France.'" A. Megglé, *Terres françaises. La Syrie*, Paris, 1931, p. 136.
48. A passenger in Gouraud's car, Catroux recounts the incident in: *Deux Missions*, op. cit., pp. 109–14.
49. Lieutenant-Colonel Catroux, "Synthèse politique," *La Situation politique et militaire au Levant à la date du 1er janvier 1927*, Paris, 1927, p. 26.
50. "So as to split the desire for unity, we have dismembered the territories comprising the kingdom of Faysal." Ibid., p. 26.
51. This policy, biased in favor of Christians and of the Maronites in particular, was roundly condemned by General Catroux: "[...] Gouraud's policy in Lebanon, which was moreover that of the French government, proved a grave psychological error [...]. In denominational terms, it was a blunder as it favored the Christian communities and was to the detriment of the Muslim, and thus deepened the traditional antagonism between them." *Deux Missions*, op. cit., p. 37.
52. Lieutenant-Colonel Catroux, "Synthèse politique," op. cit., p. 26. On Catroux, cf. Gontaut-Biron, *Sur les routes de Syrie*, op. cit., p. 155, and de Gaulle, *Lettres. Notes et carnets. Compléments 1908–1968*, Paris: Plon, p. 250: "There was a man, and, as I believe, only one, who really understood Syria and knew how to manage it, and he was Colonel Catroux."
53. Ibid., p. 26. Even before the battle of Khan Maysalun, Gouraud had already begun "buying off" notable citizens in Damascus. Such "political groundwork" cost a fortune: "The least gift is a thousand gold *livres*," Gouraud wrote in a missive to the French government. "[...] The first figure of note in Damascus to have shown himself amenable requests a down payment of a million and a half. To mobilize his tribes, the head of the Bedouin confederation [...] will set us back nearly three million. The rest are of the same stamp. We shall have to comply with this blatant blackmail or increase our own military forces." *Archives des Affaires étrangères, Syrie-Liban*, quoted by J. Hajjar, *L'Histoire politique*, op. cit., p. 330.
54. Quoted by E. Rabbath, *L'Évolution politique de la Syrie sous mandat de 1920 à 1925*, Paris, 1928, p. 268.
55. Lieutenant-Colonel Catroux, "Synthèse politique," op. cit., p. 28.
56. General Andréa, the main architect and most zealous proponent of repression, was, however, obliged to confess: "In the Djebel-Druze, [...] an entire people rose up against us and military operations of some scale had to be organized to quell them." *La Révolte druze*, Paris, 1937, p. 23.
57. "[...] overwhelmed by superior numbers, our men succumbed one by one and, when only a handful were left, the rebels rushed them and cut them down without pity, sticking the wounded with saber and dagger." Ibid., p. 53.
58. Ibid., p. 73.
59. A. Poulleau, *À Damas sous les bombes. Journal d'une Française pendant la révolte syrienne (1924–1926)*, Yvetot, n. d., p. 110.
60. Ibid., p. 99.
61. Ibid., p. 104.
62. Ibid., p. 109.
63. R. Dorgelès, *La Caravane sans chameaux*, op. cit., pp. 167 and 179.
64. L. Jalabert, *Syrie et Liban, réussite française?*, Paris, 1934, p. 162.
65. General Gamelin, "Synthèse militaire," *La Situation politique et militaire au Levant*, op. cit., p. 44. "More than three hundred streets or lanes emerge from the city into the Ghuta," wrote General Andréa. "This illustrates the kind of difficulties we have to overcome in forbidding access to the city of these bands which lean on the peasantry in the countryside and pose a threat to the peace of the townsmen." *La Révolte druze*, op. cit., p. 77.
66. Ibid., p. 44.
67. Ibid., p. 83. "At the beginning of 1926, Damascus, under the protection of its belt of iron—periodically reinforced with a cordon of fire—quickly reverted to its peacetime face." Ibid., p. 86. This language of typically military frankness is singularly at odds with the sanctimonious tones of those who claimed to be only "civilizing" Syria. Andréa, moreover, adds some intriguing details: "The engineer of the municipality and the officers assisting him proceed to lay out stakes for the new avenues in straight tranches whose ends abut houses in which we will position machine-gunners to protect the barbed wire." Ibid., p. 84.
68. G. Puaux's prose provides a choice example: "The mandate had already made strides in the area of road maintenance: sewers, new streets opened, public parks. But there remained one great task to be undertaken: the creation of ring roads [...]. These great outer boulevards will perhaps live on as the most durable creation of French Damascus; and it surely cannot be a coincidence that our genius has conceived them as much with the aim of liberalism as of hygiene and aesthetics." *Deux Années au Levant*, op. cit., pp. 130–31.
69. P. Alype, "Situation au 1er janvier 1926," *La Situation politique et militaire au Levant*, op. cit., pp. 141–42.
70. A. Poulleau, *À Damas*, op. cit., p. 233.
71. Ibid., p. 234.
72. Ibid., p. 218.
73. P. Alype, "Situation au 1er janvier 1926," op. cit., p. 199.
74. J. Kessel, *En Syrie*, Paris, 1927, p. 94. "Expedient policies, the policies of a chargé d'affaires: these are more or less [...] all we put into operation throughout the entire, overlong experiment." L. Jalabert, *Syrie et Liban*, op. cit., p. 169.
75. Article 4 of the Mandate stipulates that the agent should guarantee Syria and Lebanon against loss or leasing of whole or part of the territories of any nature, and against the establishment of any control by an alien power.
76. Quoted by G. Pilleul, "Le général de Gaulle, la Syrie et le Liban," *France-Pays arabes*, November 1990, p. 23.

77. *Le Monde*, May 1945.

78. Ibid., June 13 1945. Syria, which was merely a mandate monitored in theory by the international community, suffered none of the massacres that, from Sétif to Haiphong, via Morocco, Madagascar, and the Ivory Coast, marked the last gasp of an expiring empire. Cf. Y. Benot, *Massacres coloniaux 1944–1950: la IVᵉ République et la mise au pas des colonies françaises*, Paris: La Découverte, 2001.

79. *Le Monde*, June 26, 1945.

80. Ibid., June 13, 1945.

81. Ibid.

82. On February 14, 1945, Franklin D. Roosevelt and 'Abd al-'Aziz b. Sa'ud signed the Quincy Accords that enshrined American monopoly over Saudi crude oil in exchange for defending the regime. As to oil, G. Puaux had already written, op. cit., p. 15: "It is through there [i.e. the Levant] that the new route to the Indies runs: the one for planes and trucks through which all the sources of oil pass [...]. We have then every encouragement to remain in the Levant."

83. "The Lebanon has remained an artificial construct of our policy," wrote General Catroux. "It contained no cohesion of its own, on the contrary, it was subjected to a centrifugal force, the irredentism of Tripoli." *Dans la bataille de Méditerranée*, Paris, 1949, p. 219. In addition, Catroux attests (p. 219) to the absence of any national feeling in Lebanon and to the fact that France had constructed "the future of the Lebanon for the Maronites" (p. 240).

84. That it was an error to have severed the region and that it would have been preferable to have kept it in one piece was recognized in 1939 by the British High Commissioner, Sir Harold McMichael; cf. G. Puaux, *Deux Années au Levant*, op. cit., p. 173.

85. G. Samné had already written in 1920: "But we are aware that a Palestine detached from the unity of Syria marks the first attack on Syrian nationality, an inadmissible and unforgivable assault that would open a chasm of mistrust and hatred between the indigenous race and the immigrant Jews." *La Syrie*, op. cit., p. 426.

86. How could Syrians have benefited from this supposed French "mission," given that Lord Cromer had already averred in *Modern Egypt* that they could hardly be candidates for "civilization" as they were already perfectly civilized, incorruptible, of acute intelligence and elevated culture? Indeed, observed Cromer, an upper-class Syrian cannot be distinguished from a European of equivalent social status; cf. G. Samné, ibid., p. 544.

87. Testis, *L'Œuvre de la France au Levant (Syrie et Cilicie)*, Paris, 1921.

88. H. Bordeaux, *Yamilé sous les cèdres*, Paris, 1923, p. 2. "We all have reason to be proud of the civilizing work of our splendid colonials," Abbé E. Wetterlé wrote shortly afterwards. *En Syrie avec le général Gouraud*, Paris, 1924, p. 188.

89. Obviously, improvements in the road network had first and foremost a military objective, as R. de Contaut-Biron testifies, *Sur les routes de Syrie*, op. cit., p. 5: "The necessity of being able to impose order more easily and bring the instruments of repression—troops and materiel—more quickly into operation in disturbed areas [...] has induced the civilian authority and the military command to complete a road system that was already at an advanced stage as rapidly as possible [...]. Thus, nowhere else in the Orient is there a road system comparable to that of Syria [...]."

90. A. Raymond, "La Syrie, du royaume arabe à l'indépendance," *La Syrie d'aujourd'hui*, Paris, 1980, p. 83.

91. R. Danger, "L'urbanisme en Syrie," *L'Urbanisme*, 1937, p. 154.

92. Ibid., p. 156.

93. R. Dorgelès, *La Caravane sans chameaux*, op. cit., p. 163.

94. Ibid., p. 157.

95. Ibid., p. 155.

96. J. and J. Tharaud, *Le Chemin de Damas*, op. cit., pp. 220 and 225.

97. Declarations by Zionist officials calling for the ethnic cleansing of Palestine in order to achieve—in accordance with Weizmann's doctrine—a "nation as Jewish as England is English" are legion. Already in 1895, Herzl, who was not above urging European statesmen to make anti-Semitic statements so as to foster Zionism, wrote in his journal: "We strive to incite the impoverished population to cross the border in obtaining jobs for it in the transit country and refusing it the least employment in our own land. The process of expropriation and displacement of the poor must be conducted with discretion or circumspection." Quoted by E. B. Childers, "L'indicible rêve," *Revue d'études palestiniennes*, 15, 1998, p. 4. The result of this "cleansing" was quite the reverse of that desired by Herzl: "It is the best who have fled," declared a member of the Jewish Agency, "the leaders, the intelligentsia, the economic elite. Only the 'small fry' have opted to stay." Cf. T. Segev, *Les Premiers Israéliens*, Paris, 1998, p. 91. In 1940, Yosef Weitz, director of the Colonization Department of the Jewish National Fund, wrote: "Between you and me, it has to be clear that there is no place in this country for two peoples simultaneously [...] The only solution is a land of Israel, or at least a Western land of Israel, west of the Jordan, without Arabs [...]. No other solution is possible other than to transfer the Arabs from here to other countries nearby, and to transfer them all; not a village, not a tribe must remain." Cf. I. Shayak, "L'idée du transfert," *Revue d'études palestiniennes*, 29, 1988, p. 115. For his part, the racist Ben-Gurion averred that a land with a and a land without Arabs were two quite different things; cf. T. Segev, *1949, the First Israelis*, New York, 1986, p. 26. Anti-Arab Jewish racism in Palestine is well attested—among others, by an eyewitness, Arthur Koestler (*Promise and Fulfillment Palestine 1917–1949*, London, 1949). The Jews of Israel commonly call the Arabs "Arabushim," a term of abuse of the same order as "Yid." Jewish racism was naturally not confined to Arabs: thus, in 1972, a group of emigrants from the USSR (as befits any self-respecting disciple of Gobineau) protested against their settlement near a Yemeni Jewish district with cries of: "We did not come from the USSR to live next to Blacks." I. Halévi, *Question juive*, op. cit., pp. 281 and 270. As regards the attitude of the Zionist State and the Jewish community in South Africa in respect of apartheid, cf. R. A. Plumelle-Uribe, *La férocité blanche*, Paris, 2001, pp. 238, 240, and, above all, pp. 243–47, with the damning paragraph: "Zionists and onetime Nazis—An extremely interesting heritage." Concerning the Zionist methods of ethnic cleansing, A. Koestler reported in 1948: "The Jewish army will herd the villagers together, dynamite their houses, and put the young men in concentration camps." A. Koestler, ibid., p. 199. For his part, J. de Reynier, head of a delegation from the International Committee of the Red Cross, wrote in connection with the events of 1948: "Gripped by fear the Arabs left their homes and retrenched to their heartlands. First isolated farms, then villages, and finally whole cities were thus evacuated, even when the Jewish invader did no more than hint at an attack. Finally, some seven hundred thousand Arabs fled as refugees, abandoning everything in great haste with the sole aim of avoiding the fate of those at Dayr Yassin." *À Jérusalem un drapeau flottait sur la ligne de feu*, Neuchâtel, 1950, p. 76, and this goes on: "Haifa was emptied of twenty thousand Arabs and Jaffa of thirty thousand on April 23 and 28 [1948]. The war has not even begun yet; what will happen after May 15?" Ibid., p. 84. The ethnic cleansing got underway in earnest shortly after the UN's decision in favor of partition, well before "official" hostilities started on May 15, 1948, and far beyond the zones of southern Syria allotted to the Jewish State by the UN. To the great satisfaction of Israeli officials, moreover: "And then the landscape looked far more beautiful," one declared. "It's so wonderful, especially between Haifa and Tel-Aviv where there's not a single Arab on the horizon." Cf. T. Segev, *Les Premiers Israéliens*, op. cit., p. 69.

98. Écochard and Benshoya, *Plan directeur*, Damascus, 1968, p. 108.

99. Ibid., p.108.

100. Ibid., p. 110.

101. Ibid., p. 109.

102. Cf. G. Degeorge, "Le massacre de Damas," *Urbanisme*, no. 280, Jan.–Feb. 1995, pp. 26–29; "The Damascus Massacre," *The Architectural Review*, April 1995, pp. 68–71; "The Massacre of Damascus," *The Hindu*, March 20, 1994.

103. Interview given to AFP (French Press Agency), March 12, 1900, quoted by D. Le Gac, *La Syrie du général Assad*, Paris, 1991, p. 56.

104. A. Poulleau, *À Damas*, op. cit., p. 254.

Muslim Dynasties

"Rightly Guided" Caliphs.
632–61 C.E.

Abu Bakr	632
'Umar	634
'Uthman	644
'Ali	656–661

Umayyad Caliphs.
661–750 C.E.

Mu'awiya I	661
Yazid I	680
Mu'awiya II	683
Marwan I	683
'Abd al-Malik	685
Al-Walid I	705
Süleyman (Soliman)	715
'Umar	717
Yazid II	720
Hisham	724
Al-Walid II	743
Yazid III	744
Ibrahim	744
Marwan II	744–750

'Abbasid Caliphs.
750–1258 C.E.

Al-Saffah	750
Al-Mansur	754
Al-Mahdi	775
Al-Hadi	785
Al-Rashid	786
Al-Amin	809
Al-Ma'mun	813
Al-Mu'tasim	833
Al-Wathiq	842
Al-Mutawakkil	847
Al-Muntasir	861
Al- Musta'in	862
Al-Mu'tazz	866
Al-Muhtadi	869
Al-Mu'tamid	870
Al-Mu'tadid	892
Al-Muqtafi	902
Al-Muqtadir	908
Al-Qahir	932
Al-Radi	934
Al-Muttaqi	940
Al-Mustakfi	944
Al-Muti'	946
Al-Ta'i'	974
Al-Qadir	991
Al-Qa'im	1031
Al-Muqtadi	1075
Al-Mustazhir	1094
Al-Mustarshid	1118
Al-Rashid	1135
Al-Muqtafi	1136
Al-Mustanjid	1160
Al-Mustadi	1170
Al-Nasir	1180
Al-Zahir	1225
Al-Mustansir	1226
Al-Musta'sim	1242–1258

Tulunids.
868–905 C.E.

Ahmad b. Tulun	868
Khumarawayh b. Ahmad	883

Jaysh b. Khumarawayh	895
Harun b. Khumarawayh	896
Shayban b. Ahmad	904–905

Ikhshidids.
935–69 C.E.

Ikhsid b. Tughj	935
Unjur b. Ikhshid	946
'Ali b. Ikhshid	960
Kafur	966
Ahmad b. 'Ali	961–969

Fatimids.
909–1171 C.E.

Al-Mahdi	909
Al-Qa'im	934
Al-Mansur	945
Al-Mu'izz	952
Al-'Aziz	975
Al-Hakim	996
Al-Zahir	1020
Al-Mustansir	1035
Al-Musta'li	1094
Al-Amir	1101
Al-Hafiz	1130
Al-Zafir	1149
Al-Fa'iz	1154
Al-'Adid	1160–71

Seljuks.
1076-1104 C.E.

Atsiz	1076
Tutush I	1078
Duqaq	1095
Tutush II	1104
Irtash	1104

Burids.
1104-54 C.E.

Tughtakin	1104
Buri	1128
Shams al-Muluk Isma'il	1132
Shihab al-din Mahmud	1135
Jamal al-din Muhammad	1139
Muju al-din Abaq	1140–54

Zengids.
1154-74 C.E.

Nur al-din (Nurredin)	1154
Isma'il	1174

Egyptian Ayyubids.
1169-1252 C.E.

Al Nasir Salah al-din Yusuf (Saladin)	1169
Al-'Aziz 'Imad al-din 'Uthman	1193

Al-Mansur Muhammad	1198
Al-'Adil Sayf al-din Abu Bakr	1199
Al-Kamil Muhammad	1218
Al-'Adil II Sayf al-din Abu Bakr	1238
Al-Salih Najm al-din Ayyub	1240
Al-Mu'azzam Turan Shah	1249
Al-Ashraf Musa	1250–52

Ayyubids of Damascus.
1186-1260 C.E.

Al-Afdal Nur al-din 'Ali	1186
Al-'Adil Sayf al-din Abu Bakr	1196
Al-Mu'azzam Sharaf al-din 'Isa	1218
Al-Nasir Salah al-din Dawud	1227
Al-Ashraf Musa	1228
Al-Salik Isma'il	1237
Al-Kamil (of Egypt)	1237
Al-'Adil (of Egypt)	1238
Al-Salik (of Egypt)	1240
Al-Salih Isma'il	1240
Al-Salik (of Egypt)	1245
Al-Mu'azzam (of Egypt)	1249
Al-Nasir Salah al-din Yusuf (of Aleppo)	1250–60

Bahri Mamluks.
1250-1390 C.E.

Shajar al-Durr	1250
Aybak	1250
'Ali	1257
Qutuz	1259
Baybars I	1260
Baraka Khan	1277
Salamish	1279
Qalawun	1279
Khalil	1290
Nasir al-din Muhammad (1st reign)	1293
Kitbugha	1294
Lajin	1296
Nasir al-din Muhammad (2nd reign)	1299
Baybars II	1309
Nasir al-din Muhammad (3rd reign)	1310
Abu Bakr	1341
Qujuq	1341
Ahmad	1342
Isma'il	1342
Sha'ban I	1345
Hajji I	1346
Hasan (1st reign)	1347
Salih	1351
Hasan (2nd reign)	1354
Muhammad	1361
Sha'ban II	1363
'Ali	1376
Hajji II (1st reign)	1381
Barquq	1382
Hajji II (2nd reign)	1389–90

Burji Mamluks.
1382-1517 C.E.

Barquq (1st reign)	1382
Hajji II	1389
Barquq (2nd reign)	1390
Faraj (1st reign)	1399
'Abd al-'Aziz	1405
Faraj (2nd reign)	1406
Al-Musta'in ('Abassid caliph)	1412
Shaykh	1412
Ahmad	1421
Tatar	1421
Muhammad	1421
Barsbay	1422
Yusuf	1438
Jaqmaq	1438
'Uthman	1453
Inal	1453
Ahmad	1461
Khushqadam	1461
Bilbay	1467
Timurbugha	1468
Qa'itbay	1468
Muhammad	1495
Qansuh (al-Zahir)	1498
Janbalat	1500
Tumanbay I	1501
Qansuh al-Ghuri	1501
Tumanbay II	1516–17

Ottomans (from the reign of Selim I onwards).
1512-1924 C.E.

Selim I	1512
Süleyman (Soliman the Magnificent)	1520
Selim II	1566
Murad III	1574
Mehmed III	1595
Ahmed I	1603
Mustafa I (1st reign)	1617
'Uthman II	1618
Mustafa I (2nd reign)	1622
Murad IV	1623
Ibrahim I	1640
Mehmed IV	1648
Süleyman II	1687
Ahmed II	1691
Mustafa II	1695
Ahmed III	1703
Mahmud I	1730
'Uthman III	1754
Mustafa III	1757
'Abd al-Hamid I	1774
Selim III	1789
Mustafa IV	1807
Mahmud II	1808
'Abd al-Majid I	1859
'Abd al-'Aziz	1861
Murad V	1876
'Abd al-Hamid II	1876
Mehmed V	1909
Mehmed VI	1918
'Abd al-Majid II	1922–24

Glossary

Agha: title given to individuals of high rank, in particular to the commander of the Janissaries.

Amir: chief, he who commands or leads. gives in European languages "emir." Equivalent of the Turkish bey.

Atabeg: originally meaning a man trusted by the sultan, whom the latter would appoint as tutor to his son, later it became an honorific title conferred by the sultan on important figures in his entourage.

Bahra: chiefly, "the sea," but may also designate a river, or even a simple pool or basin.

Bazistan: equivalent of *qaysariyya* in the Turkish domain. Derives from *bazz*, "precious," and the locative case with *stan*. Originally for the sale of silk, linen, and, above all, cotton cloth.

Bimaristan: hospital, from the Persian *bimar*, "ill, sick" with the locative suffix, *stan*.

Defterdar: head of the financial administration.

Devsirme: literally, "gathering." Under Ottoman rule, the system of recruiting boys to serve in the army, at the royal palace, or in the government.

Dhimmi: "protected;" a non-Muslim subject, Christian, Jew, or Zoroastrian.

Firman: sultan's decree in the Ottoman Empire.

Fisqiyya: ornamental fountain generally placed in the *'ataba*, the lower part of the *qa'a*.

Funduq (*pl.* fanadiq): from the Greek *pandokéion*. The oldest of the terms designating an edifice built for trade. In the Middle Ages, entered Italian as *fondaco*. Today the meaning is often just a hotel.

Hadith: literally "information, news, record." In religious parlance, a story or saying supposed to have arisen with the Prophet. The Hadith is composed of an *isnad* or chain of guarantors who, in principle, have vouched for the authenticity of the saying and the utterance itself, the *watn*. The Hadith, together with the Koran itself, constitute the two pillars of Islamic law. The series of authentic Hadith constitutes the *sunna*, or "customs," of the Prophet.

Hajj: pilgrimage to Mecca.

Hara: quarter, also *mahalla* or *akhtat*.

Himaya: right of protection.

Imam: in pre-Islamic Arabia, the conductor of a caravan. May designate both he who conducts prayers and the holder of an executive power.

'Imara (*Turkish* imaret): edifice in which the poor are provided with food; similar to modern Western "soup kitchens."

Islam: submission to God.

Iwan: high vaulted hall completely open on one side to a courtyard.

Jabal: mountain.

Jihad: individual striving in the ways of the Lord (major *jihad*), but also "Holy War" (minor *jihad*).

Jiziya: poll tax imposed on the dhimmi.

Khan: Persian word that had replaced *funduq* by the thirteenth century in the Near East. Rarer in North Africa.

Kalam: initially meaning "word," "discourse," also designates Islamic theology.

Khanqah: building set aside for the reception of the Sufi.

Kharaj: rate or land tax concerning land owned by the dhimmi.

Khazna: treasury, but also simply "cupboard."

Khutba: homily at Friday prayers pronounced by the *khatib*.

Maqsura: protected area reserved for the caliph (or his representative) in a mosque. Also annexes specially for physical hygiene in the *hammam*.

Mashhad: literally, place of a martyr's death; extended to mean wherever prayers are said on (real or supposed) remains.

Mastaba: bench; also the upper part of a *qa'a*.

Mawla (*pl.* Mawali): freed slave, convert to Islam of non-Arab origin.

Maydan: hippodrome, horse-racing track.

Mihrab: niche indicating the qibla.

Minbar: sort of dais accessible by way of a short flight of steps from the top of which the *khatib* pronounces the khutbah at Friday prayers. Generally placed along the qibla to the left of the mihrab.

Mufti: juridical counselor endowed with the power to issue fatwas (decisions binding in law).

Mujawir: name given to someone staying in a mosque, a holy city, etc. Also, students at the university of al-Azhar.

Muqarnas: decorative elements characteristic of Islamic architecture springing from the division of the squinches that results in various types of vaulting either in freestone or in stucco.

Musalla: open-air prayer area.

Na'ib: lieutenant, provincial governor under the Mamluk sultans.

Pasha: during the Ottoman Empire, title attributed to governors of provinces.

Qa'a: reception hall.

Qaysariyya: derived from the Greek *kaisareia*, imperial. A *khan* in principle for the trade solely of luxury products. In Spanish gives the word *alcayseria*.

Qibla: mosque wall facing Mecca towards which Muslims kneel side by side to pray.

Ra'is (*pl.* Ru'asa'): head of corporation or guild.

Ra'iyya/ra'ayya: subjects.

Ribat: in general, fortified "monastery" in which in times of peace individuals devoted themselves to study and religious observance. Sometimes used in the place of *khan*.

Sabil: public fountain.

Sandjak: subdivision of province.

Sandjakbey: overseer of a *sandjak*.

Shahid (*pl.* shuhud): "witnesses."

Shari'a: code of canon law derived from the Koran and the Hadith.

Sharif (*pl.* ashraf): descendant of the Prophet Muhammad.

Shurta: State police.

Suq (*pl.* aswaq): market, group of shops arranged by guild. Each was placed under the authority of a head who could bear any one of a series of titles: sheikh, *'arif, naqib, kabir, amin, nazir*.

Tafsir: commentary on the Koran, exegesis.

Takiyya/tekke/tekiyyé: Sufi or dervish meeting place.

Tanzimat: secular codes introduced into the law of Muslim states.

Tasawwuf: doctrine of the Sufi; Islamic mysticism.

Ta'wil: Koranic interpretation.

Umma: entire community of (Muslim) believers.

Wali: provincial governor.

Waqf (*pl.* awqaf, wuquf): pious foundation.

Yerliyya: local forces (in Syria in particular).

Zawiya: literally, "corner," designates a Muslim religious establishment. Sometimes used in the place of madrasa or *khanqah*.

Zu'ar: low-class brigands, sometimes forming what amounted to militias; bands controlling city districts; sometimes also known as *ahdath*.

Bibliography

For a more detailed bibliography see:

DEGEORGE G. *Damas des origines aux Mamluks*, Paris: L'Harmattan, 1997, pp. 351–59; and *Damas des Ottomans à nos jours*. Paris: L'Harmattan, 1994, pp. 230–54.

Further reading:

Album des artistes en expédition de voyage au pays du Levant (exh. cat.). Paris, 1993.

Ali Bei. Un pelegri català per terres de l'islam (exh. cat.). Barcelona: Museu etnológic de Barcelona, 1996.

AL-MAKIN IBN AL-'AMID. *Chronique des Ayyubides (602–658 /1205-6-1259-60)* (Fr. tr. A.-M. Eddé and F. Micheau). Paris: Académie des inscriptions et belles-lettres, 1994.

AL-QAYRAWANI IBN ABI ZAYD. *La Risala.* Algiers: J. Charbonel, 1952.

AL-TARSUSI NAJM AL-DIN. *Kitab Tuhfat al Turk. Œuvre de combat hanafite à Damas au XIVe siècle* (Fr. tr. Mohamed Menasri). Damascus: PIFD, 1997.

ANDRÉA, General. *La Révolte druze et l'insurrection de Damas, 1925–1926.* Paris: Payot, 1937.

ARBOIT, G. *Aux sources de la politique arabe de la France. Le Second Empire au Machrek.* Paris: L'Harmattan, 2000.

ATASSI, S. *Damas à la fin de l'époque mamelouke. Éléments de topographie historique et religieuse* (typescript thesis). Lyon, 1984.

AVEZ, R. *L'Institut français de Damas au palais 'Azm (1922–1946) à travers les archives.* Damascus: PIFD, 1993.

AYALON, D. *Le Phénomène mamelouk dans l'Orient islamique.* Paris: PUF, 1996.

BEAUPLAN, R. DE. *Où va la Syrie? Le mandat sous les cèdres.* Paris: J. Tallandier, 1929.

BRÉMOND, E. *Le Hedjaz dans la guerre mondiale.* Paris: Payot, 1931.

BURNS, R. *Monuments of Syria, an Historical Guide.* London: I. B. Taurus, 1992.

CATROUX, General. *Dans la bataille de Méditerranée. Égypte, Levant. Afrique du Nord, 1940–1944.* Paris: Julliard, 1949.

—— *Deux Missions au Moyen-Orient (1919-1922).* Paris: Plon, 1958.

CAUVIN, J. *Religions néolithiques de Syrie-Palestine.* Paris: J. Maisonneuve, 1972.

—— *Les Premiers Villages de Syrie-Palestine du IXe au VIIe millénaire avant J.-C.* Lyon: Maison de l'Orient, 1978.

—— *Naissance des divinités. Naissance de l'agriculture.* Paris: Flammarion, 1997.

CHAMBERLAIN, M. *Knowledge and Social Practice in Medieval Damascus, 1190–1350.* Cambridge: Cambridge University Press, 1994.

CHARLES-ROUX, F. *France et chrétiens d'Orient.* Paris: Flammarion, 1939.

CHEVEDDEN, P. E. *The Citadel of Damascus* (doctorate thesis). Los Angeles: University of California, 1986.

COLLET, A. *Collet des Tcherkesses.* Paris: Corrêa, 1949.

CONTENSON, H. DE. *Aswad et Ghoraifé. Sites néolithiques en Damascène aux IXe et VIIIe millénaires avant l'ère chrétienne.* Beirut: IFAPO, 1995.

—— *Ramad. Site néolithique en Damascène aux VIIIe et VIIe millénaires avant l'ère chrétienne.* Beirut: IFAPO, 2000.

DEGEORGE, G. and D. CLÉVENOT. *Splendors of Islam.* New York: Vendome Press, 2001.

DEGEORGE, G. and Y. PORTER. *The Art of the Islamic Tile.* Paris: Flammarion, 2001.

DEGEORGE, G. and J.-C. DAVID. *Alep.* Paris: Flammarion, 2002.

DEVREESSE, R. *Le Patriarcat d'Antioche depuis la paix de l'Église jusqu'à la conquête arabe.* Paris: J. Gabalda, 1945.

DIB, P. *Histoire de l'Église maronite.* Beirut: Éditions La Sagesse, 1962.

DION, P.-E. *Les Araméens à l'âge du fer: histoire politique et structures sociales.* Paris: J. Gabalda, 1997.

DU VÉOU, P. *Le Désastre d'Alexandrette (1934–1938).* Paris: Éditions Baudinière, 1938.

—— *La Passion de la Cilicie, 1919–1922.* Paris: Geuthner, 1954.

EDWARDS, R. *La Syrie 1840–1862.* Paris: Amyot, 1862.

ESTABLET, C. and J.-P. PASCAL. *Familles et fortunes à Damas, 450 foyers damascains en 1700.* Damascus: PIFD, 1994.

—— *Ultime Voyage pour La Mecque. Les inventaires après décès des pèlerins morts à Damas vers 1700.* Damascus: PIFD, 1998.

FESTUGIÈRE, A.J. *Antioche païenne et chrétienne. Libanius, Chrysostome et les moines de Syrie.* Paris: E. de Boccard, 1959.

FINKELSTEIN, I. and N.A. SILBERMAN. *La Bible dévoilée, les nouvelles révélations de l'archéologie.* Paris: Bayard, 2002.

FLOOD, F. B. *The Great Mosque of Damascus. Studies on the Makings of an Umayyad Visual Culture.* Leiden: Brill, 2001.

FRIÈS, F. "Les plans l'Alep et de Damas, un banc d'essai pour l'urbanisme des frères Danger (1931–1937)," in "Figures de l'orientalisme en architecture," *Revue du Monde musulman et de la Méditerranée*, 73–74. Aix-en-Provence, 1994, pp. 311–325.

GANEM, C. *Écrits politiques.* Beirut: Dar an-Nahar, 1994.

GAUDIN, J.-P. "L'urbanisme au Levant et le mandat français," in *Architectures françaises. Outre-mer.* Liège: Mardaga, pp. 177–205.

GEOFFROY, E. *Jihâd et contemplation. Vie et enseignement d'un soufi au temps des croisades.* Beirut: al-Bouraq, 2003.

GHAZZAL, Z. *L'Économie politique de Damas durant le XIXe siècle. Structures traditionnelles et capitalisme.* Damascus: PIFD, 1993.

GONTAUT-BIRON, Comte R. DE and L. LE RÉVÉREN, *D'Angora à Lausanne. Les étapes d'une déchéance.* Paris: Plon, 1924.

HAJJAR, J. *L'Histoire politique de la Syrie contemporaine (1918–1990).* Damascus: Dar Tlass, 1993.

HEBEY, P. *Les Disparus de Damas.* Paris: Gallimard, 2003.

Histoire des troupes du Levant. Paris: Imprimerie nationale, 1931.

Hommage à Michel Écochard, Revue des Études islamiques, LIII, 1985. Paris: Geuthner, 1992.

JALABERT, L. *Syrie et Liban. Réussite française?* Paris: Plon, 1934.

LA TOURETTE, G. DE. *L'Orient et les peintres de Venise.* Paris: E. Champion, 1923.

Le Régime des Capitulations par un ancien diplomate [Anonymous]. Paris: Plon, 1898.

LEPROUX, M. *Quelques figures charentaises en Orient.* Paris: Geuthner, 1939.

Les Annales archéologiques arabes syriennes, special issue, *Damas,* XXXV. Damascus, 1985.

L'Orient de Saladin, l'art des Ayyubides (exh. cat.), Institut du monde arabe. Paris: Gallimard, 2001.

LYAUTEY, P. *Le Drame oriental et le rôle de la France.* Paris: Société d'Éditions géographiques, maritimes et coloniales, 1924.

MARDAM BEY, S. *La Syrie et la France. Bilan d'une équivoque (1939–1945).* Paris: L'Harmattan, 1994.

MASPÉRO, J. *Histoire des patriarches d'Alexandrie depuis la mort de l'empereur Anastase jusqu'à la réconciliation des Églises jacobites (518-616).* Paris: E. Champion, 1923.

MARINO, B. *Le Faubourg du Midan à l'époque ottomane.* Damascus: PIFD, 1997.

MEGGLÉ, A. *Terres françaises. La Syrie.* Paris: Société française d'Éditions, 1931.

MEINECKE, M. "Mamluk Architecture. Regional architectural traditions: evolutions and interrelations." *Damaszener Mitteilungen,* 2, 1985, pp. 163–75.

MOAZ 'ABD AL-RAZZAQ. *Les Madrasas de Damas et d'al-Salihiyya depuis la fin du Vᵉ/XIᵉ jusqu'au milieu du VIIᵉ/XIIIᵉ siècle* (typescript thesis). Université d'Aix-en-Provence, 1990.

MOUTON, J.-M. *Damas et sa principauté sous les Saljoukides et les Bourides (468–549/ 1076–1154).* Cairo: IFAO, 1994.

—— *Saladin. Le sultan chevalier.* Paris: Gallimard, 2001.

MÜLLER, V. *En Syrie avec les Bédouins. Les tribus du désert.* Paris: E. Leroux, 1931.

O'ZOUX, R. *Les États du Levant sous le mandat français.* Paris: Larose, 1931.

PÉTACHIA DE RATISBONNE. "Tour du monde ou voyages du rabbin Pétachia de Ratisbonne dans le XIIᵉ siècle." *Journal asiatique,* VII, 1831, pp. 257–307 and 353–413.

PICHON, J. *Sur la route des Indes. Un siècle après Bonaparte.* Paris: Société d'Éditions géographiques, maritimes et coloniales, 1932.

POUJOULAT, B. *Voyage à Constantinople dans l'Asie Mineure, en Mésopotamie, à Palmyre, en Syrie, en Palestine et en Égypte.* Brussels: N.-J. Grégoire, V. Wouters, et Cⁱᵉ, 1841.

PUAUX, G. *Deux Années au Levant. Souvenirs de Syrie et du Liban 1939–1940.* Paris: Hachette, 1952.

RABBATH, E. *Unité syrienne et devenir arabe.* Paris: Maral Rivière et Cⁱᵉ, 1937.

REYNIER, J. DE. *À Jérusalem un drapeau flottait sur la ligne de feu.* Neuchâtel: Éditions de La Baconnière, 1950.

RISTELHUEBER, R. *Les Traditions françaises au Liban.* Paris: F. Alcan, 1925.

ROCHEMONTEIX, P.C. DE. *Le Liban et l'expédition française en Syrie (1860-1861). Documents inédits du général A. Ducrot.* Paris: A. Picard, 1921.

ROUJON, Y. and VILAN L. *Le Midan. Actualité d'un faubourg ancien de Damas.* Damascus: PIFD, 1997.

ROUSSIER, P. *Les Derniers Projets et le dernier voyage de Domingo Badia (Post-Scriptum aux Voyages d'Ali-Bey),* extract from *La Revue africaine.* Algiers: J. Carbonel, 1931.

ROSEN-AYALON, M. *Art et archéologie islamiques en Palestine.* Paris: PUF, 2002.

SCHATKOWSKI SCHILCHER, L. *Families in Politics. Damascene Factions and Estates of the 18ᵗʰ and 19ᵗʰ Centuries.* Stuttgart: F. Steiner, 1985.

SIVAN, E. *L'Islam et la croisade. Idéologie et propagande dans les réactions musulmanes aux croisades.* Paris: A. Maisonneuve, 1968.

THOUMIN, R. *La Maison syrienne.* Damascus: PIFD, 1932.

TRESSE, R. "L'installation du premier consul d'Angleterre à Damas (1830–1834)." *Revue de l'histoire des colonies françaises,* 1936, 24, pp. 359–380.

VANDAL, A. *Une ambassade française en Orient sous Louis XV. Les missions du marquis de Villeneuve 1728–1741.* Paris: Plon, 1887.

WEBER, S. "Der Marja-Platz in Damaskus." *Damaszener Mitteilungen,* 10, 1998.

—— "The Creation of Ottoman Damascus, Architecture and Urban Development of Damascus in the 16ᵗʰ and 17ᵗʰ centuries." *Aram,* 9–10, 1997–1998, pp. 431–470.

—— *The Transformation of an Arab-Ottoman Institution. The Suq (Bazar) of Damascus from the 16ᵗʰ to the 20ᵗʰ Century,* Seven Centuries of Ottoman Architecture: "A Supra-National Heritage." Istanbul, 1999.

WIRTH, E. "Conservation or Revitalisation of the old City of Damascus." *Les Annales archéologiques arabes-syriennes,* 35, 1985, pp. 74–79.

YARED-RIACHI, M. *La Politique extérieure de la principauté de Damas de 468/1076 à 549/1154. Étude chronologique des événements d'après les chroniques arabes* (typescript thesis). Université de Lyon 2, 1992.

Index of proper names

Index of place names

List of illustrations

Page 2: Manuscrits orientaux. Bibliothèque Nationale. Paris.

Page 5: Manuscrits latins. Bibliothèque Nationale. Paris.

Page 8. Bottom left. B.: R. Thoumin, Géographie humaine de la Syrie centrale, Tours, Arrault et Cie, 1936, page 360.
Bottom right. D.: Ibid, p. 13 (modified).
Bottom. C.: M. Écochard, Les bains de Damas, Beyrouth, 1942, p. 12.

Page 9: R. Thoumin, op. cit., p. 360.

Page 11: Ibid, p. 360.

Page 13: V. Guérin, La Terre Sainte, son histoire, ses souvenirs, ses sites, ses monuments, Paris: E. Plon Nourrit et Cie, 1884, p. 385.

Page 16: H. de Contenson, La région de Damas au néolithique, Les Annales archéologiques arabes syriennes, XXXV, Damas, 1985, p. 11 et Aswad et Ghoraifé, Sites néolithiques en Damascène (Syrie) aux Xe et VIIIe millénaires avant l'ère chrétienne, Institut français d'Archéologie du Proche-Orient: Beirut, 1995, p. 15.

Page 24: J. Sauvaget, Le Plan antique de Damas, Syria, XXVI, Paris: 1949, p. 356.

Page 25: Dr L.-C. Lortet, La Syrie d'aujourd'hui: Voyages dans la Phénicie, le Liban et la Judée, 1875-1880, Paris: Hachette, 1884, p. 597.

Page 26. Top: R. Dussaud, Le Temple de Jupiter damascénien et ses transformations aux époques chrétienne et musulmane, Syria, III, Paris, 1922, planche LII, p. 228.
Bottom: Ibid, p. 226.

Page 34: K.A.C. Creswell, A Short Account of Early Muslim Architecture (revised and supplemented by James W. Allan), The American University in Cairo Press: Cairo, 1989, p. 49 et J. Sauvaget, Les monuments historiques de Damas, Beirut, Imprimerie Catholique: 1932, p. 19.

Page 58: Manuscrits orientaux. Bibliothèque Nationale. Paris.

Page 60: E. Herzfeld, Damascus: Studies in Architecture, Ars Islamica, 1942, p. 6 et Revue des Études Islamiques, Hommage à Michel Écochard, LIII, Paris, 1985, p. 33.

Page 66: J. Sauvaget, Les monuments ayyubides de Damas, II, E. de Boccard: Paris, 1938, p. 88.

Page 68: M. Écochard et C. Le Cœur, Les Bains de Damas, II, Beirut, 1943, p. 18 for the cross-section, p. 16 for the map.

Page 73: V. Guérin, op. cit., p. 413.

Page 75: J. Sauvaget, Esquisse d'une histoire de la ville de Damas, Revue des Études islamiques, VIII, Paris, 1934, planche VII.

Page 77: V. Guérin, op. cit., p. 405.

Page 78: S. Berthier, Introduction au Supplément citadelle de Damas du Bulletin d'Études Orientales, LIII-LIV, Damas, 2003, p. 32 (map by H. Hanisch).

Page 79: V. Guérin, op. cit., p. 404.

Page 84: J. Sauvaget, Les Monuments historiques..., p. 56.
Page 85: J. Sauvaget, Les Monuments ayyubides..., p. 28.

Page 90: Ibid, p. 81.

Page 91: Ibid, p. 68.

Page 95: E. Herzfeld, Damascus: Studies in Architecture. Ars Islamica, 1946, p. 24 et Revue des Études Islamiques, Hommage à M. Écochard, LIII, 1, Paris, 1985, p. 59.

Page 107: E. Atil, Renaissance of Islam: Art of the Mamluks, Smithsonian Institution Press, Washington D. C., 1981, p. 11.

Page 126–27: Musée du Louvre. Paris. This painting was part of King Louis XIV's collection.

Page 142: Revue des Études Islamiques, Hommage à M. Écochard, LIII, 1, Paris, 1985, p. 81 for the map, p. 83 for the cross-section.

Page 144: M. Meinecke, Syrian Blue-and-White Tiles of the 9th/15th Century, Damaszener Mitteilungen, vol. 3, 1988, p. 204.

Page 149: M. Écochard et C. Le Coeur, Les Bains de Damas, II, 1943, p. 72.

Page 157: J. Sauvaget, Esquisse..., Revue des Études Islamiques, VIII, 1934, VIII.

Page 161: Revue des Études Islamiques, Hommage à M. Écochard, LIII, 1, Paris, 1985, p. 66.

Page 163: V. Guérin, op. cit., p. 383. The original caption read "the Tekieh [...], a huge hospice built for the pilgrims by Sélim I^st, in the year 1516".

Page 176: Bon I.-J.-S. Taylor and L. Reybaud, L'Égypte, la Palestine et la Judée, Paris: Mame, 1835–38, p. 157 (after a drawing by Dauzats).

Page 177: Bibliothèque Nationale. Paris.

Page 183: Palais 'Azm, Damas.

Page 191: J. Kelman, From Damascus to Palmyra..., London: Adam and Charles Black, 1908, p. 120.

Page 193: R. Dussaud, Le Temple de Jupiter damascénien et ses transformations aux époques chrétienne et musulmane, Syria, III, Paris, 1922, p. 249.

Page 194: M. Scharabi, Der Suq von Damaskus und zwei traditionelle Handelsanlagen: Khan Sulayman Pasha, Damaszener Mitteilungen, vol. 1, 1983, p. 293 (modified).

Page 195: M. Meinecke, Syrian Blue-and-White Tiles of the 9th/15th century, Damaszener Mitteilungen, vol. 3, 1988, p. 204.

Page 196: Map and cross-section kindly leant to the author by the Département du Vieux Damas (Bimaristan de Nur al-din). See also Revue des Études islamiques, Hommage à Michel Écochard, LIII, 1, 1985, p. 103 for the map and 105 for the cross-section.

Page 197. Top: Private collection.
Bottom: Dr. L.-C. Lortet, op. cit., p. 588.

Page 201: D. Sack, Damaskus: Entwicklung und Struktur einer orientalisch-islamischen Stadt, Verlag Philipp von Zabern: Mainz am Rhein, 1989, p. 73.

Page 207: M. Écochard et C. Le Coeur, Les bains de Damas, II, 1943, p. 108 et J. Sauvaget, Les Monuments historiques de Damas, Beirut, 1932.

Page 219: E. Gouin, L'Égypte au XIXe siècle, Paris: P. Boizard, 1847, p. 283.

Page 224: Le Journal illustré, June 1883, p. 185.

Page 225: L'Univers illustré, no 116, August 2, 1860.

Page 226: J. Carne, La Syrie, la Terre Sainte, l'Asie Mineure, London, Paris: Fisher et fils, 1836–38, t. 1, p. 39.

Page 227: L'Univers illustré, t. 8, 1865, p. 45.

Page 228: V. Guérin, op. cit., p. 410.

Page 229: V. Guérin, op. cit., p. 408.

Page 230: Dr. L.-C. Lortet, op. cit., p. 590.

Page 234: L'illustré. Soleil du dimanche, Octobre 10, 1897, p. 6. Author's archives.

Page 235: R. Dussaud, Le Temple de Jupiter damascénien et ses transformations aux époques chrétienne et musulmane, Syria, III, Paris, 1922, planche LIV, p. 248.

Page 242: J. Sauvaget, Esquisse..., Revue des Études islamiques, VIII, 1934, X.

Page 257: Dr. L.-C. Lortet, op. cit., p. 574.

Page 258: Postcard. Author's archives.

Page 263: V. Guérin, op. cit., p. 423.

Page 271: J. Pichon, Le Partage du Proche-Orient, J. Peyronnet et cie: Paris, 1938, p. 92.

Page 272: D.S. Margoliouth, Cairo, Jerusalem and Damascus: Three Cities of the Egyptian sultans..., London: Chatto and Windus, 1907, p. 267.

Page 277: Postcard. Author's archives.

Page 279: Maktab 'Anbar's archives. Damascus.

Page 280: Postcard. Author's archives.

Page 281: Postcard. Author's archives.

Page 282: A. Poulleau, A Damas sous les bombes. Journal d'une Française pendant la révolte syrienne (1924–1926), Yvetot, Bretteville Frères, s.d., (Stironi), p. 168. Original caption: "They were three young people..."

Page 285: Postcard. Author's archives.

Page 287: J. Sauvaget, Esquisse..., Revue des Études islamiques, VIII, 1934, XI.

Page 298: Based on official maps created from 1930 to 1934.

Acknowledgments

*The author would like to extend friendly thanks
to General Mustafa Tlass, Minister of Defense
of the Syrian Arab Republic, for the flybys
over Damascus, as well as for the helicopters
graciously placed at his disposal.*

*He also expresses his heartfelt gratitude to:
Edmond El-Ajji, Sophie Berthier, Chantal de Bertoult,
Oussama Deway, Muwafaq Dughman, 'Imad Hammami,
Joseph Hanna, Lubna al-Jabri, Mahat Farah al-Khoury,
Michel al-Maqdissi, Françoise Siess, 'Ali Nahawi,
Ghassan Nasrallah, Hassan Zahabi, and to the many
Damascenes who, with a generosity, spontaneity,
and feeling for hospitality that are rarely found
outside the Orient, have been kind enough over
the years to open their doors to him.*

All the photographs are by Gérard Degeorge with
the exception of the following:
Bibliothèque nationale de France, Paris: 2, 5, 58, 66, 176,
177, 191, 224, 225, 227, 272
AKG/Erich Lessing, Paris: 126–127
ACR/Mathaf Gallery, Paris: 197
Philippe Maillard, Paris: 53, 71

Translated from the French by David Radzinowicz

Copyediting: Susan Schneider

Design and typesetting: Thierry Renard

Distributed in North America by Rizzoli International
Publications, Inc.

Simultaneously published in French as
Damas: Perle et Reine d'Orient
© Éditions Flammarion, 2004
English-language edition
© Éditions Flammarion, 2004

All rights reserved. No part of this publication may be
reproduced in any form or by any means, electronic,
photocopy, information retrieval system, or otherwise,
without written permission from Éditions Flammarion.
26, rue Racine
75006 Paris

www.editions.flammarion.com

04 05 06 4 3 2 1

FC0456-04-XI
ISBN: 2-0803-0456-9
Dépôt légal: 11/2004

Printed in Italy by Errestampa

Endpapers. Umayyad Mosque. Detail of an epigraphic band from the minaret of Qa'itbay. Mameluk period. End of the fifteenth century.